A History of the Jews
in the United States

A History of the Jews in the United States

By Rabbi Lee J. Levinger, Ph.D.

Author of *A Jewish Chaplain in France;*
Anti-Semitism in the United States;
co-author of *The Story of the Jew*

Union of American Hebrew Congregations

New York

COMMISSION ON

JEWISH EDUCATION

of the UNION OF AMERICAN HEBREW CONGREGATIONS
and CENTRAL CONFERENCE OF AMERICAN RABBIS
AS OF 1967

UNION GRADED SERIES

EDITED BY
ALEXANDER M. SCHINDLER, *National Director of Education*
UNION OF AMERICAN HEBREW CONGREGATIONS
Director of Adult Education
CHAIM I. ETROG
Director of Teacher Education
ABRAHAM SEGAL

TO

ALFRED M. COHEN

AMERICAN AND JEWISH LEADER

Editor's Introduction

The present status of American Jewish education may be partly described by the fact that many books published in recent years had to be introduced as the first of their kind.

For example, it is well accepted in recent educational theory that one of the fundamental aims of education should be to bring about an intelligent, sympathetic, yet critical understanding of the immediate environment of the child. In America, one would expect this to be reflected in the publication of many texts for children and young people on American Jewish History. This should especially be done because of the unique and in many respects remarkable part which the Jew has played in the upbuilding of America. Yet there are few books available and no full textbook on the history of the Jews in America other than the present volume by Dr. Lee J. Levinger, the first edition of which appeared in 1930.

Dr. Levinger's *History of the Jews in the United States* is an attempt to supply a text on American Jewish History for the high school department. The author presents, first of all, the basic facts in the American Jewish story. The participation of the Jews in the discovery of America, their part in the struggle for independence, their growth in and with the country, are fully described. The three

Editor's Introduction

waves of Jewish migration, which account for much of the nature of American Jewry today, are clearly presented.

One of the most significant contributions of the book, in our opinion, is the fact that fully one-third of it is devoted to a cross-section of Jewish life in America in the twentieth century. Here, all important phases of American Jewish life are treated. Our religious institutions, Orthodox, Conservative and Reform, our philanthropic institutions, our fraternal, educational and cultural organizations are presented. The Jewish labor movement and its effect on the development of American Jewish life are described.

At the end of each chapter, topics for essays, questions for discussion and debate, and readings for students and teachers have been appended. The inclusion of maps, charts, and carefully selected illustrations will prove especially useful to students. The Union of American Hebrew Congregations has spared no effort to make the book as attractive as possible from the point of view of its physical appearance. And the 1961 edition brings the story of American Jewry up to date.

We sincerely hope that this book will be found helpful in our schools, especially in the high school department, and that it will further that appreciation and understanding of American Jewish life which alone can contribute to the spiritual enrichment of our community here, and to the enhancement of Jewry throughout the world.

EMANUEL GAMORAN

Preface

THIS book is primarily a text for the study of American Jewish history in the high school classes of Jewish schools. It is hoped that it will also prove valuable for general reading and for reference.

Hence the emphasis on readableness, on the selection of outstanding points rather than inclusion of all available facts, and particularly on current movements and on leading personalities, past and present. This is primarily a book by which American Jewish youth may learn those facts which will enable them to become intelligent American Jews.

As far as possible, the author has tried to be objective throughout the book and he has discussed many disputed problems with people of different points of view. He, therefore, feels that he is justified in claiming that he has maintained an attitude of objectivity and impartiality.

The author desires to express his appreciation to those who read his manuscript and made invaluable suggestions: Dr. Emanuel Gamoran, Educational Director of the Commission on Jewish Education, Dr. David Philipson, Chairman of the Commission, Dr. Samuel Schulman, Chairman of the Committee on Youth Education of this Commission, Professor Carl Wittke, Professor of American History at the Ohio State University, Mr. Max J.

Preface

Kohler, vice-president of the American Jewish Historical Society; also to Rabbi Louis I. Egelson, Assistant Director of the Department of Synagogue and School Extension, and to Mr. M. Myer Singer of the Department who is responsible for the typography and design of the book.

LEE J. LEVINGER

Columbus, Ohio
May, 1930

To the Revised Edition

During thirty-one eventful years, many epochal changes have occurred in the world and not least in American Jewry. In addition, our attention was focused on our own past by the tercentenary celebration in 1954.

In the revision of 1949 we found it necessary to add two chapters, dealing with the period between the two World Wars and with the Second World War. Moreover, the entire survey of Jewish life in America was rewritten at that time.

The chief supplement to the 1961 edition has been a section on the growth of suburbia, with its effect on Jewish life. References to current events have been brought up-to-date. For this last, the author owes deep thanks to dozens of busy organization officials who gave him recent and authoritative figures on their activities.

LEE J. LEVINGER

Los Altos, Calif.
July, 1961

Contents

INTRODUCTION

PART I

JEWS WHO SETTLED IN THE COLONIES

Contents

xii

Contents

Contents

xiv

Contents

Contents

xvi

Contents

Maps and Charts

Illustrations

Illustrations

Illustrations

INTRODUCTION

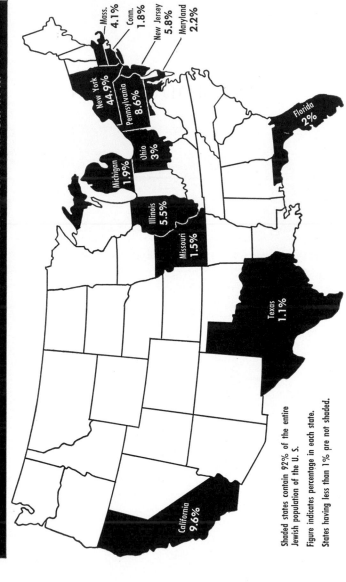

GEOGRAPHICAL DISTRIBUTION OF THE JEWISH POPULATION IN THE U.S. (1940)

Mass.
4.1%

Conn.
1.8%

New Jersey
5.8%

Maryland
2.2%

New York
44.9%

Pennsylvania
8.6%

Florida
2%

Ohio
3%

Michigan
1.9%

Illinois
5.5%

Missouri
1.5%

Texas
1.1%

California
9.6%

Shaded states contain 92% of the entire
Jewish population of the U. S.

Figure indicates percentage in each state.

States having less than 1% are not shaded.

CHAPTER 1

The Jews Who Live in the
United States Today

I. THE JEWISH PART IN AMERICAN HISTORY

WHEN we read American history or study it in our schools, there is seldom much mention of the Jews. Thoughtless people might judge from this that the Jewish people have had little to do with the history of the United States, or that the Jews are newcomers who arrived after others had founded the nation and made it great.

But this happens to be far from the facts. Jews have lived in the land that is now the United States of America long before it won its freedom; they have worked for it, sacrificed for it, and loved it at every period of its great history. But they came as families or even as separate persons, not in large groups, like the Pilgrims or the Cavaliers; they did not have a whole colony of their own, like the Quakers in Pennsylvania or the Catholics in Maryland. Therefore they are often lost to view among the individuals of many different races and religions who lived in America and helped to make it what it is today.

We will want to study this book to find out some-

3

thing about the Jews of the United States today, where they came from, how they got here, and what they have done in this country. We will want to know whether they have contributed much or little to America in peace and war; whether they have neglected the heritage of their fathers, or have built great Jewish institutions in the New World.

II. AMERICAN JEWRY AT PRESENT

EVEN in the twentieth century, the Jews are by no means the largest of the many elements of population in the United States. In 1959, they constituted about 5,367,000 of the 177,500,000 citizens of this nation, a large and important body in itself but a small percentage of the entire people. Still, this comprises the largest number of Jews living in any country of the world, and almost one-half of all the Jews on earth. These people live chiefly in all the large cities of the United States, but they have smaller groups scattered everywhere, a Jew in nearly every village as one of its business men, in many a country district as one of the farmers.

The city of New York alone has over two million Jews as part of its great population, the largest number of Jewish people ever gathered together in any city since our history began, more than Jerusalem ever held in its greatest days. Other great cities also have large numbers of Jews, their number varying according to the size of the city as a whole and the nature of its special industries.

4

Jews in the United States Today

The Jews are divided by their work and their wealth into almost the same groups as other Americans. They have their rich and their poor, large numbers of poor immigrants who must be helped to get a start in the new land, as well as many rich men and women who are ready to give them their chance. They have professional men, business men, manufacturers, and workingmen. They often live near each other for company in one section of a city. They often enter the same fields of business where they have acquaintances. For example, the garment industries are largely owned by Jewish manufacturers.

These Jews do not all agree in religion, or politics, or personal feelings. They work together for charity, however, and they have wonderful hospitals, orphan asylums, and many other kinds of institutions to help the unfortunate and the needy. Some of them belong to orthodox, some to conservative, and some to reform synagogues; these three religious groups have their separate national unions of congregations, conferences of rabbis, and schools for the training of rabbis. Many American Jews are Zionists, devoted to the Jewish nationality, and striving for the welfare of the State of Israel. Others are not interested in Zionism, or disbelieve in the organization of Jews as a nation, preferring to constitute only a religious body.

Still others, and a very important body, too, are interested in the Jewish nation, though not the Jewish religion, but most of all in the welfare of human beings

5

History of the Jews in the United States

in general. These Jewish "secularists" are working in the cause of the laboring classes and of peace between nations.

Great numbers of Jews, coming from lands where they spoke Yiddish, still cultivate that language in America. There are Yiddish newspapers, Yiddish books, and Yiddish theaters, and a literature of very high quality is being produced in that tongue here in America. Other Jews are studying the ancient Hebrew language, the holy tongue in which were written the Bible, the Mishnah, and the prayer book. This is now the spoken language of the Jewish settlers in Israel and is spoken and written by a number of their friends and sympathizers in America.

There is a great movement for Jewish education in America, beginning with the many Hebrew schools and religious schools connected with congregations, the communal Talmud Torahs, the schools for Jewish teachers, and ending with five colleges for the training of rabbis. The epoch-making Jewish Encyclopedia was written in America. The translation of the Bible into English by Jewish scholars, and the other important works of the Jewish Publication Society of America, are an enduring monument to Jewish learning.

This great body of American Jews, with all its different groups, different opinions, and different activities, has naturally been a great influence among the Jews in other lands. The rebuilding of Palestine, which has enlisted the efforts of Zionists in every country, has had

6

Jews in the United States Today

much support and a great amount of financial help from American Jewry even though most of the immigrants to the ancient home of Israel have been the persecuted Jews of eastern Europe and of North Africa.

The only complete unity ever achieved among American Jews has been for aid of our brothers abroad. This began during the First World War, when three groups were formed among reform, orthodox, and secular Jews to collect money; these joined together in the Joint Distribution Committee to use the funds wherever they might do the most good. At the same time the Zionist movement was raising great sums for use in Palestine. By 1933, these two great causes joined in the United Jewish Appeal, which later included the United Service for New Americans as well. The American Jews, uniting to save the lives of their brothers overseas and to help establish the new state of Israel, found at the same time that unity was possible among themselves. No single organization has been able to speak for united Jewry, not even the American Jewish Conference which was organized during the Second World War. But the United Jewish Appeal has been able successfully to represent all American Jews in working for world Jewry.

One of the outstanding trends of the present day is this striving for unity, and we shall see in this book the many efforts now being made by various groups in that direction.

We do not need to be reminded that the Jews of America have not only their Jewish life, but, like all other American citizens, contribute to American life in general. They belong to various political parties, in which they vote and sometimes hold office. They have their inventors, their writers, their musicians and artists. In time of war they send their full quota to fight for America. They have their business leaders in many lines of endeavor. In other words, the Jews of America are complete partakers in American life, and at the same time possess certain Jewish institutions, too. They combine in themselves the age-old Jewish tradition of worship and loyalty, and the newer American life of progress and freedom. Their Judaism and their Americanism reinforce each other.

III. WHERE THE AMERICAN JEWS CAME FROM

THESE Jews came to the United States from every land under the sun, for the Children of Israel dwell everywhere. They came for the same reasons that our other immigrants have come since the very discovery of the New World. Some came, like the French or Spanish, for love of adventure or desire for colonization. Some came, like the Germans and Irish, because they were very poor in the Old World and wanted to establish homes where they could provide a better livelihood for their families. Above all, the vast majority of them came like the Quakers and the Pilgrim Fathers as refugees from religious persecution, seeking a land where they might worship God in their own way. As a modern writer, herself a Jewish immigrant, has said: "Every immigrant ship is

Jews in the United States Today

another Mayflower, and Ellis Island is just a new name for Plymouth Rock " (Mary Antin: *They Who Knock at Our Gates.*)

The first Jews who came to America were from Spain and Portugal, some of them coming to this country directly, and others after wandering to several other lands on their weary search for a permanent home. Since the year 1492 these Jews had been fugitives, trying to find a place of security east or west, north or south. Naturally some of them tried the New World, so that the first and for a long time the only Jewish immigrants to America were Spanish Jews. Another factor that led these people to America was the colonizing activity of the Spanish and Portuguese at that early date. It was natural that people from these lands should come to America, first because there they would find colonists whose language they spoke, and secondly, because of the comparative ease of obtaining passage.

Now and then a wanderer came from England, Germany, or even Poland, but fully half of the early Jews were of Spanish origin. Then came a change, and from 1815 on the Jewish immigration came largely from Germany and other countries of central Europe. For this was the time of the great German immigration to America, when thousands of Germans of all religions fled their native land for the New World. It was the time when the revolt of 1848 had been repressed and those who wanted freedom had to seek it in a foreign land. It was also a period of great poverty in Germany, when multitudes desired a fresh start in a new home. Hence the German Jews came to America, along with other Germans, seeking opportunity, freedom, and above all liberty to worship according to the dictates of their conscience.

During all this time, there were very few immigrants from eastern Europe. But this immigration increased in 1881 when the terrible May Laws were promulgated by the Czar of Russia. Since that time persecutions have piled up in eastern Europe, taking the form of discriminatory laws against the Jews, anti-Semitic parties in politics and mob violence. Since then great masses of Jews have fled from Russia, Austria, Roumania and nearby lands, of whom the greatest number fled to the United States. They, too, came for a chance to make a living, for freedom from tyranny, and most of all for liberty to be themselves and to live as Jews. At the same time the Jews were not the only new arrivals from eastern Europe. Large numbers of peasants also, especially of the different minority nationalities, came for the same reasons. Tyranny was heavy on them all, poverty was bitter to them all, but both poverty and tyranny bore most terribly on the Jews.

One might think of Jewish history in America in terms of certain figures, showing the increase of the numbers of Jews in this country. After the Revolution there were 3,000 Jews in the new nation. In 1840 there were 15,000; in 1881, a quarter of a million; and in 1959, there were 5,367,000 all together. They increased much like a series of steps, each one immensely larger than the one before.

10

Jews in the United States Today

With many individual exceptions, these steps roughly represent different countries from which the Jews came.

The first fifteen thousand represented largely the Sephardim, the Jews from Spain and Portugal; the next two hundred thousand or more are the German Jews; the next three and a half million are the Jews from eastern Europe. Thus the descendants of the earliest settlers form the smallest group of Jews in the United States, the next largest is formed by the descendants of the German Jews, while the largest of all is composed of the latest to arrive, those from eastern Europe, and their children. Of course, there are also small bodies of Jews from Persia, Turkey and all sorts of countries, who have sent a few of their representatives to this great gathering-place of the nations, America.

IV. CHARACTERISTICS OF THE THREE MIGRATIONS

NATURALLY, each of these three groups of immigrants had its own characteristics, depending on the sort of Jewish life these people had led, the kind of national surroundings they had known in their former homes. The first migration, that of the Spanish Jews, consisted of a few families, drifting in from time to time. They were chiefly merchants; some of them were wealthy merchants, engaged in commerce with other lands. They settled in the thirteen original colonies in a few leading commercial cities, and had five congregations in all at the time of the Revolution. They were strictly observant Jews, and most of their institutions were for their reli-

11

gious life. The typical community began with a cemetery when a few families came to a town; as soon as
there were ten men in the community for services, they
established a synagogue; finally they organized to help
the poor, and to help each other in time of sickness or
death.

The German Jews who arrived next were very different
in several respects. Most of them were poor when they
first came. They usually began in the new land as peddlers wandering from house to house and from farm to
farm, often with their entire stock of goods on their
backs. By industry and courage they overcame the ob-
stacles of poverty, a strange language, and the natural
suspicion for unknown foreigners. Many a one started
by buying a horse and wagon with which to carry on
his peddling, then a little store, then a larger business
of one kind or another. The result is that many of the
very old men who are leaders in business, in charity, and
in public work among American Jews today were among
these pioneers, while a surprising number of the active
middle-aged Jews of the present, judges, physicians and
bankers, are their sons, reared and educated in America.

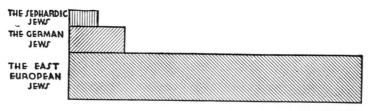

THE THREE WAVES OF JEWISH MIGRATION

Jews in the United States Today

Comparatively few of these German immigrants were scholars or professional men in their old homes, but many of them had a certain amount of both German and Jewish culture, due to the fine schools in Germany during their youth. Many of these men read books and had modern ideas. Some of them had belonged to the rising new reform movement in Germany. Thus it came about naturally that liberal Judaism in America was fathered by these poor immigrants from Germany. They originated, likewise, social institutions, such as the B'nai B'rith and the Young Men's Hebrew Association. They founded philanthropic institutions—orphan asylums, homes for the aged, hospitals, and relief societies. All these, of course, were very small in their beginnings; all of them were needed by some element in the growing Jewish community. They organized nation-wide Jewish institutions, notably the Union of American Hebrew Congregations, and through it the Hebrew Union College, in Cincinnati, the oldest seminary for training rabbis in America. They grew steadily in wealth, education, Jewish influence and public standing.

The distribution of the German immigrants was different from that of the Spanish. They did not stay in a few cities on the Atlantic seaboard, for they found a great continent just opening up to settlement. So they went ahead with the pioneers into every part of the growing nation. Naturally, they went largely to the same cities and sections where their non-Jewish comrades from Germany were settling. In this way Cincinnati became one of the most important Jewish centers in the United States, because it was a center of German settlement. These Jews settled in remote sections of the west and south; most of the Jewish communities of the country were founded during this period by some of these German immigrants.

Finally there came the great mass of immigration from eastern Europe. The Jews from Russia, Poland, Austria, Roumania and related lands came neither as scattered individuals nor as family groups. They represent the transplanting of practically entire communities, rich and poor, learned and ignorant together. The German immigrants had been chiefly the poor or the dissatisfied, for those with advantages at home hesitated to leave. So were the early immigrants from Russia. But after 1881 in Russia few Jews could be safe or prosperous; whole settlements were often ordered out of the villages where they had lived for generations, and driven to strange cities where they had no homes and no means of livelihood. This new migration was different, not only in its vastly greater numbers, but also in its nature. The new wave of migration centered in New York City, and spread out from that center. There are now Russian Jews in many other cities as well, but a great body of them still remains in that tremendous Jewish community.

These east European Jews were, for the most part, either orthodox or Zionists; or socialists and not religious at all. Very few of them belonged to reform synagogues, although very soon a milder modification of orthodoxy,

14

called conservative Judaism, arose among them. They possessed a great deal of Jewish culture, as their rabbis and also many laymen were learned in the Bible and the Talmud; but they had fewer scholars in Russian or other modern tongues. This was due to the lack of public schools in Russia and the exclusion of Jews from many of the private schools, so that they had to rely entirely on their own Jewish schools and their own Jewish learning. Their culture, then, was either Yiddish or Hebrew. The Yiddish newspapers and theaters, the Zionist sentiment and organizations, the Hebrew schools and Talmud Torahs, owe their origin to the Russian Jews, exactly as the reform synagogues and their religious schools, charities and lodges, originate with the German Jews, and as the first orthodox synagogues originate with the Spanish Jews.

V. THE MINGLING OF ELEMENTS IN AMERICAN JEWRY

AMERICAN Jewry represents all these three, not as separate groups, but as they now live intermingled and largely united. The differences pointed out are historical only, and exist now only in small part. Jews of Russian origin have a great influence through their overwhelming numbers, which Jews of German origin often equal because they came to America first, and consequently have acquired more wealth and are better adjusted to conditions in this country. Meanwhile the little Spanish community has largely been absorbed into the greater masses, retaining its separate identity in only a few cities.

History of the Jews in the United States

In the rest of this book, we shall try to see in detail how all this came about, and how the Jewry of America came to be. We shall try also to see what influence the Jews have had in American history, what great men they have produced in this country, and how much they have been able to accomplish for the benefit of their country. Finally we shall study the Jewish community of today, which is both interesting and important to all of us.

REVIEW QUESTIONS

1. How many Jews are there in the world? In the United States? In New York City?
2. Name some of the national movements among American Jews; some of the institutions which represent these movements.
3. Why are Jews mentioned so seldom in your American history in school?
4. From what lands did the Jews come to America? For what reasons?
5. Sketch the growth of the Jewish community of the United States.
6. Describe the three groups of Jews which came to America.

TOPICS FOR REPORTS

It may be most interesting to see the Jewish community of America in small, in its reflection in your own city; for example:

1. Study the Jewish community of your own city, as to numbers, residence, lines of business, Jewish institutions, and so on.
2. Find out the significant dates in the history of the Jews of your city, the first arrivals, the date of founding the various synagogues and other institutions, and the other matters of interest.

16

Jews in the United States Today

3. Study their origin, the country from which they came, their present connection with various countries, such as relief for war sufferers, relatives in other lands, or aid for Palestine.
4. Make a brief survey of world Jewry in its numbers, location and world movements, so as to see where American Jewry fits into these. For example, which are the great Jewish communities of the world, and which of them are in the United States? This is beginning in the opposite way, but it can be equally useful.
5. Name three American Jewish institutions, such as the B'nai B'rith the National Jewish Hospital, or any others; give their date of origin, purpose, and the work they are doing. This will lead you directly into the whole of American Jewry also.

REFERENCES

Every school library should contain a minimum of reference works for the more thorough study of this text book. Unfortunately, much of the material is unavailable, and most of the accessible material is more suitable for teachers than pupils, or can be used by the latter only under guidance. Indispensable works are:

FOR PUPILS

Index to articles on this field in Funk and Wagnalls' *Jewish Encyclopedia.*

Index volume of the American Jewish Historical Society Publications.

A standard history of the United States.

Philipson, David, *The Jew in America,* (a tract giving an excellent brief summary). Union of American Hebrew Congregations.

Levinger, E. E. and L. J., *The Story of the Jew* (for a background of Jewish history). Behrman.

Wiernik, Peter, *History of the Jews in America,* 1931 edition Jewish Press Publishing Co.

History of the Jews in the United States

FOR TEACHERS

Sachar, A. L., *A History of the Jews*. Knopf.
Margolis, M. L. and Marx, A., *A History of the Jewish People* (for a Jewish historical background). Jewish Publication Society.
Sachar, A. L., *Factors in Modern Jewish History*, U.A.H.C.
Raisin, Max, *History of the Jews in Modern Times*. Hebrew Publishing Co.

FICTION FOR PUPILS

Asch, Sholom, *America* (out of print). Bloch.
Levinger, E. E., *The New Land*. Bloch.

A variety of biographies and works on special topics are available, referred to in the different chapters. The biographies are practically all suitable for pupils. Many of these, if not all, should be in the school library. I suggest such books as these:

BIOGRAPHIES

Adler, Cyrus, *Jacob H. Schiff, His Life and Letters*. Doubleday Doran.
Antin, Mary, *The Promised Land*. Atlantic Monthly Press.
Kohut, Rebekah, *My Portion*. Seltzer.
May, Max B., *Isaac Mayer Wise, A Biography*. Putnam.
Philipson, David, *Max Lilienthal, American Rabbi*. Bloch.
Straus, Oscar S., *Under Four Administrations*. Houghton Mifflin.

SPECIAL TOPICS

Kayserling, M., *Christopher Columbus and the Participation of the Jews in the Spanish and Portuguese Discoveries*. Longmans Green, new edition Dobsevage.
Levinger, Lee J., *A Jewish Chaplain in France*. Macmillan.
Levinger, Lee J., *Anti-Semitism in the United States*. Bloch.

18

Jews in the United States Today

Peters, Madison C., *The Jews Who Stood by Washington.*

Philipson, David, *The Reform Movement in Judaism.* Macmillan.

Straus, Oscar S., *Origin of the Republican Form of Government in the United States.* Putnam.

Wolf, Simon, *The American Jew as Patriot, Soldier and Citizen* (out of print). Levytype Co.

The fifty volumes of the American Jewish Historical Society and the fifty volumes of the American Jewish Year Book contain a great store of source material and statistics.

Many local histories and other useful works are referred to throughout this book. Few periodical references are given because these, however valuable, are seldom available.

Every city has great possibilities for laboratory work in the history and status of its own Jewish community. This can be undertaken as a class project for the year with this book as a background.

For contemporary problems, some Anglo-Jewish newspapers should be at hand, and a file of one of them will prove invaluable to use with the annual summaries in the Year Books.

PART I
Jews Who Settled in the Colonies

CHAPTER 2.

Jews Who Helped Columbus

I. THE BEGINNING OF AMERICAN HISTORY

AMERICAN history, as we usually think of it, begins in Spain, at the time when Ferdinand and Isabella, the king and queen, decided to assist Christopher Columbus in his voyage of discovery to the west. The history of the Jews in America begins at the very same time, for there were then many Jews in Spain. Some of them had influence at court and favored the plans of the great discoverer; some aided him with scientific knowledge; some accompanied him on his first voyage into the unknown waters to the west. Some, indeed, without their own knowledge or consent, contributed to the expenses of the second voyage of Columbus which were largely paid out of the money taken away from the Spanish Jews in the year 1492.

That year was an especially important one both to Spain and to the Jews. It was the year of the final triumph of the Christians over the Mohammedans in that land, after they had held the greater part of Spain for almost eight hundred years. During those centuries one Christian king after another had struggled against them. Now at last Granada, their final stronghold, was taken;

23

Spain was a Christian country; Ferdinand and Isabella were its undisputed sovereigns.

They wanted all their subjects to accept their religion, which was that of the Roman Catholic Church. For that reason they had established the terrible Inquisition (that is, inquiry or investigation), which was intended to investigate the loyalty to the church of any Catholics who might be suspected. The Inquisition became a great instrument of oppression and cruelty, torturing and executing thousands of people, among them many who were suspected of clinging to Judaism. Finally in 1492 Ferdinand and Isabella passed an edict that all Jews in Spain must either be baptized or leave the country forever.

It was a sad choice after these many happy centuries of prosperity, learning, and devotion to Spain. The Jews of Spain had been throughout the Middle Ages the aristocracy of Israel. They had attained great wealth, some of them becoming members of the king's court; others owned large estates, since Spain was almost the only country in the Middle Ages where a Jew might own land. The Moslems especially had been tolerant and cultured rulers. The Jews had possessed many privileges in Spain, so that they naturally clung to that country as their home and fatherland.

In that Golden Age of Spanish Jewry, appeared the finest outflowing of Jewish genius of any period of Jewish history since the Prophets. There were Solomon ibn Gabirol, poet and philosopher; Ibn Ezra, the wandering scholar, with his keen reason and his ready wit;

24

Jews Who Helped Columbus

Judah Halevi, apologist for Judaism and sweet singer of Zion, who finally turned his face eastward to die in the Land of Israel. There was Maimonides, master of Jewish law and of world science, one of the greatest philosophic minds of the entire Middle Ages, who was born in Spain but fled the growing persecutions and lived during his great manhood in Egypt. There was Nachmanides, the keen thinker who debated for Judaism against the representatives of the Church. Such men as these were not only great masters of the Jewish law, but also scientists, poets and philosophers.

When the decree of expulsion was announced, the Jews were compelled to adopt Christianity or to leave their native land in which they had prospered. Many chose to remain. As a consequence, some of the noblest Spanish families of today have Jewish blood. Thousands of these converts, however, kept up their Judaism secretly, in the face of constant danger to their lives from the Inquisition. These secret Jews, or Marranos, as they were called, were the weaker and less loyal part of the Spanish Jews. Yet even they retained much love for their own Jewish religion. Wherever possible, they celebrated the Sabbath and festivals; they hid away their Hebrew prayer books; often for generations they kept alive the memory of their own customs as Jews. The Marranos suffered terribly from the anger of the Inquisitors, who were suspicious of the sincerity of their conversion and set many spies to observe whether they still practiced Jewish customs. A former Jew might be thrown into

25

prison because of an anonymous letter, or because a servant had seen him putting on clean garments on a Saturday. Once in prison, he was subject to torture and in
many cases even to burning at the stake, while the
Church confiscated his property.

Most of the 300,000 Spanish Jews, however, were
made of stronger stuff. They sold their property for what
little it would bring and left their ancient homes. They
wandered to Portugal, France, northern Africa, Italy,
and Turkey, seeking everywhere to find a home where
they might remain Jews. Their voyages were filled with
sorrow and privation; thousands of them died on the
way; some had their children taken away by force and
brought up as Christians.

Certainly the world needed a land of freedom just
then. The Jews above all longed for a land where they
might find liberty to live in happiness, to keep their
families together, to worship the God of Israel. Even
Spain, the land in which they had flourished for so long,
had now become their bitterest persecutor. But neither
the sad fugitives nor the haughty and triumphant monarchs knew that land of refuge was to be discovered that
very year.

For just one month after the decree of expulsion, the
monarchs issued Letters Patent to Christopher Columbus to seek lands and islands in the western ocean. Just
one day after the final expulsion of the Jews from Spain,
the three tiny caravels of Columbus set out from the port
of Palos. The expulsion took place on August 2nd, which

26

Jews Who Helped Columbus

was Tisha b'Av, the anniversary of the destruction of the Temple in Jerusalem. Emilio Castelar, a modern Spanish statesman, writes: "It chanced that one of the last vessels transporting into exile the Jews expelled from Spain by religious intolerance, passed by the little fleet bound in search of another world." It is our pride that Jews had much to do with that discovery which, without their foreseeing it, finally won for them a new refuge, a home for a far larger Jewish community than medieval Spain had ever boasted.

II. CHRISTOPHER COLUMBUS

EVERYONE is familiar with the few leading facts in the life of Christopher Columbus, the great explorer who first found the way across the seas to the west, and who, in search for the ancient civilizations of India and China, discovered instead the new world of America. According to his own statement, he was born in Genoa, Italy, went to sea at an early age, travelled as far south and north as seamen ever dared in those days, learned how to make maps and how to navigate a ship. Finally he became convinced that the earth was round and that the east might be reached by sailing west. With this great idea he tried to find a patron who would outfit an expedition to sail westward.

After several years of effort at the court of Portugal, then the leading nation in the world for exploration, he turned to Spain. There he studied, waited and pleaded for seven weary years until the sovereigns listened to him.

27

History of the Jews in the United States

A few students believe that Columbus was of Jewish blood, though he has always been known as a Catholic. They say that no Spanish Jew could ever have expected aid from the king and queen of Spain, so he claimed to be a Christian from Italy. The Italian form of his name was Colombo, a very common name in northern Italy, but its Spanish form was Colon, and there was a family by that name of Jewish blood. We know neither the exact place nor date of his birth, which some people think shows that he had something to hide. A number of Jews were his firm friends and were believers in his great life-hope, but that is no proof at all that he himself was a Jew.

Nor is there proof in other details which bolster up the theory: that Columbus wrote either in Spanish or Latin, not in Italian; that he gave Spanish, not Italian names to the places he discovered; that his mother's name was Fontenarossa, and that a Jewish family of that name, some of whose members were brought before the Inquisition, lived in Galicia, in northern Spain. The interesting thing is, however, that not Jews but Spaniards are trying to prove this theory, in order to claim the great discoverer as of Spanish birth. A royal commission was appointed to study the subject, and its judgment was that "there is no proof that Don Christopher Columbus was born in Galicia." Since that time a Madrid newspaper offered a large prize to anybody who could prove from documents the Spanish birth and origin of Columbus.

In fact, it has not been proved that Columbus was a

Jews Who Helped Columbus

Spanish Jew. He himself claimed to be an Italian Catholic, and certainly very definite proof would be needed to contradict this statement. We should be very proud to claim this great explorer and intrepid spirit as a Jew, if the facts warranted it, but it is not possible to do so without real proof, especially against his own statement. At present the claim seems to be without foundation.

III. JEWISH SCIENTISTS

THERE is no doubt, however, that Columbus received much information from Jewish voyagers and scientists. We must remember that he studied every available book and map and talked with every possible traveller, trying always to get more information about the lands in the west, the form of the earth, or the best route to follow as an explorer. While he was in Portugal he studied the charts of Jefudah (that is, Judah) Cresques, who was known as the "map Jew." Cresques had been born in the Spanish island of Mallorca, where a number of Jews were seamen and others were mapmakers. He was converted by force during a persecution, one of the many which came to the Jews in those days. Later Prince Henry the Navigator, the great royal explorer of Portugal, established a school of navigation and called him, under his new name of Maistre Jaime of Mallorca, to be its head. One of his maps was sent to Paris as a present to the king of France, and we can find a copy of it in the Jewish Encyclopedia. (Vol. 3, opposite page 678.)

When Columbus was at the court of Portugal, he

studied these maps. There he met also, among other
scholars, the court physician, Joseph Vecinho. This Jew
had translated, from Hebrew into Spanish, the astronomi-
cal tables of Abraham Zacuto, his former teacher. Columbus obtained a copy of them, which he carried and
used on his voyages, and left behind in his working
library when he died. But Vecinho did not favor the
ambitious schemes of the explorer. We cannot imagine
how brave and clear-sighted a man had to be to follow
such a new idea, especially when it was the idea of a
man who was neither a prince nor a scholar, but only a
sailor, a wandering adventurer. So the junta, or commission, which studied the plans of Columbus, brought in an
unfavorable report, due largely to the opposition of Vecinho. The explorer followed his vision to the court of
Spain.

Among the men he met there was Abraham Ben Samuel Zacuto, the teacher of Vecinho, who made up for his
pupil's rejection of Columbus' dreams by accepting them
whole-heartedly, and giving all the information and personal encouragement in his power. Zacuto was an unusual
man in every way. He was a professor in the University
of Salamanca, Spain, and wrote Hebrew books on astron-
omy and Jewish history. He was of the brave group who
refused to become Catholics in 1492, but went instead to
Portugal. He was received there at first with the dignity
so great a scholar deserved, but when Portugal turned
against the Jews he had to flee to Tunis and later to
Turkey. He died in exile, a loyal Jew; he saw the suc-

cessful voyages of Columbus and Vasco de Gama, which he had helped to bring about; but he chose to suffer, while those who accepted Christianity—or even pretended to accept it—were rewarded.

We are now interested to know that Columbus believed that the part of Asia where he was to go was the same as the land of Arzareth, which is mentioned in the Fourth Book of Ezra in the Apocrypha, and that, therefore, he expected to find there the ten lost tribes of Israel. This queer idea of Fourth Ezra was taken from the book of Deuteronomy where the Jews are told that they will be driven to "another land"—Erez Ahereth. Columbus, like many people, believed in all these ancient prophecies and expected this one to be fulfilled by his own voyage.

IV. JEWISH FINANCIAL HELP

THE closest Jewish friends of Columbus and two of his greatest backers in his first expedition were two Marranos of Spain who were in high favor at the court of Isabella. They were Luis de Santangel, chancellor of the royal household, and Gabriel Sanchez, chief treasurer of Aragon. They were both very rich men who had saved their wealth and their position by formal conversion during the persecutions of the Jews. In fact, several near relatives of Santangel had been put to death by the Inquisition; he himself had only been saved, after doing penance, by the personal friendship of the king. As a reward for his faithful service to the king, and especially for his part in financing the expedition of Columbus,

31

Santangel was later exempted by decree from any charge of apostasy against himself, his children or grandchildren.

These two men befriended the bold adventurer during his seven years at the Spanish court, when his plans were considered, first by a scientific commission, then by a practical body; the latter rejected them because of his excessive demands for the title of Admiral and a share in all the profits of any new lands to be discovered. At last, in 1492, the monarchs decided adversely on the advice of this commission. Columbus turned his mule away from Granada, to join his brother Bartholomew at the court of France and begin his pleading and his explaining over again. But when he was two leagues away, a messenger overtook him—the monarchs had changed their minds, he was to return to court, to be made Admiral, to be given ships and men!

We can imagine the spirit with which he turned back to the court. He was no longer a hopeless adventurer but an Admiral of Spain, with a great task of discovery ahead. We do not know exactly what happened in that final interview which reversed the decision of the king and queen. But we do know that among the pleaders for Columbus were Gabriel Sanchez, Juan Cabrero, the chamberlain of Ferdinand and another convert from Judaism, and the chief among them all, Santangel himself. He argued that the risk of the expedition was small in case of failure, while the gain of a successful voyage would be incalculably great. All the new lands with their trade; all the chance of converting the natives to Chris-

Jews Who Helped Columbus

tianity would be the profit, while the title and pay of Columbus would be a trivial reward for such a service.

When this reasoning was successful, the question of the cost of outfitting the expedition arose. Isabella spoke of pledging the crown jewels, which had been previously pledged to finance the war against the Moors. But in this case that was not necessary, for Santangel believed so strongly in the cause that he offered to advance the money. As Professor Herbert B. Adams, a great American historian, has said: "Not jewels, but Jews, were the real financial basis of the first expedition of Columbus."

In addition to the money raised as a fine by the people of Palos, where the three ships were outfitted, the remainder of the cost of this expedition was advanced by Santangel. His old account books still exist with the records of 17,000 florins, about 5,000,000 maravedis, which he loaned the king at this time and which was later repaid. This sum, by which the discovery of a new world was assured, amounted to $20,000 in modern money. Of course, we must remember the vastly greater buying power of money then than now.

When Columbus had made this wonderful first voyage and had discovered the new world, which he always thought was only an unknown part of the coast of Asia, his first letters describing his discovery were sent to Luis de Santangel and Gabriel Sanchez. These letters were duplicates, written in Latin, and covered all the events of the expedition; they were printed soon afterward and some copies of them exist today.

History of the Jews in the United States

It has been said that other Jews were interested in Columbus during his years in Spain, especially Abraham Senior, the chief farmer of the taxes, and Don Isaac Abravanel, scholar, statesman, and loyal Jew, who clung to his religion and therefore was no longer in the land of his birth when the Admiral returned. He was an exile in Italy, and the later history of his famous family lies entirely in that land.

We are interested in one more fact concerning the financing of the second voyage. The first had been paid for by Santangel, who was later repaid by the king. The second was paid for by the king out of the confiscated goods and money of the banished Jews, for even the debts which Christians owed to Jews were taken over by the government for the benefit of the royal treasury.

V. JEWS ON THE FIRST VOYAGE

OF THE hundred and twenty men on the first voyage of Columbus, five and perhaps six were Jews by birth, although, of course, only converts to Christianity were taken on the expedition. Among them were Roderigo Sanchez, of Segovia, a relative of Gabriel Sanchez, who was sent as inspector at the special request of the queen; Alfonso de la Calle, who was named after the *Calle* or Jewish quarter of the Spanish towns; Marco, the surgeon; and Mastre Bernal, the physician of the party, who had done penance before the Inquisition in 1490 as an adherent of Judaism. Bernal, with a number of others of the expedition, later engaged in a conspiracy

34

against the Admiral, when only the firm friendship of Santangel saved Columbus from complete disgrace.

It is said that the first sailor who sighted land was a Jew. Columbus himself claimed the honor because he had seen moving lights the night before, while this sailor, Rodrigo de Triana, sighted the actual land at two o'clock in the morning. On returning to Spain the prize of 10,000 maravedis was given to the Admiral instead of the sailor; the latter, we are told, went to Africa and returned to his original religion. This story, however, is not vouched for by all the authorities of that time.

It seems more certain that the first white man who stepped on the soil of San Salvador, the first little island to be reached, was Luis de Torres, a converted Jew, the interpreter of the fleet. As Columbus had expected to reach Asia, he was eager to have a capable interpreter along; so he took Torres, who understood Hebrew, Chaldaic and some Arabic, and could thus converse with some of the peoples of Asia. When land was sighted, the interpreter Luis de Torres was naturally the first man to go ashore. He was followed by the Admiral with his captains and seamen, eager to thank God for the successful termination of their bold venture and to claim the land discovered in the name of the king and queen of Spain. This took place on October 12th, 1492, on the Jewish festival of Hoshanna Rabba.

As they had reached neither Japan nor India, but only a little island in the West Indies, and as the people were naked tribes instead of the ancient civilizations of the east, the interpreter never had a chance to use his knowledge of languages. When the fleet reached Cuba, which the Admiral thought was the mainland on account of its size, Torres was sent with one companion to search for the capital city of the Great Khan of Tartary, to deliver to him a letter from the royal pair of Spain. This little trip of twelve leagues into the interior of Cuba, the first expedition of any kind taken by white men in America, led them only to rude villages of straw huts; but it brought other knowledge of real importance. For on this trip De Torres saw the natives smoking tobacco, which he described to Columbus and later took back to Europe. De Torres also named the turkey in a Hebrew letter to his old home, calling it "tukki," the Hebrew for peacock.

Luis de Torres may not have found India, or spoken Arabic to the inhabitants; but his lively and accurate descriptions of the country were used by Columbus. He himself was so impressed with the new land that he settled there, received a grant of land from a native chief and a pension from King Ferdinand, and finally died in his home in Cuba.

It seems providential that Jews from the very beginning should have helped to discover America. In the year of their exile from their happiest and most beautiful medieval home, they helped to find the land which was to be their refuge and home in modern times. They aided Columbus with their wealth of scientific knowledge. A group of converted Jews gave him the powerful support of their influence at court and advanced the money which

Jews Who Helped Columbus

made his first great voyage possible. Five Jews were on that first voyage, including the man who was first to step upon American soil. As if predetermined, the voluntary gifts for the first voyage were followed by the confiscation of Jewish goods which paid for the outfitting of Columbus' second expedition. At every turn we find Jews doing their part in the great discovery. At the very moment Spain was driving out its Jewish citizens, they were helping Spain to find and colonize a new world. None could look forward through the centuries to the time when Spain would have lost her great American possessions, while the persecuted Jew should have here a home, which combined much of the learning and prosperity of medieval Spain and the freedom that belongs only to modern America. But it was many a year until the new spirit of this new land triumphed, freed it from the despotism and bigotry of the old world, and proclaimed it as a refuge for all mankind, including the weary wanderers of the house of Israel.

Review Questions

1. Why did the Jews need a refuge in 1492?
2. Do you believe that Columbus was a Jew? Why?
3. Was it right for the Marranos to pretend to be Christians? Was there any excuse for them?
4. Tell what Columbus learned from one Jewish scientist.
5. What Jew helped Columbus most? Why?
6. Why are we interested in the part played by Luis de Torres in the first voyage of Columbus?

History of the Jews in the United States

TOPICS FOR REPORTS

1. The Inquisition. Graetz, vol. IV, pp. 483–485. *Jewish Encyclopedia,* vol. VI, pp. 587–603. *Encyc. Brit.*
2. The Marranos. Aguilar, Grace, *The Vale of Cedars.* Graetz, vol. IV, pp. 180, 182, 197, 199, 202–256. *Encyc. Brit.*
3. The Golden Age of the Jews in Spain. Graetz, vol. IV, pp. 271–276. *Jewish Encyclopedia,* arts. on Spain, Abraham Ibn Ezra, Nachmanides, Jehuda ha Levi, Levinger, E. E. and L. J., *Story of the Jew,* chap. viii.
4. The Life of Columbus.
5. Great Explorers before Columbus.

REFERENCES FOR PUPILS

Peters, Madison C., *The Jews in America,* chap. i. John C. Winston Co.

Wiernik, Peter, *History of the Jews in America,* Introd., chap. i.

Graetz, H., *History of the Jews,* vol. IV, pp. 367, 368, 378. Jewish Publication Society.

Levinger, E. E. and L. J., *The Story of the Jew,* chap. ix (for the European background of the period).

Jewish Encyclopedia, arts. on Discovery of America, Cresques, Columbus, Luis de Santangel, Vecinho, Abraham Zacuto.

Aguilar, Grace, *The Vale of Cedars* (a novel of the Inquisition in Spain).

Levinger, E. E., "In the Night Watches," *The New Land.*

Any good life of Christopher Columbus.

REFERENCES FOR TEACHERS

Kayserling, M., *Christopher Columbus and the Participation of the Jews in the Spanish and Portuguese Discoveries.*

Burke, U. R., *A History of Spain.* Longmans Green.

McEntire, W. F., *Was Columbus a Jew?* Stratford.

Adler, E. N., *Auto da Fé and Jew.* Oxford.

38

CHAPTER 3.

Jewish Settlers in Spanish America

WHEN we follow Jewish migrations to the New World, we naturally wonder in what section to look for them. We find at once that the earliest Jewish settlers went to the section that first was settled, and that Jews appear among the pioneers of almost every colony in order. Whenever the authorities permitted, the first Jewish pioneers followed the routes of the explorers into the new colonies as they were opened up; those who migrated after them followed the newly established routes of trade into commercial centers.

I. IN SPANISH TERRITORY—INQUISITION RULES

THE first century and a half after the discovery of the New World brought only a continuation of the terrible conditions that confronted the Jews in Spain and Portugal, for these nations were the first colonizers and rulers in Mexico and South America. Many years elapsed until the Dutch were freed from Spain and set forth to acquire colonies where they practiced the same toleration as was practiced in their own homeland; it took many more years before England adopted a liberal policy toward the Jews living on English soil, or gained possessions across the seas.

History of the Jews in the United States

The unfriendly attitude of the Spanish and Portuguese toward their converts, "the New Christians"—who were always suspected of secret adherence to Judaism—was not changed when they crossed the Atlantic. As Jewish history in Spain ends with the Inquisition, so Jewish history in America begins under the same cloud of cruelty and bigotry. The Inquisition was formally established in the West Indies in 1511 and in South America in 1516.

At the same time, laws were made against the New Christians going to the colonies. Nevertheless, the first man to obtain permission from the King of Spain to trade with the New World—in the year 1502—was a convert, Juan Sanchez of Saragossa, a nephew of Gabriel Sanchez. This Juan Sanchez belonged to a famous family of Marranos. His father and many other relatives had been burned at the stake for observing Jewish customs. His kinsman, Luis de Santangel himself, boasted the prized possession of a royal decree exempting him and his family from all questioning or accusation by the Inquisition.

Law after law was promulgated in Spain forbidding Jews, Mohammedans, or converts from these religions to go to the New World, through fear that they not only might become rich there, but might also escape the rules of the Church. But these laws must have been evaded constantly, for in South America there was at once felt a need for the Inquisition in order to detect converted Jews and others who were not loyal to the Catholic faith. This included the Indians, converted in large num-

Jewish Settlers in Spanish America

bers by force, and then killed by the thousands for continuing their own religious customs, even when they did not understand anything at all about the Christian religion. Soon there were also Protestants to seek out, as the Protestant Reformation occurred in this same century and influenced people in every country. But always there was exceptional suspicion and exceptional jealousy of the converted Jews. Whenever a Marrano became rich, spies were set upon him, for if he could be proved loyal to Judaism his property could be taken away and he himself imprisoned or even put to death. Secret testimony, even the evidence of frightened and bullied children, was used against the suspects; they were tortured to force confession; they were defended only by servants of the Inquisition, appointed for that purpose; spies were imprisoned with them to extract confessions by pretending sympathy; the prosecutors were at the same time the judges.

Yet the loyalty of these people to Judaism was so profound that they risked all this to keep even a few of the old religious customs of their fathers. Men and women whose grandparents or great-grandparents had been unwilling converts to Christianity still taught their children the Shema, still gathered secretly to fast on the Day of Atonement, still married according to the Jewish law and still rested on the Sabbath day. Even though they went to Church and pretended to be Christians, they kept the feasts and fasts of Judaism in the secrecy of their homes.

History of the Jews in the United States

This secret Judaism, opposed by the power and trickery of the Inquisition, could have but one ending in America as in the Old World. Many of the Marranos were convicted, most of them to imprisonment, banishment, confiscation of their property, or public penance dressed in the Sanbenito (a long garment ornamented with figures of devils); some of them were burned to death at an auto da fé or "act of faith," as the public execution was called. The first burning of a Jew in America occurred in Mexico City in 1574; from that time on there were many others burned at the stake in Mexico, Peru and throughout the Spanish dominions.

Some of these unfortunate sufferers because of their lingering loyalty to Judaism were both interesting and important in themselves, apart from their sad fates. There was the rich and noble family of Carabajal, of which the head was Don Luis de Carabajal y Cueva, governor of one of the districts in Mexico toward the end of the sixteenth century. He settled his own district with colonists from Spain, including several secret Jews, and also brought his sister, her family, and many other relatives to Mexico. But even in that distant colony his protection did not help them. In 1590 his sister, Francisca Nunez de Carabajal, was arrested on suspicion of being a Jewess. She was tortured until she confessed and then again until she betrayed her husband and children. They all recanted and were condemned to imprisonment; but five years later they were tried again, convicted of backsliding, and she, her four daughters and her son

42

THE INQUISITION
From a painting of about 1500.

Luis were all burned at the stake in 1595. The younger Luis de Carabajal was the first Jewish author in the New World, for while in his prison he wrote his autobiography and some Jewish hymns.

In 1642 the Inquisition in Mexico arrested a thirteen-year old boy named Gabriel de Granada, together with his mother and sisters. Poor little Gabriel was kept in prison for three years as a helpless victim. He was sometimes tortured to make him betray others, at other times promised his freedom if he gave their names, with the result that he finally named many of his relatives and friends, who were arrested and punished in their turn. There must have been a number of secret Jews in the city at that time, for 107 were accused in this one trial alone. Gabriel was finally freed, exiled from the colony and sent to Spain, where he had to live in certain sections, stay away from the chief cities, and do various penances under the control of the Inquisition. It is sad to read the court records of his trial, which have been published by the American Jewish Historical Society (Vol. 7).

A man of a different stamp was Francisco Maldonado de Silva, who was arrested in Lima, Peru, on the testimony of his own sister. He was a young man of thirty-three who had been born in America, was both a physician and a poet. He had been a devout Catholic up to eighteen years of age, but at that time he came to feel that Judaism, not Christianity, was the true religion. For twelve years he was kept in prison where he wrote and studied constantly, held many arguments about religion

44

with the priests and monks who were sent to bring him back to Catholicism, and even succeeded in converting two Catholic prisoners to Judaism!

As he would not recant, De Silva was burned to death with ten other Jews at the greatest auto da fé ever held in America, at Lima, Peru, in 1639. Of all the executions held by the Inquisition—and this horror continued until 1806—this was the most important. Beside the eleven Jews who were put to death, more than fifty others were condemned to various other penalties. As those punished included the richest man in Peru and several others of wealth, it is possible that the Inquisition desired their property as much as their conversion.

So, generation after generation, Spanish and Portuguese Marranos tried to find freedom in the New World, but were followed, captured and tormented by their persecutors.

II. IN PORTUGUESE CONTROL—SECRECY AND DANGER

THE Portuguese had the same attitude toward the Jews at home as did their neighbors of Spain; they forbade professing Jews to live in their land and sought out secret Jews through the Inquisition. However, they did not establish that dread office in all its power in their dominion of Brazil. Instead, they had spies there; anyone reported as a Judaizer was sent back to Portugal for trial and punishment. Thus many American Marranos were condemned in Portugal but the burnings and other horrors were not carried out in America.

45

History of the Jews in the United States

In one way the policy of the Portuguese was different from that of the Spaniards. While the Spaniards always forbade Marranos from settling in their over-seas
dominions, and the latter could do so only by bribery or
in secret, the Portuguese sent a great many Marranos
as well as criminals (we can see what they thought of the
Jews at that time) among the first settlers. In the one
case, the Jews were forbidden what, in the other, they
were forced to do; they never had the right to make their
own choice as human beings.

Even in those early days of the first explorers and
colonizers, certain men of Jewish descent were prominent
in the industry of the New World. In 1548 the sugar cane
was imported from Madeira into Brazil by several Portuguese Marranos and for two centuries after that their
families were connected with the sugar industry of
Brazil.

We cannot wonder that the Jews hated and feared
their proud rulers from the Iberian peninsula, and that
they greeted with all possible enthusiasm the people of
another nation, which was both fair and friendly to the
Jews.

III. WITH THE DUTCH—A MOMENT OF FREEDOM

HOLLAND, after gaining her freedom from Spain and the
Inquisition, was one of the few countries in the world
where the Jew had a chance. William the Silent was both
a liberal and a far-seeing man; he stated that "he should
not suffer any man to be called to account, molested or

46

injured for his faith or conscience." This was partly because the Dutch were Protestants, who had suffered from the Inquisition themselves. Perhaps their ruler also understood that the Jewish merchants would help to bring prosperity to his little but progressive country. Of course, Jews were not full citizens in Holland in those early days, in the sixteenth and seventeenth centuries. They were allowed to live there, to worship in their own way, and to engage in many kinds of business, especially with foreign countries. They were still regarded as aliens, however, were excluded from certain trades, and were forced to pay a special tax instead of serving in the militia. Complete freedom and equality of all religions was not known anywhere at that time, but the Dutch were nearer to it than any other people of Europe.

Many Spanish and Portuguese Marranos fled to Holland, where they could return openly to the religion of their fathers. The Jewish community of Amsterdam soon became large and rich, as it remains to this day, including even at the beginning rich merchants, great scholars and world-famous thinkers. The Dutch were constantly at war with Spain and Portugal and made a number of attempts to capture some of their American colonies. Naturally the Marranos already settled in the New World did their utmost to help their protectors from Holland. In 1631 the Dutch captured Recife, at that time the capital of Brazil, now called Pernambuco and still an important city. Many of the secret Jews living there and in other parts of South America took advantage of the

47

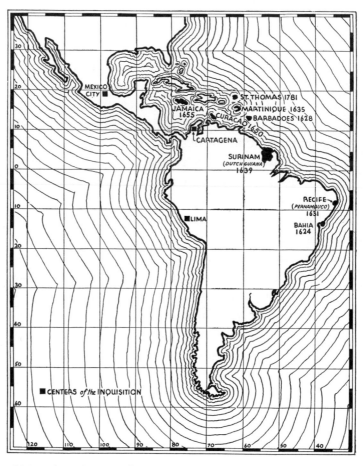

EARLY SETTLEMENTS OF JEWS IN CENTRAL AND SOUTH AMERICA

opportunity and openly returned to Judaism; thus Recife possessed the first Jewish community on American soil.

The settlement of Jews increased rapidly from every source until some authorities claim it contained about 5,000 souls. The largest and most important group of colonists came from Amsterdam in 1642, and included 600 people. Among them were two Jewish scholars who became the first American rabbi and chazan, or cantor —Isaac Aboab da Fonseca and Moses Raphael de Aguilar. These people settled partly in Recife, partly in other Dutch settlements; they must have planned a great Jewish center in South America. There was even an effort to bring Rabbi Manasseh ben Israel, the famous rabbi of Amsterdam, to the New World. Manasseh is an interesting figure, not only because he was a scholar and wrote many books, but especially because he approached Oliver Cromwell, the ruler of England at that time, and induced him to permit Jews to settle in England, from which they had been banished for almost four hundred years. It is hard to imagine the possible difference in the history of the Jews of England if Manasseh had gone to Brazil instead of remaining to accomplish his great work in Europe.

The Jews of Recife formed a congregation, called Kahal Kodesh, the Holy Congregation; they built fine homes, established sugar mills, and began an extensive trade with Holland and other countries. But just as their prosperity and freedom seemed assured, and their future appeared most rosy, their fate was again changed. The war between Holland and Portugal took a different turn; the Portuguese laid siege to Recife.

At first the Jews discovered a Portuguese conspiracy against the Dutch and averted the danger. Then the siege began. Jews at once volunteered for the defense in large numbers; the Dutch later acknowledged in full their bravery and their sufferings. One of the Pinto family defended a fort single-handed until he was entirely overwhelmed by the forces of the enemy. Wealthy merchants raised all the money they could to contribute supplies to the defenders. The sufferings of the Jews were described by Rabbi Aboab in a book entitled Zecher Rab, the Great Remembrance. Thus the first Hebrew book written in America was a story of suffering due to the loyalty and the persecution of the Jews. Aboab wrote: "Many of the Jewish immigrants were killed by the enemy; many died of starvation. Those who were accustomed to delicacies were glad to be able to satisfy their hunger with dry bread; soon they could not obtain even this. They were in want of everything, and were preserved alive as if by a miracle."

In 1654 Recife fell and the Jews were forced to leave at once. Most of them returned to Holland, among them Joseph Velosino, who is interesting to us because he was the first Hebrew author who was born in America. Others went to the various Dutch colonies in the New World: Surinam, Cayenne, Curacao, and probably New Amsterdam. Some of these districts have had Jewish communities since that date, that is, for over two cen٠ turies and a half.

Surinam, or Dutch Guiana, had the largest and most interesting of all these old Jewish settlements. The first Jews were already settled there in 1639 during the time when the Recife community was flourishing. Guiana was owned during this period, sometimes by the English, sometimes by the Dutch, and both gave the Jews the same rights they enjoyed under the Dutch at Recife. We notice this liberalism especially because it was so unusual. At the neighboring colony of Cayenne the Jews settled under the Dutch but had to leave the moment that territory was captured by the French. In 1665 the Jews of Surinam received a splendid grant of privileges from the British governor, Lord Willoughby, granting them the free exercise of the Jewish religion, allowing the rabbis to settle law suits according to the Jewish law,

SAVANNAH OF THE JEWS—SURINAM

and even granting British citizenship to foreign-born Jews. These privileges were continued when the Dutch took back the colony two years later, and most of the Jews remained in their little trading city on the coast, between the sea and the jungle.

But some of them were bolder pioneers than that. They began to clear the jungle and to lay out sugar plantations in this tropical wilderness, using imported negro slaves for the work. In 1680 Samuel Nassi, the richest man in the colony, donated an island far up the river to his people; many of them moved there from the seaport, and built there a Jewish colony, far away from the rest of the world, in the midst of the jungle. This was known as the Savannah (or plain) of the Jews, and was the first Jewish city built in the New World, and one of the few built anywhere in modern times. We do not know the thoughts of its founder, but he must have had some idea of a separate Jewish nation, with its own farms and its own rich trading city.

The settlers imported bricks, furniture and books from Holland in return for their sugar cane. Within five years of the founding of the Savannah they built their synagogue, with a wide stairway and an elaborate entrance, calling their congregation Berakah veShalom (Blessing and Peace). The settlers engaged, not only in farming and trade, but also in warfare. The negro slaves who were imported from Africa were unhappy in slavery; some of them escaped from time to time to the jungle, and finally they were numerous enough to form armies

52

and attack the white settlements. In this border warfare the Jewish settlement was at the most dangerous point, nearest the jungle. Jewish troops were raised, who carried their share of this fierce war, winning many times. But at last after a century the rebel slaves won, the Jewish town was deserted and the Jews went back to the seaport. Today there are only a few ruins of masonry and broken stones in the midst of the luxuriant jungle, where once was the Savannah of the Jews.

Through all this period the Nassi family was the leading one among the Jews, and ranked high in the colony as a whole. David Nassi had been one of the founders of the colony. Samuel Nassi, donor of the Savannah, was the richest planter in Surinam; he was known as Capetin because he fought against a French fleet. Later on another David Nassi was commander against the slave insurrection; after repeated victories he was killed in battle at the age of seventy-one.

All these Jews came either direct from Spain or Portugal, or via Holland, or other American colonies. There were not enough German Jews to form a congregation until 1734, almost a century later. The first Jewish theatre of modern times was built here by some of these German Jews. Both old congregations still exist in Surinam, both strictly orthodox; they still include a few families of the original settlers.

Another settlement of the same early period was at Curacao in the Dutch West Indies in 1650. When the Portuguese recaptured Brazil many Jews came to

Curacao, where they became active both as planters and as merchants. In fact, Peter Stuyvesant, who was governor of New Amsterdam at that time, complained violently to the Directors of the Dutch West India Company, asking for his own colonies the same privileges as those of the "Usurius and Covetus Jews." The first Jewish congregation was founded as early as 1656. The Jewish community of Curacao flourished and became the mother of a number of other Jewish settlements, both in the West Indies and in Newport, Rhode Island.

IV. WITH THE ENGLISH—TOLERATION

MOST of the early Jewish settlements, as we have seen, were in the territory held by Holland; but in a few places Jewish colonists came into contact with the English. In later times, as the English program of colonization grew at the expense of other nations, most of the Jews in the New World came finally under the British rule. In earlier days the British would have treated Jews much as the French did, with expulsion, although neither country ever subjected its people to the Inquisition. But at this period, during the middle of the seventeenth century, England had just undergone a great revolution under Oliver Cromwell which resulted in increasing freedom for everyone. Jews were allowed to return to England after an absence of about 400 years. Therefore we hear of the grant of privileges to the Jews of Surinam in 1665.

In Barbados, Jews were probably among the first

Jewish Settlers in Spanish America

settlers in 1628. When the British captured Jamaica in 1655, a number of secret Jews who were living there were glad to come out in the open as Jews at last. They had had difficulties under the Spaniards, but at least they had escaped the Inquisition because Jamaica had been at first the personal property of the family of Columbus, rather than a colony of the Spanish crown. The English called these Jews "Portugals" and at once gave more rights to them than to the Spanish Catholics. Jews came from Recife when the Portuguese captured it, from Surinam and even from England itself. The Jews of Jamaica were active in the vanilla and sugar industries as well as in foreign commerce; some of them were among the richest men in the island and usually they paid most of the taxes.

There were a few legal restrictions at first, as in England itself. Jamaica was the first British territory to abolish the discriminations against Jews voting and holding office. This was done in 1831, and only four years later Alexander Bravo was elected to the Assembly, later becoming Receiver General. In fact, so many Jews achieved distinction in Jamaica that this became one of the arguments in favor of complete equality in England itself.

So throughout the seventeenth century little settlements of Jews sprang up wherever a moment's liberty was given them. Everywhere they accompanied or followed the very first explorers. Expelled by the French, oppressed by the Portuguese, hounded and persecuted by the Spanish, they grew prosperous and happy under the rule of the English and especially of the Dutch. It need not surprise us, therefore, that the first Jewish settlement in North America was in a Dutch colony, and that Jews settled and flourished in English colonies even before the Revolution which was to bring them freedom.

It would be an interesting study for us in North America to trace the slow growth of Jewish communities in South and Central American lands since they won their freedom from Spain and Portugal. At present there are about 250,000 Jews living in these various nations, about 200,000 of them living in Argentina. The greatest settlement in that country, which brought many other Jews to the district, was established by the Jewish Colonization Association with money given for that purpose by Baron Maurice de Hirsch. We shall hear of this work in its proper place in this history. Since the World War, owing to the limitation of immigration to the United States, many other settlers have found their way to Mexico and Cuba, and some to South America.

REVIEW QUESTIONS

1. What were the motives that brought the Spaniards to America? What were the motives that brought the Dutch to America? What were the motives that brought the English to America? What were the motives that brought the Jews to America?
2. Why did it take so long to provide a refuge for the Jews in the New World?
3. Describe the first Jewish settlement in America.

Jewish Settlers in Spanish America

4. Tell about one prominent family of Jews or Marranos in South or Central America.
5. Compare the treatment of Jews in the colonies of five different Nations.

TOPICS FOR REPORTS

1. The Jews in Holland. *Jewish Encyclopedia*, vol. IX, pp. 228–233. Graetz, vol. IV, pp. 661, 667, 668, 685; vol. V, p. 34. Margolis and Marx, chap. lxv.
2. The Jews in England. *Jewish Encyclopedia*, vol. V, pp. 161–174. Graetz, vol. III, pp. 356, 409–416, 515–516, 571, 587–592, 640–646. Margolis and Marx, chap. lxv.
3. The Jews of Latin America Today. *American Jewish Year Book*, 1917–18, art. by Harry O. Sandberg.
4. The Growth of Religious Toleration.
5. Colonization in the Western Hemisphere during the period 1492–1660.

REFERENCES FOR PUPILS

Wiernik, Peter, chaps. ii–viii.
Vandercook, John W., "Jungle Jews," *Menorah Journal*, March, 1928.
Jewish Encyclopedia, arts. on Isaac de Fonseca Aboab, Moses Raphael de Aguilar, America, Bahia, Barbadoes, Brazil, Carbajal, Curacao, Cuba, Jamaica, Martinique, Recife, South and Central America, West Indies.

REFERENCES FOR TEACHERS

Hyamson, A. M., *History of the Jews in England.*
Wolf, Lucien, *Mission of Manasseh ben Israel to Cromwell.*
Wolf, Simon, *The Jew as Patriot, Soldier and Citizen,* pp. 442–484.
Publications of the American Jewish Historical Society.
Kayserling, M., "The Earliest Rabbis and Jewish Writers of America," vol. III, pp. 13–20.

History of the Jews in the United States

Kohut, George Alexander, "Early Jewish Literature in America," vol. III, pp. 103–148.

"A Trial by the Inquisition in Mexico, 1642–45," vol. VII.

Hilfman, P. A., "Notes on the History of the Jews in Surinam," vol. XVIII, pp. 179–208.

Hilfman, P. A., "Some Further Notes on the History of the Jews in Surinam," vol. XVI, pp. 7–22.

Oppenheim, Samuel, "An Early Jewish Colony in Western Guiana, 1658–66," vol. XVI, pp. 98–186.

Davis, N. Darnell, "Notes on the History of the Jews in Barbadoes," vol. XVIII, pp. 129–148.

Judah, George Fortunatus, "The Jews' Tribute in Jamaica," vol. XVIII, pp. 149–178.

Lea, *Inquisition in the Spanish Dominions.*

Adler, E. N., *Auto da Fé and Jew.*

Wolf, Simon, *American Jew as Patriot, Soldier and Citizen*, pp. 443–498, art. by George A. Kohut on "Sketches of Jewish Loyalty, Bravery and Patriotism in the South American Colonies and the West Indies."

CHAPTER 4.

How the First Jews Came to North America

I. NEW AMSTERDAM, 1654

WHEN South America was closed to Jewish settlers through the victory of the Portuguese over
the Dutch, the Jews had to find other places of refuge,
other abiding places for their constant hope of freedom.
Some returned to Amsterdam for the liberty they had
known there. Some went to the British colonies in the
Barbados and Jamaica. Some sought the Dutch colony to
the north in New Amsterdam, now known as New York.

Where did they come from, these first Jews to settle
in our continent? How did they reach these shores? Why
did Jews begin to come to the land that some day was
to become a dear home for so many of their descendants?

In September 1654, twenty-three Jews, men, women
and children, entered the harbor of New Amsterdam on
the bark St. Charles, probably from Cape St. Anthony in
Brazil. The captain was a Frenchman, Jacques de la
Motte. These people must have been very poor, as refugees would naturally be who had lost their possessions
in the wars. For the first we hear of them is that they

were unable to pay the full amount of their passage money, that their little household goods were sold at auction to pay part of it, and that two of the men were imprisoned as surety for the rest.

Peter Stuyvesant, the Dutch governor of the colony, was angry to see these people trying to enter his little town. We can imagine him stamping about on his silver-banded wooden leg and cursing wildly as he was accustomed to do on less important occasions. He had even complained long before to his directors, the heads of the Dutch West Indies Company in Amsterdam, about the ruinous competition

COMMEMORATION MEDAL OF THE 250TH ANNIVERSARY OF THE SETTLEMENT OF THE JEWS IN THE UNITED STATES.

of the Jews living in British colonies. Evidently he had no love for the children of Israel. At once he wrote his objections to Amsterdam. But as the newcomers wrote at the same time and were backed by the Dutch Jews, the directors could consider the whole question and decide it fairly. Naturally they tried to make their colony as much like the mother country as possible, and Holland had the most liberal policy toward the Jews of any nation in those days, as we have seen above. So when

60

Stuyvesant asked that "the deceitful race be not allowed further to infect and trouble this new colony" citing their poverty as a reason, the directors decided against him.

Their reply was sent in April, 1655. They said that "this would be unreasonable and unfair, especially because of the considerable loss sustained by the Jews in the taking of Brazil, and also because of the large amount of capital which they have invested in the shares of this company. . . . These people may travel and trade to and in New Netherlands, and live and remain there, providing the poor among them shall be supported by their own nation." This is the charter of Jewish settlement, and the beginning of Jewish liberty in the United States. The condition laid down, to care for their poor, was kept by the original settlers, and the great Jewish community which followed never forgot this promise.

The governor and his supporters were not at all satisfied. Even before this order came, they had tried to drive all the Jews from the colony because one of them had kept his shop open on Sunday. Naturally this expulsion was stopped by the same order that permitted the Jews to settle. Other petty persecutions and oppositions went on from time to time, as we shall see in the rest of this chapter.

II. EARLIER ARRIVALS

THIS first settlement of a group of Jews was both preceded and followed by bold individuals. Jacob Barsimson came to New Amsterdam directly from Holland on

61

the ship Peartree, as early as August, 1654, a month ahead of the larger group of Jews. We know that others came from Holland during the same winter, for certain orders and letters the next summer speak of the Portuguese Jews from Brazil and the Dutch Jews who came directly from the mother country. Other immigrants came from both places as time went on.

Jacob Barsimson of Holland, then, seems to have the honor of being the first Jewish settler in what is now the United States. Here and there are records of possible Jews in other colonies at an early date, but we know too little about them to establish the facts. But the first Jewish community in North America was that of New Amsterdam, which has other "firsts" as well, the first Jewish cemetery, the first congregation, and the first synagogue. We shall now follow the slow development of the tiny Jewish community in the little colony at the very tip of Manhattan Island, under the Dutch until 1664, and after that under the English until the Revolution.

III. TEN YEARS IN NEW AMSTERDAM

DURING these ten years the Jewish community acquired a cemetery though not a synagogue. It was the first step in their communal life. In July 1655 Abraham de Lucena, Salvador Dandrada, and Jacob Cohen petitioned the governor and directors of the colony for the right to establish a Jewish cemetery. They were told that they might have one when there was need; this need arose in

How the First Jews Came to North America

the following year and a tract of land was set aside for them from the colony lands. The site was outside the village, which means that it was north of Wall Street, where the Dutch built the city wall; it was near the present location of Chatham Square, on the New Bowery. Only a small part of the cemetery, with a few of the tombstones, still exists. One of the most interesting original studies in American Jewish history is a visit to this old Jewish burying ground as well as to the second one established, on what is now West 11th Street, near 6th Avenue.

The names given in the petition are Spanish ones, which shows that these Jews or their families came origi‑ nally from Spain or Portugal. As Abraham de Lucena's name is first in this as in several other documents, he must have been the most influential man in the little Jewish community. The inscriptions on the tombstones are in both Hebrew and Spanish, which shows us that these Jews used Spanish as their mother-tongue, but likewise were strictly orthodox and employed Hebrew on their tombstones. Their poverty is shown by the small stones they put up, but that was not peculiar, as almost everybody was poor in the new colonies of those days, and the stones are just as small and plain in any ceme‑ tery of that period.

But the founding of a synagogue was denied. Peter Stuyvesant wrote to Amsterdam, giving his personal ob‑ jection, which was that it would lead to Lutherans and Catholics putting up churches as well. In other words,

63

he wanted only his own particular church to have full rights. In this the directors of the company agreed with him. The Jews were allowed to worship privately in their own homes but not to build a house of worship.

In the same way, the Jewish merchants were allowed to trade with the Indians, both up the Hudson toward Albany, and up the Delaware (which they called the South River); but they were not allowed to engage in retail trades or in certain crafts. Stuyvesant wanted to prohibit all trading by the Jews; but the directors in Holland laid down the rule that was actually followed. The bigoted governor tried to prevent the Jews from buying real estate, but was overruled on appeal to Hol-

OLD JEWISH CEMETERY, WEST TWENTY-FIRST STREET,
NEW YORK, N. Y.

land. However, he did not object to their paying taxes; the Jews were assessed heavily, along with the rest of the colony, for the building of the city wall at the present site of Wall Street.

The most interesting character of this early American Jewish history is Asser Levy, one of the original settlers from the St. Charles. Levy was a bold, independent spirit, always insisting on justice for himself, always in court with one suit or another, and at the same time defending Jewish rights as well. As early as 1655 he objected to paying a special tax instead of standing guard with the other burghers, in defending the colony against the Indians. The request was refused at the time but it must have been granted later, for we hear of Levy serving under arms in the train bands. In 1657 he applied for citizenship on the ground that he was a burgher of Amsterdam in Holland. The governor denied this request also, but again an appeal of the entire community to the Dutch West Indies Company was successful, and the Jews of New Amsterdam were granted exactly the same rights as they had enjoyed in Amsterdam. These rights gave them tolerance rather than complete freedom; but they were far in advance of the rights given the Jews by other nations, and were one step toward the liberty embodied later on in the Constitution.

IV. A CENTURY UNDER GREAT BRITAIN

WHEN New Amsterdam became New York little change was made in the status of its inhabitants. Jews were still

History of the Jews in the United States

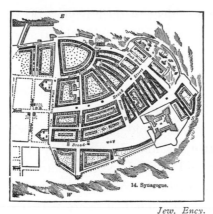

Jew. Ency.

tolerated, not accepted as full citizens, but on the other hand they were not persecuted or discriminated against. The toleration in England was followed in the colony. The number of Jews in New York increased very slowly during this period.

Still progress came slowly but surely. First, in 1682 the Jews of early New York rented a house for a synagogue, so that the worship conducted privately in their homes might now be public in a house of God. It was probably a little, rude house with only one room, not very different from the homes of the settlers or the churches of their neighbors. For these people were pioneers, not only for Judaism, but also for America; they underwent the privations and knew the triumphs of the pioneers. This first synagogue was located on what is now Beaver Street, between Broadway and Broad Street. It was founded in accordance with a liberal decree of the Duke of York, which went beyond the charter of the colony in 1683. This charter had allowed freedom of worship to any Christians; but the Duke permitted it "for any persons whatsoever," which included the Jews.

66

How the First Jews Came to North America

By 1728 the little congregation were ready to build a house of worship. They organized as the Congregation Shearith Israel, or Remnant of Israel, and erected the first regular synagogue in North America on Mill Street, where a mill then stood. It was a little stone building with a wooden fence around it. It stood at the present site of South William Street, where the great banks and office buildings contain nothing to remind us of the Dutch burghers and the pioneer Jews of those early days. But the congregation still exists as the oldest Jewish congregation in the United States and one of the oldest bodies for worship of any kind. Naturally, its present synagogue is "up-town" on Central Park West, and not in the original place of settlement; but it is still orthodox, observing the Sephardic ritual as it did from the beginning. The first Chazan or reader of services was Saul Brown, one of the business men, who was admitted to the burgher right in 1685.

In 1727 the General Assembly of the colony passed an act that when the oath of abjuration, or allegiance, to Great Britain was to be taken by a Jew, the words, "on the true faith of a Christian," might be omitted. This was very important because it gave the Jews a chance

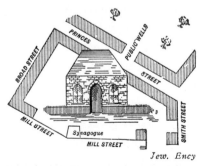

Jew. Ency

SKETCH AND SITE OF OLD MILL STREET SYNAGOGUE, NEW YORK, N. Y.

67

to become naturalized, and took religion a little more out of governmental control, making it a little more the free right of each citizen. Of course, this did not give the Jews all the rights they enjoy now. They could not hold office in the colony. Just ten years later a case arose when the English law of the time was applied, and Jews were not allowed to act as witnesses in a court or to vote for members of the General Assembly.

During this time the wealth of the Jews and their numbers slowly increased. They traded with the West Indies and with Portugal, and probably brought back some of their coreligionists with them. There must have been a few Jews from other lands, too, in the colony, for the Rev. John Sharpe in 1712 uses this fact as one of his arguments for establishing a school and library in the little town. "It is possible also to learn Hebrew here as well as in Europe, there being a synagogue of Jews, and many ingenious men of that nation from Poland, Hungary, Germany, etc." Even though the good minister may have been exaggerating a little, he probably had some basis for this statement.

About thirty years later, New York was visited by a Swedish traveller, Peter Kalm, who wrote a fine account of the colony. This is what he says of the Jews he found there: "There are many Jews settled in New York who possess great privileges. They have a synagogue and houses, great country seats of their own property, and are allowed to keep shops in town. They have, likewise, several ships which they freight and send out with their goods; in fine, the Jews enjoy all the privileges in common to the other inhabitants of this town and province." These privileges were all the more remarkable in that day, for they were not granted in any European nation except Holland and England.

In 1711 when money was being subscribed for the steeple of Trinity Church, one of the most interesting buildings of down-town New York even today, several Jews were among the donors. They must have been able to contribute by that time, as well as broad-minded enough to give money toward a Christian church building.

The first part of the eighteenth century found Lewis Gomez a leader among the Jews by reason of his wealth and public spirit. He was born in Spain of a family of Marranos, escaped from the country as a grown man, and lived openly as a Jew in New York. He was one of the chief merchants of the little town, and his ships which carried American produce to the Old World and traded in foreign lands, often brought back other Marranos who settled in the New World as Jews. He had five sons, who carried the name of Gomez on through the period of the Revolution. One of them was an old man at that time, but volunteered as a soldier, saying, "I think I can stop a bullet as well as a younger man."

During the last half of the eighteenth century, the leading Jew was Hayman Levy, who traded with the Indians, buying their furs in return for civilized products. Hayman Levy was the first employer in America of one John Jacob Astor, later the great merchant prince of New York. The future millionaire received at that time one dollar a day for beating furs.

But this brings us to the next topic, the American Revolution.

REVIEW QUESTIONS

1. Who were the first Jews in North America? Trace their entire journey as far as you can.
2. Outline the communal life of the oldest Jewish community, what its institutions were and their growth.
3. Name outstanding Jews of the various periods from the landing to the Revolution.
4. Explain the development in Jewish rights from the attitude of Peter Stuyvesant to the fullest toleration enjoyed. How far did that fall short of present Jewish rights in New York?

TOPICS FOR REPORTS

1. Sketch the settlement of the various European nations in North America.
2. Show the reasons why the Dutch gave the Jews toleration in their colonies.
3. Outline the history of early New York from its settlement to the Revolution.
4. Study whether the Jews of New York have kept their promise to care for their own poor. Prove by present conditions.
5. Compare the growth of the early Jewish community in New York with that of your own city in its beginnings.

History of the Jews in the United States

REFERENCES FOR PUPILS

Jewish Encyclopedia, arts. on New York City, Hayman Levy, Peter Stuyvesant, Gomez Family, Asser Levy.

Wiernik, Peter, chap ix.

Levinger, E. E., "When Katrina Lost Her Way," *The New Land.*

REFERENCES FOR TEACHERS

Daly, *Settlement of the Jews in North America* (out of print), pp. 1–58. Philip Cowen.

Markens, Isaac, *The Hebrews in America,* pp. 1–21. Printed by the author.

Ency. Americana, art. by Max J. Kohler, "Jews in America."

Brodhead, J. R., *History of the State of New York.* Harper.

Goodwin, M. W., *The Dutch and English on the Hudson, Yale Chronicles of America,* vol. VII. Yale University Press.

The Two Hundred and Fiftieth Anniversary of the Settlement of Jews in America, Commemorative Volume. New York Cooperative Co., also Pub., Vol. XIV.

Publications of the American Jewish Historical Society.

    Kohler, Max J., "Beginnings of New York Jewish History," vol. I, pp. 41–48.

    Kohler, Max J., "Phases of Jewish Life in New York before 1800," vol. III, pp. 73–86.

    Oppenheim, Samuel, "The Early History of the Jews in New York, 1654–1664," vol. XVIII, pp. 1–92; "More about Barsimson," vol. XXIX.

    Phillips, Rosalie S., "A Burial Place for the Jewish Nation Forever," vol. XVIII, pp. 93–123.

Volumes XXI and XXVII are the Lyons' collection, including Minute Books of Shearith Israel Congregation and the Notebooks of Rev. J. J. Lyons.

CHAPTER 5.

A Thriving Jewish Community
Before the Revolution

I. NEWPORT, RHODE ISLAND

IF, without knowing the facts, we would try to reason out where we should find the second settlement of Jews in what is now the United States, we would look for two things: religious freedom and a busy seaport. The first was necessary if Jews were to be allowed even to enter a colony; the second would provide a location where they might establish a business.

The second Jewish settlement in what is now the United States (though not the second point where individual Jews arrived) was at Newport, Rhode Island. Of all the English colonies this alone offered the Jews complete toleration to a Jew as a resident, citizen, and worshipper. Some colonies allowed Jews to settle but not to vote, others to vote but not to worship openly. Many of the colonies did not want Jews on any terms. But Roger Williams, pious clergyman and bold thinker, made no distinction between members of his own church, of other Christian churches, or even the outcast sons of Israel. His colony was the first and only one which made no religious distinction of any kind. Even Pennsylvania,

72

which had no state church, made a distinction between Christians and non-Christians in the right of voting; while every other English settlement had an official church, some of them Puritan, some Church of England.

But when Newport was founded in 1636, the daring theory was propounded that there should be no connection of any kind in the new colony between church and state. The church was not to receive support from taxes or from the police power of the colony. Neither was the church to dictate governmental policies, nor to exclude people of other churches from the settlement. Most people predicted that this would mean the moral ruin of the colony or the public downfall of its church, perhaps both. But Roger Williams thought differently! We will see in chapter nine how his ideas a hundred and fifty years later became part of the fundamental law of the United States.

There is an old tradition that a few Jews came to Newport in 1658, just four years after the settlement in New Amsterdam, and that they began the Masonic order in the United States. This last seems very unlikely, for Masonic lodges were not founded in America for many years after that. But there were certainly Jews in this liberal colony very early, for their present cemetery was founded in 1677. It is therefore the oldest Jewish cemetery still existing in the United States, as the earlier one in New York has almost been lost with the growth of the city, and only a corner of it survives. This old cemetery has attracted much attention, for it

HEBREW CEMETERY, NEWPORT, R. I.

is a romantic spot, with its tombstones bearing inscriptions of Hebrew and Spanish names. Near it is the quaint little synagogue, also the oldest now existing in the United States; it was built in 1763, and was later endowed by the great philanthropist, Judah Touro.

Longfellow wrote a poem on "The Jewish Cemetery in Newport" at a time when no Jews at all were living in the city. Emma Lazarus, an American Jewish poet of the same period, wrote one entitled "In the Jewish Synagogue at Newport." It will be worth while to read these entire poems to compare their messages; but a quotation from each is all that we can give here. Longfellow wrote, using his knowledge of Jewish life and of the Hebrew language:

Jewish Community Before the Revolution

"Gone are the living, but the dead remain
   And not neglected; for a hand unseen
Scattering its bounty, like a summer rain
   Still keeps their graves and their remembrance green.

How came they here? What burst of Christian hate,
   What persecution, merciless and blind,
Drove o'er the sea—that desert desolate—
   These Ishmaels and Hagars of mankind?

Pride and humiliation hand in hand
   Walked with them through the world where'er they
      went,
Trampled and beaten were they as the sand,
   And yet unshaken as the continent."

Emma Lazarus, speaking for her own people, whom she loved so well, wrote in a similar strain:

"What prayers were in this temple offered up,
   Wrung from sad hearts that knew no joy on earth,
By these lone exiles of a thousand years,
   From the fair sunrise land that gave them birth!

Natheless the sacred shrine is holy yet
   With its lone floors where reverent feet once trod.
Take off your shoes as by the burning bush,
   Before the mystery of death and God."

History of the Jews in the United States

The romantic and touching beginnings of this Jewish community were followed by a period of real importance in the fifty years immediately before the American Revolution. At that time Newport was a more important port than New York, following only Boston and Philadelphia. Much of its commerce was traceable to the Jews from the West Indies and other lands. These were wealthy and influential men, with business connections in their former homes as well as in several of the other colonies. There were at least sixty Jewish families in Newport before the Revolution, with a permanent rabbi, Isaac Touro, as well as occasional visiting rabbis and scholars. Ezra Stiles, later the distinguished president of Yale University, has left interesting records of the Jewish community. He was a student of Hebrew and of Judaism, and had several close friends among the Jews of Newport during his twenty years as Congregational minister in that city. It is most interesting to read his account of religious discussions with some of the rabbinical scholars whom he met, his description of the synagogue and of its dedication exercises, and his tribute to Aaron Lopez, the leading Jew of the community.

Most of the Jews of Newport had Sephardic names, though some seem to have come from Holland or the West Indies. The Lopez family came from Portugal about 1750, the Rivera family from Spain; both of them had fled, a few fugitives at a time, to escape the Inquisition. We can hardly imagine the loyalty and heroism of these exiles. After two and a half centuries as Marranos, with the daily fear of the Inquisition, they had finally fled to a land where they might live openly as Jews, like their ancestors eight generations before. They were all naturalized, that they might conduct commerce under the British flag; those who had difficulty with the narrow immigration policy of certain Newport magistrates were easily naturalized in either New York or Massachusetts. These Newport Jews were among the leading business men of their day both in wealth and in pioneer projects; they were largely responsible for the high standing which Newport had as a seaport, and which it lost at the Revolution.

One of these men, Jacob Rodriguez Rivera, introduced the sperm oil industry in America. This proved a much better mode of lighting than the old tallow candles, and indirectly Rivera advanced the whaling industry as well. For a century thereafter whaling was among the leading industries of New England; it has left its impression deep in the history and literature of our country.

Aaron Lopez was a merchant and shipper of unusual standing; just before the Revolution he had thirty ships sailing back and forth to the West Indies, to Europe, and to the whaling fisheries. Ezra Stiles wrote in his diary after Lopez's death: "He was a Merchant of the first eminence; for Honor and Extent of Commerce probably surpassed by no Merchant in America. He did Business with the greatest ease and exactness—always carried about with him a sweetness of behavior, a calm Urbanity, and agreeable and unaffected Politeness of manners.

History of the Jews in the United States

AARON LOPEZ

Without a single Enemy and the most universally beloved by an extensive acquaintance of any man I ever knew." Remember that this was written in his own diary, not for the public, and you will see the real estimate this Christian scholar held of the Jewish merchant.

Even in Rhode Island there was some discrimination, for the courts did not naturalize Jews even when authorized by the British act of 1740.

The end of the Newport Jewish community came suddenly, with the Revolution. Most of the Jews were strongly attached to the cause of liberty, even Aaron Lopez, with his thirty ships at the mercy of the British navy. The commerce of Newport was destroyed when the port was taken over by the British; all sympathizers with the cause of freedom had to flee. Rabbi Touro went back to Jamaica, where he died; some Jews hurried to New York or Philadelphia, then held by the colonists. But part of the Jewish community followed Aaron Lopez to Leicester, Massachusetts, where they constituted the first Jewish settlement in that state. In

Jewish Community Before the Revolution

his will Lopez founded the Leicester Academy. This was at a time when large philanthropic gifts were very rare indeed.

These Jews remained in Leicester during the Revolution, conducting there certain types of business; when peace came some of them returned to Newport. But the leader of them all, Aaron Lopez, lost his life in quicksand on the way; he was brought back for burial in the little Jewish cemetery. During the Revolution other cities had taken the trade of Newport, and it never was restored. The older people died in Newport, the younger ones such as Judah Touro went to other cities, and Newport Jewry disappeared. The famous synagogue is now in use again; but the worshippers are a newer generation of Jews from eastern Europe, not descendants of the Marranos of those early days.

II. MASSACHUSETTS

NEWPORT was the only New England town with a permanent Jewish settlement prior to the Revolution, but occasional individuals or even families settled in various parts of the New England colonies, and many others passed through them. The cause of this difference rests on the different types of government. Plymouth was a democratic little group of people who thought alike and shared a common sacrifice for a common cause; it had no place for anyone who differed even slightly from the faith and practice of the Pilgrims. The Puritan settlements of Massachusetts Bay, New Haven and Connecticut were founded as Bible Commonwealths; they aimed to be theocracies like Israel under the rule of Moses, when God was the real ruler of the people. In such a community, Church and State were one and the same. The proper worship of God was one of the chief aims of the civil rulers. For this reason, the Puritans would not tolerate in their towns the Quakers, or Roger Williams, or anybody else who differed from them in religion. Sometimes they were terribly severe to these poor folk, whose consciences impelled them to a different faith; sometimes they were milder, but still insisted on their leaving the colony.

This is why no Jewish settlement grew among the Puritans, such as those in Dutch New Amsterdam or radical Rhode Island. The first record of a Jew in Massachusetts dates from 1649, when a certain Solomon Franco was directed to leave the colony for Holland, from which he had come, and a small weekly allowance was given him until he could take ship. There are other records later on, of one Jew who became a Christian in 1702 at Charlestown and another whom Cotton Mather, the famous minister, tried unsuccessfully to convert. The best known of the few Jews in Massachusetts before the Revolution was Judah Monis, who became a Christian; he was instructor in the Hebrew language at Harvard College and published for his classes the first Hebrew grammar in North America. Judah Monis had studied in Amsterdam and Leghorn; in 1720, when he was thirty-seven years old, he was awarded the degree of M.A. at

דִּקְדּוּק

לְשׁוֹן עִבְרִית

DICKDOOK LESHON GNEBREET.

A

GRAMMAR

OF THE

𝕳𝖊𝖇𝖗𝖊𝖜 𝕿𝖔𝖓𝖌𝖚𝖊,

BEING

An ESSAY

To bring the 𝕳𝖊𝖇𝖗𝖊𝖜 𝕲𝖗𝖆𝖒𝖒𝖆𝖗 into 𝕰𝖓𝖌𝖑𝖎𝖘𝖍,

to Facilitate the

INSTRUCTION

Of all thofe who are defirous of acquiring a clear Idea of this

Primitive Tongue

by their own Studies;

In order to their more diftinct Acquaintance with the SACRED ORACLES of the Old Teftament, according to the Original. And Publifhed more efpecially for the Ufe of the STUDENTS of *HARVARD-COLLEGE* at *Cambridge*, in NEW-ENGLAND.

נֶחְבַּר וְהוּגַת בְּעִיּוֹן נִמְרָץ עַל יְדֵי

יְהוּדָה מוֹנִישׁ

Compofed and accurately Corrected,

By JUDAH MONIS, M. A.

BOSTON, N. *England*

Printed by JONAS GREEN, and are to be Sold by the AUTHOR at his Houfe in *Cambridge.* MDCCXXXV.

TITLE PAGE OF JUDAH MONIS' GRAMMAR

Harvard, being the first Jew to receive a college degree in North America, as well as the only one to receive a Harvard degree before 1800. Two years later, at the urging of the Reverend Increase Mather, he became a Christian; soon afterward he was appointed instructor of Hebrew at Harvard and continued in this position for forty years. Hebrew was a required subject then, as most of the students were preparing for the ministry, and the college authorities laid great stress on a thorough knowledge of the Old Testament. In 1735 Harvard College published Monis's Hebrew grammar, using Hebrew type which they had imported for the purpose. The life of Monis is not typical of his people; but it is an example of how at least one Jew appeared in every new settlement at some time or other, and of how many of them found a place where they might fit in the new land.

III. CONNECTICUT

THERE are records of Jews being given temporary permission to reside in Hartford as early as 1659 and 1661, but there was no Jewish community there, perhaps no Jewish family living there permanently for almost a hundred years after that. About the middle of the eighteenth century there were Jews living in several Connecticut towns, the Pinto family settling in New Haven in 1759. They were well-known merchants who distinguished themselves during the Revolution. The Rev. Mr. Stiles did not like them, however, because of their lack of religion. He wrote in his diary in 1772:

Jewish Community Before the Revolution

"The summer past a family of Jews settled here, the first real Jews (except two Jew Brothers Pinto who renounced Judaism and all Religion) that settled in New Haven. They came from Venice. . . . This is the first Jewish worship in New Haven."

So a few Jewish pioneers appear in every colony along with the Dutch, the Puritans, and the Quakers. In the next chapter we shall see the beginnings of Jewish settlement in Pennsylvania and the South.

REVIEW QUESTIONS

1. Why did Jews come to some colonies before others? Did the same causes operate in South America? Illustrate.
2. What sort of records have we of the earliest Jews in New England? Date them.
3. Discuss one important Jew of early New England. Explain why he was important.
4. What is the importance of individual wanderers, or of temporary settlements, in a study of Jewish history?

TOPICS FOR REPORTS

1. Trace the difference in theory of government in Massachusetts, Connecticut and Rhode Island.
2. Compare the two poems by Longfellow and Emma Lazarus, in regard to ideas, style and Jewish sympathy.
3. Compare the Marranos who returned to Judaism and Judah Monis who became a Christian, in their motives, lives and standing.

REFERENCES FOR PUPILS

Wiernik, Peter, pp. 71–75, 98–99.
Harris, M. H., *Modern Jewish History,* pp. 134–136. Bloch.

History of the Jews in the United States

Jewish Encyclopedia, arts. on Connecticut, Massachusetts, Newport, Judah Monis.

Levinger, E. E., "A Place of Refuge," *The New Land.*

REFERENCES FOR TEACHERS

Publications of the American Jewish Historical Society.

Kohler, Max J., "Jews of Newport," vol. VI, pp. 61–80.

Jastrow, Morris, "Jews in the Diary of Ezra Stiles," vol. X, pp. 5–36.

Huhner, Leon, "Jews of New England," vol. XI, pp. 75–99.

Daly, pp. 77–86.

Markens, Isaac, pp. 33–45.

Kohut, George A., *Ezra Stiles and the Jews.* Philip Cowen.

Straus, Oscar S., *Roger Williams, the Pioneer of Religious Liberty.* The Century Co.

CHAPTER 6.

How the Jews Scattered Through
the Colonies

THE most conspicuous feature of Jewish history
since the destruction of the Temple in the year 70
has been the scattering of the Jews from land to land
the whole world over. If we look closely, we shall see
the same fact in the history of the Jewish people in our
own country. They appear, from time to time in our
story, going here and there as conditions permitted—
in times of persecution as single pioneers, in times of
freedom as little communities of traders.

I. PENNSYLVANIA, THE SETTLEMENT OF WILLIAM PENN

WILLIAM PENN as a Quaker knew the bitterness of persecution himself; but unlike the Puritans, he sympa-
thized with the situation of others. He gave his newly
founded colony a charter of toleration, by which people
of all nations and all faiths were welcomed. In reply to
this, many Germans of persecuted Christian sects found
a home in early Pennsylvania, along with some other
English dissenters beside the Friends themselves, and a
sprinkling of Jews. True, the illiberal influences of the
British court, to which Penn's successors yielded, enforced a law that only Christians might vote or hold

65

office. But the Jews, accustomed to far more severe restrictions than this in other lands, considered the Quaker colony a most desirable home.

Jews came to Pennsylvania, not only from Spain and Portugal, but also from England and Germany, along with the persecuted Christian sects. Jewish history is full of surprises for us if we estimate in advance the probable results and compare them with the actual events. So in early Pennsylvania we find the names of many Ashkenazic or German Jews along with the Sephardic ones which were more usual at this period. Also we find early Jewish settlements, not only in Philadelphia, where we would expect one, but also in Lancaster and Easton, where even today the Jewish communities are not very large. Of course, this refers only to settlers who came to live in the colony; Jewish traders had been there as early as 1656, when three of the recent settlers in New Amsterdam petitioned for permission to trade with the Indians on the South River (which we now call the Delaware).

There were Jews in Lancaster, Pa., as early as 1730, before the town was organized. The most important Jewish merchant of that tiny community was Joseph Simon, who came there in 1735 and built up a great business— for those days—trading with both the Indians and the colonists. He was among those men who suffered greatly in the Indian raid of 1763 at Bloody Run, and who were awarded as payment, great tracts of Indian lands in the western territories now known as West Virginia and

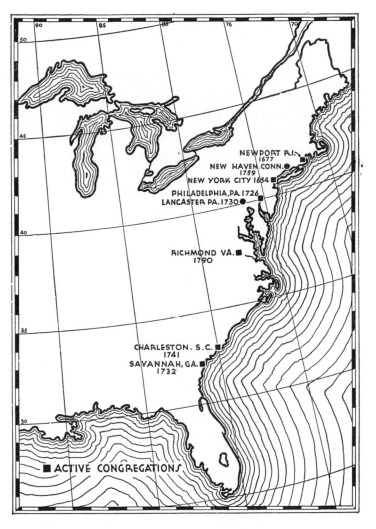

NEWPORT R.I.
1677
NEW HAVEN CONN.
1759
NEW YORK CITY 1654 ■
PHILADELPHIA, PA. 1726 ●
LANCASTER PA. 1730 ●

RICHMOND VA. ■
1790

CHARLESTON. S.C. ■
1741
SAVANNAH, GA. ■
1732

■ ACTIVE CONGREGATIONS

FIRST JEWISH SETTLEMENTS IN THE UNITED STATES

Illinois. Owing to the outbreak of the Revolution, they were never able to take possession of what was practically an empire. Although Joseph Simon was a member of the congregation in Philadelphia, where many of his family resided, he also established a Jewish cemetery and congregation at Lancaster in 1747. Several other families followed him there, some of them his relatives. He was one of the men who supplied the Continental army with necessities during the Revolution. He died in 1804, at the advanced age of ninety-two years, and was buried in Lancaster cemetery. But by that time, most of the Lancaster Jews had moved to larger cities; the cemetery was not used until 1855, when there were ten new families in the town and a synagogue was finally built.

Naturally, Philadelphia itself attracted Jews as well as other settlers of persecuted faiths. It was the capital of the new colony and its chief town. The first Jewish settlers of whom we are certain were living in Philadelphia in 1726, but there may have been earlier settlers whose names do not happen to appear on any deeds to property or other legal documents. Their cemetery was acquired in 1740. They did not hold any religious services until the year 1745, which shows how small the community must have been, and then they did not have any regular organization. Barnard Gratz, one of the early members of a family that was famous later on, was one of their first leaders.

The best-known Jewish family of colonial times was

88

How the Jews Scattered Through the Colonies

the Franks—English Jews. Most of its members were ardent in the cause of the Revolution; but David Franks, the eldest leader of the family at the time, was a strong Tory, and one of the agents for the British commissary. He married a non-Jewess, but was also a member of the Jewish congregation. One of his daughters, Rebecca, was known as a belle of early Philadelphia; she was one of the two queens of the Meschianza, the great ball which the British soldiers held while they occupied Philadelphia; she was also one of the wits of her day, and many accounts of early Philadelphia give extravagant praise (in the stilted language of the time) to her clever tongue and beauty. She married General Sir Harry Johnson of the English forces.

Several of the other Philadelphia Jews, such as Col. David S. Franks, Col. Isaac Franks, Major Benjamin Nones, and especially Haym Salomon, will receive full mention in chapter eight, as their chief interest to us later day Americans is the part they played in the American Revolution.

In 1782 the number of Jews in Philadelphia was considerably increased by refugees from New York, as well as other places. They finally carried out their old ambition to build a synagogue. It was a little one, dedicated on the Sabbath of Repentance; its first rabbi was the patriot rabbi of New York, Gershom Mendez Seixas. He remained in Philadelphia until the war was over and then he moved back home. It was named Mikveh Israel (the Hope of Israel), and followed the Spanish ritual, as it still does after almost a century and a half. In 1788 the congregation experienced financial difficulties, due to the number of Jews who moved back to their former homes at the close of the war, so it appealed for aid to the non-Jews of Philadelphia. It is remarkable that a Jewish congregation felt able to do this, and just as remarkable that it received enough assistance to carry it over its hard times. Benjamin Franklin gave five pounds, the largest sum donated, true to his principle of befriending all religions, so long as they seemed to make for morality and good citizenship.

II. MARYLAND—TOLERATION FOR ALL CHRISTIANS

MARYLAND is unique among the original colonies in being founded by a Catholic, Lord Baltimore, and in extending a great amount of religious freedom; this went so far that the Protestants actually came in, outnumbered the Catholics and later disfranchised them. The Act of Toleration of the province, however, was not as liberal to Jews as to Christians, for it said that "no one professing to believe in Jesus Christ shall be molested." That means that no Jews who professed their religion were admitted. It means also that we can have no certain records of their arrival, for they would have had to conceal their faith if they wanted to live in Maryland.

For example, there was Mathias de Sousa who arrived in the province as early as 1634 with the first settlers; but we have no proof that he was a Jew. If he was, he preceded the New York settlement by twenty years.

How the Jews Scattered Through the Colonies

There was Jacob Lumbrozo, a physician from Portugal, who is mentioned in several legal documents as "ye Jew doctor." He arrived in Maryland in 1656—two years after the first New York group—purchased land, practised medicine and traded with the Indians until his death ten years later. In 1658 he was brought to court on a charge of blasphemy, the only known prosecution of a Jew for that offense in the United States; he was accused of being a Jew and of attacking the foundations of the Christian religion. In his reply Lumbrozo did not deny his own faith, but he did deny having attacked that of others. The case never was tried, however, and it did not harm his status in the colony, for Lumbrozo later received letters of denization (a sort of partial naturalization), and owned considerable property when he died in 1666.

There were other Jewish settlers, or at least passing traders and travellers during all this time, but no permanent settlement of Jews in Maryland until the Revolution, when the city of Baltimore began its great growth and attracted some Jews among the rest of its population. Maryland was one of the last states in the Union to withdraw its laws discriminating against the Jews, as we shall see in chapter nine.

III. VIRGINIA—AN ESTABLISHED CHURCH

VIRGINIA duplicated the conditions of England before the time of Cromwell; the Church of England was its official religion and no other was really recognized. Jews

could not enter England until the Lord Protector admitted them; nor could Jews enter Virginia. Of course,
there were always a few who managed to enter either as
traders or settlers. There seems to be no real proof of
Jews living in early Virginia, except names, which are
always unreliable as evidence. Biblical names are sometimes of German or English Puritans; Spanish names may
belong to Spanish Jews or to Spaniards. There are no
settlers in Virginia whom we can positively identify as
Jews until after the Revolution, when Isaiah Isaac is
found living in Richmond; the first congregation of that
city was founded in 1790. So Elias Legardo, who came
to Virginia in 1621, may possibly be the first Jew in
North America; or the honor may belong to De Sousa
in Maryland a few years after; but the true pioneers
both as known Jews and as a Jewish community were the
New Yorkers of 1654.

IV. SOUTH CAROLINA UNDER OFFICIAL TOLERATION

THE constitution of the Carolinas was written by the
great English philosopher, John Locke, who in his lib-
erality arranged toleration for "Jews, heathens and dissenters." So here was another English colony giving
permission, if not an invitation for Jews to settle within
it. Records exist from the earliest days of the little colony
of the Jews who found their way to that remote section
of the world.

There is an old book written in 1707 by a former
governor of Carolina, in which he tells how he had cap-

tured some Indians as early as 1695; they spoke Spanish, and he had a Jew as interpreter. Imagine it—a Jew
interpreting Spanish between an English governor and
Indian prisoners in that early day in Charles Town (as
it was then called). Two years later four Jews were
naturalized in the colony, and one of their naturalization
papers still exists, that of Simon Valentine, a prominent
merchant who had come to South Carolina from New
York. The first real influx of Jews was in the year 1741,
from the neighboring colony of Georgia; how they came
there and why they left will appear in the next section of
this chapter. In 1750 several more Jews arrived from
London.

By that time there were enough Jews in Charles Town
to form a congregation, which was therefore organized
after the Jewish New Year of 1750 under the name, Beth
Elohim, House of God. This congregation is still in existence and is therefore the third oldest Jewish congregation in the United States today, coming after New York
and Newport. The present one at Savannah, Ga., is
fourth, that at Philadelphia fifth, and that at Richmond,
Va., sixth in order. These six were in existence during
the first administration of George Washington as President, and were the six which sent him greetings during
his first administration. All of them were strictly orthodox, as this was before the rise of Reform Judaism in
Europe; all of them followed the Sephardic ritual, even
though there were some Ashkenazim among their members.

In 1773 Francis Salvador, a brilliant young English Jew of great wealth, settled on a plantation in South Carolina. He was a member of the Provincial Assembly which decided to secede from England, one of the three Jews to be representatives in such a body in America. He died as a patriot in a skirmish with the British in 1776 at the very beginning of the Revolution. A man of brilliance and promise, with wealth, personality, and intellect, his short life and tragic death make an unusually romantic story.

V. GEORGIA—A MIXED HISTORY

GEORGIA was founded by General Oglethorpe, another of the broad-minded humanitarians whom we find from time to time in early American history. Just after the arrival of the first ship bearing the governor and his company in 1732, another ship arrived in Georgia bearing forty Jews of Spanish and Portuguese extraction. A few German Jews came only a year later. The Portuguese Jews were men of considerable property and initiative; they had gone first to England and then to the southern colony where they hoped to engage in business and to cultivate the vine, with which they were familiar. The German Jews were poor people who had gone to England to make a living, and who were being assisted with money to come to the new colony, like most of the early Christian colonists of Georgia. Thus there were two little groups of different kinds of Jews, living separately in this new colony.

94

How the Jews Scattered Through the Colonies

At first the trustees were opposed to Jews coming to the colony, as they wanted to have a model colony, and control immigration themselves. Their charter prohibited Catholics on account of the nearness of the colony to Catholic territory in Florida, but did not mention Jews. So Oglethorpe, who was much more liberal than his trustees in London, defended the Jews who came to the colony, gave them a chance to settle, and was justified by their conduct in the colony.

The Portuguese Jews founded their congregation in Savannah in 1734. In 1740 there was a crisis in the colony on the question of negro slavery, which was opposed by the trustees and desired by the colonists. They objected to doing all the hard work themselves when neighboring colonies had slaves to work for them. At this time many Christians and Jews left Georgia; the Jewish congregation in Savannah was practically broken up, and the one in Charleston, South Carolina founded. But the people drifted back again when the trouble was settled, and new families joined them. The Savannah congregation was reorganized in 1774 and still exists, the fourth oldest in the United States. Joseph Ottolenghi was a member of the colonial assembly in 1761–5.

At the time of the Revolution, there were five Jewish congregations in the United States, located in those colonies which had been most tolerant toward the Jews from the beginning. These were, in order of founding, New York, Newport, Charleston, Savannah, and Philadelphia. In every case Jews had settled in each of these colonies because of their existing laws and the type of government; in addition, each had a seaport town where Jewish merchants could work and make a living. A few random settlers have been discovered in five colonies, as we have noticed: Massachusetts, Connecticut, Delaware, Maryland, and Virginia, though in several of these cases the Jews were converted to Christianity before being allowed to stay. We have no record of Jews before the Revolution, in three colonies: New Hampshire, New Jersey, and North Carolina. Altogether there were about 2,500 Jews in the thirteen colonies, almost all of them merchants and traders, almost all of Sephardic origin, and for the most part living in the main seacoast towns.

REVIEW QUESTIONS

1. Mention some important service which was done by a Jew, or Jews, in two of the above colonies.
2. Where did the Jews come from to the southern colonies? Trace their travels, and the reason they wandered as they did.
3. Give an illustration of the unusual or unexpected appearance of Jews among the early settlers.
4. Give one doubtful case of early Jewish immigration; explain the reason for our doubts.
5. Who was the first Jew to be elected a representative in any colony? Look up his life, and see why he was so distinguished.

TOPICS FOR REPORTS

1. Work out the family tree of some important colonial family, such as the Franks or Gratz family; mention the important members and why they are notable. Look in the Jewish Encyclopedia.

96

How the Jews Scattered Through the Colonies

2. Trace the origin and growth up to 1800 of one of the six early congregations of the country.
3. Trace the development of some industry in colonial days, and show the Jewish element in it.
4. Compare in their attitude to Jews the various Christian bodies in colonial times; is this identical with their general attitude of toleration, or were there differences when they considered the Jews?

REFERENCES FOR PUPILS

Wiernik, Peter, pp. 75–79.
Jewish Encyclopedia, arts. on Charleston, Pennsylvania, Lumbrozo, Georgia, J. Pinto, Abraham de Lyon, Maryland, Savannah.

REFERENCES FOR TEACHERS

Altfeld, E. M., *Jewish Emancipation in Maryland.*
Daly, pp. 64–76.
Elzas, Barnett, *The Jews of South Carolina* (out of print), chaps. ii–iii. Lippincott.
Markens, Isaac, pp. 45–83.
Morais, *Jews of Philadelphia.*
American Jewish Year Book 1926, art. by A. M. Friedenberg, "The Jews of America, 1654–1787." Jewish Publication Society.
Publications of the American Jewish Historical Society.
Huhner, Leon, "The Jews of Georgia in Colonial Times," vol. X, pp. 65–96.
Huhner, Leon, "The Jews of South Carolina from the Earliest Settlement to the End of the American Revolution," vol. XII, pp. 39–64.
Necarsulmer: "Jews of Lancaster," vol. IX.
Abrahams, Edmund H., "Some Notes on the Early History of the Sheftalls of Georgia," vol. XVII, pp. 167–186.
Huhner, Leon, "The Jews of Virginia from the Earliest Times to the Close of the Eighteenth Century," vol. XX, pp. 85–106.

PART II
How the Jews Grew
with the Nation

CHAPTER 7.

Jewish Influence on the New Republic

I. DIRECT INFLUENCE

THE fathers and founders of the American Repub‑ lic knew few Jews personally, and learned very little from them. The three thousand Jews, or less, living in the thirteen colonies were not leaders of thought as a rule. This was one reason why the Christians were not ready to learn from them. The influence of the Jews on American civilization, while very great, was chiefly in‑ direct, through the Bible, especially the Old Testament. This influence came through two groups: the Puritans and the Deists. It touched the ordinary lives of the peo‑ ple, as well as their religion, their laws and constitutions. When the time came for revolution and freedom, the Hebrew Scriptures were the great inspiration of the leading thinkers; they were quoted on every hand, and won many friends for the cause of freedom among the pious farmers and traders of the colonies.

In what way was this Jewish influence manifest? Let us examine the foundations of American history to see where it appears and how important it proved to be.

The direct influence of Jews was exerted chiefly

101

through their activity as traders. They introduced certain types of trade; they improved others; they carried on several more. But for a long time they were not permitted to engage in every type of business. Therefore they naturally specialized, and most Jews were found in one particular kind of commerce. This kind was vitally important to a new and poor country, which had only potential wealth and needed every kind of goods, for the Jews engaged largely in commerce between nations and between colonies.

It is hard for us to realize nowadays how isolated each little settlement was at the beginning. People traded largely with their neighbors and exchanged goods for goods. Clothes, candles, soap, almost everything was manufactured in the homes. But people needed sugar, finer materials for clothing, bricks for buildings, furniture, and many other means of luxury and comfort. These had to be imported, and the people who rendered this service were important factors in the beginnings of American prosperity. In addition, each colony was very largely isolated from the others in communication by land; bad roads and slow, tedious means of travelling made trading very difficult. But each colony was on the sea-coast, and coast-wise trading was comparatively cheap and easy. Therefore the exchange of products between Massachusetts and Virginia, for example, was a great help to both, almost as great as the importation of foreign supplies. Finally, the great and growing slave trade, then conducted under the approval of the British government in order to supply the colonies with laborers for their fields, was flourishing at the time, even though the growing moral sense of the American people was later to rebel against it and to destroy slavery in the terrible Civil War.

Jews were early active in these three branches of commerce—import, inter-colonial trade, and the slave trade. The first Jewish settlers of Newport had relatives and business partners in the West Indies and established a trade with those islands at once. They soon added to this the carrying of slaves from Africa and a certain amount of European import business. The Jews of New York and Charleston likewise engaged in foreign and domestic trade, to an extent entirely out of proportion to their numbers. Thus the few colonial Jews were an important factor in the beginnings of American prosperity.

II. THE JEWS AND THE PURITANS

THE Puritans, who were among the early and most important settlers of New England and who largely established the character of the future America, based their religion, their character and their daily life on the Old Testament, the Jewish Bible. They did not know many Jews personally, but they were deeply interested in the Jewish people, past and present, the Hebrew language and the Jewish law. In England, at the time of Oliver Cromwell, the Puritans were in control and their ideas were dominant; the same type of people, with the same ideas, controlled New England twenty years earlier and carried out much the same policy there.

In England, Cromwell showed his interest in the Jews by allowing them, at the petition of Rabbi Manasseh ben Israel of Amsterdam, to re-enter the country from which they had been exiled since 1290. The Puritan enmity to kings was based on their study of the Jewish Bible: they believed that only God was the real King, and the perfect government must be a theocracy or government by God. The Puritans, or many of them, believed that the end of the world was at hand, and that before that time the Jews must be brought together from the four corners of the earth. Many Puritans also considered the Indians to be the Lost Ten Tribes of Israel and tried to convert them to Christianity. Still others considered the British themselves to be the latest descendants of those Lost Ten Tribes.

In New England the same ideas were uppermost in the minds of the people. One is familiar with the large number of Old Testament names among them, even such unusual ones as Hezekiah and Ezekiel. Many of them studied Hebrew, which was a special interest of their ministers; Hebrew was taught at Harvard College as early as 1655, at the very beginning of higher education in the New World. The leading men of the colony, such as Cotton Mather, Increase Mather and Ezra Stiles, studied Hebrew there. The Puritan influence, then, made for a love of the Old Testament and brought Jewish ideas into the very foundations of American life.

104

Jewish Influence on the New Republic

One of these Jewish ideas was the importance of law; another, the love of freedom: the Puritan combined respect for law and the demand for freedom much as the Jew has done throughout his long and thrilling history. The Pilgrims came to New England in 1620 to find their own freedom of worship; they immediately established a law of their own, basing it on the Old Testament, not on the English Constitution of their day. The Puritans, arriving soon afterward, came with the special purpose of establishing a theocracy like that of the Jewish people in the wilderness days and in Palestine before they had accepted a king. The Plymouth Colony Code of Laws in 1636, the Massachusetts one in 1647, and the Connecticut Code of 1650 were all based on the laws of Moses. Not only were their civil and criminal laws based on Jewish statutes but their political constitution as well, with its government by elders, by a council of citizens, and so on. In the New Haven Code, adopted in 1639, over half the statutes came straight out of the Old Testament.

The Puritans established feasts and fasts after the Jewish model, especially the feast of Thanksgiving, which we still celebrate as a great American festival, and which was copied directly from the feast of Sukkoth, except that the difference in seasons between New England and Palestine made Thanksgiving come two months after Sukkoth. Thanksgiving was, like its original, a feast of harvest and of Thanksgiving to God, the Giver of the harvest.

THE

WHOLE

BOOKE OF PSALMES
Faithfully
TRANSLATED *into* ENGLISH
Metre.

Whereunto is prefixed a difcourfe declaring not only the lawfullnes, but alfo
the neceffity of the heavenly Ordinance
of finging scripture Pfalmes in
the Churches of
God.

Coll. III.
*Let the word of God dwell plenteoufly in
you, in all wifdome, teaching and exhort-
ing one another in Pfalmes, Himnes, and
fpirituall Songs, finging to the Lord with
grace in your hearts.*

Iames v.
*If any be afflicted, let him pray, and if
any be merry let hiw fing pfalmes.*

Imprinted
1640

Jewish Influence on the New Republic

III. THE DEISTS

NOT only were the Puritans, the most devout Christians in America, especially interested in the Jews, but the most liberal religious thinkers also introduced Jewish ideas. These were the Deists, or free-thinkers of the time, men like Benjamin Franklin, Thomas Jefferson and Thomas Paine, who believed in a God of nature rather than the personal God of Christianity. There were also Theists, or liberal Christians such as John Adams and James Madison.

All these men laid less emphasis on the New Testament and the life of Jesus than on the Old Testament, with its belief in one God and its teaching of a moral life; they thus inclined toward many Jewish views. As several of these men were very important in the time of the Revolution, and wrote and spoke in favor of their ideas, they brought the Jewish teachings near to the people as a whole. Benjamin Franklin's religious ideas, in his Autobiography, had these special points: "the existence of the Deity; that He made the world and governed it by His Providence; that the most acceptable service of God was the doing good to man; that our souls are immortal; and that all crimes will be punished, and virtue rewarded, either here or hereafter." We notice that Franklin's rationalism rejected many ideas of the Christian religion but included most of those which Christianity and Judaism hold in common. In pursuance of these ideas, Franklin was friendly to all religions:

when the Congregation Mikveh Israel of Philadelphia appealed to the Christians of that city for aid, Franklin headed the list of givers.

IV. THE BIBLE AND FREEDOM

THE Old Testament was one of the great inspirations of those who fought for freedom, as well as of those who were working out the American theory of equal rights and of tolerance for every religion. The European theory which prevailed in almost every colony, was that the state should maintain the true religion; the only ground for argument was which religion was true. We have seen how one colony, however, was established on a new idea, that of exact equality for all men of all religions, before the law.

Roger Williams, the founder of Rhode Island, claimed that the basis for his new theory was in the Old Testament; he was a devout minister and a student of Hebrew. So was Thomas Hooker, the liberal leader in Connecticut. So was the pious Quaker who inscribed on the great bell of 1753 the words from Leviticus (XXV, 10), "Proclaim liberty throughout the land, unto all the inhabitants thereof," the words which were fulfilled almost a quarter of a century later when this Liberty Bell rang out for the adoption of the Declaration of Independence. One of the first designs proposed for a seal of the United States, by a committee consisting of Jefferson, Franklin and John Adams, showed Israel crossing the Red Sea, with Pharaoh pursuing and Moses

108

already safe on the other side; the motto was "Rebel‑ lion of tyrants is obedience to God."

All these are significant of a general tendency to con‑ nect the hopes of liberty with the life of the people of Israel and with the Old Testament promises. A great historian, Lecky, says: "It is at least an historical fact that in the great majority of instances the early Protes‑ tant defenders of civil liberty derived their political prin‑ ciples chiefly from the Old Testament, and the defenders of despotism from the New. The rebellions that were so frequent in Jewish history formed the favorite topic of the one—the unreserved submission inculcated by St. Paul of the other." (Rationalism in Europe, revised edi‑ tion 1919, Vol. II, p. 168.)

Many people in the infant nation even believed that they were basing the structure of the new Republic, not on the British Constitution, but on that of Israel in an‑ cient Palestine. Oscar S. Straus, a noteworthy American Jew who will appear again in a later part of this book, made a study of *The Origin of the Republican Form of Government in the United States,* in which he shows that a book much studied at this time claimed that the three-fold form of government—executive, legislative, and judicial—came from the Hebrew Commonwealth, in its Shofet, or chief executive, its Sanhedrin or Senate, and its Congregation or popular assembly. This may not have been correct history, for the American institutions came directly from the British ones, but it is significant as showing what the American people were thinking, and

History of the Jews in the United States

how their ideal of liberty was bound up with their study in the Bible. There were, of course, other strains of thought that made for liberty in the eighteenth century, the works of French and English thinkers among the rest.

Still, Mr. Straus concludes: "In the spirit and essence of our Constitution, the influence of the Hebrew Commonwealth was paramount, in that it was not only the highest authority for the principle, 'Rebellion of tyrants is obedience to God,' but also because it was in itself a divine precedent for a pure democracy as distinguished from monarchy, aristocracy, or any other form of government. By that means and to that extent, it had a decisive influence in guiding the American people in the selection of their form of government." (p. 79–80.) The strongest expression of this idea has been credited to a non-Jew, Lecky, who said: "Hebraic mortar cemented the foundations of American democracy." The few Jews then living in the colonies did their part; the great ideas given by Judaism to the world played an even greater role in the founding of the American Republic.

Review Questions

1. Is the indirect influence of the Jews in America important? Why?
2. How did the Puritans use the Bible in everyday life?
3. Would the study of Hebrew and the Old Testament make men more friendly toward Jews? Did the Christians try to help the Jews, to convert them, or to exploit them? Illustrate.

Jewish Influence on the New Republic

4. Tell how Jewish trade was of value to the colonies.
5. What were the ideas of freedom in the colonies at first? At the time of the Revolution? What was the Jewish share in them?

TOPICS FOR REPORTS

1. Trace the New Testament idea of authority (Romans 13.1–70) and the Old Testament ideas of freedom (I Samuel 8; Judges 8; 22, 23; Exodus 18, etc.).
2. Study the Puritans and their relation to the Jews and the Old Testament.
3. Work out the relation between the laws of Moses and the laws and constitutions of the New England colonies.
4. Describe the liberal religious movements (such as the Deists) and show the similarity to Judaism.

REFERENCES FOR PUPILS

Wiernik, Peter, pp. 71, 80–84.
Feuerlicht, Morris M., "The Influence of Judaism on the Founders of the Republic," *Year Book of the Central Conference of American Rabbis,* vol. XXXVI.
Feuerlicht, Morris M., *Judaism's Influence in the Founding of the Republic* (tract). U.A.H.C.

REFERENCES FOR TEACHERS

Straus, Oscar S., *Origin of the Republican Form of Government in the United States.*
Newman, Louis I., "Hebraic Aspects of American Puritanism," *Jewish Influence on Christian Reform Movements,* pp. 631–646. Columbia University Press.
Newman, Louis I., and Morris, Richard B., "The Jewish Tradition at the Birth of America," *American Hebrew,* September 30, 1921, pp. 480 ff.

111

History of the Jews in the United States

Adams, James T., *Founding of New England*. Atlantic Monthly Press.

Publications of the American Jewish Historical Society.

Kohler, Max J., "Jewish Activity in American Colonial Commerce," vol. X, pp. 47–74.

Huhner, Leon, "The Jews of New England Prior to 1800," vol. XI, pp. 75–80.

Pool, David de Sola, "Hebrew Learning Among the Puritans of New England Prior to 1700," vol. XX, pp. 31–83.

Friedman, Lee M., "Cotton Mather and the Jews," vol. XXVI, pp. 201–210.

CHAPTER 8.

Jews in the Founding of the Republic

I. THE JEWISH SYMPATHIES

THE great majority of the Jews in the thirteen struggling colonies were ardent in the cause of liberty. They had suffered so long and so tragically from being deprived of liberty that any movement for freedom enlisted their hearty support, and every form of tyranny their bitter resistance. The American Revolution was largely a movement of poor people, but there were a few wealthy men, like George Washington, who threw in their lot with the ragged Continentals. Among these were several rich Jews, who not only lost great fortunes, but also risked their lives for the cause.

Of course, the Jewish colonials were not unanimous, any more than were the rest of the American people at that time. Here and there a settler from England might feel loyal to his former home, or might wish to avoid a desperate war which seemed impossible to win. The most prominent of these men was the elderly David Franks of Philadelphia, who was mentioned in chapter six. He had to flee the colony for his life when the British troops evacuated it; but it is interesting to see that he returned after the Revolution and lived in Philadelphia until the end of his days, so that his opposition must have been forgiven by the American officials.

Nine Philadelphia Jews were among the merchants of that city who signed the Non-Importation Resolution against British goods in 1765. On this list appears the name of David Franks—afterwards a Tory. There are also the names of such ardent patriots as Barnard and Michael Gratz. There were only three Jews elected to any of the Continental assemblies or congresses—the law forbade that almost everywhere. The leading exception was Francis Salvador of South Carolina, a most important man in declaring and organizing rebellion in that colony; he seemed destined also for a great military career until his tragic death at the age of twenty-nine at the very beginning of the war.

What, then, was the nature of Jewish participation in the struggle for liberty? Was it hearty or weak, did it involve many Jewish patriots, and was it really important to the new nation?

Because of the small and scattered communities of Jews in the colonies, there could be no mass movement among them, and no organized system of loyal support to the nation, such as there was during the World War. But we know of over forty Jews who fought under Washington, as well as a number of others who served in other ways. I shall tell here the interesting stories of several of these Jewish soldiers, so that we shall see just what sort of men they were,—how brave and eager they

Jews in the Founding of the Republic

were for freedom, and how much they gave for its defense! We will notice also that they came from all the various points where the Jews lived—Newport, New York, Philadelphia, Charleston and Savannah.

II. REVOLUTIONARY SOLDIERS

Two outstanding patriots were cousins, members of the Franks family; in fact, they were related to David Franks, the famous Tory. The first of these is Lieutenant-Colonel Isaac Franks, who had a varied career in the field and received his high rank as an officer of Pennsylvania militia after the war. He volunteered at the beginning of the war, when he was only seventeen years old, and served at first with a regiment of New York volunteers. He was captured by the British, but managed to escape, made a dangerous crossing of the Hudson, and received various promotions in the infantry and quartermaster department. In later days his house in Germantown was occupied by the first President during the yellow fever epidemic in Philadelphia. We have many original documents concerning Isaac Franks, as well as his portrait, painted by the great Stuart. For many years he was a prosperous citizen of Philadelphia and later of Lancaster; finally in his old age he became poor, applied for and received a pension for his services in the army.

David Salisbury Franks (the middle name distinguishes him from his older relative, the Tory), had just as interesting a career. He was a young merchant from

England and was in business in Canada at the time of the American expedition there, early in the Revolution. He had previously been in trouble because of his sentiments; now he boldly joined the troops from the United States and when they retreated he went back with them. He rose to be a major on the staff of General Benedict Arnold and was one of his two leading aides. When Benedict Arnold turned traitor, there was natural suspicion against everyone who had been associated with him. Although he was not implicated particularly, Major

COL. ISAAC FRANKS

Franks asked the commander-in-chief for a court of inquiry so that he might prove his innocence. His request was granted and he proved his innocence completely. He was exonerated by the court, held his rank in the army, and was later entrusted with several diplomatic missions, such as carrying the official copy of the treaty of peace across the sea to the American representatives in Paris. His final rank on retirement from the service was Lieutenant-Colonel.

The Franks family were of Hanoverian origin. Some of

116

the Jews who enlisted on the side of the new nation were German, either earlier immigrants or deserters from the Hessian mercenaries. We will soon discuss one of French, and another of Polish birth who both served America well in her weakness and her need. The largest group of Jewish soldiers from any one colony was that of South Carolina, because that colony had a regular militia in which every able-bodied man was enrolled. Thus it happens that twenty-six Jews served in the company of Captain Lushington, who commanded the men from a certain section of Charleston. They did excellent service, particularly during the siege of the city by the British; after its capture some of them were imprisoned and many expelled from the city. Because of the large number of Jews enrolled, Captain Lushington's command was often referred to as the "Jews' company."

In Georgia there were two prominent Jews, Mordecai Sheftall, who was appointed Deputy Commissary-General of Issues for the Southern Department, and when captured by the British, was treated with unusual severity; and David Emanuel, a soldier whose capture, escape and return to the field make a thrilling story. It is likely that Emanuel was a Jew although we do not have his name on any congregational roll, as we have the names of the Sheftalls and Franks. But if he was really a Jew, as seems probable, he was the first by over a hundred years to be elected governor of a state, for he was governor of Georgia in 1801, and the largest county of the state was named after him.

History of the Jews in the United States

In Connecticut there were the four Pinto brothers, of whom three were in the colonial forces. Far back in that early day two of these Pinto brothers were graduates of Yale; one of them, Solomon, was an officer in the Connecticut regiment. Wherever a few Jews lived, one or another was sure to distinguish himself by some unusual position or action; it is surprising to see how early in American history two Jews appear as graduates of an American college. This shows not only the enterprise of the Jews, but also the liberalism of the college, for at that time very few universities in Europe admitted Jews.

One of the notable Jewish officers of the Revolution was born in France, in the city of Bordeaux, and came to Philadelphia in 1777. Benjamin Nones served first as private under Pulaski, then under De Kalb, and finally as major and staff officer under Lafayette and Washington. He went through the entire war, from the early campaign in the south to the final ones which ended the struggle. He was cited by General Pulaski for valor in action, in the following letter written by a captain of the staff: "Benjamin Nones has served as a volunteer in my company during the campaign of this year and at the siege of Savannah in Georgia, and his behavior under fire in all the bloody actions we fought has been marked by the bravery and courage which a military man is expected to show for the liberties of his country, and which acts of said Nones gained in his favor the esteem of General Pulaski, as well as that of all the officers who witnessed his daring conduct."

Jews in the Founding of the Republic

After the war Nones returned to Philadelphia, married and raised a large family. He was president of the Congregation Mikveh Israel for many years. In addition, he ran for office; we have a most interesting campaign letter in which he tells that he is accused of being a Jew, of being a Republican, and of being poor; he proudly states that he is all three of these terrible things, but that in his opinion these make him still more worthy of election.

III. PATRIOTS IN PEACEFUL WAYS

NOT all of the population fight during a war: there are many other necessary duties for some of the citizens. During the Revolution the Jews contributed their full share of patriots off the battle field as well as on it.

I wonder whether we give all the honor he deserves to Gershom Mendez Seixas, the young rabbi of Congregation Shearith Israel of New York. When the British captured that city, he refused to remain and left with the sacred Torah and the greater part of his congregation. At first he moved only as far as Stratford, Conn.; later he went to Philadelphia and served the congregation there during most of the struggle. Philadelphia, after 1778, was the great refuge of patriots from every part of the thirteen colonies, and before long there was such a large and flourishing congregation there that a new synagogue was erected and dedicated by Rabbi Seixas. After the war he returned to New York, where he served his former congregation again until the day of his death, thirty-two years later. He was a trustee of King's College, now Columbia University, for over twenty-five years; he was also one of the ministers of various denominations who took part in the first inauguration of President Washington, and was repeatedly honored as a patriot and a citizen. Born in New York, he lived there most of his days and did a great work in that city for two generations.

A number of Jewish business men advanced varying sums of money to the Continental government during and after the Revolution. This was a most patriotic act, for they stood a very good chance not to get it back, owing to the poverty and confusion of the government; in case of the defeat of the colonies, they were certain never to see it again. But the government needed money desperately to pay troops, buy supplies, and keep up the war, and there are many records of Jews as well as Christians, who gave their wealth as freely as some of the men we have been studying served in the field.

We do not need to remember all their names, though what they did was certainly deserving of honor. To mention only a few, there were Joseph Simon and Aaron Levy in Lancaster, Pa. (Aaronsburg, Pa., was later named after him); Philip Minis of Georgia, who advanced $7,000 to pay the troops in the South; Isaac Moses of Philadelphia, who pledged 3,000 pounds when Robert Morris needed it the most, and so on through the various colonies where Jews lived.

But the one who did more for the cause of the Revolu-

Jews in the Founding of the Republic

tion than any other Jewish civilian or soldier, was Haym Salomon of Philadelphia. He came from Poland in 1772, —the first Polish Jew of whom we have record in North America,—and opened a business in New York. When the British took that city, they imprisoned him as a sympathizer with the Revolution; but they soon learned of his knowledge of different languages and made him interpreter. In this capacity he assisted French and American prisoners to escape, and finally he himself escaped to Philadelphia, where he lived the few remaining years of his life. He died suddenly in 1785 during the terrible confusion at the close of the war and before the adoption of the Constitution leaving his young wife, Rachel Franks of the famous Franks family, with four little children. All his estate was in the form of various securities of the Continental government, which at the time were practically worthless; his poverty-stricken family received nothing but the furniture of their home. After the government was established and government obligations were again valuable, bills were repeatedly brought up in Congress to repay his family, were investigated and recommended by committees of both the House and Senate, but always failed to be passed by Congress.

Salomon's official title was "Broker to the office of finance" of the United States: that is, he was the broker through whom Robert Morris, the Superintendent of Finance, sold the securities of the weak infant government. He was also broker to the French army in America and transacted their business affairs. In Morris' finan-

121

cial diary, Salomon's name appears seventy-five times. He even endorsed personally the bills of exchange of the government, putting his own credit in danger. He handled several hundred thousand dollars for the government, but died a bankrupt and left his family destitute. It seems that he was never very wealthy himself, just a hard working business man and a devoted patriot.

Salomon advanced money to several of the delegates at the Continental Congress, for many of them were poor and their States did not always send them their expense money on time. In fact, James Madison, afterward President of the United States, wrote back to Virginia: "I have been a pensioner for some time on the favor of Haym Salomon. I am almost ashamed to reiterate my wants so incessantly to you. The kindness of our friend near the coffee house is a fund that will preserve me from extremities, but I never resort to it without great mortification, as he obstinately rejects all recompense. To necessitous delegates he always spares them supplies."

There were others of these needy delegates who received his assistance, as appears from their correspondence and the history of the times.

The following quotations are from some of the Congressional committees of investigation: (29th Congress, 1846) "From the evidence in the possession of the committee, the patriotic devotion of Haym Salomon to the cause of American independence cannot be questioned."

In 1850 another committee reported: "The committee from the evidence before them, are induced to consider

Jews in the Founding of the Republic

HAYM SALOMON (*right*) WITH GEORGE WASHINGTON (*center*) AND ROBERT MORRIS (*left*). STATUE LOCATED ON WACKER DRIVE, CHICAGO

Haym Salomon as one of the truest and most efficient friends of the country at a very critical period of its history."

In our own day a monument was erected to his memory in Chicago, showing Salomon together with George Washington and Robert Morris.

IV. WASHINGTON AND THE JEWS

AFTER the adoption of the Constitution and the election of Washington as the first President of the United States, the six little Jewish congregations wanted to express their loyalty to him and to the government of which he was the head. They sent him letters of loyalty and congratulation, written in the high-sounding language of the time, one from the congregation at Newport, one from Savannah, one from Charleston, the fourth a joint letter from the congregations of New York, Philadelphia, and Richmond, Va., (the newest congregation of the six). To these letters the President replied in words which have become classic and which every Jewish boy and girl in America ought to know. This is part of the letter to the Newport congregation.

> It would be inconsistent with the frankness of my character not to avow that I am pleased with your favorable opinion of my administration, and fervent wishes for my felicity. May the children of the Stock of Abraham, who dwell in this land, continue to merit and enjoy the good will of the other Inhabitants; while every one shall sit in safety under his own vine and figtree, and there shall be none to make him afraid. May the father of all mercies scatter light and not darkness in our paths, and make us all in our several vocations here useful, and in his own due time and way everlastingly happy.
>
> G. Washington

EXCERPT FROM LETTER OF GEORGE WASHINGTON TO THE HEBREW CONGREGATION OF NEWPORT, R. I.

"The citizens of the United States have a right to applaud themselves for having given to mankind examples

124

Jews in the Founding of the Republic

of an enlarged and liberal policy worthy of imitation. All possess alike liberty of conscience and immunities of citizenship. It is now no more that toleration is spoken of as if it were by the indulgence of one class of people that another enjoyed the exercise of their inherent natural right, for happily, the government of the United States, which gives to bigotry no sanction, to persecution no assistance, requires only that they who live under its protection shall demean themselves as good citizens in giving it on all occasions their effectual support. May the children of the stock of Abraham who dwell in this land continue to merit and enjoy the good will of the other inhabitants, while every one shall sit in safety under his own vine and fig tree, and there shall be none to make him afraid."

To Savannah Jewry Washington wrote: "May the same wonder-working Deity, who long since delivered the Hebrews from their Egyptian oppressors, planted them in the promised land, whose providential agency has lately been conspicuous in establishing these United States as an independent nation, still continue to water them with the dew of heaven and make the inhabitants of every denomination participate in the temporal and spiritual blessings of that people whose God is Jehovah."

Review Questions

1. State the reasons why Jews should have been particularly loyal to England, or particularly interested in the Revolution, or both.

History of the Jews in the United States

2. Give the biographies of three Jewish patriots from three different colonies.
3. Why were Jews especially active in non-military aid to the colonies? Give examples.
4. Why is it important that Washington wrote letters to the Jewish congregations? Analyze the contents of the passages quoted from his letters.

TOPICS FOR REPORTS

1. A biography of some Jewish soldier in the Revolution.
2. A biography of some non-military patriot, such as Seixas or Salomon.
3. The Jews of some one colony in the Revolution, such as South Carolina or Pennsylvania.
4. Washington and the Jews.
5. Portraits of Early American Jews; read article, retell, show portraits to class, etc.

REFERENCES FOR PUPILS

Wiernik, Peter, chaps. xii-xiii.
Peters, Madison C., *The Jews in America,* pp. 39–50.
Harris, Morris H., *Modern Jewish History,* pp. 140–143.
London, Hannah R., *Portraits of Jews by Gilbert Stuart and Other Early American Artists.*
American Jewish Year Book 5665, art. by N. Taylor Phillips, "Gershom M. Seixas."
American Jewish Year Book 5684, art. by Hannah R. London, "Portraits of Early American Jews."
Jewish Encyclopedia, arts. on Franks Family, Salomon Family, Francis Salvador, Aaron Levy, Haym Salomon, Solomon Pinto, Washington's Letter to Newport in facsimile.
Levinger, E. E., "Down with King George," "The Last Service," "The Generous Giver," *The New Land.*

126

Jews in the Founding of the Republic

REFERENCES FOR TEACHERS

Markens, Isaac, pp. 126–127.
Wolf, Simon, *The American Jew as Patriot, Soldier and Citizen,* pp. 12–61.
Russell, Charles E., *Haym Salomon and the American Revolution.* Cosmopolitan.
Baron, H. S., *Haym Salomon.* Bloch.
Elzas, B., *The Jews of South Carolina,* chaps. iv–v.
Kohler, Max J., "Haym Salomon, the Patriot Broker of the Revolution—His Real Achievements and Their Exaggeration." Privately printed.
McCall, Samuel W., *Patriotism of the American Jew.*
Publications of the American Jewish Historical Society.
  Friedenwald, "The Jews in the Journal of the Continental Congress," vol. I, pp. 65–89.
  Adams, "A Sketch of Haym Salomon," vol. II, pp. 5–20.
  Rosenbach, A. S. W. and Wolf, "Aaron Levy," vol. II, pp. 157–164.
  Hollander, J. H., "Some Further References to Haym Salomon," vol III, pp. 7–12.
  Abraham, L., "Correspondence between Washington and Jewish Citizens," vol. III, pp. 87–96.
  Kohler, Max J., "Incidents Illustrative of American Jewish Patriotism," vol. IV, pp. 81–100.
  Jastrow, M., "Documents Relating to Col. Isaac Franks," vol. V, pp. 7–34.
  Rosenbach, A. S. W., "Documents Relating to Maj. D. S. Franks," vol. V, pp. 157–190.
  Huhner, Leon, "Francis Salvador," vol. IX, pp. 107–122.
  Straus, Oscar S., "New Light on the Career of David S. Franks," vol. X, pp. 101–108.
  Huhner, Leon, "The First Jew to be Governor of a State," vol. XVII, pp. 187–196.

127

CHAPTER 9.

The Land of Religious Liberty

I. THE EUROPEAN THEORY TRANSPLANTED

W E ARE accustomed to take the idea of religious freedom in America as necessary and natural. Even going back to the Founders, we read the words of Washington to the Jewish congregations, or the theory of Jefferson on personal freedom, and we take it all for granted.

But at the beginning of the national life the ideas of religious liberty, of the separation of church and state, of a free church in a free state, of the right of Jews, Quakers, or Catholics to vote—such points as these were far from accepted, and only the radicals really fought for them. They were finally achieved, partly through the leadership of radicals like Jefferson and Thomas Paine, advanced thinkers who read the works of Voltaire, Locke and other philosophers of France and England. The practical reason for the adoption of religious liberty at that time was the need for compromise between the many small and the few large sects, each of which would have liked to rule the country.

Every colony was, of course, settled by people from Europe; each group brought along its own ideas. One of

The Land of Religious Liberty

the most constant and strongest of these ideas was that there could be only one true religion, and that the government of any state or nation ought to support and insist on that true religion. The real difficulty was in deciding which religion was the true one. In England, Holland or Germany, it was decided by the Protestant king who was the head of the national church; in France, Italy and Spain the people accepted the Catholic church, with the Pope at its head. Everywhere there were smaller sects, such as Baptists or Quakers, who claimed the right to worship God in their own way. In addition, there were in most countries a few Jews, who did not accept even the chief dogmas of Christianity that united the various warring sects; these Jews also insisted on their own faith and would not give it up, either through fear of the Inquisition or through the inducements of the Protestant preachers.

Because each church thought it had the only true faith, there were religious wars in Europe which did not end until 1648, after the settlement of many of the colonies in America. Every nation in Europe had its official church, which was supported with money and authority by the government. The people felt that if the state religion was the only true faith, the government should support it in every possible way.

The American colonies were founded on this idea. The New England colonies were established as theocracies, patterned after ancient Israel, except that their religion was Protestantism of the Congregational variety.

129

History of the Jews in the United States

So there were official Congregational colonies—Massachusetts, Plymouth, New Haven, Connecticut, and New Hampshire; official Church of England colonies—Virginia, North and South Carolina; four colonies which had had the Church of England forced on them—Maryland, at first under Catholic rule, but with freedom of worship for all Christians; New York and New Jersey, which had been founded under the Dutch Reformed Church; and Georgia, founded with almost complete religious liberty, even for Jews. Only three had never had state churches: Rhode Island, founded by Roger Williams; Pennsylvania, by William Penn, and its offshoot, Delaware.

Which of the two leading faiths should rule the new nation? Should the smaller groups, Baptists, Quakers, Mennonites, Catholics, Jews, have the right to live under toleration, to worship in their own way, to vote or hold office as citizens? Not a country in Europe gave the last right to Jews at that time; not every country gave even the first one. Most of the colonies did not admit Jews as residents. Others admitted them on sufferance.

How did it happen that a new theory of liberty came into the world here in this new land? What was that new theory like, and how could it possibly have grown from such a background? How was it that America, first of all the nations in the world, offered every right of a man and a citizen to the children of Israel? And what was the process by which those rights were offered by America and accepted by the Jew?

130

The Land of Religious Liberty

THE new theory of religion was originated in America by a radical Protestant minister, Roger Williams. In 1636 he founded Rhode Island, with a charter that provided that no person should be "any wise molested, punished, disquieted, or called in question for any difference in opinion in matters of religion." The government should have concern only with law and crime, not with the private beliefs. That is why Jews settled in Newport so early. It is also the starting point of the American theory of religious freedom. We can hardly realize how radical this was. People considered it to be the extreme of anarchism with reference to both church and state.

"Massachusetts set up its theocratic state with its chief interest in the Church; Virginia established its civil state, with the church as a subject member; while Rhode Island boldly denied the purposes and premises of both, placing an impassable gulf between the State and the Church and relegating to the individual conscience and to voluntary association all concern and action touching the Church and religious matters." (Cobb: Rise of Religious Liberty in America, page 70.)

William Penn a few years later introduced a similar liberty into his colony of Pennsylvania. He gave a guarantee of religious liberty for all who "acknowledged one Almighty and Eternal God to be the Creator, Upholder and Ruler of the world." Thus he included Jews and all varieties of Christians, excluding only unbelievers.

131

History of the Jews in the United States

This was a new step in the history of the world. Spain had insisted that all must belong to the one Church of the King and Queen. Holland had taken a great step forward by declaring that the Church of its rulers was the true Church, but others (such as Jews) might live in the country if they obeyed its laws. Rhode Island, and later the United States of America, said that religion is a matter for each man to decide for himself, and the government has no right to meddle with it for or against. The new step was from toleration to freedom. As Thomas Paine said: "Toleration is not the opposite of intolerance, but the counterfeit of it. Both are despotisms: the one assumes to itself the right of withholding liberty of conscience, the other of granting it."

The new nation, then, had a double question in religious matters,—the competition between the various sects, and the new theory of complete separation of Church and State. Like most other questions decided in the Constitutional Convention of 1787, the opposition between religious sects was settled by a compromise: none of them were to be connected in any way with the Federal government. Article VI, section 3 of the Constitution says: "No religious test shall ever be required as a qualification to any office or public trust under the United States." The first amendment to the Constitution, adopted in 1789, adds a further point: "Congress shall make no law respecting an establishment of religion, or prohibiting the exercise thereof!"

Thus the United States can have no official religion,

The Land of Religious Liberty

can make no discrimination between people of different religions or of no religion at all as citizens, voters, or officeholders. Every new state thereafter wrote the same kind of provisions into its Constitution or Bill of Rights. But these clauses did not affect the original states where changes could come about only through the action of the people of those states themselves.

III. RELIGIOUS LIBERTY IN THE STATES

THE decisive struggle for religious liberty was waged in Virginia in 1776 and in 1785, two years before the adoption of the Federal Constitution. The clause then included in the Virginia state constitution, helped in determining the national policy two years later; it influenced liberal thought in France and England; it was definitely intended to free Jews from any limitation of their freedom to worship God in the way of their own ancestors, even though at that time there were only six Jewish families in the city of Richmond. The original clause was by George Mason and James Madison. The author of the final clause was Thomas Jefferson, who asked that his authorship of the "Virginia Law to Establish Religious Freedom" should be one of the three points to be mentioned on his tombstone. At the time of the passage of the law, Jefferson was ambassador in France, and James Madison, another future President of the United States, was its chief advocate in the legislature and before the people.

Not all the people in Virginia agreed with them.

133

History of the Jews in the United States

Patrick Henry believed in political more than in religious liberty, and led the fight to keep some connection between the state of Virginia and the Episcopal church. There was a six years' struggle from the original drafting of a bill for religious freedom by Jefferson until it was finally made part of the governing law of the state. Even then the legislature might have been against it, but Madison appealed to the people as a whole and they supported the cause of complete religious liberty. Jefferson was happy in France, and wrote back how the liberals in France and throughout Europe were studying the example of America. Only a few years later in the French Revolution, religious liberty was introduced for the first time on the continent of Europe for Christian, Jew and non-believer, and Virginia was pointed to as a precedent.

New York adopted the first comprehensive law on religious liberty in 1777. Other states lagged behind these in changing their charters and inserting the new American principle of religious freedom. The very last to adopt it was New Hampshire in 1877, although the restriction had been a dead letter even there long before. There were two especially interesting situations in this long struggle for equality: one in North Carolina in 1809, and one in Maryland in 1826.

North Carolina had not adopted the Virginia clause of religious freedom, but instead had inserted in her state constitution in 1776, along with provisions for liberty of worship for every faith, a prohibition on office-holding for those who "shall deny the being of God

The Land of Religious Liberty

or the truth of the Protestant religion or the Divine authority, either of the Old or New Testament, or who shall hold religious opinions incompatible with the freedom and safety of the state." This was aimed at atheists and Catholics, but of course, included Jews, Quakers and some other groups as well. It seems to have been a dead letter from the beginning, for a Catholic was elected governor in 1781 and a Jew, Jacob Henry, was elected and served in the state legislature in 1808. The next year, however, an opponent tried to have Mr. Henry unseated on the ground of this old Constitutional provision. He defended himself in an exceptionally able speech, by which he justified himself and Judaism and held his position in the legislature. This speech was very widely circulated at the time, was quoted in the similar fight in Maryland a few years later, and was printed in a collection called "The American Orator."

I quote part of this speech, not only because its ideas are important and true, but for the picture they give us of the times: "If a man should hold religious principles incompatible with the freedom and safety of the state," he said, "I do not hesitate to pronounce that he should be excluded from the public councils of the same. But I should really be at a loss to specify any known religious principles which are thus dangerous. . . . Nothing is more easy to demonstrate than that conduct alone is the subject of human laws, and that man ought to suffer civil disqualifications for what he does, and not for what he thinks."

History of the Jews in the United States

Mr. Henry was justified both by his own defense and by a legal twist in the interpretation of the Constitution; by similar methods Catholics also were allowed to hold office, even as high as justice of the supreme court of the state. In 1835 the law was made more liberal by substituting "Christian" for "Protestant," but Jews were still excluded in theory from office-holding. The final change, putting into law what was already long sanctioned in practice, did not come until after the Civil War, in 1868. In this long struggle for religious freedom, Jacob Henry must be remembered as one who fought well for his own people and for all who desire liberty.

In Maryland, however, there was a different leader, not a Jew defending his own rights, but a Scotch Presbyterian who did not know any Jews, and who fought for only one thing, freedom for every man to worship God in his own way and still be a full citizen of the state. Thomas Kennedy of Maryland is another man who deserves remembrance because of his service to religious liberty. The Maryland Constitution of 1776 required "a declaration of a belief in the Christian religion" for holding office in the state. In 1797 Solomon Etting, Bernard Gratz and several other prominent Jews of Baltimore, petitioned the legislature to change this provision; they stated that "they are a set of people called Jews and that they are thereby deprived of many of the invaluable rights of citizenship, and praying that they be placed upon the same footing with other good citizens." As we notice, Catholics and Quakers were not

136

excluded, as in North Carolina; here, only the Jews and free-thinkers, who did not accept the Christian religion, were under the ban.

The bill was brought up repeatedly in the legislature and always failed to pass until the cause was taken up by Thomas Kennedy. This fighter for human rights was born in Scotland in 1776 and came to Maryland in 1811; he did not live in Baltimore, where about 150 Jews then resided, but in the western part of the state. He stated his own convictions on the subject: "There are no Jews in the country from which I come, nor have I the slightest acquaintance with any Jew in the world . . . There are few Jews in the United States; in Maryland there are very few, but if there were only one, to that one we ought to do justice . . . A re-

HEROES OF RELIGIOUS LIBERTY
Top to bottom: Thomas Jefferson, James Madison, Roger Williams, Thomas Kennedy

137

ligious test can never be productive of any good effect, it may prevent the honest, the conscientious, from accepting an office, but the depraved, the ambitious, will not be stopped by so feeble a barrier." As an amendment to the Constitution, the bill to emancipate Jews and make them full citizens had to pass two sessions of the legislature; the first time it passed was in 1822. But in the next election the fight was carried into Kennedy's home county, he was defeated for reelection, and his "Jew bill," as it was called, failed with him. In 1826 he campaigned for the "Jew bill," was triumphantly reelected, introduced his bill in the legislature, and saw it carried for a second time, thus becoming a law. He had overcome opposition of terrible bitterness and violence, and he had fought— we must remember—only for the Jews, as all Christians were already equal before the law in Maryland. Both as Jews and as liberty-loving Americans we are to-day glad to remember and honor Thomas Kennedy, as a sincere lover of liberty and an ardent worker for human advancement.

REVIEW QUESTIONS

1. What were the reasons for including religious liberty in the Federal Constitution?
2. In which states were Jews equal citizens before the Revolution; in which states merely tolerated; in which discriminated against?

The Land of Religious Liberty

3. Why were some states slower than others in following the Federal Constitution? Name the last two, with dates.
4. Give the history of religious liberty in one of the three states: Virginia, North Carolina, Maryland.

TOPICS FOR REPORTS

1. What is liberty? What is the importance of religious liberty?
2. The history of religious toleration in the Old World and the New.
3. How did religious toleration turn into religious liberty? Give examples.
4. Study the speech of Jacob Henry, work out its ideas in sequence, and show the similar ideas of Washington, Jefferson, Franklin, Madison, etc.
5. Work out some contribution of the Jews to the struggle for their own, and general religious liberty.

REFERENCES FOR PUPILS

Wiernik, Peter, pp. 84–85, 112–121.
Straus, Oscar S., *The American Spirit*, Century Co.

REFERENCES FOR TEACHERS

Cobb, Sanford H., *The Rise of Religious Liberty in America.*
Schaff, Phillip, *Church and State in the United States*, Putnam.
Altfeld, E. M., *The Struggle for Religious Liberty in Maryland.* M. Curlander.
Luzzati, L., *God in Freedom*, supplementary American chapters by Irving Lehman and Max J. Kohler.
Publications of the American Jewish Historical Society.
Kohler, Max J., "Phases in the History of Religious Liberty in America," vol. XI, pp. 53–74, vol. XIII.

History of the Jews in the United States

"Civil Status of the Jews in Colonial N. Y.," vol. VI.
"The Doctrine That Christianity Is a Part of the Common Law and Its Parent Judicial Authority in England," vol. XXXI.
Huhner, Leon, "The Struggle for Religious Liberty in North Carolina," vol. XVI, pp. 37 ff.

CHAPTER 10.

The First Wave of Immigration: From Spain

W E HAVE now come to the end of the first part of our story, and are ready to see just what these early settlers were like, and what they accomplished in the United States. We are also ready to see the new settlers who were beginning to arrive and who soon exceeded them in numbers and later in importance.

I. HOW AND WHENCE THEY CAME

OF THE three successive "waves" of Jewish immigration to America, the first was not really a "wave" at all. It was simply a slow but steady flow of a few individuals or families at a time, beginning with the passengers of the St. Charles back in 1654 and continuing by twos and threes right through American history. If we go over the names of the early settlers, as we have done several times with their leaders, we notice that most of them are Spanish or Portuguese in form, and we therefore conclude that the first immigration period consisted chiefly of Sephardic Jews. But not exclusively, nor did they stop at any given time when another wave of immigration began. Sephardic Jews are still coming to America, little by little, as they have all along. They were merely lost to view in the much larger masses of German and Russian Jews, who did come by actual mass movements, owing to special conditions in their old homes.

Occasional Jews came, even in the early period, from Germany, as for instance the Lancaster colony, or from Germany via England, as did the Franks family, or from Poland, as did Haym Salomon. Later on there were often enough of these others to form a second synagogue, with the Ashkenazic (or North European) ritual, such as the Congregation Rodeph Shalom of Philadelphia in 1802 and the Congregation B'nai Jeshurun of New York in 1825 and Anshe Chesed of New York soon after. More often, the newcomers joined the existing synagogue, as in the case of Beth Elohim of Charleston, which in 1800 was the largest in the United States, and in which there were names other than Spanish ones.

In numbers, the Jews of those early days were very few; our best estimates run from 3,000 after the Revolution to 15,000 in 1840. As this shows, Jewish immigration was very slow, even slower than that of the United States as a whole, for during this period the general immigration varied from 8,000 in 1820 to 84,000 in 1840. The increase of Jews did not even keep up with that of the general population, and the few Jewish immigrants were never a large factor in the United States at that time.

These people were evidently the most enterprising and adventurous Jews, the ones who loved liberty so much that they were willing to make the greatest sacrifices

142

The First Wave of Immigration: From Spain

and take the greatest risks in order to obtain it. They could come from a place of oppression or of toleration to a land of freedom. But they also knew that they could do this only by parting from relatives and friends, braving a long ocean voyage, settling in a comparative wilderness, coming to a community of few Jews, struggling with new modes of making a living, and learning a new language. All honor to the heroic few who took the risks, made the sacrifices, and founded American Jewry for us, the millions of the twentieth century.

Some of the newcomers were peddlers or small merchants, trading from place to place or owning little stores. But often there were wealthy Jews like Aaron Lopez, or the Franks family; soon we find others who made money in America by serving the needs of the growing American communities. But their wealth was very modest compared with the rich men of the present, for the country as a whole was poor in money and rich only in the undeveloped possibilities of forests, fields, and mines. These rich Jewish importers and traders were welcomed in the various communities, as they had been in Newport before the Revolution. As the country west of the Alleghenies opened up, there were more and more poor Jewish immigrants along with the poor immigrants of other faiths, and there were more and more Ashkenazic Jews among the settlers. As a whole, the Spanish Jews were certainly wealthier on their arrival than the later comers; it took some years in the new land for these to catch up with their more fortunate brothers. We shall see the same thing later on in this history, in the comparison of the German and Russian Jews.

The Sephardic Jews were proud of their history, of the great men they had produced in the Spanish peninsula, and of the high standing of their ancestors. They considered themselves the aristocracy of Jewry, and held themselves somewhat apart from their more humble brothers from northern and central Europe. At first they would not intermarry with Ashkenazic families, though they welcomed them into their synagogues, where additional members were very badly needed, and where no Jew was excluded from worshipping.

The travels of the Sephardim on their way to America would make a history of exploration. Some came directly from Spain or Portugal, where they had lived as Marranos. Some came from Holland or England, whither they had fled in order to return to Judaism. The very first settlers came from South America, and from time to time since then Sephardic Jews entered the United States from Jamaica, the Barbadoes, Curacao, and other parts of South America and the West Indies. Now the most recent arrivals of the Spanish-speaking Jews come from the Levant, from Turkey, Greece and Egypt, where their ancestors have lived since that terrible day in 1492 when they were driven forth from Spain.

II. THEIR INSTITUTIONS

THE Jewish communities were too small in those days to require any great amount of organization, such as we have now, of charity, religion, education, and social life. There was ordinarily just one Jewish institution, the synagogue, in which all Jewish activities centered. In connection with the synagogue there was a cemetery, a school, some provision for charity and some social activi-ties. The synagogue was, then, the center of Jewish life for the entire community; every Jew belonged to it, and every Jewish interest flowed out of it. The synagogue had a president, or parnass, a board of trustees, a treasurer, and a chazan or cantor. This last often had his own busi-ness to conduct, and in addition, volunteered his services in the synagogue. But as soon as the congregations grew large enough, they engaged professional Hebrew scholars, who could chant the service, teach Hebrew, preach a sermon in English, slaughter the cattle according to the Jewish law. Sometimes the chazan tried to do all these things himself. But the growth in membership and wealth in the congregations made for more officials, with sub-division of duties. Rabbi Gershom Mendez Seixas was an eloquent preacher as well as a cantor; but most of the congregational functionaries were not able to preach, either because of lack of general education or because they were not proficient in English. Every congregation was completely self-controlled, with no national associa-tion of any kind.

The synagogue buildings seem mostly to have been in the colonial style; the oldest of them now standing, the one at Newport, is a very fine example of this real Ameri-can architecture. They were intended for orthodox services, so they had the reader's platform in the center, and a separate place for the women, either in a gallery or at the rear or even (in a small, simple building) at one side of the synagogue. The service was strictly orthodox, of course, and was in the Sephardic ritual, which had certain differences from the Ashkenazic one, both in the arrangement of the prayers, in certain special prayers or hymns, and in a different pronunciation of the Hebrew. One reason for the founding of special German synagogues when there were enough German Jews was this difference in the service; another was the social difference, because people coming from the same country

Jew. Ency.

TOURO SYNAGOGUE, NEWPORT, R. I.

146

The First Wave of Immigration: From Spain

naturally felt more at home with each other than they did with the proud Sephardic aristocrats.

Practically every congregation conducted some kind of Jewish education; as this was before the days of the free public school throughout the nation, this often included some kind of general school training, too. The New York congregation, Shearith Israel, established a Hebrew school as early as 1731, and in 1755 turned it into a regular day school, a parochial school, where the chazan taught Hebrew, Spanish, English, writing and arithmetic. This school continued until 1840 as a regular school, when it finally limited its work to religious and Hebrew instruction only. It was reorganized in 1802 as the Polonies Talmud Torah, and still exists under that name as a Jewish religious school. This was the natural and necessary progress everywhere; at first a parochial school when that was the only way that Jewish children could receive an elementary education; then, when public schools developed, the Jewish children attended them, and the congregational school became supplementary, meeting either afternoons or on Sundays.

Rebecca Gratz, an outstanding Jewish woman, whose whole biography will be told in chapter twelve, founded the first Jewish Sunday School in Philadelphia, in 1838. This was natural, as Philadelphia was the home of the Protestant Sunday School movement, which had begun there in 1791. Miss Gratz, having observed how the Christians taught their children religion one day a week, began the same system for Jewish children. Many of these

147

Jewish children were not at that time learning anything about Judaism or the Hebrew language, as they did not attend the Jewish parochial schools which at first offered the only kind of Jewish instruction. So this was a great step forward in Jewish education. It meant that Miss Gratz and other earnest men and women taught them Hebrew, the Jewish religion, and Jewish customs and worship. This system rapidly spread through the country, as Jewish children everywhere began to attend public schools instead of the Jewish parochial schools.

There was very little Jewish charity in these early days, for there were no great classes of rich and poor Jews, as there are now. Instead, people simply helped each other in need. This was usually attended to by the synagogue officials as the only representative officers of the Jewish community. So that charity, as well as education and religion, began and ended in the synagogue.

III. THE SPREAD OF JEWISH SETTLEMENTS

IT IS interesting to see the spread of Jewish settlements at this early period,—how Jews put in a sudden appearance, first in one city, then in another far away, just like the other pioneers; how congregations slowly spring into being in one section of the nation and in another; how the first few adventurous pioneers turn into little Jewish communities, and finally into one great Jewish community of the United States. We are not yet bewildered by an embarrassment of riches, as in later periods when there were so many immigrants and so many cities

148

involved; we can still see the different tiny shoots from which the future greatness was to grow.

For example, there was Richmond, Va., where few Jews lived before the Revolution, but which had a congregation among the six which wrote congratulations to the first President. The first record of a Jew there, is of Isaiah Isaac, who sued for a debt in 1769. In 1782 there were three other Jewish names, especially Jacob I. Cohen, a business partner of Isaac's, who had been a revolutionary soldier in South Carolina, and who afterward became one of the leading Jewish business men of the country. Jacob Cohen advanced money to James Madison when he was a delegate to the Continental Congress, as Haym Salomon had done; he was elected master of a lodge of Masons, and after he moved to Philadelphia was elected president of the Mikveh Israel Congregation. When he died in 1823 he left a bequest to the Richmond Congregation, and ordered that all his slaves be set free. In the year 1790, when the Congregation Beth Shalom of Richmond was already existing (we do not know the exact date of its organization) there were 171 white men in the city, and 29 of them were Jews. The first synagogue was built in 1822; the ritual was Sephardic, but the congregation was mixed, including some Jews from England, Germany and Holland. The German Congregation Beth Ahabah originated in 1839 and became a separate congregation in 1841. The first cemetery dates back to the year 1791, when the land was deeded to the congregation by Isaiah Isaac.

149

History of the Jews in the United States

The earliest Jew known to live in Baltimore was Jacob Levy, who had a store there in 1773, and who was authorized by Congress to sign bills of credit, with the value of money. The most important Jew of the early days was Solomon Etting, who was born in Lancaster, Pa., came to Baltimore after the Revolution, and became a leader in business, in the Jewish community, and in the city as a whole. The cemetery was founded in 1786, and the land was formally conveyed in 1801. Owing to the discrimination against Jews in the Maryland law, they were not able to incorporate, and perhaps there were not enough families, either. At any rate, the first service we know of was held in a private home in 1829. Later they incorporated as the Baltimore Hebrew Congregation; a burial society was organized in 1832 and a charity society in 1846. By that time, as we see, the community was growing large and complex and had many different needs.

The first Jewish settler in New Orleans, La., seems to have been Judah Touro, one of the worthies about whom we shall study in chapter twelve. He came to New Orleans in 1802 from Newport, R. I., while Louisiana was still French territory. As the first burial ground was not laid out until 1828, we see how slowly the little community had grown up. Jews came from Jamaica, England, Holland and Germany; American Jews as well moved there from Charleston, Baltimore and later down the river from Cincinnati. The first congregation sprang from the burial society; it still bears the name of Judah Touro, like so many other Jewish institutions in New

150

Orleans and also in Newport, which was his birthplace.

Next after New Orleans comes Louisville, Ky. The first Jewish pioneer along the trail of Daniel Boone seems to have been a German Jew from Berlin, in 1814. By 1832 enough Jews had followed him to start a congregation. Of course, we cannot think of these pioneer congregations in terms of our present-day ones; it took exactly ten Jewish men to make a congregation; they could hold holyday services in one of their homes, with one of their own number as reader. They could buy a small lot on the outside of the town as the nucleus of a cemetery, at a time when land values were very low. Then they merely waited until the growth of cities, the westward movement of progress, and the rise of trade brought more Jews along to join them. From such beginnings as these arose all the western Jewish communities, exactly like the early eastern settlements of colonial days.

St. Louis Jewry originated with a Bohemian Jew in 1816; its first congregation was organized in 1839, by which time many German Jews were settling that city along with the German Christians. For in this period the German Jews were steadily increasing, and their big centers came to be the main centers of German population in the United States.

This was especially true of Cincinnati, which was destined to play as important a part in the middle period of Jewish immigration as Newport did in the first, or New York in the third period. Much of the history of the German Jewish period rises from the Cincinnati community. Peculiarly enough, however, the first settlers here were not German, but English Jews, coming in 1817; their first congregation was formed in 1824, before the Germans had really begun their exodus to America or their settlement in the Ohio valley. The first Jew in this community was Joseph Jonas, a young watchmaker, who was born in England and had just come to America with the express purpose of settling in the western territory. The Jews of New York had tried to dissuade him from settling among gentiles away from all Jewish contacts; but he pressed on, took the two months trip from the east and down the Ohio valley. His brothers followed, then other acquaintances from England, two or three German Jews—so the community grew. The first holyday service was held in 1819, with only five men in place of the regular minyan, but they did not want to wait longer; they wanted to pray to the God who had caused them to prosper in the new land, and to found a Jewish congregation there. The cemetery was acquired in 1821 to bury a man who confessed on his death-bed that he was a Jew, though he had not lived as one. Twenty Jewish men signed the articles in 1824 for the Congregation Bene Israel, which received articles of incorporation from the General Assembly in 1830. As the community was very poor, they wrote to the congregation at Charleston for assistance in building their synagogue.

Joseph Jonas, who enjoyed writing and speaking, wrote memoirs of his early experiences in Cincinnati. He was the first Jew whom most of the people there had

152

ever seen; some of them actually came for long distances just to look at him. One old Quaker woman said to him: "Art thou a Jew? Thou art one of God's chosen people. Wilt thou let me examine thee?" She turned him round and round and at last exclaimed, "Well, thou art no different to other people!"

Cleveland was not settled by Jews until a Bavarian Jew came there in 1837; the first congregation dates from 1839.

And so one community sprang up after another as we approach the second period, that of German immigration. The pioneers spread into the west and south; usually there were a few Jews among them. Wherever Jews settled, they at once founded the institutions of Judaism, a cemetery, a synagogue, soon afterward a school, a charity society.

There is one more city I want to mention, where the Jewish connection is almost legendary, and goes back to the very early days of the pioneers, back near the Revolution. This is Montgomery, Ala., whose present Jewish community dates from the German period, in the 1840's, but whose founder is said to have been a Jew, Abraham Mordecai. The city of Montgomery was begun in 1814, but Mordecai lived on its site as early as 1789. He was born in Pennsylvania, came south as an Indian trader, married a squaw, and lived in that section for sixty years. Mordecai built the first cotton gin in Alabama, in order to introduce the culture of cotton in the state. This was burned by the Indians, and its owner injured in a fight with them a year or two later. But he recovered, served in the War of 1812, and lived to an extreme old age among the Creek tribe.

IV. THE WAR OF 1812 AND THE MEXICAN WAR

Two wars occurred during this general period, in which the Jews again did their share in proportion to their small numbers and the minor character of both struggles. In the War of 1812 there is definite record of 43 Jews who served in the armed forces, beside a special group in Baltimore, who were enlisted in the home defense force of that city when it was attacked. Beside Commodore Uriah P. Levy, who is important enough to have a full biography in the next chapter, the most important Jewish officers were Captain John Ordroneaux of New York, who commanded a privateer and captured a number of enemy vessels; and Captain Mordecai Myers, who served in the northern army with special distinction. Captain Myers saved many lives during a lake storm and was badly wounded in the shoulder at the battle of Chrysler's Farm.

As in every pioneer movement where they were not especially excluded, Jews appeared in Texas under Mexican rule and had a part in the revolt which led to the American war against Mexico. There was one, Samuel Isaacs, among the first settlers of Austin in 1821; there were two others living in Velasco in 1831; there was a German Jew, Adolphus Sterne, among the first settlers of Nacogdoches in 1824. He was a fighter against Mexico,

The First Wave of Immigration: From Spain

a member of the Texas Congress when Texas was an independent nation, and one of the first representatives of Texas in the United States Congress after annexation. Several Jews fought under General Sam Houston, while his surgeon general was Moses Albert Levy. The first Jewish cemetery in Texas was established in the city of Houston in 1844, and the first synagogue in the same city in 1854, which shows the very slow growth of the Jewish community beyond the few adventurers and pioneers of the early days.

Mr. Simon Wolf has listed 56 Jews in the American army and navy during the Mexican war, not many more than in the earlier wars, when the Jewish population had been far smaller. The only outstanding one of these was David Camden de Leon, who was an army surgeon of long experience in Indian wars. He was called the "fighting doctor" after he had led a charge of cavalry when the commanding officer had fallen. He earned the rank of Major and was twice commended by Congress for gallantry in action. As a Southerner, he resigned at the outbreak of the Civil War to enter the Confederate army; here he was Surgeon General, and organized the medical service.

REVIEW QUESTIONS

1. Characterize the Spanish Jews as a whole.
2. Characterize their settlement in America; where did they come from and for what purpose? Where did they settle?
3. Describe their early institutions. Give reasons.
4. Name two early settlements in the west or south, with

155

their founders, and describe the growth of the community.
5. How did the Jewish school system start in America?
6. How did the Jewish charities begin?
7. Summarize the service of Jews in the War of 1812; the Mexican War.

TOPICS FOR REPORTS

1. The Jews of the Ohio Valley, early settlements.
2. The Jews of Baltimore or of Richmond till 1840.
3. Abraham Mordecai.
4. The history of the Sephardim from the earliest times till their settlement in America.
5. The Sephardic community of the United States today.
6. A typical Jewish school of the early days.

REFERENCES FOR PUPILS

Wiernik, Peter, pp. 104–127, 158–163.
Jewish Encyclopedia, art. on America, vol. I, pp. 495–501, 512–513, arts. on Judaism in America, Cincinnati, Cleveland, Baltimore, St. Louis, New Orleans, Richmond, Kentucky.
Levinger, E. E., "Three at Grace," *The New Land.*

REFERENCES FOR TEACHERS

Dushkin, Alexander, *Jewish Education in New York City,* pp. 28–53. Bureau of Jewish Education, N. Y.
Blum, Isidor, *The Jews of Baltimore,* Historical Review Publishing Co.
Ezekiel, H. T. and Lichtenstein, G., *History of the Jews of Richmond, Va.* H. T. Ezekiel.
Wolf, Simon, pp. 67–75.
Morais, Henry S., *The Jews of Philadelphia.* Levytype Co.
Rosenbach, H. P., *The Jews of Philadelphia Prior to 1800.*

156

The First Wave of Immigration: From Spain

Publications of the American Jewish Historical Society.
    Cohen, Henry, "Settlement of the Jews in Texas," vol. II,
    pp. 139 ff.
    Philipson, David, "Jewish Pioneers of the Ohio Valley," vol.
    VIII, pp. 43 ff.
    Messing, A. J., Jr., "Old Mordecai, The Founder of the City
    of Montgomery," vol. XIII, pp. 71 ff.
    Huhner, Leon, "Jews In the War of 1812," vol. XXVI, pp.
    173 ff.

CHAPTER 11.

Outstanding Jews of the First Half of the Nineteenth Century

I. JUDAH TOURO, 1775-1854

IN THIS early period of our history, there were several people so interesting in their lives and so important in their deeds that it is worth our while to stop and learn more about them. They are very different sorts of people, too: a business man and philanthropist; a politician and writer; a soldier of fortune; a rich woman who engaged in charity and education; a poor blind woman who wrote poetry.

The first of these is the first of all the Jewish philanthropists in America, leader of a line which now includes Jacob Schiff, Nathan Straus, and Julius Rosenwald. Judah Touro was the son of the rabbi of Newport, R. I., and was born the day before the battle of Bunker Hill. At his father's death, he was brought up by his uncle, Moses Michael Hays of Boston, a prominent merchant, and a friend of many leading non-Jews of the city. When he was twenty-seven years old he settled in New Orleans, then still a French possession. For over fifty years he lived there, working day by day in his store, opening the place every morning at precisely the same time, so that neighbors could set their watches by his comings and goings. A precise, formal little man, scrupulously honest, he imported goods from his friends in New England, sold them at a small profit, and then invested that profit in New Orleans property and in ships. So his fortune grew rapidly, while he continued his small, careful business and watched it grow.

This, however, did not measure the whole soul of the man, but merely his outside appearance. For he was a volunteer for the defense of New Orleans in 1815, served under General Andrew Jackson, was wounded and actually left for dead on the battlefield. But a young Virginia gentleman, Rezin D. Shepherd, carried him in, nursed him back to health and became his life-long friend. Shepherd was one of the four executors of Touro's will almost forty years later, and the one to whom the residue of the estate was left after all special bequests had been paid. But as he was also a rich man, he simply added this amount to the different charitable gifts in the will.

Perhaps because of his share in America's struggle for liberty, Touro was always interested in the Revolutionary War. An effort had been made to erect the Bunker Hill Monument but the movement languished for thirteen years. Then Amos Lawrence of Boston offered $10,000 for the purpose and Judah Touro of New Orleans sub-scribed the same amount on condition that the remaining thirty thousand was raised. With this sum coming from a Jew in that far section of the country, the rest was speedily subscribed. In 1843 the Monument was dedicated. Daniel Webster delivered the chief address on that occasion, and special homage was paid to these two men who had given the largest sums for the Monument. These verses were read on that day and became popular through the country:

JUDAH TOURO

Amos and Judah—venerated names!
Patriarch and prophet press their equal claims,
Like generous coursers, running neck and neck,
Each aids the work by giving it a check.
Christian and Jew, they carry out a plan—
For though of different faith, each is in heart
    a man.

The list of Judah Touro's other gifts is a long one; many of them were given so modestly and secretly that they are still unknown. He founded the Jewish congregation of New Orleans, and gave $40,000 for the synagogue; he also purchased a Christian church which was in debt and leased it to the congregation rent-free. In

160

his will he left varying sums to practically every Jewish congregation and charitable society in the United States, for he seemed to know them all; to Sir Moses Montefiore of England, the great philanthropist, for the poor Jews of Jerusalem; to found a Jewish hospital in New Orleans; to buy the Old Stone Mill left by the Northmen at Newport, and now surrounded by Touro Park; and to a huge number of non-Jewish charities of different kinds in New Orleans. Both Newport and New Orleans, where he was born and died, have named streets in his memory.

The inscriptions on many tombstones are known to exaggerate, but his actually sums up the man:

"By righteousness and integrity he collected his wealth;
In charity and for salvation he dispensed it.
The last of his name, he inscribed it in the book of philanthropy
To be remembered forever."

REFERENCES

Jewish Encyclopedia, art. on Judah Touro.
Publications of the American Jewish Historical Society.
  Kohler, Max J., "Judah Touro, Merchant and Philanthropist."
Wiernik, Peter, pp. 144–147.
Wasserman, Jacob, *Judah Touro.*

II. MORDECAI MANUEL NOAH, 1785–1851

THE second of our Jewish worthies was the greatest possible contrast to the first. He was expansive, large-

161

handed, visionary, equally ready with his tongue, his pen and his sword, always engaged in some novel scheme, always in some kind of fight with some kind of opponent. Mordecai Manuel Noah was noted in his day as politician and public man, journalist and playwright, patron and friend of the Jewish cause, dreamer of a Jewish nation whether in Palestine or in America. He was hated and despised, admired and feared; the only emotion he never aroused was indifference.

Mordecai Manuel Noah was born in Philadelphia, the son of a revolutionary soldier; it is said that General Washington was a guest at the wedding of his parents. When he was about four years old, his father disappeared, leaving him in the care of a grandfather; Mordecai was then apprenticed to a trade, but managed to learn a good deal about writing, as he preferred being a newspaper man and dramatist to anything else in the world. When he was only fifteen he was a reporter and at twenty-five an editor. He got an early start as a dramatist by rewriting old plays for an amateur theatrical group. In later life he was editor of several leading New York newspapers, author of a half dozen successful plays, friend of every actor and public man in the city of New York, and very infiuential in the politics of the city, state and nation. He was a dandy, in spite of his stoutness; a social leader, much sought after for his power and public standing.

None of his books or plays are read any more, but those which are preserved in old chronicles or in the

162

MORDECAI MANUEL NOAH

publications of the American Jewish Historical Society are very interestingly written, while his speeches must have been most impressive when he delivered them with his natural and characteristic fire and energy.

Noah had a varied career in the holding of public office. He was at various times sheriff of New York County, judge of the New York Court of Sessions, Surveyor of the Port of New York, and United States Consul to Tunis. In regard to the first office, the story is told of a political opponent who said, "It would be a pity to have a Jew hang a Christian," to which Noah retorted: "Fine Christian that had to be hanged!"

Those were shifting days in political parties, so that Noah, one of the early members of Tammany Hall, and a leading political writer all his life, is found in various political fights and sometimes on changing sides. He was an active Mason, a Major in the New York State Militia, an officer of the Jewish congregation and president of the Jewish charities.

163

His most important political office, and one connected with his intense Jewish feeling, was that of consul to Tunis. He asked for this office in 1811 so that he might represent his country and at the same time study the situation of the Jews in Europe and Africa. In 1813, after he had refused the post at Riga, he finally received, at the appointment of President Madison, the post he desired at Tunis. Those were stirring days in the Barbary States; rights of civilized nations had to be defended constantly, either by bluff as in the case of Noah, or by force as in the case of Stephen Decatur. In addition, Noah had to ransom Americans taken prisoner by the pirates, and to interpret and apply treaties; he even cited an earlier treaty made by Joel Barlow, to show that the United States is not a Christian nation but one in which all religions are equal, and as such it deserved preferred treatment by the Mohammedans.

There was some difficulty about Noah's exceeding his instructions in regard to the ransom money, and he was recalled; it took him over a year to get the matter settled and to show that he had done the best possible thing under the circumstances. As a matter of fact, Noah had a peculiar attitude toward money all his life; he was generous to a fault, both with his own money and that of other people. He gave his royalties for a play to the actors after the theatre had burned down; he gave his salary as sheriff to the widow of his predecessor; all his life he was a poor newspaper man, but as generous as a prince.

164

Finally he became a prince of a kind. In 1825, he thought he saw a great opportunity to rescue the house of Israel from their world-wide oppressions, to settle them in a new land, and to build a great city and behind it a great new empire. He had seen the Jews abroad, then terribly oppressed during the reactionary period from 1815 to 1848, and knew that such a home was needed. In default of Palestine, which was not obtainable at the moment, he would found a worthy substitute on Grand Island, in the Niagara River opposite the village of Buffalo. Noah persuaded a Christian friend to purchase sufficient land on the island, and decided to lay out there a city which he named Ararat, in allusion to his own name.

As high priests and kings were out of date in America, Noah went back to the period of the Judges for his model; as there was no authority to elect the first judge, and no worthy rival for the office, he appointed himself the first Governor and Judge over Israel. In 1825 he went to Buffalo, then a little village of 2,500 people, to dedicate the new city. Clad in his judicial robes of crimson, he marched in a long procession with the militia, the politicians, the Masons and the people of the town. There were not sufficient boats to permit an actual crossing to the island—in fact, Noah probably never went to the island at all.

So the cornerstone was brought into an Episcopal church, and the dedication exercises took place there, with Mr. Noah as Governor and Judge delivering a long speech, in which he invited Jews from all the countries of the globe, and also the American Indians—whom he believed to be the lost Ten Tribes of Israel—to settle in this new city of Ararat.

He also issued a proclamation to that effect: "In his name do I revive, renew and reestablish the government of the Jewish Nation, under the auspices and protection of the constitution and laws of the United States of America . . . And I hereby enjoin it upon all our pious and venerable Rabbis, our Presidents and Elders of Synagogues, Chiefs of Colleges and brethren in authority throughout the world, to circulate and make this, my Proclamation, and give it full publicity, credence and effect."

But nobody regarded this Proclamation. No Jew ever settled on Grand Island. Neither Noah nor anyone else ever built a house there, but only a temporary monument, which has since been destroyed. The Jews did not flock to the new refuge, nor did the Indians. Mordecai Noah returned to New York and printed his great address and proclamation in the newspapers.

Twenty years later he delivered another address, which he also printed. This dealt with the need of the Jews for the ancient land of Israel, and pointed forward to the movement of Zionism, which had its inception fifty years later.

All his life Noah was an optimist, a dreamer, an enthusiast, and many times he espoused good causes and anticipated future developments.

Outstanding Jews, First Half Nineteenth Century

REFERENCES

Makover, A. B., *Mordecai M. Noah, His Life and Works*.
Zangwill, I., "Noah's Ark," *Ghetto Tragedies*.
Levinger, E. E., "Across the Waters," *The New Land*.
Wiernik, Peter, pp. 128–134.
Daly, pp. 104–138.
Wolf, Simon, *Selected Addresses and Papers*, pp. 108–154.
Jewish Encyclopedia, art. on Mordecai Manuel Noah.
Publications of the American Jewish Historical Society.
   Kohler, Max J., "Early American Zionist Projects," vol.
   VIII, pp. 84–118.
   "Address by Mordecai M. Noah at the Dedication of the
   City of Ararat," vol. XXI, pp. 221–252.

III. URIAH PHILLIPS LEVY, 1792–1862

OUR third hero of American Jewry is still a different sort of man. For Uriah P. Levy was bold, adventurous, hard-headed, fiery, far different from the genial, hopeful and versatile Noah. Levy also was born in Philadelphia and died in New York; but he spent the intervening years as sailor before the mast, officer on merchant vessels and in the navy, he was six times court-martialled but always restored to rank, and died a Commodore, the highest ranking officer in the United States Navy.

When he was only ten years old, young Levy sailed as a cabin boy, and rose through the ranks until he was master of a sailing vessel before he was twenty-one. The end of this chapter in his career came in a mutiny, which left him penniless in a foreign land; but he managed to get home, accuse the mutineers, and have them all

167

brought back to the United States and convicted.

By that time the War of 1812 had broken out and he volunteered, receiving a commission as sailing master. He captured several prizes, but finally was himself captured by the British and kept as a prisoner until the end of the war.

URIAH P. LEVY

In the navy Levy encountered a double prejudice, as a Jew and as a sailor promoted from the ranks. He always claimed that the former was the more decisive one of the two, and that his troubles were due, neither to his humble beginnings nor to his fiery temper, but solely to his loyalty to the faith of Israel.

But it is certain that there were unpleasant episodes in plenty. He fought a duel and killed his opponent. In Paris he heard a French officer and civilian hiss the name of President Jackson, so he promptly challenged them both, extracting apologies both to himself and to his nation. He was tried six times by court-martial and repeatedly degraded in rank. At one of these times he happened to be in Brazil and was offered a high position

168

in the Brazilian navy by the Emperor himself. But he proudly declined, saying that the humblest position in his country's service was preferable to royal favors. He insisted on a chance to vindicate himself, had a special commission of inquiry appointed by Congress, proved his complete loyalty and efficiency as an officer, and was reinstated as Captain.

He died a Commodore just after the outbreak of the Civil War. He asked that his tombstone might record that "he was the father of the law for the abolition of the barbarous practice of corporal punishment in the United States Navy." Evidently his experience as a cabin boy and sailor made him sympathetic toward the seaman in a practical way.

Uriah P. Levy was so ardent an admirer of Thomas Jefferson, that he donated the statue of him which now stands in Statuary Hall in the Capitol at Washington. For many years, Levy owned Monticello, which is now established as a Jefferson memorial, according to the idea of Uriah P. Levy and that of its later owner, his nephew, Congressman Jefferson M. Levy. A Jew, a duellist, a naval officer—how many surprises and contradictions there are in the history of the house of Israel!

REFERENCES

Wiernik, Peter, pp. 238–241.
American Jewish Year Book 5663, Biography by Simon Wolf, pp. 42–45.
Levinger, E. E., "The Lucky Stone," *The New Land.*

History of the Jews in the United States

THE lives of two Jewish women who were noted far and wide in their own day, still have a lingering interest for us. Rebecca Gratz was a member of the famous Philadelphia family; she was beautiful, rich and c h a r m i n g—a social leader; she was also a woman of unusual ability, as organizer and worker for a dozen charitable and religious movements, both Jewish and non-sectarian. She lived to the great age of 88, and became a legend even before her death.

REBECCA GRATZ

The legend is a romantic one. First, it told how she had been in love with a Christian but refused to marry him because she was a Jewess, and therefore remained single all her life. This seems more than likely, for Rebecca Gratz certainly had all the attractions which bring many offers of marriage, and there must have been some special reason which kept her unmarried.

Second, the legend, which seems to be based on facts all the way through, tells that Rebecca Gratz was the

170

Outstanding Jews, First Half Nineteenth Century

original of the character of Rebecca in Sir Walter Scott's "Ivanhoe." Washington Irving was a great friend of the Gratz family, as was also Matilda Hoffman, the young woman to whom he was engaged. During the last months of her life Matilda Hoffman was nursed by Rebecca Gratz. One bed-room of the Gratz home was known as the "Washington room" because it was always used by Washington Irving when he came to visit Philadelphia. A few years after the death of Matilda Hoffman, Irving went to Europe, visited Scott, and described the visit in one of his essays. He spoke of Rebecca Gratz to the great novelist—her beauty, pride, wealth, her devotion as a nurse to Matilda, her loyalty to her religion and her refusal to marry a Christian. These are precisely the qualities which are described in "Ivanhoe," and the ones for which Scott's Rebecca has become such a popular heroine; "Ivanhoe" was published just a few years after the visit of Washington Irving, when this conversation was still fresh in Scott's mind.

But Miss Gratz herself outgrew the romantic legend of her life, though it is still the thing for which we all like best to remember her. She became a leading worker for charity and education in all Philadelphia. She brought up a family of orphans on the death of their mother. She was secretary of the Female Association for the Relief of Women and Children in Reduced Circumstances (a non-sectarian society) in 1801, and organizer and secretary of the Female Hebrew Benevolent Society in 1819. She was also a founder of the Philadelphia Orphan

History of the Jews in the United States

Asylum and its secretary for forty years; founder of the first Jewish Sunday School in America and its president and superintendent for twenty-six years. She gave of herself for the good of others,—particularly for the sick, for women and for children. If she was really the original of Scott's Rebecca, she was also a fine copy of that lovely character in her own life story.

REFERENCES

Wiernik, Peter, p. 107.
Jewish Encyclopedia, art. on Gratz Family.
Morais, H. S., *The Jews of Philadelphia.*
Markens, p. 76.
Levinger, E. E., "The Princess of Philadelphia," *The New Land.*
Philipson, David, *Letters of Rebecca Gratz* (edited by).
Publications of the American Jewish Historical Society.
    Jacobs, Joseph, "The Original of Scott's Rebecca," vol. XXII, p. 53.
    Philipson, David, "Some Unpublished Letters of Rebecca Gratz," vol. XXIX, p. 53.

V. PENINA MOISE, 1797–1880

DURING the greater part of Rebecca Gratz' life there was a younger Jewish woman, living in Charleston, South Carolina, who was almost as well known the country over. This was Penina Moise, the daughter of a French Jewish family, (Moise being the French form of Moses) and one of the popular writers of poetry in that day. She was one of a large family, whose father had died early, so that she had to work very hard in the home and pick up

172

her education by stealth. That is how she ruined her sight, reading late at night by firelight or moonlight. During most of her life, Miss Moise had to play nurse to a paralyzed mother, and always she had to battle against poverty. Considering the few methods of earning money which were open to women in those days, her ability and power are amazing.

Penina Moise was chiefly known in her own day as a poet; even today many of her hymns are sung in the Jewish synagogues and schools. She contributed serious and humorous verse to leading publications of the day, such as Godey's Ladies Book, and published some of them in book form. She was a noted leader in literary circles in Charleston, which had an old tradition of culture, so that she had a sort of salon, similar in many ways to the famous ones of Europe. For the last twenty-five years of her life Penina Moise was blind and in pain; still she and her sister conducted a private school, where she taught from memory and the pupils read to her from the books she knew and loved. Even up to the end she dictated her poetry which appeared regularly in the magazines.

Penina Moise was also a teacher and the second superintendent of the Sabbath School at Charleston, which was organized only a few months after the one in Philadelphia. There were no text books in the English language for Jewish children, so Miss Gratz wrote out the lessons for her own school every week and made a copy which she sent to Charleston; then the Charleston teachers copied that, and had something to teach their children the next Sunday.

REFERENCES

Elzas, B., *Jews of South Carolina*, pp. 181–184.
American Jewish Year Book 5666, art. by Lee C. Harby, "Penina Moise, Woman and Writer," p. 17.

REVIEW QUESTION

1. Sketch the life of each of the five Jewish notables in this chapter.

TOPICS FOR REPORTS

1. Find some other interesting Jew of the period, and report on his life and work.
2. Describe the Jewish community of New York in the time of Major Noah, with its 500 Jews in a city of 60,000.
3. Describe the Jewish community of Charleston before the Civil War.
4. Look up some of the poetry of Penina Moise, especially in the Union Hymnal.
5. Find some of the writings or speeches of Mordecai Noah, and report on them.
6. Report on the character of Rebecca in "Ivanhoe," and compare it with our account of Rebecca Gratz.

CHAPTER 12.

The Second Wave of Immigration: From Germany

WHAT is the reason for the abrupt shift of Jewish immigration from the Spanish to the German Jews? Why were these newcomers so much more numerous, that they supplanted the Sephardim? Were they the same type as the Sephardim, or were there important differences? What did the German Jews bring to America, and what did they contribute to Jewish life in America? Questions such as these are suggested by the title of this chapter, implying that there was a new wave of Jewish immigration in the middle of the nineteenth century.

I. WHO THESE IMMIGRANTS WERE

THE Spanish Jews had been largely rich and cultured people, with a proud history. The German Jews were chiefly the rank and file of the population, poor or middle class workmen, merchants, with rarely a professional man among them. The Spanish Jews came to North America as a separate group, with very few Spanish Christians, though the two groups had migrated together to South America. The Russian Jews (the third wave, whom we will discuss later) came alone, without Russian Christians, due to special Jewish causes. But the German Jews came as part of a great German migration, which began in 1815 or even earlier and continued until the 1890's. So there were general reasons for Germans to leave their fatherland for America at that time, while certain special reasons applied to the Jews in particular. Of the 5,000,-000 German immigrants, about 200,000 were Jews.

The number of Jews in America rose from 15,000 in 1840 (mostly Sephardim) to 250,000 in 1880 (mostly Germans). Again, we must not think that the two waves of immigration were entirely distinct. We have already seen that some German Jews settled in New York, Lancaster, and Philadelphia,—for instance, Joseph Simon and the Gratz family, in very early days; others appeared in Charleston and joined the Sephardic congregation. But their number was small, and usually their influence was smaller still. On the other hand, the German immigration did not stop in 1860 or 1890; it merely slowed down, and was lost to view in the far huger influx of the third wave, that from Russia and Eastern Europe. Comparatively few Russian, Polish, Austrian, Bohemian and Roumanian Jews found their way to America during the German period; but there were a few, and they must not be forgotten, for in the Spanish period they included a Haym Salomon and in the German period a Michael Heilprin.

The reasons for the migration from Germany are to be found, naturally, in Germany. After the Napoleonic wars Germany was bitterly poor, worn out by war, with

Second Wave of Immigration: From Germany

few opportunities for increase of wealth and with little hope for the future. There were a number of small, separate states, without any central government; each of these states took advantage of the opportunity to suppress all liberal thought, all striving for liberty, and to maintain a petty autocracy of its own. In some of these states the medieval laws against the Jews, which had been suspended during the supremacy of Napoleon, were revived in all their rigor. The nation was backward in government and industry, militaristic and brutal in politics, and particularly severe against the Jews.

Hence, Catholic, Protestant and Jew fled from Germany to find freedom in America. These people were lovers of liberty and came to a new world to seek it. The German non-Jews settled largely in the middle west, though some remained in the eastern cities; a great many of them purchased farms or obtained them free as homesteads. At the same time, the German Jews were drawn along with this mass movement, except that few of them settled on the land. Some remained in the eastern cities, but many were among the first settlers in a number of cities and country towns in the west and south, and with their little stock of goods, often carried on their backs, they opened up many a new region to trade.

Of the Jews in different parts of Germany, the largest group came from Bavaria, because there the anti-Jewish laws were most severe. The Bavarian Jews had to pay heavy taxes, were not allowed to be citizens, had special laws to burden them and control their place of living, their

177

business, and their travelling about. Worst of all, they were not allowed to marry when they wished, as only a certain number of Jewish marriages could be held in a certain period of time. Some of the immigrants were engaged couples who married as soon as they reached America and at once founded homes in the new land. These restrictions ceased about the middle of the century, so that the immigration of German Jews practically stopped in 1860, while that of non-Jews kept up much longer; after that date, Jews merely represent their share in the general movement, for there were no special disabilities under which they labored at that time.

II. THEIR GENERAL CHARACTERISTICS

THESE German Jews were in many ways different from the proud Spaniards of earlier days. They had been forced to live for generations in ghettoes, to wear a special Jewish costume or badge, to run away from Christian persecution and to pay and bribe the officers of the law. Those who came to America were at first poor in worldly goods, weak in learning. The wealthy and educated managed to get along in Germany, but the poor people hurried to get away. Later, after 1848, a new element came, both among Jews and non-Jews, the "forty-eighters"; that was a year of revolt in Germany and in much of Europe. But the revolt was put down, and many of the most liberal and best educated people in Germany fled to a new world. The most prominent among the non-Jews in that group was Carl Schurz.

178

Second Wave of Immigration: From Germany

ADOLF KRAUS

But there were a number of Jews also, such as Dr. Abraham Jacobi, and they contributed a fine element to the growth of American Jewry. After 1850 there was a return to the earlier situation,— the immigrants were again usually poor traders who left nothing behind except despair, and whose chief assets in their new homes were industry and hope.

We can see the poor beginnings of these Jewish immigrants in this typical story told by Adolf Kraus, later a leading lawyer and public man in Chicago, and international president of the B'nai B'rith. He was a sixteen year old boy from Bohemia, knowing little English and without a job. "It was a bitter cold day. I was hungry and all the money I had left was two pennies. I went into a store to see what I could buy for this money. I saw large, beautiful apples there and asked the grocer how much he wanted for an apple. 'Two cents,' said the grocer. 'That is all the money I have. Could you not sell me one of the smaller ones for one cent?' The grocer looked at me and said, 'You can have two apples for a cent.' Since that time I have eaten a good many apples, but

179

I have never since eaten an apple that tasted so good as those two which the grocer gave me on that occasion." Then the boy walked on and found a job cleaning horses; he did not know how at first, but he was very willing to learn.

The German Jewish immigrants were hard working, enterprising, and were generally good business men. Their usual way was to start out peddling with a pack; the first few weeks' profit paid for the original goods, the next few for a horse and wagon. After that there were two purposes for saving: to send for their relatives and give them a start in America; to invest in a store in some likely spot, which they found through their business trips. By that time the family would be over from Europe, to help in the store and to develop the business. This business might grow into a huge success, so that many of the wealthy Jewish families in the United States today can trace their rise from the German migration, and from these humble beginnings.

Most of these immigrants were ignorant both of Jewish and of American culture. Such little learning as they had was of German literature and life, and there was not much of that, for this was before the day when the German public schools were opened to the Jews. A marked change is found among the small group of more recent German immigrants, since 1880, for they are full exponents of German culture. Dr. Isaac M. Wise tells of asking for a Mishnah in an orthodox synagogue in New York shortly after his arrival in the 40's; the sexton laughed at

Second Wave of Immigration: From Germany

him, thinking only a greenhorn would ask for a Hebrew book in America. Wise complained bitterly of the equal lack of Jewish and American learning among the members of the first congregation that he had in Albany, and contrasted them with the superior Spanish Jews of Charleston.

But the German Jews wanted to learn. They were ambitious for education for their children, and sometimes for themselves as well. They brought from Germany, if not much learning in their own heads, a vast respect and desire for it; the learned professions were their greatest admiration. They came from a civilization which—in spite of its medieval survivals, such as autocracy and anti-Jewish laws—was in many ways as modern as that of America. They merely had to learn English and get used to a few privations of the frontier before they were thoroughly at home. They were liberals to a man, according to the definition of that term in their day; against autocratic government, against slavery, and for the right of the individual to develop as he pleased. They were used to German system and German organization, and carried that attitude with them.

They had, with this individualism and love of liberty, quite a touch of provincial narrowness, too. Their first synagogues were often composed of people from the same part of Germany. They experienced prejudice on the part of the proud Spaniards, and, though so recently out of the ghetto themselves, they passed on the same prejudice to the Jews from Poland and Galicia. They were sturdy, sober, hard-working; they were not dreamers and had little use for dreamers. They were builders of the country, of the cities, and of Jewish institutions.

III. WHERE THEY WENT

THERE were only a few Jewish communities in the Sephardic period, and some of these, as we have seen, were partly begun by Germans. But there were many communities organized during the German period, in almost every city of importance in the United States, and in many smaller ones as well. The German Jews scattered themselves, for they were business men, and each one looked for a location; they did not mass together in great cities, as did the Russian Jewish workingmen later on. I know personally German Jews settled in Georgetown, Delaware; Paducah, Kentucky; and Mitchell, South Dakota. If I were better acquainted through the country, I have no doubt I could add all sorts of out-of-the-way places to that list. If you study your own Jewish community, unless it is one of the few already mentioned, it is practically certain that it was first established by Jews from Germany.

The following are a few of these many Jewish settlements which multiplied from 1840 on. Chicago was incorporated as a town in 1836, and the first Jew settled there in 1837. The first cemetery was organized in 1845, and so was the first holyday service; they had exactly ten men for the minyan, so when one of them left the room the service had to stop. By 1847 there was a congrega-

182

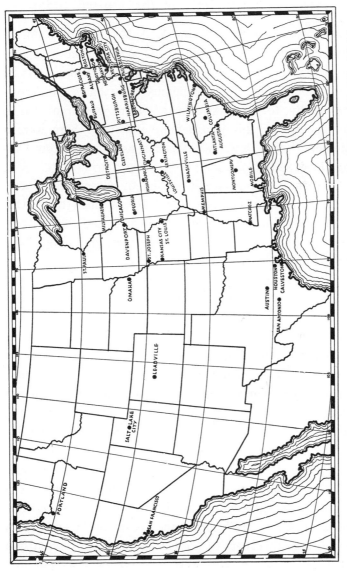

HOW THE GERMAN JEWS SETTLED THROUGHOUT THE COUNTRY UP TO 1865.

tion of twenty members, the K A M (Kehillath Anshe Maariv, Congregation Men of the West). The first synagogue, where the great Chicago postoffice now stands, was built in 1851. The community must have been growing rapidly, for the first charity society was organized in the same year; this is a definite sign that there were a number of poor Jews, who needed assistance. Now Chicago has 282,000 Jews.

Cincinnati, being largely settled by Germans, became a center for the German Jews, from which they scattered to the various sections of the west and south. Most German Jewish families, wherever they are living, have some kind of connection or relationship in Cincinnati. As we have seen in a previous chapter, the first Jews to settle in Cincinnati were from England, and the first congregation, Bene Israel, was founded in 1824 under their leadership. But by 1841 there were enough German Jews to organize their own congregation, the Congregation Bene Jeshurun. Only a few years later Cincinnati's leadership in Jewish affairs was made definite when two prominent rabbis accepted the pulpits of these two congregations, Isaac M. Wise in 1854 and Max Lilienthal in 1855. Much more will be said of these two men, especially of the former, in our chapter on reform Judaism.

In 1849, when gold was discovered in California, Jews were among the earliest settlers there, journeying over the long, weary trail across the continent or coming by boat from all corners of the earth where Jews might live. That very year services were held on Yom Kippur in a

Second Wave of Immigration: From Germany

tent and a store in San Francisco; in 1850 two congregations were organized, one by German and American, the other by English and Polish Jews. A dozen mining camps had temporary congregations in this period which were as short-lived as the camps. Two Jews were members of the state legislature in 1852, while two others, Solomon Heydenfeldt and Henry A. Lyons, were Associate Justices of the Supreme Court of California.

It is unnecessary to mention more names and dates; statistics on any particular city may be found either in the Jewish Encyclopedia or in some local history. But most of the original communities belong in this German-Jewish period, from Memphis, Tenn., to St. Paul, Minn.; from Indianapolis, Ind., to St. Louis, Mo., and on to Portland, Ore. The father of the famous Straus brothers, Isidor, Nathan and Oscar, came from Rhenish Bavaria in 1852 as one of the "forty-eighters," peddled through Georgia with a horse and wagon, (he skipped the first stage of the pack) opened a store in Talbotton, Georgia, and sent for his family within two years. From this humble beginning came Macy's in New York, Abraham & Straus in Brooklyn (two great department stores), the philanthropy of Nathan Straus, and the public service of Isidor and Oscar Straus. This is typical of what many German Jews have done on a smaller scale.

IV. WHAT THEY ACCOMPLISHED

MANY of the great business enterprises, especially the department stores, which are owned by Jews, are the

185

product of this German Jewish migration and grew from the peddler's pack. For a while that seemed to be all the German Jews were accomplishing, except for the establishment of their own congregations and mutual benefit societies. This was natural, for it takes time to learn a new language and customs, as well as to earn sufficient money for leisure. This was the necessary first step before branching out; the German immigrant had to have an income so that his family could live; at the same time he wanted to look forward to a better future. So it happened that the German immigrant of the first generation did not enter politics or the professions to any great extent.

That step came later, after the financial basis had been established, and in most cases it was not taken by the immigrants themselves but by their children, born, or at least educated, in America. Oscar S. Straus studied law at Columbia; Henry Morgenthau attended the College of the City of New York; Justice Irving Lehman, of the Court of Appeals of New York State, attended Harvard, —all three were sons of German immigrants. Occasionally, usually among the "forty-eighters," we find a man who went into public life on his own account, without waiting for a generation and for the accumulation of a fortune; such men were Simon Wolf and Adolf Kraus.

But, in addition to their occasional entrance into medicine, law, and politics, the enduring work of the German Jews was the creation of the Jewish institutions of the United States. The Sephardim were few, wealthy, and in

186

little communities: their needs were small and centered in the synagogues. The Germans were numerous, widely scattered, and had many poor among them; their needs were many and varied. In addition, they had a secular tendency, to organize apart from the influence of religion. They were the great organizers of American Jewish life in every community and in the nation as a whole. From them come the lodges, the unions of congregations, the great charitable societies, the orphan homes, and all the rest. They were skilled in organizing, and seem often to have formed an organization and written a thirty page constitution, just for pleasure.

In addition, many of them were rationalists; they wanted to figure out everything by their own reason, instead of taking their ideas from the teachings of the past; they wanted to build everything up systematically and logically. From them came the reform movement in America as a national influence, although its little beginnings had been among the Sephardim of Charleston. From them came the social and philanthropic institutions, not as part of the synagogue, but as something important in themselves. These Germans had come to this country for freedom to live their own lives, to think their own thoughts; this they did, creating new forms of organization to carry out their new ideas.

Let us take the typical organization of a German Jewish community anywhere in the country. First, of course, came the cemetery and immediately afterward, the little congregation, which soon tried to build its synagogue.

187

But very closely afterward was a society for mutual help; the poor immigrant might fall sick and need temporary aid, or he might die and his family be in want. So there were little weekly or monthly dues, a small payment in case of need, and the duty of sitting up with the sick or dead. But this was not all; there were also immigrants wandering in search of a home and location, or fallen on hard times when away from their own city; the German Jews got together a little sum of money to help them and put somebody in charge. Finally, there was always some kind of a congregational school, usually held once a week, so that the children might learn what it meant to be a Jew, even in the strange, new land to which their parents had taken them; the German Jews speak constantly of the "preservation of Judaism in America" as one of their chief cares.

Then the little group of poor peddlers grew up. They built a fine temple to take the place of the little frame structure; they engaged a rabbi to preach in German and (if possible) in English, and to conduct their religious school. They did not need the mutual benefit society any longer, for they had insurance and money in the bank. So the mutual benefit society became a lodge for social events and for intellectual improvement, and the little charity society became an organized philanthropy, to look after the needs of the poor in the community, of the orphan, the widow and the sick. The distinctive characteristic of the German Jews is their love of organization; they took Jewish life out of the synagogue alone, and gave it a dozen centers about which it has revolved ever since.

This great work of building up the little societies for self-help into imposing philanthropies was largely accomplished during the fifteen years from 1865 to 1880; by that time the earlier immigrants had mostly established themselves and were no longer poor and weak. The tide of Jewish immigration had largely slowed down; as the ghettoes of Germany had been abolished, the German Jews had an opportunity at home, and the terrible oppressions of the 1880's had not yet begun to drive the Russian Jews forth in such tremendous numbers. The German Jewish community was fairly well adjusted to America and had a chance to make something great out of its petty beginnings of the twenty years before. From this period date many of the great organizations and great buildings of the American Jew, although so many of them had their nominal origin before the Civil War. The B'nai B'rith had its greatest growth; the Hebrew Union College its origin, at this time. It was a breathing spell after the German Jews themselves had come and before they were called upon to help others, as they were during the Russian Jewish immigration. Then they organized special societies to help the immigrants, to scatter them about the country, and centers for their Americanization. After a first stage of self-help, and a second stage of building up Jewish communal life, came the third stage of helping others. The poor German peddler had become a rich merchant and a community leader.

History of the Jews in the United States

1. Why did the German Christians come to America? The German Jews? Were there any differences in their reasons, the places they went, the things they did?
2. Describe the German Jewish immigrants.
3. Give their number and distribution.
4. Tell how they succeeded and why.
5. Describe their institutions and the reasons for them.
6. What was their contribution to American Jewish life?

TOPICS FOR REPORTS

1. Study the Jewish background in Germany; show why the Jews had their special characteristics, why they left Germany, why they stopped migrating when they did.
2. Study your own Jewish community; find out when the German Jews came and what they did; see how far your city was typical according to the description in the chapter.
3. Read the life of some Jewish immigrant of this period, such as Oscar S. Straus, Henry Morgenthau, Adolf Kraus; give the typical features according to the chapter, and the special ones of the individual.
4. Study some important Jewish community in the United States, to see what the German Jews accomplished during the period from 1840 to 1880.

REFERENCES FOR PUPILS

The best material for this period is often in the form of biographies, congregational and local histories. See such books as:
Straus, Oscar S., *Under Four Administrations*. Houghton Mifflin Co.
Morgenthau, Henry, *All In a Lifetime*. Doubleday Page.
Kraus, Adolf, *Reminiscences and Comments*. Tony Rubovitz.
Kohut, Rebekah, *My Portion*. Seltzer.

190

Second Wave of Immigration: From Germany

Wise, Isaac M., *Reminiscences*. Bloch.

Wiernik, Peter, pp. 140–157, 242–244.

Jewish Encyclopedia, arts. on the settlements of various states and cities, such as California, Indiana, Illinois, Chicago, Cincinnati, and parts of the article on the United States.

REFERENCES FOR TEACHERS

Eliasoff, "The German Jews in America," *Deutsch Amerikanische Geschichtsbaletter*.

Publications of the American Jewish Historical Society.

Kohler, Max J., "The German-Jewish Migration to America," vol. IX, pp. 87 ff.

Bernheimer, Charles, *The Russian Jew in the United States*, p. 10.

Szold, Henrietta, *Elements of the Jewish Population*, John C. Winston Co.

Voorsanger, Jacob, *Chronicles of Emanu-El (San Francisco)*. G. Spaulding Co.

Stern, Myer, *The Rise and Progress of Reform Judaism, from the Records of Temple Emanu-El (New York)*. Pub. by the Author.

Wirth, Louis, *The Ghetto* (with reference to the Chicago community), chaps. ix, x. University of Chicago Press.

Meites, H. L., *History of the Jews of Chicago*.

Goldstein, Israel, *A Century of Judaism in New York—Congregation B'nai Jeshurun*.

Davis, Edward, *The History of Rodeph Sholom Congregation, 1802–1925 (Philadelphia)*.

Heller, Maximilian, *Souvenir Jubilee of Temple Sinai, 1872–1922 (New Orleans)*.

Rubinstein, Charles, *History of the Har Sinai Congregation of the City of Baltimore, 1918*.

Philipson, David, *The Oldest Jewish Congregation in the West, B'nai Israel, Cincinnati*.

CHAPTER 13.

The Civil War: Jews in the North and South

I. THE SYMPATHIES OF THE JEWS

THE great issue of slavery divided Jews, as it did members of other religious bodies in the United States. As the Jews had no church organization or rulership, there was nobody to speak for them officially and they took opposite sides, for and against slavery, according to their personal views and interests. Judah Touro, who loved human beings more than he did institutions, had no use for slavery even though he lived in a slave state; he owned only one slave in his life, taught him his business and freed him with enough money to make him self-supporting; the slaves who waited on him daily in the home where he lived were all freed and given a start in life.

But other Jews, more conventional and less humanitarian, did keep slaves, both in the early days of Newport and in the middle of the century in the South. Naturally, the old families of Sephardic Jews in the South were strong adherents of their own states and of slavery. On the other hand, the new German immigrants in the North—both Jews and Christians—were ardent for every

The Civil War: Jews in the North and South

kind of liberty, including that of the negro; it was these German immigrants who kept Missouri in the ranks of the Union.

And so when we read of the exploits of John Brown for the abolition of the slave traffic in Kansas in the 50's, it is surprising but natural to find among his little band of fanatics and martyrs the names of three young Jewish immigrants from Austria and Germany, who fought beside the stern Puritans in Kansas and who served later as soldiers in the Civil War.

DAVID EINHORN

Sculpture by Enrico Glicenstein, in Temple Emanu-El, New York City

The one pronouncement that was sometimes considered an official statement was in favor of slavery. It was a sermon by Rabbi Morris J. Raphall of New York on the occasion of the national fast day in January, 1861, just before the inauguration of President Lincoln. This article was reprinted and circulated all over the country, so that many people who knew that Christian churches were divided on the subject and were breaking up into separate bodies for and against slavery, thought that the

193

History of the Jews in the United States

Jews all held with Rabbi Raphall that the Bible permitted the holding of slaves. At this moment, two men,
who had been ardent abolitionists all along, stepped forward to express a different view of Jewish teaching. One
of these was a rabbi in Baltimore, Dr. David Einhorn,
who had come over from Austria just six years before
and who was at that time the most radical reform leader
in the United States. Dr. Einhorn in his pulpit and in his
weekly publication attacked slavery most bitterly, declaring that it was contrary to the laws of God and the
teaching of humanity. Remember that this was done in
Baltimore, where the great majority of people were
southern in sympathy. The expected happened; Dr.
Einhorn's name was among those listed for attack by the
mob in April, 1861, and he had to flee to Philadelphia
with his family to prevent outrages such as were suffered
by many Union sympathizers. There he was one of the
ardent supporters of the Union during the entire Civil
War. The other of these Jewish abolitionists was a writer,
Michael Heilprin, who refuted Rabbi Raphall in a long
article in the New York Tribune, showing that slavery
had not been a part of Jewish life for hundreds of years,
and that the humane teachings of Bible and Talmud were
directly against the modern form of negro slavery, as
practised in America. There were other rabbis, politicians and leaders of the Jews who expressed views against
slavery.

But it happened that at that time two Jews were particularly identified with the cause of the South, because

194

The Civil War: Jews in the North and South

as members of the United States Senate they defended slavery: David Yulee of Florida and Judah P. Benjamin of Louisiana. David Yulee, whose original name had been David Levy, was a Senator from Florida from 1845 till 1861, when he resigned to join the Confederacy. He was the first Jew to serve in the United States Senate. Judah P. Benjamin, Senator from Louisiana from 1852 till the outbreak of the war, was a most eloquent speaker and defended slavery against Daniel Webster in a great debate, which led a northern preacher to call him "an Israelite with an Egyptian heart." We shall hear more of Benjamin before this chapter is over, for he was the outstanding Jew in American public life during the Civil War.

II. ABRAHAM LINCOLN AND THE JEWS

As THE Jews of the North were nearly all ardent in the Union's cause, it is natural to find them as supporters and occasionally as friends of Abraham Lincoln. Three Jews were present at the 1860 Republican convention which nominated him, two of them voting for Lincoln and the third not voting because his delegation (from Missouri) had been instructed to vote for another candidate. This third man, Moritz Pinner, had been editor of an abolitionist newspaper. One of the others was Lewis N. Dembitz, a lawyer of Louisville, Kentucky, who wrote books both on legal and Jewish subjects, and whose nephew and namesake, Louis Dembitz Brandeis, became a Justice of the Supreme Court of the United States.

History of the Jews in the United States

One of the influential supporters of Lincoln in the campaign was Abraham Kohn, city clerk of Chicago. After the election Mr. Kohn sent Lincoln an American flag, with the Hebrew words painted on it which had been the encouragement of Joshua in ancient times: "Be strong and of good courage; be not afraid, neither be thou dismayed; for the Lord thy God is with thee whithersoever thou goest."

A close friend of Lincoln for many years was another Illinois Jew, Abraham Jonas of Quincy. We have heard of Jonas' brother before, for he was the first Jew to settle in Cincinnati. Abraham Jonas was more of a wanderer, for he came from England and lived in Cincinnati, in Kentucky and finally in Illinois. He was the first grand master of the Masons of the state of Illinois, a lawyer, a member of the state legislature, and postmaster at Quincy. One of Lincoln's first official acts as president was to reappoint Jonas as postmaster. Several years later, in 1864, the President had an opportunity to do him a greater and more difficult favor. It happened that Jonas had one son in the Union army and four in the Confederate forces, and that one of these latter was a prisoner of war at the time when his father was dying at home. The family appealed to the President, and he promptly gave the young man a parole so that he might be with his father, Lincoln's old friend, in his last hours.

Simon Wolf tells another typical story of how Lincoln pardoned a Jewish soldier charged with desertion. Here is the incident from his book, *The Presidents 1*

196

The Civil War: Jews in the North and South

Have Known (page 6: "The whole scene is as vividly before me as in those early hours of the morning. (It was two o'clock.) The President walked up and down with his hands hanging by his side, his face wore that gravity of expression that has been so often described by his historians and biographers, and yet greeted us as if we were his boon companions. Corwin (a Congressman) told him why we had come. He listened with deep attention, and when Corwin had exhausted the subject, the President replied, 'Impossible to do anything. I have no influence with this administration,' and the twinkle in his eye was indescribable, 'Stanton has put his foot down and insists on one of two things, either that I must quit or he will quit.' Corwin turned to me and said: 'I told you, my dear friend, that it was hopeless,' and was about to leave the room. I said, 'Mr. President, you will pardon me for a moment. What would you have done under similar circumstances? If your dying mother had summoned you to her bedside to receive her last message before her soul would be summoned to its Maker, would you not have been a deserter to her who gave you birth, rather than desert in law but not in fact to the flag to which you had sworn allegiance?' He stopped, touched the bell; his secretary, John Hay, who time and again spoke of that occurrence, came in; he ordered a telegram to be sent to stop the execution, and that American citizen of Jewish faith led the forlorn hope with the flag of his country in his hands at the battle of Cold Harbor and was shot to death fighting heroically and patriotically for the country of his birth. When months afterwards I told the President what had become of that young soldier, he was visibly moved and with great emotion said, 'I thank God for having done what I did.' "

As we notice here, Simon Wolf was already an important man in those days; he had access to the President and was frequently consulted on matters that concerned the Jews or other German immigrants; he developed into a most useful public servant and prominent Jewish leader as years went on.

A special incident which aroused the Jews of the country terribly during the war was a general order (known in history as Order No. 11) issued by General Grant during his advance into the South in December, 1862. He had been troubled by traders (many of them Jews) going with the troops, and it was charged that some of them also traded with the enemy, and took money into the Confederacy. As the easiest way to prevent this, he summarily abolished all traders from the army from that time on. But unfortunately General Grant, who was a soldier and not a politician, worded his orders to include "the Jews as a class," and ordered all Jews expelled, with all other traders, from the district controlled by his armies. Of course, this aroused the Jews, as many of them were Union sympathizers and Union soldiers, and two delegations set out for Washington. The first was Cesar Kaskel, a young merchant who had been born in Germany and was at the time living in Paducah, Ky.; if this order were enforced he and all the Jewish residents

198

The Civil War: Jews in the North and South

of the town with their families would have to vacate.
President Lincoln received him at once, heard his com‑
plaint, and remarked: "And so the children of Israel
were driven from the happy land of Canaan?" "Yes,"
replied Kaskel, "and that is why we have come unto
Father Abraham's bosom, asking protection." "And this
protection they shall have at once," said Lincoln, who im‑
mediately sat down and revoked the order. A few days
later the second delegation, Rabbis Isaac M. Wise and
Max Lilienthal, with a few leading laymen, arrived from
Cincinnati. They found that the order had already been
revoked, and called to thank the President, who told them
again of his equal love and interest in all human beings,
irrespective of religion or race. Years afterward when
General Grant was running for the office of President,
many Jews opposed him on the ground of Order No. 11,
while others, such as Simon Wolf, supported him, claim‑
ing that he was not personally responsible for the order,
or that he had written it in the heat of a military cam‑
paign and without due thought, which last seems to be the
fact. Certainly, Grant was not an enemy of the Jews in
any sense and as president continued the same friendly
relations, personal and official, which have been charac‑
teristic of the presidents from Washington on.

III. JEWS IN THE ARMIES

YEARS after the Civil War a writer in a magazine made
some statement attacking the patriotism and courage of
the Jews during that conflict. So Simon Wolf, who had

lived in Washington through the war and knew many of the facts, set out to collect all the information he could regarding American Jews in the armies; he was not able to get every fact because many of the states did not have full records, and many soldiers were not listed by their religion but only by their home city. But the results he accomplished, and which he published in a big book entitled *The American Jew as Patriot, Soldier and Citizen,* are very interesting indeed and disprove every slander made against Jewish patriotism.

Mr. Wolf lists by name over 6,000 Jews who served in the Union armies, and 1,200 in the Confederate forces, a total of about 7,500 from less than 200,000 people, many of them recent immigrants. The larger number were in the Union army because most of the German immigrants, as we have seen, lived in the North. On the whole, the service of the Southern Jews was the more distinguished, as they were old residents of their own states, and many cases are known where four or five brothers served in the Confederate ranks. The highest ranking officers, however, were in the North. It is interesting to notice that the largest settlements of Jews, as shown by their numbers in the army, were New York (1,882 soldiers), Ohio, Illinois and Pennsylvania; while the Southern states which led were Louisiana (224 soldiers), South Carolina, Mississippi and Georgia. There were 23 staff officers, known to be Jews, in the Confederate army. The first Surgeon General of the Confederacy was David de Leon, and the Quartermaster General was A. C. Meyers.

The Civil War: Jews in the North and South

Four Jews attained the rank of general officer in the Union army. The highest of them all was Frederick Knefler of Indianapolis, an immigrant Jew born in Hungary, who volunteered as a private soldier in Indianapolis and rose to be colonel of the 79th Indiana regiment; he was repeatedly cited for bravery in battle and promoted for his ability; his highest actual rank was Brigadier General, to which the temporary rank of Brevet Major General was later added. General Knefler went through all the important battles in the west and was on Sherman's well-known march to the sea. After the war he settled down in Indianapolis again, was active in the Jewish community, and held a Federal appointment in the pension service.

Three Jews were full colonels and brevetted brigadier general; Leopold Blumenberg of Baltimore, Md., Philip J. Joachimson of New York City, and Edward S. Solomon of Chicago. The last-named is the best known of the three, because after the war President Grant appointed him governor of Washington territory, where he served for four years. So this patriot adds another military hero and another state governor to the list of distinguished American Jews.

Seven Jews were awarded for distinguished gallantry on the field of battle the Congressional Medal of Honor, the highest honor that can be given to an American soldier. Much later, during the World War, this distinction was continued among the Jewish soldiers. Mr. Wolf lists 316 soldiers who were wounded, 336 who were killed in

MONUMENT IN HONOR OF JEWISH SOLDIERS (BROOKLYN)

action, and 53 who were captured, 17 of whom died in prison. And he concludes from all these authenticated figures that the Jews certainly contributed their full share to the nation in the great struggle and that, if all the Jewish soldiers could be known, their percentage in the armies would be far above the Jewish proportion of the general population.

For the first time in American history, rabbis were appointed to serve the troops in field and hospital along with the chaplains of other faiths. President Lincoln was willing to appoint them as soon as the need was pointed out to him, but he was limited by the law, which said that ministers of Christian denominations should serve as chaplains in the army. This law was altered in July, 1862, to include ministers of all faiths. The President then appointed two rabbis as hospital chaplains, Jacob Frankel of Philadelphia and Bern-

202

hard H. Gotthelf of Louisville. In addition, Rabbi Ferdinand L. Sarner was elected chaplain of the 54th New York Infantry; he served through the war and was wounded at Gettysburg.

IV. JUDAH P. BENJAMIN

AGAIN, as in the Revolution, the most outstanding service rendered by a Jew was not in the army but in civil life. This time, however, it was not a financial genius, a Haym Salomon, but a statesman, Judah P. Benjamin. He still remains the most important Jew in public life in the United States, although Oscar S. Straus and Louis D. Brandeis have since had distinguished, but somewhat different records.

In addition, Benjamin had a checkered career, with plenty of ups and downs; he was admired and praised by friends and foes in the North and South, and in England as well. He made and lost several fortunes. He was lawyer, author and statesman, United States Senator, Secretary of three departments in the Confederate Cabinet, and was offered a seat in the Supreme Court of the United States.

Judah Philip Benjamin was born in 1811 of an old Sephardic family in British territory in the West Indies. He was brought to the United States at the age of seven when his parents moved to Charleston, South Carolina. He attended Yale for two years and is accounted one of her distinguished students, although he was never graduated. When he was seventeen years old he moved to New Orleans and studied law in a lawyer's office, according to the practice at that time; when he was twenty-one he was admitted to the bar. The next year he married a Catholic girl. Benjamin was never much interested in Jewish matters, but he always remained a Jew and defended his people boldly when opponents in politics or law tried to create prejudice by calling him a Jew.

JUDAH P. BENJAMIN

He was elected by Louisiana to the United States Senate in 1852 and reelected six years later, only resigning after the secession of his state from the Union. Before that time he had made a fortune or two in law practice and lost them in sugar plantations when the Mississippi overflowed its banks. When he was Senator he was offered an appointment as Associate Justice of the Supreme Court by President Pierce, but refused it as he preferred to stay in the turmoil of legal practice and political life, and also as he desired the huge income of the law practice for the use of his family. He had the reputation at that time of being one of the leading orators of the Senate, a man to be compared with Daniel Webster and John Calhoun. Unfortunately for his reputation, his great

The Civil War: Jews in the North and South

powers of mind and speech were largely employed in defense of slavery in that turbulent decade of the fifties, when events were rapidly moving toward the Civil War. The fight for slavery was lost as it deserved to lose, and as a result, the great ability and devotion of many of the people enlisted in its cause are frequently overlooked or forgotten.

When Benjamin was fifty years old, his state seceded from the Union; he promptly resigned from the Senate, delivered a thrilling farewell address, and went home to begin a second and entirely different career, one of sacrifice and leadership in a cause that was destined to failure. Jefferson Davis, his former colleague in the Senate, appointed him Attorney-General, then Secretary of War, and finally Secretary of State. Benjamin was the most trusted advisor of the President of the Confederacy until the war was lost; the two defeated leaders fled from Richmond together as the Union troops entered the city. Benjamin has often been called by historians "the brains of the Confederacy," and whether or not he really deserved such praise, there is no doubt that he labored constantly and brilliantly in a cause he could not possibly hope to win against such odds. He used to be at his desk at eight in the morning and leave it, day after day, at one or two the next morning; through it all he preserved his calm, his courtesy, and his cheerful smile.

As Secretary of War, Benjamin was blamed for the loss of a battle because he did not get ammunition to the troops in time, and he was censured by a vote of the

Confederate Congress. The fact is that there was no ammunition to send, but this fact could not be made public; so Benjamin smiled and took the blame, and President Davis, who knew the facts, promptly promoted him to Secretary of State. It must be admitted that he was far more popular and successful in this post than as Secretary of War; he had not known much about military strategy and had not deferred enough to the proud Southern generals. As Secretary of State he tried to gain recognition from England and France, appealing to the British mill owners, who needed southern cotton for their mills. It is just now being realized how near Benjamin came to success in this attempt; the sentiment of Great Britain was divided between the moral and financial motives, against slavery and for cotton. But the North held the lines of communication so that Benjamin found it hard to get letters to his ambassadors, and made little progress. Then came Gettysburg and Vicksburg; the warfare favored the North, and Benjamin's task became impossible. Nobody would recognize a beaten rebellion. So he stayed and worked, kept up the morale of the people and advised with Jefferson Davis, until the last day when he burned his official papers and fled.

Most of the Confederate leaders finally took the oath of allegiance to the United States, but Benjamin would not. He journeyed to England, resumed his British citizenship, and took up the practice of law in Great Britain, beginning at the age of fifty-five a third career. He was done with politics and office-holding for good; from now on he was simply a lawyer. So ably did he apply himself to his profession that his book on Sales is still a recognized authority in the law schools; he was acknowledged as one of the leading barristers of England, made an income of $100,000 a year, and when he retired after sixteen years, his third career was crowned with a great banquet in his honor by the Bench and Bar, the first affair of its kind in England. He died in Paris at the age of seventy-three, where his Catholic wife had him buried according to the rites of her church.

Benjamin was a great man and a great American, but he was not a great Jew. Rabbi Isaac M. Wise met him in Washington while on a visit to Daniel Webster there; they discussed religion and Wise found himself largely in agreement with Webster, who was a Unitarian of Puritan ancestry and could quote the Bible for every point he made. But Benjamin opposed them and had little proof for his assertions; Rabbi Wise was a bit ashamed that the Christian statesman knew the Bible so well while the Jewish statesman knew it so badly. Benjamin, being a cultured man, quoted Shakespeare in his speeches, but he could not quote the Bible.

Benjamin was hot-headed and quick to resent an insult, whether delivered against him or his people. When a Senator in debate called him "that Jew from Louisiana," he replied at once: "It is true that I am a Jew, and when my ancestors were receiving their Ten Commandments from the immediate hand of Deity, amidst the thunderings and lightnings of Mt. Sinai, the ancestors of my opponent were herding swine in the forests of Great Britain." A similar reply was made in Parliament by Benjamin Disraeli, the great Prime Minister of England, who was born a Jew and to whom Judah P. Benjamin has often been compared. It was a brave and true reply, but just as superficial as the attack, for both of these men thought more of the achievements of their ancestors than they did of serving their people.

REVIEW QUESTIONS

1. What were the sympathies of the Jews on the question of slavery? Why? How did they show their sympathies?
2. On which side did more Jews fight and why? Give numbers.
3. Did the Jews serve in the Civil War in proportion to their number in the general population?
4. Name one Jewish soldier in the Civil War and tell about him.
5. Tell one story of contact between Lincoln and some Jew.
6. Show an instance of discrimination against Jews in Civil War.
7. Tell about Judah P. Benjamin's career.
8. Give the religious arguments for and against slavery.

TOPICS FOR REPORTS

1. The life of Benjamin Disraeli, Lord Beaconsfield; compare this with the career of Judah P. Benjamin; compare their characters.
2. What was Abraham Lincoln's attitude toward religion? Toward various peoples of different race or religion from his own? Give examples.
3. Study the history of one state or city, finding out the number of Jews who served from it in the Civil War, and all about them. There may be such a history of your own state or city, as a number are now in existence.

The Civil War: Jews in the North and South

Wiernik, Peter, pp. 206–237.
Raisin, Max, *A History of the Jews in Modern Times,* pp.
276–292. Hebrew Publishing Co.
Markens, Isaac, *Abraham Lincoln and The Jews.*
Levinger, E. E., "A Present for Mr. Lincoln," *The New Land.*
Jewish Encyclopedia, arts. on Judah P. Benjamin, Edward S.
Solomon, Michael Heilprin, David Einhorn, Anti-Slavery
Movement in America.

Wolf, Simon, *The American Jew as Patriot, Soldier and Citizen* (the bulk of the volume).
Butler, Pierce, *Judah P. Benjamin.* G. W. Jacobs and Co.
Bradford, Gamaliel, *Confederate Patriots,* chap. v. Houghton
Mifflin Co.
Pollak, G. *Michael Heilprin and His Sons.*
Hertz, Emanuel, *Abraham Lincoln, The Tribute of the Synagog.* Bloch.
Kohler, K., (edited by) *Einhorn Memorial Volume.* Bloch.
Mielziner, Ella M., *Moses Mielziner,* reprints much of the
valuable material here cited.
Publications of the American Jewish Historical Society.
Wolf, Simon, "The American Jew as Soldier and Patriot,"
vol. III, p. 21.
Kohler, Max J., "Jews and the Anti-Slavery Movement," vol.
V, p. 137; vol. IX, p. 45. "Judah P. Benjamin, Statesman and Jurist," vol. XII, p. 63.
Isaacs, Myer S., "A Jewish Army Chaplain," vol. XII, p.
127; "A Bird's-eye View of Jewish Activity During the
Civil War," vol. XXIX, pp. 117–126.
Lebowitch, J., "U. S. Grant and the Jews," vol. XVII, p. 71.
Markens, Isaac, "Lincoln and the Jews," vol. XVII, p. 109.
Huhner, Leon, "Some Jewish Associates of John Brown," vol.
XXIII, p. 55.

CHAPTER 14.

The Basis of Judaism in America

W HAT was the background for American Judaism
as we have it today, with its many synagogues,
different kinds of congregations, its rabbis, colleges, and
schools? How did the Jews manage to organize and build
in such a remarkable manner? How does it happen that
we have today orthodox, reform and conservative Jews
in America, not worshipping all together as Jews were
accustomed to worship in the earlier periods of our
history?

I. THE ORTHODOX SYNAGOGUE

MODERN American Judaism all springs from the orthodox synagogue. We have already discussed the synagogue
of the Sephardic Jews; now it becomes apparent that the
German immigrants, for the most part, had exactly the
same kind of synagogues. True, the German pronunciation of Hebrew was different, and the German Jews had
some extra prayers, and also omitted some of those which
appeared in the Sephardic ritual. Naturally, they felt
more at home in their own synagogues, not only because
they were among friends who spoke the same language,
not only because there was nobody there to look down on
them as newcomers, but also because of the familiar

210

sound of their accustomed prayers read with the well-known accent.

Few of these Jews were really learned in the great ancient books of Judaism, any more than are the majority of Jews nowadays. But they believed unfalteringly that these works contained the important truths of life, and that the principles laid down in them would never be altered. They believed that it was wrong to make any change whatever in the services, even to alter one local custom which had been observed for three or four generations, because they knew that their parents and grandparents were wise and good people, and that anything observed by them must be good for their descendants. Their view and their conduct made for piety more than progress. It was the idea of honest, God-fearing Jews, who followed implicitly the teaching of Jewish tradition.

That is to say, they kept the Sabbath very strictly, were particular to pray three times a day, wearing their tefillin, and never ate anything that was not kosher. Their beliefs were outlined in the Thirteen Articles of Maimonides; they believed in one God, in the prophets and in the future coming of the Messiah. Many of these beliefs and practices are still held by Jews, but there are other practices which have been kept by some Jews and changed by others. This separation into orthodox and reform Jewry is one of the two important facts of our history in the middle of the century, next only to the basic fact of the increase in the number, wealth and influence of the American Jews themselves.

History of the Jews in the United States

SOME of the German immigrants, however, brought over a different kind of religion; in fact, the idea had preceded them in its influence. The reform movement in Judaism had begun in Germany in the early years of the century; first in a school conducted by Israel Jacobson about 1810, then in the famous Hamburg Temple in that great German city in 1818. These earliest reformers had in mind chiefly the hope of making their services a little more beautiful and a little more modern. They made few changes, if any, in their daily life; but they did shorten the prayerbook, introduce into it some prayers in their daily speech, the German tongue, have German sermons which all the people might understand, and an organ and choir. Naturally, there was terrible opposition and hatred on the part of the strictly orthodox who felt that these people were hurting Judaism. There was also a certain amount of support from historians like Leopold Zunz, who proved that there had been in the past some changes in Judaism, including new ideas, new laws and new prayers.

So, timidly and carefully, the early reformers tried to express a modern idea of Judaism: that there is such a thing as growth and change in the religious life of a people; that they considered themselves German citizens rather than members of a Jewish nation, longing for a return to Palestine; that they hoped for a golden age for all humanity in the future rather than for a Messiah,

212

The Basis of Judaism in America

who would come and save the Jewish people and make them supreme. These ideas, which came to be the viewpoint of many Jews later on, were just glimpsed by the beginners. Their first effort was simply to beautify their synagogue service.

In Germany such movements as this ran in danger of being suppressed by the government, for after the time of Napoleon the whole of Europe was terribly conservative and reactionary, and anything new, even in the field of religious thought, was regarded as the seed of another French Revolution. But in America, which was founded by a Revolution, and where religion was entirely free from any interference by the government, the new idea could develop whenever people were ready to accept it.

III. THE FIRST REFORM CONGREGATION IN AMERICA

IT HAPPENED, peculiarly enough, that the first movement for reform in the Jewish religion in America came in the old Sephardic congregation of Charleston, South Carolina, in 1824. At that time the Congregation Beth Elohim was the largest and richest in the United States; it included a large proportion of German Jews, although it had been founded by the Sephardim and followed their ritual, as well as their custom of complete religious domination over the members of the congregation. A number of the younger men petitioned the trustees for certain changes in the service, such as shortening the prayers, reading some of them in English, and adding an

213

English sermon to explain the meaning of the Jewish religion to those who did not understand Hebrew. When the trustees rejected this petition without even discussing it, members began to withdraw until there were fifty in a new organization, the "Reformed Society of Israelites," led by Isaac Harby. They had no rabbi but worked out a service after the example of the one in Hamburg, shortening the orthodox ritual and adding many English translations, while some of the members preached occasionally. This first society lasted just eight years when lack of money and the bitter opposition of the main congregation caused it to disband. But a few years later the reforms came into the congregation itself.

Rev. Gustav Poznanski was the new cantor and preacher of the congregation. He was a Polish Jew who had lived some years in Hamburg and had known the Hamburg Temple itself. When the Charleston synagogue burned down in 1838 he advocated putting an organ into the new building —a very radical step in the eyes of the orthodox —and the majority of the congregation sustained him. So the new synagogue was built for what we

TEMPLE BETH ELOHIM, CHARLESTON, S. C.

214

The Basis of Judaism in America

would now call a conservative congregation, that is, one which admits the possibility of change in the law of the Talmud, but which is willing to make very few such changes. An orthodox congregation is one which is loyal to the traditional religion and law in every detail. A reform congregation is one which makes a number of highly important changes in order to adapt the expression of the religion to growing thought. Of course, as Jews are not under compulsion in their religion, an individual may not agree with his own congregation in every way, but may be more orthodox or more liberal than the majority of the members of his own synagogue.

In Charleston at that time the orthodox minority was very strong, so when Congregation Beth Elohim voted to install an organ, many of the members resigned and formed a strictly orthodox congregation; the two did not unite again until after the Civil War, when the community became much poorer and they needed each other very badly. In the meantime there was terrible bitterness on both sides, as was usual in those days whenever somebody introduced an innovation. The extreme bitterness of those days is over now, as most people realize that there is room for various interpretations of Judaism, and that more than one party can be good Jews. But in the early times the orthodox party often called the other group innovators, destroyers of the religion of their fathers. They in turn called the first, ignorant reactionaries, who were perpetuating an outworn conception of religion.

History of the Jews in the United States

THE early Charleston movement did not endure, partly because it was not properly prepared, partly because it had no leader. Young, active, progressive men they were, but there was no one among them with a thorough knowledge of Judaism, who could explain the new ideas by tongue and pen, teach the children, instruct the willing adults, and defend his group against criticism. When such a man was found in Poznanski, the movement, while not victorious, became much more aggressive and successful. That was the history of the reform congregations from that time on. First, a society of young people organized to stand by the new ideas in Judaism— a Reform Verein, as they called it in German. Then a rabbi undertook their leadership; usually he was a man from the slowly developing reform party in Germany. Later, a reform congregation took its place beside the older orthodox congregation of the community. We can trace this in several cities by the growth in the number of the German liberals from the forties on. We must remember also that there was no religious authority of any kind among the Jewish people or in the American government (as there had been in the governments of the various German states), so that every congregation could do exactly as it pleased, could accept the opinions of its own rabbi as its final authority, and could have a Judaism of its own. It took years of this individualistic striving before three clearly marked groups of congregations

216

The Basis of Judaism in America

stood out in America, the reform, the conservative and the orthodox. Because they were the newest and most aggressive, the reform congregations were the first to unite in a national body.

The history of almost any city in the United States during this period is most interesting. The first reform society was the Har Sinai in Baltimore in 1842; then came the Emanu-El of New York in 1845; the congregation in Albany, N. Y. under Rabbi Isaac M. Wise, in 1846; the two congregations in Cincinnati, in 1854 and 1855; the Keneseth Israel congregation of Philadelphia about the same time; and Sinai Temple of Chicago in 1858. These, which are now among the great reform con‧ gregations of the United States, were then little societies of cultured and would-be-cultured German immigrants, liberals in desire, men who wanted to be loyal to Judaism and at the same time progressive and modern in their own generation.

The leaders of these congregations were rabbis born and educated in Germany; some of them came to the new land as flaming young liberals, determined to devote their lives to the double work of religion and freedom in a free land. Others, such as Dr. David Einhorn of whom we have heard before, came as mature men, already famous preachers in Germany. David Einhorn served in Baltimore, Philadelphia and New York; Max Lilienthal, who preceded him, in New York and Cincinnati; Isaac M. Wise, the next to arrive, in Albany and Cincinnati; Samuel Adler in New York; Bernard Felsenthal

217

in Chicago; and Samuel Hirsch in Philadelphia. In their
time each of these men made great contributions to the
life of the Jews in the United States and also to the advancing cause of liberalism among Jews and Christians.
The most important of them in work accomplished was
Isaac M. Wise, and his achievements will be discussed
at length in the next chapter. The most interesting and
romantic career was that of Max Lilienthal, who preceded
him to America, and became later his close friend and
coworker in Cincinnati.

Dr. Lilienthal had two distinct careers in two different countries. The first began at the age of twenty-
three as a brilliant young German rabbi and Ph. D.,
when he was called to Russia as teacher of the Jewish
community of Riga, with the most extravagant promises
of the kind treatment the Russian government wanted
to extend to the Jews. For five years he lived in Russia,
first establishing in Riga a successful Jewish school after
the German model, in which the children learned both
Jewish and general subjects. Then he was called to St.
Petersburg and worked with the minister of education on
a similar plan for the entire empire of the Czar. Finally
he toured through the Jewish communities of Russia and
made friends for himself and for this proposal, an extremely difficult matter because of the suspicion with
which the Russian Jews regarded any move of the government. This suspicion was justified; it is probable that
the Czar wanted only to convert the Jews to the Greek
Catholic Church and not at all to educate them in a

modern manner. It is likely that Lilienthal was ordered to accept that religion himself if he wanted advancement or even to continue his work in Russia. At any rate, he resigned suddenly from what he had thought would be a great life-work and came to America with his bride when he was just thirty years old.

In America he was at first the rabbi of three little orthodox German congregations in New York City. His opinions became steadily more liberal, so he resigned this work and engaged in teaching. But his great opportunity was still ahead. In 1855 he was called to Cincinnati as rabbi of the Congregation Bene Israel, where he lived and worked for twenty-six years until his death. His friend Isaac M. Wise had moved to Cincinnati as rabbi of another congregation just the year before, so that Cincinnati became the center of reform Judaism in America as it was of the German immigration. Tall, handsome and aristocratic, Max Lilienthal presented an unusual figure in the Jewish pulpit; he had a doubly interesting life: a training in Germany, a brilliant failure under the conditions of Russian autocracy, and a brilliant success in America with its political and religious freedom.

V. ISAAC LEESER, LEADER OF ORTHODOXY

As we noticed before, the reform movement did not have everything its own way; the great majority of Jews were orthodox at the beginning, and very many of them remained orthodox all along. Their outstanding leader, a much older man than any of these reform rabbis, and one who began his American career long before any of them, was Isaac Leeser, a German rabbi of a Portuguese congregation in Philadelphia.

Isaac Leeser was not strictly a rabbi; he was a layman, largely self-taught, and he came to Richmond, Va., from Prussia in 1824, when

RABBI ISAAC LEESER

he was just eighteen years of age. This was long before any reform rabbi arrived in America, just the year of the first timid reform experiment in Charleston. Leeser began working for his uncle in Richmond. Soon he read articles attacking and criticising the Jews, who were practically without ability or courage to defend themselves. So the young man, who had learned English just a few years before, sat down and wrote a defense of the Jewish people and also a full explanation of their religion and laws as he understood them, to make the whole matter plain. This made the young man instantly prominent in the little Jewish community of the United States, and he was elected—without his application—reader of the important Mikveh Israel Congregation of Philadelphia in

220

1829, when he was just twenty-three years old. He lived in that city for almost forty years as rabbi of two different congregations, editor, writer, translator, and preacher. He was the outspoken opponent of innovations in the synagogue, the advocate of unity in Israel, the defender of the Jewish people against outside attack, the most important Jewish leader in the east, as Isaac M. Wise was in the west. His was not an exciting life, but a most useful one to the Jewish people.

The record of Isaac Leeser's life can be found in his works. Most important of all, he translated the Bible from Hebrew into English, so that Jews who did not possess a knowledge of the holy tongue might be able to read it in a Jewish version, without the many references to Christianity which were introduced into the King James version. He saw the need for Jewish education in America, and because there were no text-books, he either wrote his own or translated them from the German. He did a tremendous amount of this sort of writing and translation, much of it useless now, but all immensely valuable in its own time. In 1843, he founded the first Jewish periodical of any importance in America, the Occident, and published it every month for twenty-five years until his death. He wrote much of its contents himself but included writings of other Jewish leaders as they came to America; Isaac M. Wise and many another first appeared to the American public in the pages of the Occident. For half its life, the Occident was the only Jewish periodical published in the United States, until the founding of the Israelite by Isaac M. Wise in 1854; this first publication played an important part for American Jewry.

Isaac Leeser was not orthodox in the fashion of eastern Europe; he was more what we could call today conservative. He believed in modern education. He introduced an English sermon in his congregation, and good order during services, but he would not have a word except Hebrew uttered in prayer. His translation of the Bible was written for study outside, not in the synagogue. He hoped ardently for unity among all Jews in America, attended a conference in Cleveland in 1855 in that hope, but when he saw that Dr. Wise and others persisted in their reform views, he attacked them unsparingly in his paper. He was the first to insist on the use of English for sermons and school-teaching instead of the German used by most immigrants. For Leeser united enthusiasm for American liberty with bitter memories of the Germany of his day, with its oppression of the Jew. He founded a dozen or more Jewish institutions in Philadelphia: Charitable organizations, religious schools, a Jewish Publication Society, a college for the training of rabbis, and so on. His name is found almost as often in connection with Jewish organizations in that city as is the name of Benjamin Franklin in connection with general organizations. Many of the organizations founded by Leeser still exist; others were too early for their time, such as the last two mentioned above. Due largely to Isaac Leeser, the east remained the stronghold

of orthodoxy while the middle west, especially Cincinnati, became the home of reform.

Review Questions

1. Describe the early synagogue in America. Give its theory.
2. What was the theory and the background of reform Judaism?
3. How did reform congregations start in America? Give one example.
4. Name one reform rabbi of the early days; tell where he lived.
5. Give the life of the outstanding orthodox leader of this period.

Topics for Reports

1. The history of some important reform congregations up to 1880.
2. The life of one of the reform rabbis listed in this chapter.
3. A biography of Isaac Leeser.
4. A report on the Leeser Bible.
5. A definition of reform, orthodox and conservative Judaism.
6. Music in the orthodox and reform synagogues.

References for Pupils

Wiernik, Peter, pp. 164–192.
Raisin, Max, pp. 251–253, 269–274.
Philipson, David, *Max Lilienthal, American Rabbi.* Bloch.
Wise, Isaac M., *Reminiscences,* pp. 1–175.

References for Teachers

Philipson, David, *The Reform Movement in Judaism* (the authoritative work for this and the following chapter; for America, see chapter 12; the first 11 chapters containing the German development). Macmillan, 1931.

History of the Jews in the United States

Elzas, B., *Jews of South Carolina,* chaps. ix, xi.

Felsenthal, Emma, *Bernard Felsenthal, Teacher in Israel.* Oxford University Press.

Kohler, K., (edited by) *Einhorn Memorial Volume.*

Moise, *Isaac Harby and the Charleston Jewish Reform Movement.* (1931, In press.)

Leiser, Joseph, *American Judaism.*

Lilienthal, Mrs. S., *Records of the Lilienthal Family.*

Year Book of the Central Conference of American Rabbis.
   Englander, Henry, "Isaac Leeser," vol. XXVIII, p. 213.
   Kohler, K., "David Einhorn," vol. XIX, p. 215.
   Silverman, Joseph, "Samuel Adler," vol. XIX, p. 415.

Blum, Isidor, *The Jews of Baltimore.*

Ezekiel, H. T., and Lichtenstein, G., *History of the Jews of Richmond, Va.*

Stern, Myer, *The Rise and Progress of Reform Judaism, from the Records of Temple Emanu-El* (New York).

CHAPTER 15.

The Growth of Reform Judaism

WE ARE now at the formative period of Jewish institutions in America. The Jews had been here long enough to learn the language and customs, and acquire a certain amount of wealth. They were now ready and able to erect great institutions, religious, charitable and social. This chapter will try to bring out why the dominant note of their religious development was along the line of reform Judaism in the period from 1840 to 1880, and just what that growth was like. The next chapter will ask similar questions about the charities and social institutions which grew at the same period. We will see what they were like, and why they followed their special line of growth rather than some other line.

In regard to reform Judaism, the whole story can be told most easily in connection with the life of one man, Isaac M. Wise, whose name has already come into this story. He was typical of the reform element in American Jewry, particularly of the reform rabbis: a strictly orthodox education in Europe, a young man's stirrings of doubt and the desire for progress, a migration to America to make that progress possible. Then came the slow upward struggle as teacher, preacher, editor, reformer, organizer, until when he died at the age of eighty-one, the work of the founders was completed, and reform Judaism stood where it does today, except for the natural increase of numbers and influence which another quarter century brought with it. At the same time, the conservative development in Judaism followed ten years behind, and the orthodox another ten behind that. Today we see all three standing together, but in the historical order we must take them one at a time.

I. EARLY DEVELOPMENT OF THE REFORM IDEA

ISAAC MAYER WISE was born in Bohemia (now Czecho-Slovakia), in March, 1819. As you remember, there was always an element of immigrants from the lands near Germany; the "German" immigration was not all from Germany itself. Young Wise's father was a village school teacher and shochet; at the age of five, the boy began to study Hebrew; at six, the Talmud; and at nine, he had to leave home for more advanced teaching than his father could give him. At first, his life was that of the typical yeshiva bochur (Talmud student) of eastern Europe up to the present day: he was boarded out in charitable families, studied the traditional Jewish literature in Hebrew, and became a tutor to young children in order to pay his own way. Then came a law requiring students for the rabbinate to have a modern education as well as a traditional Hebrew one. The young student exchanged Hebrew for Greek instruction with another young man who was preparing for the Catholic priest-

226

The Growth of Reform Judaism

RABBI ISAAC M. WISE

hood, passed his examinations for the various years of the gymnasium (high school) and studied for a year at the University of Vienna. When he was twenty-three years old he was ordained as rabbi and took a position in a little town in Bohemia.

The tyranny of the government and the medievalism of the Jews were both hard on a young liberal in Bohemia in 1843. He attended a conference of reform rabbis in Germany, where he saw the growth of liberal thought in that country and came under the influence of such a man as Abraham Geiger, the great German reform leader. In a second-hand bookshop in Prague he bought a set of American newspapers containing the debates on the Federal Constitution of 1789. He said many years later: "That literature made me a naturalized American in the interior of Bohemia. It inspired in me the resolution to go to America." So in 1846, when he was twenty-seven years of age, taking his young wife and baby, Isaac M. Wise left Bohemia without a passport and journeyed to ward the new world, his heart full of burning eagerness to raise the mental and spiritual standards of his brethren there, to teach them Judaism and to teach it in an enlightened way.

At that time, in the forties, the German Jews in America were still comparatively few and still very poor; two-thirds of them could not read English; their congregations were small and struggling, strictly orthodox with only three exceptions. Leo Merzbacher was rabbi of Temple Emanu-El in New York,—which now has such a tremendous congregation housed in such a magnificent edifice. At that time it was located in a private house at Grand and Christie Streets, way down town in the immigrant section, and the rabbi received the salary of $200 per year. This was a miserable income even though living was far cheaper than it is today. Max Lilienthal was rabbi of three little orthodox congregations in New York City and received $600 a year from the three of them. Isaac M. Wise was called to officiate as rabbi for the tiny congregation in Albany, N. Y., where he lived for eight years.

In discussing the beginnings of the reform movement in America, it has been shown that some of the great congregations began as Vereine, societies of young liberals. But even a greater number arose out of early orthodox congregations, which little by little altered their ideas and their practices. This was the situation especially when a strong leader arose, like Wise in Albany. Many of the congregation followed him, desired his English sermons, his more orderly and attractive services, even though these things were innovations. But the opposition was intense, the president of the congregation actually knocked the rabbi down on Rosh Hashanah when he rose to take the Torah from the ark, and the congregation broke into two sections, one remaining strictly orthodox, the other going with Wise, and adopting what would today be considered a conservative ritual.

Meanwhile, Wise's own ideas were going ahead from this stage of timid pioneering to real constructive reform. He was introduced to a wider public of American Jews by Isaac Leeser in the Occident. There he wrote on two subjects: first, the need for progress in ideas, and second, the need for rabbis who were trained in America and could speak in English, and for a union among American Jews to provide a college for rabbinical education. In this last effort, Leeser agreed with him perfectly, although he was not in accord with the first half of Wise's appeal.

II. THE PERIOD OF GROWTH

In 1854, Isaac M. Wise was called as rabbi of Congregation Bene Yeshurun of Cincinnati. He was then thirty-five years of age, young, eager, ambitious. For twenty years he had to invest his labor, his ideas, his enthusiasm before returns began to come in. These twenty years correspond with the period of slow but steady growth of the German immigrants from poverty to comfort, from ignorance to American education and viewpoint. At the same time, they spread throughout the United States, and a generation of their children grew up and were taught in American schools. The things which were unthinkable in the forties and too difficult in the fifties worked themselves out in the seventies. The life of Isaac M. Wise is typical of this slow process. He was at once the leader and the expression of the growth of American Jewry. The rationalism of the German Jew, his loyalty to Judaism, his desire for knowledge, and his growing wealth and power of organization, all appear in the life of this man.

This intervening period was not only one of scattering and strengthening of the Jews; it was also the period of rampant individualism. Every congregation had its own rules; apparently half the rabbis wrote and printed their own prayerbooks, each one a little different from that of his neighbor. Everybody was experimenting, trying to grow in ideas as well as in external power. This was a necessary stage but a dangerous and a difficult one. Rabbi Wise from the outset longed to establish Judaism in America, with its own college for training rabbis, its own papers and leaders and thinkers, with a unified body of congregations and of rabbis. But at first, the immigrants continued to come to the United States, and to scatter; they had to settle down and grow up in the new land before they could really unite or even stand firm, whether as reform Jews or as Jews at all.

It is remarkable what Isaac M. Wise accomplished

The Growth of Reform Judaism

in those years in Cincinnati: he founded an English paper, the Israelite, which still exists as the American Israelite; he founded a German paper, the Deborah, for the majority of Jews who did not yet read English; he wrote a new prayerbook, which he called the Minhag America, because he hoped it to be the American prayerbook, corresponding to the Minhagim (or customs) of the Sephardim, the Germans and the Polish Jews; he tried to found a college for rabbis, Zion College, in his second year in Cincinnati. In pursuit of these aims he wrote sermons, articles, histories, novels and even plays expressing his ideas of Jewish life. He travelled about the country, preaching in dozens of cities and dedicating a number of new synagogues. With his colleague, Dr. Lilienthal, who came to Cincinnati to the Congregation Bene Israel, Rabbi Wise made the Jews known and respected in the Middle West, and at the same time increased their self-respect. He called conferences of rabbis and of congregations, one in Cleveland as early as 1855, and others in 1869 and 1871, trying to bring the Jews nearer together, to unite them, and to found his college for rabbis. It was a period of incessant labor with very few immediate results. Rabbi Wise himself grew respected and nationally known, his congregation became larger and more enthusiastic in his support. The time was slowly approaching for the realization of his dream, for the erection of great Jewish institutions in America, that American Jews might at the same time become more American and remain loyal in the religion of their fathers.

History of the Jews in the United States

FROM 1865 to 1880 there was very little Jewish immigration; new laws had been passed in Germany which gave the Jews a chance in their homeland, so very few of them came to America any more. At the same time, the terrible persecution of the Jews in Russia had not yet begun and very few Russian Jews were coming to America, except the rare pioneers from that great Jewish population. With no problem of immigration to face, the Jews in the United States had a chance to put their house in order. All the little synagogues and charities that were started by the poor immigrants of earlier days now grew up, not only in numbers, but in wealth and importance. Other institutions were started during this period, including the chief educational ones and the national unions of local synagogues.

So this was the time when all the foundation work of Isaac M. Wise began to show results. The Jews of America were now ready for it—in ability to pay; in desire for American rather than German methods and ideals; in education and the desire for educated leaders. Rabbi Wise had found in 1855 that Cincinnati alone could not support a college; he now decided that it was necessary to form a union of the congregations in order to start one. So this time he began with the congregations; in 1871 the first meeting was held. Not all the congregations of America responded at first, for Rabbi Wise was a moderate reformer, so that the orthodox on one side

232

The Growth of Reform Judaism

and the extreme reformers on the other stayed away. But the Union of American Hebrew Congregations began. Four years later, in 1875, the Hebrew Union College opened in the basement of a temple, with thirteen students, two instructors including Wise himself, and some Hebrew Bibles and prayerbooks as the library. Every year another grade had to be added, with new courses and occasionally with new instructors. After four years, there was a first graduation from the preparatory department, and in 1883 the first graduation from the college when four rabbis were ordained, and for the first time, rabbis who were born in America (with one exception) and educated in America went forth to serve American congregations. These four men were Israel Aaron, for many years rabbi of Buffalo, N. Y.; Henry Berkowitz and Joseph Krauskopf, who occupied pulpits in the two great reform temples of Philadelphia; and David Philipson, who became the successor of Max Lilienthal in Cincinnati, and who served in that city until his death at the age of eighty-seven. The College today has seven buildings, and the best facilities of any Jewish seminary in the world. The graduates of the Hebrew Union College-Jewish Institute of Religion total almost 1,000. Most occupy pulpits or serve Jewish institutions in all parts of this country, while a few are rabbis in Canada and England. The greatest work of Isaac M. Wise was as organizer, teacher and president of this college, for twenty-five years.

We have seen before how Wise, Leeser and others

tried to bring about unity among the rabbis and how impossible this was at the outset. Orthodox and reform rabbis could not work well together in those days when the two groups were so bitter against one another; even those of the same group were not used to working together but each one was accustomed to doing things exactly as he liked. Finally in 1885, Dr. Kaufmann Kohler of New York, a member of the Einhorn wing of reform Judaism and far more radical than Rabbi Wise, called a conference of reform rabbis only, which met in Pittsburgh and formulated a platform of the beliefs of reform Judaism. Four years later, Rabbi Wise was able to organize the Central Conference of American Rabbis, with a nucleus of his own graduates and those European-trained rabbis who wanted to join with them. Rabbi Wise was president of this Conference until his death in 1900.

The structure of reform Judaism in America was thus complete: a union of congregations, a college for training rabbis, a conference of rabbis. The great organizer had done his work during the important decade and a half of Jewish organization and the years following. This was his special eminence: welding people of different opinions and temperaments into a working unity for a common cause; erecting institutions and buildings, firing people with enthusiasm, and gaining permanent results. The conservative and orthodox wings followed this same method and practically the same type of organization when they accumulated the numbers and wealth to organize their work on a national basis.

The Growth of Reform Judaism

Some of the reasons for this special skill as an organizer lay in Isaac M. Wise's remarkable personality, and power to convince, to persuade, to inspire enthusiasm; his tremendous ability to work, even in extreme old age; his vision of the sort of thing the American Jews actually needed in order to become real Americans and remain real Jews. Still another reason lay in the fact that he was a moderate reformer, strong enough for the principle of reform but not at all extreme in its application. That meant that he could win the support of many factions which an extremist would not even desire. He fought hard enough against that type of orthodoxy which he felt was medieval in its refusal to grow with the times; he had refused an easy entrance into the legal profession and a governmental appointment back in his Albany days in order to devote himself to the enlightenment of his people. But he based his college on traditional Jewish learning, and he himself lived all his life as a pious, though not an orthodox, Jew. Finally, we cannot overlook the fact that Rabbi Wise was also a fine Jewish scholar and a direct and effective thinker. The many books, editorials and sermons from his pen show his broad background and his easy use of the whole of his knowledge for the practical purpose to which he devoted his life.

IV. OTHER RELIGIOUS DEVELOPMENTS

WE HAVE followed this entire development, which was really national, from the viewpoint of one city, Cincinnati, and of one man, Isaac M. Wise. This is the easiest way to grasp it, if it is only remembered that the movement itself concerned many cities, with their growing congregations and their own leaders. Dr. Wise's support at first was largely in the middle west and south, while the east was the center of two extreme tendencies —conservative Judaism and radical reform. To both these, Dr. Wise seemed a compromiser, as indeed he wanted to be, for only by compromise can people of many different opinions be brought to work together. It is impossible in this book to tell about all these different leaders and all their different congregations; any particular ones which may be of special interest may be found in the individual congregational records or in the Jewish Encyclopedia.

The name of Dr. David Einhorn of Philadelphia has already been mentioned. But there were younger men who followed him,—Gustav Gottheil in Temple Emanu-El of New York; Kaufmann Kohler in Temple Beth El of New York, and Emil G. Hirsch in Sinai Temple of Chicago. The two New York congregations moved uptown, erected splendid temples on upper Fifth Avenue, and became centers for the reform sentiment among the eastern Jews. On the Pacific coast the little beginnings had grown until a beautiful Temple Emanu-El in San Francisco was erected, having as its rabbi Jacob Voorsanger, the leader of Judaism in that far section. Kaufmann Kohler became in 1903 the successor of Isaac M. Wise as president of the Hebrew Union College, so

236

The Growth of Reform Judaism

his career is of special interest. He was another of the brilliant radical rabbis from Germany, where he was born in 1843, a generation later than Wise. Bred in orthodoxy, he also became filled with reform ideas in his university days, and came to America when he was twenty-six years old to officiate as a rabbi in this country.

Dr. Kaufmann Kohler

He married a daughter of Dr. Einhorn, was rabbi in Detroit, Chicago, and finally in New York for twenty-four years. When he was sixty years old, he was elected president of the Hebrew Union College, and moved to Cincinnati where he lived for the following eighteen years, acting in this capacity and also as a professor in the College. In 1921 he retired from this office and moved to New York, where he died in 1926, at the age of eighty-three years. Dr. Kohler was primarily a scholar, as Wise had been primarily an organizer. He wrote dozens of articles and several important books and was an editor of the Jewish Encyclopedia; his teaching and preaching both were full of original ideas. His greatest work was the *Jewish Theology,* a complete historical

237

study of the beliefs of Judaism in the past and at the present time.

The seventies were the period of the reformers, but the conservative Jews were also making efforts at this time which were to succeed later on. In 1867, Isaac Leeser tried to found a college, called Maimonides College, in Philadelphia; but it lasted just six years. It was intended to train American rabbis, like the Hebrew Union College a few years later, but its policy was conservative. In 1886, a full decade after the founding of the Hebrew Union College, the Jewish Theological Seminary of America was established in New York by Sabato Morais, the successor of Isaac Leeser in Philadelphia, and Alexander Kohut of New York, two prominent conservative leaders of that generation. Beside them, the name Marcus Jastrow, another Philadelphia rabbi, must be added.

The strictly orthodox development came in the nineties, and we will consider that when we take up the Russian Jewish immigration, which it represented.

V. THE PRINCIPLES OF REFORM JUDAISM

WE HAVE already discussed something of the principles of reform Judaism, how it differed from the earlier orthodoxy and what it was really striving for. But we must be careful not to consider it as entirely separate from the older synagogue or something entirely new in the world. The underlying basis of Jewish belief and conduct is the same; orthodox and reform Judaism represent merely

The Growth of Reform Judaism

different modes or interpretations. They do not have two entirely different beliefs, or customs, as is the case between Judaism and Christianity; each has the same attributes, but there is a difference of emphasis, as to what is more or less important.

Certain beliefs, of course, are the common possession of all Jews. For example, all Jews believe in one God; in Israel as a chosen people; in a life to come. All Jews believe in the moral law as expressed in the Ten Commandments, and in some kind of reward and punishment according to how those commandments are kept or broken. All types of Judaism are based on the study of the great works of the Jewish past, especially the Bible. But the difference of emphasis is very plain in both the synagogue worship and the daily life of the people.

For example, orthodoxy lays great stress on the religious value of tradition, the teaching of the great men and the experience of the Jewish people in the past; reform recognizes this also, does not break away from it, but lays more stress on the apparent needs of the present day. Reform places more emphasis on the Bible, particularly the prophets; orthodoxy on the Talmud, particularly on the legal parts of it—but both study and need all the great Jewish books and leaders of the past. Orthodoxy stresses the ceremonial, reform the ethical law, but both possess the two of them. This difference of emphasis, of interpretation, may be more clearly understood if the resolutions of the Pittsburgh Conference of reform rabbis in 1885 are considered;

239

these resolutions are not authoritative because there is no final authority in reform Judaism, but they are a very important formulation and very well presented. A summary of this platform follows:

The Bible is not considered a divinely dictated book, with every word and syllable true, but a record of the religious history and inspiration of the Jewish people; reform Judaism is not opposed to modern science, but is glad for every new truth added to the truths of the Bible. Reform does not accept every law because it is in the Bible or the Talmud; it accepts the moral law as a whole, but only some of the ceremonial laws. Therefore it rejects the binding power of the laws of food, dress and priestly purity. Some reform Jews observe the laws of kashruth because they like them, or because they honor the tradition of the Jewish people, but not because they consider them necessary. The Pittsburgh platform especially rejects the coming of a Messiah, the miraculous return of the entire Jewish people to Palestine, and the restoration of sacrifices; it substitutes the gradual coming of a Messianic age of peace and good will among all human beings. It rejects heaven and hell as places of physical reward and punishment, but proclaims the immortality of the soul, that the spirit of man can never die. Particularly it insists on the importance of the spirit of the Bible with regard to rich and poor, capital and labor, those problems which are so pressing in our own time.

Naturally, the orthodox opposed such a platform very

The Growth of Reform Judaism

strongly, for they believed in the binding value of tradition and the experience of the past, as well as in the divine inspiration of the Torah, word by word. Naturally also, the reformers applied this general principle of progress in many ways; they took off their hats in synagogue, read part of the prayers in English, installed organs, had a choir of men and women, had men and women sit together in the pews instead of sending the women up to a gallery. Many of them added a service on Sunday morning, others late Friday evening, beside the regular services at the regular times; their sermons were preached in English; they confirmed girls as well as boys on Shabuoth instead of having the old Bar Mitzvah, when the boys alone received special teaching at the age of thirteen, and each boy was called up to read the Torah alone on the Sabbath of his birthday. They dropped the second day of the holydays, adopted originally because of the uncertainty, outside of Palestine, of the exact date of the holiday, and retained as a distinction between the Jews of Palestine and those of other lands.

This new interpretation of Judaism, then, had many details different from the old, but there were also more fundamental differences. Many reform Jews observe the greater part of the traditional law. The real difference is in the theory of religious progress of the reformers, as opposed to the theory of divine revelation of the orthodox; the liberty of opinion and choice of the one, the religious authority of the other. The conservative, of course, comes in between, holding to as many traditions

History of the Jews in the United States

as he can but dropping those few which seem to him untenable.

Only within the last few years has there been any coming together, so that now orthodox, conservative, and reform Jews are working together on practical matters, and are recognizing each other as Jews, parts of the same great historic people, who differ a little in their manner of living and worshipping in this modern day.

REVIEW QUESTIONS

1. Describe the early life of Isaac M. Wise; give reasons for his change in attitude.
2. What did Wise accomplish in Albany? In Cincinnati?
3. In what way is Wise typical of the German Jewish movement? How do his accomplishments parallel the progress of the Jewish community in America?
4. Give the principles of reform, conservative, orthodox Judaism. Give the points they have in common.
5. Describe the founding and growth of the Hebrew Union College.

TOPICS FOR REPORTS

1. The beliefs of Judaism in general; the reform, conservative and orthodox interpretations.
2. The biography of a rabbi mentioned in this chapter, beside Wise.
3. The growth of the reform movement in some one city.

See the references to the preceding chapter, most of which apply to this period also.

REFERENCES FOR PUPILS

Raisin, Max, pp. 253–268.
May, Max B., *Isaac M. Wise, A Biography.*

The Growth of Reform Judaism

Jewish Encyclopedia, arts. on Judaism in America, Isaac M.* Wise, Conferences (Rabbinical), Einhorn, David; Hirsch, Samuel; Hirsch, Emil G.; Adler, Samuel.

REFERENCES FOR TEACHERS

Rosenau, William, "Sabato Morais, An Appreciation," *Year Book of the Central Conference of American Rabbis,* vol. XXXIII, p. 356.

Wise, Isaac M., *Reminiscences.*

Studies in Jewish Literature, In Honor of Kaufmann Kohler (for his biography). Hebrew Union College.

American Jewish Year Book.

    Enelow, H. G., "Kaufmann Kohler," vol. 5687.

    Feldman, Abraham, "Joseph Krauskopf," vol. 5685.

    Rosenau, William, "Henry Berkowitz," vol. 5685.

    Schwartz, S. D., "Emil G. Hirsch," vol. 5686.

Philipson, David, *The Oldest Jewish Congregation in the West, Bene Israel, Cincinnati.*

Hirsch, Emil G., *My Religion,* Macmillan.

Leiser, Joseph, *American Judaism.*

Philipson, David, and Grossmann, Louis, *Isaac Mayer Wise— Life and Selected Writings.*

Moses, Adolph, *Yahvism.*

CHAPTER 16.

How Jewish Lodges and Charities Were Formed

IF you consider the Jewish people of your own city, you notice that they have many organizations beside the synagogue, with its school and its cemetery. They have a lodge or several lodges, a club or several clubs, perhaps a Jewish newspaper, certainly many societies for charitable purposes, and probably a Federation of these into one larger organization. So the last question we want to discuss about this great German period is how almost all of these organizations beside the synagogue came into being and grew into their present form and size.

I. THE GERMAN CHARACTER

THE German Jews were great organizers and they had a need for organization. They loved the synagogue, as appeared in the last two chapters, and put in a tremendous amount of work in developing their reform ideas and institutions. But they had also a secular tendency, a desire to take things out of the synagogue, and develop separate societies for charity and for social purposes. They were used to organization in their former homes.

244

How Jewish Lodges and Charities Were Formed

They wrote long constitutions with all possible eventualities in them; I have found one of 15 printed pages for a Frauenunterstützungs Gesellschaft in Paducah, Ky., printed by Bloch in Cincinnati in 1870. And as the number of Jews, particularly of poor Jews, increased, more services had to be performed for them. The poor Jews had to be helped at least until they learned the language; their children or old people needed care; the self-supporting members of the community wanted a mutual benefit association, or a place for meetings for debate and self-improvement, or a way to celebrate their occasions of joy. The German Jews had their societies for these various purposes, outside the synagogue.

II. THE JEWISH CHARITIES

JEWISH charity is very ancient, and is based on the idea of the brotherhood of Israel, which demands that each person help the other as a matter of justice, for all alike are children of God. Whenever help was needed by poor Jews, orphans, the sick or immigrants, there would always be somebody with a little money to bring assistance. The first Jewish philanthropy in this country, apart from help given by one person to another, or from the synagogue funds—that is, the first organized philanthropy—was a Jewish Orphans' Home in Charleston as early as 1801; it is hard to imagine that there were poor orphans among the Jews of Charleston as early as that.

The New York charities began in 1820, when a very

245

old Jewish veteran of the Revolutionary War fell sick and the Jews of the city decided to look after him; they used to visit him, collected a sum of money to care for his needs, and tended him carefully. When he died two years later, $300 of this money was left; with this money the Jews of New York started a Hebrew Benevolent Society to care for other unfortunates in the future. Just a few years later, in 1832, an orphan asylum was opened: but it was naturally a very small undertaking, and in 1860, when it became associated with the Benevolent Society, it had just thirty children in a rented house. Meanwhile, there were other kindly people who started other small societies—for free burial, for furnishing fuel, for Purim dainties, and so on. Many people felt that this method was haphazard and careless, that it did not give the really necessary help to poor people, and at the same time cost the Jews of the city a great deal of extra money. The *Jewish Messenger,* the only Jewish newspaper of New York in those days, published many articles and editorials on the subject, in favor of a better method of handling philanthropic affairs. So in 1874 the United Hebrew Charities was formed, with most of the Jewish charities of the city joining. It had charge of relief for poor families, for the sick, for orphans, for the new and ignorant immigrant; for each of these needed a different kind of help. For the orphans a great institution was built on Amsterdam Avenue in 1884; in 1941 it merged with others to become the Jewish Child Care Association of New York. Today most children needing help live in foster homes, not "asylums." For the sick a Jews' Hospital was begun as early as 1857; in 1870 a great building was erected and the name changed to Mt. Sinai Hospital. So in New York City where little organizations had been founded by poor immigrants in the forties and fifties to help themselves, there existed great charitable organizations in the seventies, with fine large buildings, and with a program to take care of the growing needs of the Jews of New York.

This was fortunate because the period of no immigration soon passed, and the problems and needs of the Jews increased many times beginning with 1880. But during the fifteen years from 1865 to 1880 the great philanthropies were founded, and the little ones grew up, so that the American Jews were as ready as they could be for the terrific needs of the time ahead.

This same process went on in every great city. In Philadelphia, for instance, there was a Jewish Foster Home in 1855, a Jewish Hospital Association in 1865, and a Jewish Maternity Association in 1873. The United Hebrew Charities of Philadelphia was formed in 1869 out of six existing organizations, of which some went back in their history to the early days of Rebecca Gratz and the others dated from the middle period and the influence of Isaac Leeser. In Chicago the United Hebrew Relief Association began in 1859, the Jewish Hospital in 1868 (it was destroyed by the Chicago fire in 1871 and later rebuilt), and then, in the last part of the century,

(ABOVE): THE OLD. The Jewish community used to care for orphans in bleak barracks-like halls such as the Hebrew Orphan Asylum of New York, built in 1884 to accommodate 1600 children.

(BELOW): THE NEW. Most dependent Jewish children now live in foster homes. Others live in residential schools like the Pleasantville Cottage of the Jewish Child Care Association of New York.

How Jewish Lodges and Charities Were Formed

various orphan homes, old people's homes, and so on. In Cincinnati the charities began in 1838 and the hospital in 1845, at the beginning of the German period, but their great growth came later on. All over the country the small beginnings were turning into great, wealthy institutions, with many supporters; they faced great public problems, and usually met those problems very well. At the same time national Jewish organizations were forming to carry on various kinds of Jewish work, including charity, on a nation-wide scale.

III. THE LODGES

THE first Jewish lodge to be formed in America, and still the most important in its influence and work, was the Independent Order B'nai B'rith (Sons of the Covenant). It was started in 1843 by twelve poor Jews of New York, headed by Henry Jones, and their first name and ritual were in German, for they called themselves Bundes Brüder. At first they sought their social life in the lodge room and their mutual benefit outside. The order grew slowly in different parts of the country; the ritual was translated into English; by 1858 they had 3,000 members. Then came the great period of growth of all Jewish institutions; the B'nai B'rith was at the top of the wave and during the post-Civil War days it had 20,000 members and divided up into several Grand Lodges in different parts of the country. Evidently the German Jews wanted to band together in such an organization, where they could take out insurance, conduct literary meetings, work for Jewish ideals without any distinction between orthodox and reform Jew. As immigrants and Jews, they were not ready for American non-Jewish orders, even if these organizations had been ready to accept them, which was not always the case. But they were glad to have a Jewish order to represent them and to include them all.

The second stage came in the great period of construction. The members of the B'nai B'rith no longer needed the order for insurance,—they belonged to regular insurance companies; nor for aid when they were sick —they had money in the bank. But they knew that there were many Jews in actual and daily need, so they turned their attention toward charity. They founded an orphan asylum in Cleveland as early as 1868; an old people's home in Yonkers; other orphan homes in Atlanta and Erie; a home for old and young in New Orleans. Then the B'nai B'rith took over national charitable agencies, the National Jewish Hospital for Consumptives in Denver in 1900, and later the Leo N. Levi Memorial Hospital in Hot Springs, Ark.

After this philanthropic work and right along with it, the B'nai B'rith began to make special efforts to protect and aid Jews everywhere: in Roumania, in Russia, and wherever they needed help. The final step in this was the creation of the Anti-Defamation League to protect the good name of the Jew throughout the United States.

The B'nai B'rith spread to foreign lands in 1882 when a lodge was chartered in Berlin, Germany. Since that time lodges have been organized in England, Palestine, Turkey, Austria, and other lands. There are now (1961) seven Grand Lodges in the United States and four abroad, with the Constitution Grand Lodge in which they are all represented.

The present, or third stage in the development of the B'nai B'rith is its interest in education. Secrecy, which for so long was a precious possession of every member and the bulwark of the organization, has been abolished. Social service is now being conducted in penitentiaries; B'nai B'rith Hillel Foundations are being established in universities for religious, educational and social activities among the students; many schools of different types are aided and some have been founded.

One of the interesting contributions of the B'nai B'rith was the erection in 1876, the centennial year, of a statue of Religious Liberty by the Jewish sculptor, Moses Ezekiel, in Fairmount Park, Philadelphia.

The B'nai B'rith has been taken up in great detail because it was the first of the fraternal orders, because it is still the most important, and because its development is being followed by others in their turn. The Free Sons of Israel followed in 1849; the Order Brith Abraham was organized in 1859, when the B'nai B'rith was already well grown up; then came the Kesher shel Barzel, the Independent Order Brith Abraham, which now is the largest of them all, and a number of others. Many of these orders were composed largely of the Russian immigrants, as opposed to the B'nai B'rith,

251

which was long the stronghold of German Jewry. Of course, at the present day these distinctions are being steadily lost in an American Judaism, so that all organizations are becoming constantly more mixed and all Jews in America are becoming constantly more like each other. Each of these organizations began with sick benefits, insurance, and the educational work of the lodge meeting. Now they are turning away from self-help to charity for others. It seems probable that they also will follow the course of the B'nai B'rith, turn to Jewish education as a chief object, and abolish secrecy, thus changing from mere fraternal lodges into great educational societies.

IV. THE JEWISH PRESS

In the early days it was a very brave and a very useful thing to establish a Jewish newspaper; brave, because there were very few possible subscribers, Jews who could read English and still cared to read a Jewish paper; useful, because only through the written word could ideas be spread throughout the country. The first Jewish paper of importance (there was an earlier one in 1823, which was short-lived) was the Occident, which Isaac Leeser founded in 1843 in Philadelphia and conducted for the rest of his life; for many years it represented Judaism in America. Isaac M. Wise had his first hearing in its columns; and when he founded the American Israelite in 1855 in Cincinnati and Chicago as a reform organ, the Occident continued as a conservative

How Jewish Lodges and Charities Were Formed

or orthodox paper, opposing Dr. Wise's reform ideas but working with him in defense of the Jew. Wise founded also a German paper, the Deborah—as a matter of fact, much of the reading of the German immigrants was in the German language, and newspapers in German flourished for many years.

In New York there was Einhorn's *Sinai,* a reform paper founded in 1856, which ran for six years; the *Jewish Messenger* was founded in 1857, and united in 1902 with the *American Hebrew,* another conservative organ that had been begun in 1879.

At the same time, there were efforts to publish Jewish books in America. The present Jewish Publication Society of America, which was established in Philadelphia in 1888, was the third attempt. The first, begun by Isaac Leeser in 1845, published 14 books, but its plant was destroyed by fire and it never recovered from the blow, as there was not at that time the strength in American Jewry to surmount difficulties of the kind. A second attempt was made in 1873 in New York, but lasted only two years. American Jewry was beginning to feel the need for Jewish books, but was not yet grown up to the point where it could publish and buy them. In fact, the present Jewish Publication Society is not flourishing in a financial way, although it is doing a splendid service to the Jews of America. Perhaps this is because books are not as interesting to look at as big buildings for temples and for charities, and are not as touching in appeals for help as orphans or the aged.

History of the Jews in the United States

THESE German Jews saw also the need for unity in Israel, and for defense of Jewish rights in this country and abroad. So in 1859, when the terrible Mortara case in Italy was affecting Jews the world over, the Jews of America organized the Board of Delegates of American Israelites, on the model of the Board of Deputies of British Jews. At this same time the French Jews were organizing their Alliance Israelite Universelle. The call came from New York, and Jews of twelve other cities joined in the new organization; both Isaac Leeser and Isaac M. Wise were active in it from the beginning.

This Board of Delegates had any number of interests, in Jewish education, charity, and the gathering of statistics; but its chief work lay in defense of the Jew. As we have seen, there was such work to do in America in advocating the appointment of army chaplains and in opposing such orders as Grant's Number 11. As we shall see in chapter twenty, there was much more work of the kind in connection with Jewish rights in Switzerland, Roumania, Russia and other lands, sometimes the rights of American citizens who had gone there, sometimes of the native Jews. In each case it was the business of the Board of Delegates to represent the American Jews to the government at Washington.

We can see how the German Jews dominated Jewish life in America at that time, and how generally they tended toward reform by this fact: in 1878, when the

254

How Jewish Lodges and Charities Were Formed

Union of American Hebrew Congregations was beginning to flourish, the Board of Delegates gave up its separate existence and amalgamated with the Union. There was no need for two such organizations at the time; one could practically represent all the Jews of the United States. For forty-five years after that, Simon Wolf was the representative of the joint body in Washington, and in important crises other prominent men went to the capital to assist him.

Meanwhile, other Jews came to America and became prominent. The work of the Union grew to huge proportions on its strictly religious side, while other bodies were growing up in the twentieth century to take up the political and public work. In 1925, the Board of Delegates as a part of the Union was finally dissolved, and its work left to the bodies that had developed for that special purpose, especially the American Jewish Committee and the American Jewish Congress. But it must be remembered that during its existence both separately and for many years affiliated with the Union, this Board of Delegates was a great force to express the mind of the American Jews and help them achieve some kind of a unity from within.

VI. JEWISH EDUCATION

ONE of the constant interests of the same men who organized these other types of Jewish work was in Jewish education. They knew that if their children grew up in America without knowing what it meant to be a Jew, all

History of the Jews in the United States

their synagogues, charities, and lodges would be ineffective; the Jews of America would disappear without Jewish knowledge. So these pioneers tried to do everything at once, and succeeded only in part. It must also be remembered that these different movements overlapped and were started often by the same men and during the same period. Isaac M. Wise was chiefly interested in reform Judaism, but he was also president of District No. 2 of the B'nai B'rith, he founded a newspaper, built up a school for children and a college for rabbis. Isaac Leeser was a rabbi and writer along religious lines; he was also an editor, vice-president of the Board of Delegates, founder of many charitable movements in Philadelphia, and founder of the Hebrew Education Association of that city in 1848. Even a lay worker like Rebecca Gratz was equally busy in her day with her relief for poor women and children and her Jewish Sunday School. So the separation of activities in this chapter is only for convenience in study; actually the various movements proceeded with the growing numbers, wealth, and self-consciousness of the Jews of America.

We have already seen the attempts to start a Hebrew College in Philadelphia, Cincinnati and New York. But, of course, that was a late stage of Jewish study. Before they could enter a college, boys had to know something about the Hebrew language, the Bible and Jewish history. The facilities for such study were very poor; there were only a few school rooms in synagogues and those were in dark basements; there were few rabbis and

256

How Jewish Lodges and Charities Were Formed

teachers, few text-books, and very few schools of any
kind. Then with the growth of the public schools, the
Jewish children attended them instead of the parochial
schools and as a result, had no Jewish education at all.
What could the Jews do to teach their children about
their people and their faith?

There were two solutions, beside the training schools
for rabbis: religious schools were established for children, either on Sundays or weekdays, and Young Men's
Hebrew Associations for the young people. We have
followed this educational development from the early
Jewish parochial schools, through the beginnings of the
Jewish Sunday School in Philadelphia, under Rebecca
Gratz, and the Hebrew Education Society of that city
under Isaac Leeser. These were the first religious schools
in the field. The Society opened a little school with
twenty-two pupils in 1851, and expanded bit by bit. In
New York the Hebrew Free School Association was organized in 1868 and gave rise gradually to a number
of important schools of different kinds: the Hebrew
Technical Institute, the Technical School for Girls, and
even the Educational Alliance. But the Association's first
and most significant work at the time was the establishment of schools for Jewish children. Classes were held
in the afternoons after public school work, and on Sunday mornings. While most of the German congregations
had Sunday schools only, and taught Bible and religion
without Hebrew, the afternoon schools taught Hebrew
as well and were preferred by the strictly orthodox.

257

History of the Jews in the United States

The great development of the mid-century, then, was the cessation of Jewish parochial schools, and the building up of Sunday Schools among reform, and daily afternoon classes among orthodox Jews. Both of these were quite new to Jewish life. They sprang up in America as an answer to the peculiar situation of many Jewish children who attended public schools for their general instruction, as had never been permitted in Europe in those days. They are still the chief kinds of Jewish schools in this country, by which Jewish children can learn about the great deeds of their people and the great faith which inspired their forefathers.

In 1874 the first Young Men's Hebrew Association was organized in New York by a group of young German Jews who longed for some kind of self-culture, especially along Jewish lines. One of those young men was Oscar S. Straus; there were others who made their mark, along with him, in later days. A year later a similar organization was begun in Philadelphia. They were modelled more or less after the Young Men's Christian Associations, as we might guess from their names. They were not religious, but cultural, so that the members might meet, enjoy each other's society, and exchange ideas about all sorts of subjects: just the sort of club that young people always form, and are still forming. But these new clubs struck an important note for that day; they were intended to unite Americanism and Judaism, a comparatively new experiment, and one that was still more or less doubtful. This was what the reform Jews were trying to do along religious lines; it was also what the Y. M. H. A.'s tried along cultural lines.

It was no accident that, coming from the same group of German Jews during the same two or three decades, the two reached practically the same philosophy, and the Y. M. H. A.'s up to very recently expressed to the Jews as a whole the attitude of the American-born Jew of German parentage. They represented the view of successful middle class people, getting to be thoroughly at home in America, feeling a little superior to the new immigrants who were beginning to come again in greater and greater numbers. For the seventies with their stability and their consolidation marked the end of the German period; in the eighties, with the influx of large numbers, the Eastern European period of Jewish History began.

REVIEW QUESTIONS

1. Enumerate different kinds of Jewish institutions that grew up during the middle of the nineteenth century.
2. Describe the growth of the German Jews as a community.
3. Describe the growth of Jewish charity.
4. What was the origin of the fraternal orders? Describe their development.
5. Give reasons for Jewish periodicals; their history.
6. What type of Jewish education was developed by the German Jews for children, for young people?

TOPICS FOR REPORTS

1. The theory of Jewish charity—as justice. Illustrate from modern charities in America.

259

History of the Jews in the United States

2. Read and report on some Jewish newspaper of the present day, preferably one of those founded in the early days. Tell its usefulness to the Jewish community.
3. Report on the life of one of the early fraternal leaders: Julius Bien, Leo N. Levi, or Adolf Kraus.
4. What was the value of a Board of Delegates? Study the various methods by which Jews can defend their rights in a democracy; compare with the method of the Middle Ages (the shtadlan).
5. The Mortara case.

References for Pupils

Wiernik, Peter, pp. 242–254.
Raisin, Max, pp. 283–285.
B'nai B'rith Manual, 1926, pp. 274–276, 301–313, 319 ff. Independent Order of B'nai B'rith.
Kraus, Adolf, *Reminiscences and Comments.*
Jewish Encyclopedia. Many articles, such as American Israelite, Occident, Periodicals, B'nai B'rith, American Jewish Publication Society, and cities, personalities, etc.

References for Teachers

Bogen, Boris D., *Jewish Philanthropy.*
Fifty Years of Social Service, The History of the United Hebrew Charities of New York City.
Dushkin, A. M., *Jewish Education in New York City,* pp. 38–62.
Leo M. Levi Memorial Volume.
Publications of the American Jewish Historical Society.
  Kohler, Max. J., "The Board of Delegates of American Israelites," vol. XXIX, p. 75.
Yearbooks of National Conference of Jewish Social Service.
Frankel, Lee K., "The Last Fifty Years of Jewish Philanthropy" in *Jewish Charity,* Feb., 1905.
Wolf, *Selected Addresses and Papers;* "History of the Board of Delegates or Civil Rights."

CHAPTER 17.

The Third Wave of Immigration: From Russia

W E ARE now prepared to study the third wave of Jewish migration to America, to see wherein it was different from the two earlier ones, to find out why the Jews came from Russia, what they were like, when they arrived, what were their occupations, where they lived, what their special institutions were, and what was their particular contribution to Jewish life in America.

I. THE SIZE OF THE RUSSIAN MIGRATION

OF COURSE, this migration was not entirely from Russia. It also included Jews from Poland, Galicia, Roumania and all over eastern Europe. They were generally spoken of as Russian Jews, because those from Russia were the largest proportion, because they were all from eastern Europe near Russia, and because their language and customs gave them a fairly well-marked unity, as contrasted with the Spanish and German Jews.

It is equally clear that these Jews did not start coming in 1881. There were Haym Salomon during the Revolution, Michael Heilprin during the Civil War, and many other individuals from time to time. The B'nai

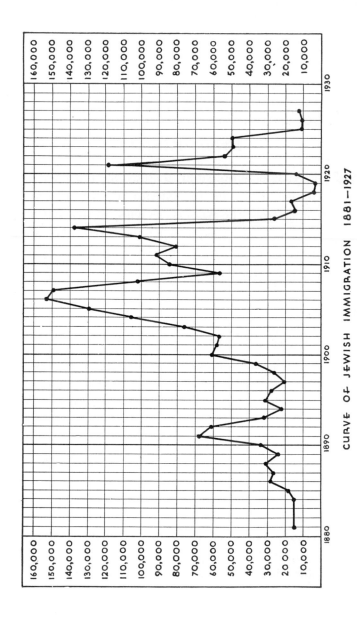

160,000
150,000
140,000
130,000
120,000
110,000
100,000
90,000
80,000
70,000
60,000
50,000
40,000
30,000
20,000
10,000

1880   1890   1900   1910   1920   1930

CURVE OF JEWISH IMMIGRATION 1881—1927

The Third Wave of Immigration: From Russia

Yeshurun congregation, organized in New York in 1825, had many Polish members as well as German and English. During a famine or mob violence against the Jews in Russia, more would come to America. Their first little synagogue in New York had been founded as early as 1852. But they were hardly enough to form a distinct element in the population, which up to 1880 was chiefly German, with a few of the old Spanish families still standing out.

Now suddenly the east-European Jews began to come in tremendous numbers, far beyond those of the early Jewish migrations. Let us consider the figures, as near as we have them. From 1790 to 1840—a period of fifty years —the population of the United States as a whole increased from 4,000,000 to 17,000,000 or 325%; during the same half century the Jewish population increased from 3,000 to 15,000 or 400%. Thus, in the Spanish period the increase was about the same as that of the nation as a whole. During the next forty years the national population increased from 17,000,000 to 50,000,000 or 200%, but the Jewish population increased from 15,000 to 250,000 or 1400%. During the German period, then, the Jews increased seven times as fast as the population of the country as a whole, and became fifteen times as numerous as they had been. During the next forty years from 1880 to 1920, the United States changed from a nation of 50,000,000 to one of 106,000,000, an increase of 112%; but at the same time the Jewish community increased from 250,000 to 3,500,000, an increase of 1300%.

1790	1840	1880	1959
			U.S. 177,500,000
		U.S. 50,000,000	
	U.S. 17,000,000		
U.S. 4,000,000			5,367,000 JEWS
3,000 JEWS	15,000 JEWS	250,000 JEWS	
Less than ¹/₁₀ of 1%	¹/₁₀ of 1%	½ of 1%	3%

CHART 6

COMPARISON OF U.S. AND JEWISH POPULATION AT VARIOUS PERIODS

The Third Wave of Immigration: From Russia

That is, during the Russian period of immigration American Jewry increased eleven times as fast as the population of the nation as a whole, and became fourteen times as large as it had been before the period began.

These figures give some idea of the huge bulk of the immigration of Russian Jews. During 40 years from 1881 to 1920, two million Jews entered the United States, while practically none left to return to their former homes. Seventy per cent of all these immigrants came from Russia, 25 per cent from Austria-Hungary and Roumania. During eight of these years, there were over 100,000 immigrants a year. The numbers are staggering when we remember that the whole United States at the time of the Civil War had only 200,000 Jews. By the time of the World War, there were that many Jewish young men in the American armies alone.

Of the 4,200,000 Jews in the United States in 1928, fully 3,500,000 were of east European birth or descent; the vast majority of these had been here less than fifty years. A half million were of German descent (very few of German birth), and most of their families had been in America more than seventy years. The differences which existed at their immigration and which exist in part still, are due to these numbers, to the different length of residence in America, and to the different background in the countries whence they came.

II. THE EUROPEAN BACKGROUND

THESE Russian and Polish Jews, and those from the nearby countries, were parts of the greatest and most

thickly settled body of Jews in the world, constituting
the great Jewish belt, from the Baltic Sea to the Black
Sea, right across eastern and central Europe. Even now
a fifth of the world's Jews still live in that belt; in
1880 there were far more, well over one-half. The Jews
had lived in many of these lands from time imme-
morial, before there had ever been a Russia or even a
Poland. They had entered some of them from the east,
from Babylonia and Persia, when the people were still
barbarous. Other sections, such as Poland and Lithuania,
had been largely settled from the west by German Jews,
driven out by persecution after the Crusades from the
many little German states of the Middle Ages. So some
of them were of the same stock as the Spanish Jews;
others were merely transplanted German Jews. A much
smaller element consisted of descendants of the Chazars,
a Tartar tribe of the Crimea which was converted to
Judaism back in the ninth century.

Practically all these Jews spoke Yiddish, a German
dialect which they had carried with them from Germany
into Eastern Europe; for in Germany they had learned
the language of the country and received much of its
culture, and they never adopted the Polish language or customs. Many of them knew Hebrew also
as a holy tongue, could read the prayerbook, and Bible;
the most advanced students could read the Talmud in
the original language. As there were no public schools
in any of these lands, the Jews established their own
schools; practically every Jewish boy learned to read

Hebrew, while all, boys and girls alike, spoke ordinarily in Yiddish. The two languages are printed alike in Hebrew letters; but most of the words and all the grammar are entirely different.

These Jews of eastern Europe were bitterly poor. They were the poorest and most oppressed element in a poor and downtrodden nation. They were as poverty-stricken as the Russian peasant, and had to endure special laws besides, which discriminated against their religion, their business ventures, their comforts and their safety. They had to pay special taxes as Jews; were obliged to live in certain parts of the country, known as the Pale of Settlement and were forbidden to live in other parts; could not own or rent farms, had to engage in certain lines of business and were forbidden to enter others. As these countries were more backward in industry than America or western Europe, all the people, except the nobility, were more or less poor; but the Jews were the poorest of all.

In their poverty and trouble these Jews were deeply loyal to Judaism. They were orthodox with a piety and an intensity which the Jews living in comfort in America could never rival. By the mere act of joining the Russian Church they could escape from all their privations, could live in the capital or travel freely through the country without having to show passports and offer tribute at every turn, could enter any business they wanted, and have their sons attend any school or university. But hardly any of them ever went the way of the apostate,

267

as so many had done in the easier but more tempting conditions of Germany and Austria. They were intensely loyal, sometimes even fanatical in their Judaism. Of course, they were not all agreed in its interpretation any more than they were to agree later with the reform Jews of America. Some were Chassidim, emphasizing prayer and joyful communion with God; others Misnagdim, emphasizing study and obedience to the Law. Some of the young people had even turned to the Haskalah, and tried to adapt the new learning of the outside world into the Hebrew language and into their own Jewish life. The highest standing in the Jewish community belonged always to the scholar in Jewish lore, not to the man of wealth or of modern education.

At the end of the nineteenth century, Russia and Poland were still largely medieval countries, in industry, government and religion. For one thing, they did not have an equality of citizenship, but ground down the serfs and the Jews; for another, they included various nationalities, each with its own laws, but paying taxes to the central government. Among these were the Jews. The Jew in Germany felt that he was a German, in America that he was an American; but the Jew in Russia was a Jew and not a Russian at all. He had his own courts, his own local community organization, with its own Jewish heads. He lived in a Jewish neighborhood of a city, or in a Jewish village, and hardly ever met a gentile except in business, or if the gentiles came to collect taxes or to attack the Jewish quarter. The Russian

The Third Wave of Immigration: From Russia

Jew on the whole, was never at home in Russia; he had his great numbers, his Jewish schools and academies, his history of hundreds of years in the land,—but he never became a Russian, and seldom was treated as a friendly alien.

The German Jews had come over to America with the German Christians, but the migration from Russia was strictly a Jewish migration; they came alone. The Russian Christians came later and in much smaller numbers. This was because of the special persecutions which made the Jews long to leave Russia. Poverty alone was not enough; such a mass migration,—the movement of a people across seas to a strange world,—could only be the result of oppression by the government, the danger of violence, and a vast disturbance of Jewish life in Russia itself.

There were two of these factors at the beginning of the period,—pogroms in 1881 and the May Laws in 1882. As both these were repeated many times in the following forty years, it is necessary to explain them at the outset. A pogrom is a massacre, or some outbreak of mob violence, incited by the government. It is hard for us to imagine this; in America, any outbreak of a lynching mob is against the sheriff or the police, and in many cases the officials are able to stop it. But in Russia in the days of the autocracy there was constant fear of a revolt, and the government often tried to prevent it—and successfully—by making the Jews the scapegoats, blaming every evil of society on them, and turning the ignorant and the violent against them. This occurred in 1881, in 1892, and in 1903 to 1905, and again during and after the World War. At every one of these outbreaks, some of which were unbelievably terrible, thousands of Jews who lived near the cities were affected; and other thousands in distant parts of the huge Russian empire took their small belongings and fled to America.

In addition, there were the infamous May Laws of 1882, by which many thousands of Jews who had been living in villages for generations were uprooted and forced to crowd into the already crowded towns and cities. It was an economic attack on the Jews, undermining the prosperity and the varied occupations of some of them, and forcing them all into the same narrow circle of homes, of business, and of opportunity. In this intense privation of many of the Jews, and this threat of dispossession against the rest, many turned for a new opportunity in a new world. Every time another restrictive law was passed, and there were many such times, the results could be seen in the increased emigration the following year.

III. CHARACTER OF THE RUSSIAN IMMIGRATION

THE character of the Russian immigration, just like its time and its numbers, can be traced to the situation of the Jews in Russia under the combined rule of the autocracy, the nobility and the Orthodox Russian Church. These rulers openly announced their program,

The Third Wave of Immigration: From Russia

which was to kill one-third of the Jews, drive one-third out of the country, and convert one-third to the Ortho-dox Church, thus solving the Jewish problem in Russia by abolishing the Jews. This solution recalls the one of Isabella of Spain, of whom we read at the very beginning of American Jewish history.

This immigration of Russian Jews was by families, not by separate individuals. Often the man came over first, worked for a little while, and then sent passage money to his wife and children; in many cases the whole family came at once. There are more women and children among the Russian Jewish immigrants than among any other group, for whole families came to America, since nobody cared to leave his dear ones in such danger. They came to stay; a smaller percentage of these immigrants return to their native lands than of any other group, according to the statistics of the Bureau of Immigration. The Jews hated and feared Czarism; they longed for the freedom and opportunity of America; they brought their families, settled down to stay forever, and became citizens as soon as possible.

But, unlike the migration of German Jews, these families did not represent a special class of the poor, or a special class of the intellectual rebels. This was a national migration on a grand scale. Whole towns moved to America, rich and poor, old and young, the Talmud scholar and the village loafer. In a novel by Sholom Asch, called *Uncle Moses*, we see how this worked out, for the entire village moved to New York and took

271

jobs in the factory started by Uncle Moses, the first of their villagers to come to America. In the *Lithuanian Village* by Kobrin, we see the other side, the whole village departing, bit by bit, for the strange world of America, and leaving their native village deserted.

The German Jews had been largely liberals, anti-slavery Republicans. The Russian Jews, coming from a land of medievalism, had very few liberals; they were chiefly divided into extreme orthodox and flaming radicals, revolutionists. The orthodox were conservative in politics and economics, extremely strict in their religion; they had made terrible sacrifices for their faith, and they aimed to preserve it in every detail. They loved the religion of their fathers, and they imported ultra-orthodoxy of the Russian type into America, establishing it beside the reform and conservative synagogues already flourishing. Zionism found its great appeal in America among these Russian Jews, who were imbued with the Jewish tradition, and who knew the bitterness of persecution. In addition to the orthodox, there were the rebels, usually Socialists in politics, trades union men in economics, doubters or deniers of all religion. This was the natural answer of the educated young men of Russia to the extreme medievalism of Russian life in all three fields, politics, economics and religion. Many of these people became wealthy and conservative in America; some became liberals in the American sense; but many of them remained radicals through all their later history. They sent Meyer London to Congress, subscribed

The Third Wave of Immigration: From Russia

for the Yiddish daily, the Vorwärts (Forward), and became one of the most advanced groups in American life and thought.

The Russian Jews thus brought to America two sets of characteristics: first, the homely democratic virtues of loyalty, piety, devoted family and group life, and the touch of fervor which the Americanized German Jews so badly needed; second, the note of rebellion which was forced on them in Russia and which many preserved in America. The German was contented; the Russian orthodox likewise; the Russian radical (in temperament or theory) could not be contented, but looked always for something else to challenge and to change.

These Russian Jews made in their own lives a leap of five centuries. Mary Antin's beautiful book, *The Promised Land,* shows the experiences that a little Russian girl went through when she came to America. Of course, the transition for the older immigrants was much harder. The Russian Jew came from autocracy to democracy; he knew nothing of political parties, of voting, of self-government; he had known the police only to bribe or flee them; he had known the Czar only as the object of forced homage and private curses. He had to change at once into a citizen of a republic, had to join a party, to vote for president. In Russia he could not even form a private association, like a lodge or club, could gain no experience at self rule, except in the synagogue. Here at once he formed a multitude of associations, lodges, and societies; most of which promptly

273

failed owing to lack of experience, although the second crop succeeded. In Russia there had been a medieval business and economic life; most of the people were peasants, the Jews mostly traders and skilled workmen. But in America the Russian immigrant entered the most advanced economic system in the world, with huge factories, specialization in every line; he had to learn a new trade, find a new job, get used to a new kind of work.

Finally, in Russia there had been a medieval atmosphere of thought, no freedom of expression, even very few modern ideas in science or politics. In America there was every variety and every current of modernism, the theory of evolution, the hope for universalism. It was a tremendous leap for people to come into a modern from a medieval world, to traverse in their own lifetime the space it had taken Europe and America four hundred years to travel. The marvel is that they were able to readjust themselves, to become at home in America, and to integrate themselves as part of American Jewry.

Those young Russian Jews who had dipped into modern thought at all did not read the sort of books that were most important in America, books dealing with the world as it is, with modern science and history and politics. They read Russian literature, which dwells so largely on one's own mind and soul, on introspection. These books are interesting and important; Americans read them very frequently in translation; but they are almost as far removed from American life and needs as

274

are the study of the ancient Hebrew books, the Talmudic laws, and the mysteries of the Kaballah. The modern type of Russian youth was thus as far removed from American conditions, in one way, as the old-fashioned type was in another.

We can understand this sort of transition best by example; so I want to quote a little from the introduction of *The Promised Land,* written by Mary Antin: "All the processes of uprooting, transportation, replanting, acclimatization, and development, took place in my own soul. I can never forget, for I bear the scars. It is painful to be consciously of two worlds. . . . I am only one of those whose fate it has been to live a page of modern history. We are the strands of the cable that binds the Old World to the New. As the ships that brought us link the shores of Europe and America, so our lives span the bitter sea of racial differences and misunderstandings. . . . I began life in the Middle Ages, and here am I still, your contemporary in the twentieth century, thrilling with your latest thought."

IV. WHAT THE RUSSIAN JEWS DID IN AMERICA

MOST of the Russian Jews settled in New York and other eastern cities, and became workmen—the tailors, glaziers, and cigarmakers and those who had been merchants or traders in towns and villages of Europe. They were not all traders like the Germans, who scattered themselves in order to succeed in business. So at the outset they drifted into the needle trades in great numbers, and filled

History of the Jews in the United States

E. M. Lilien
AT THE SEWING-MACHINE

all the factories with Russian Jewish workers. Later they branched out, entered other lines of business; many were able to open factories of their own. But at first they were terribly crowded, overworked, and underpaid. The sweatshop was a characteristic evil; the small manufacturers gave out the garments to be sewed, and the workmen took them home, where the whole family might help, in the narrow, unsanitary East Side tenements.

The great majority of the Russian Jews, as many as 72 per cent of them, settled in New York City, where they were at first crowded together owing to their poverty and their desire to be with their countrymen. Later they expanded throughout New York City and the various surrounding cities; some of them scattered through the great industrial cities of the nation, where they might find work. But fewer of them found the small towns than had been the case among the Germans; more of them clung to the great cities, the factory work, if possible the ownership of factories themselves. Most conspicuous of

276

all was the enormous Jewish community of New York, which now numbers over 2,100,000, and which in its present form is largely the creation of Russian Jews.

Of course, there were attempts to scatter these Jews through the country, and especially to settle them on farms. In the eighties and nineties several farm colonies were founded in Louisiana, in South Dakota, in Connecticut and New Jersey. Most of them soon broke up, for the newcomers were ignorant of farming, especially in a new land and under strange conditions; they also had the handicap of limited funds and often of poor land. Only a few remain today, notably the one at Woodbine,

E. M. Lilien
TEARS ON THE IRON

New Jersey, which owed much to the help of Baron Maurice de Hirsch. This great German philanthropist desired to help the Russian Jews; he founded great funds to help them leave Russia, to settle them on the land in the United States and in the Argentine, to teach them trades and agriculture. The institutions thus

277

History of the Jews in the United States

founded helped many individuals to get a foothold in the new land, and also helped by serving as an example to the German Jews of America as givers, and to the other immigrants as an incentive. Later on there were founded from this same fund a Jewish Agricultural and Industrial Aid Society to assist would-be farmers, and an Industrial Removal Office to help Jews leave New York and settle through the land. But all these efforts could help only a few; the great mass of Russian Jews began as workmen in New York.

The children of these immigrants and often the immigrants themselves, very soon began to study in American colleges. As Russian universities had been closed to them, they grasped the opportunity for education when they had a chance to get it. Among the Jews of Russia, doctors and lawyers had constituted a sort of a nobility, with special privileges from the government, and had earned the admiration of their fellow-Jews to whom they were a credit. They retained these sentiments on coming to America; it was the greatest wish of any Russian Jew to see his son enter one of the professions. Soon they became crowded with clever boys, ambitious to succeed.

But this marked the second stage in the history of the Russian Jews, the stage of independence and self-help. At first the German Jews in pity for their co-religionists, had given them charity lavishly which some of them needed. Then the immigrants became self-sustaining, sent for their relatives and friends; soon most of the newcomers had relatives or friends to help them, and

278

The Third Wave of Immigration: From Russia

BARON MAURICE DE HIRSCH

needed little if any charitable aid. Then the German Jews began to found institutions to Americanize the Russian Jews, and incidentally to make them as much like themselves as possible. This was the second stage, and the reasons for it are clear. The German Jew felt that these new immigrants were so shockingly poor, ignorant, and foreign. Not knowing Yiddish, he looked down on it as an inferior form of the German which he himself had spoken on arrival. They, whose manners were still largely foreign, felt that the Russian Jews were foreigners and had uncouth manners. So, in entire kindness but with frequent misunderstanding, they tried to "civilize" and "Americanize" these Russian immigrants.

The third stage was the natural rebellion. After a while the Russian Jew began to feel both economically and culturally independent and resented domination. He rebelled against the control and even the guidance of the Germans, and began to found the distinctive institutions of his own life in America, which we shall study in

279

Todros Geller

MAXWELL STREET (FROM *The Ghetto* BY LOUIS WIRTH)

the next chapter. The fourth stage, in which we are now living, is one of growing cooperation and even of union between the German and Russian Jews, and the founding of organizations to represent American Jews as a whole.

REVIEW QUESTIONS

1. What were the reasons for the Russian Jews' coming to America?

280

The Third Wave of Immigration: From Russia

2. Describe their numbers, compared to the previous "waves" of immigration.
3. What were the special characteristics of the Russian immigrants? Compare with non-Jewish immigrants of this period; with Jewish immigrants of the period before.
4. What were their occupations?
5. Where did they live and why?

Topics for Reports

1. The immigration statistics, especially of Jews, during the various periods.
2. The Jews in Russia and Poland.
3. A description of the "Ghetto" of some American city, preferably New York.
4. The life of some Russian Jewish immigrant, such as Mary Antin.

References for Pupils

Wiernik, Peter, pp. 254–305.
Raisin, Max., pp. 293–344.
American Jewish Year Book for immigration statistics. Use the latest number available.
Much of the material for this period is in fiction form. See:
Antin, Mary, *The Promised Land.*
Asch, Sholom, *America.* Bloch.
Yezierska, Anzia, *Hungry Hearts.*
Yezierska, Anzia, *Bread Winners.*
Frank, Helena, *Yiddish Tales.* Jewish Publication Society.
Bogen, Boris D., *Born a Jew.* Macmillan.

References for Teachers

Joseph, S., *Jewish Immigration into the United States, 1881–1910.* Columbia University Press.
Bernheimer, Charles S., *The Russian Jew in the United States* (1905). John C. Winston Co.

281

History of the Jews in the United States

Friedlander, I., *The Jews of Russia and Poland* (a handy brief summary). Putnam.

Dubnow, S. M., *History of the Jews of Russia and Poland,* vol. II, chaps. xxiii, xxvii: vol. III, chap xxxiii. J. P. S.

Jewish Communal Register of New York City, 1917–1918. Bureau of Jewish Education.

Noble, *Russia and the Russians.* Houghton Mifflin Co.

Commons, John R., *Races and Immigrants in America.* Macmillan.

Stephenson, G. A., *History of American Immigration, 1820–1924.* Ginn & Co.

Steiner, E. A., *On the Trail of the Immigrant.* F. H. Revell.

Wirth, Louis, *The Ghetto,* chaps. x, xi. U. of Chicago Press.

Blaustein, Miriam, *Memoirs of David Blaustein.* McBride, Haft and Co.

Sabsovitch, K., *Adventures in Idealism.* Privately printed.

Asch, Sholom, *Uncle Moses.* Dutton.

Cahan, Abraham, *The Rise of David Levinsky.* Harper.

Goldstein, Herbert S., *Forty Years of Struggle for a Principle. The Biography of Harry Fischel.* Bloch.

Judean Addresses, vol. II; A. Leroy-Beaulieu, "Jewish Immigrants and Judaism in the U. S.," pp. 33–51; Henry Moskowitz, "A Quarter Century of the Jewish Immigrant in America," pp. 160–9.

CHAPTER 18.

The Cultural Institutions of the Russian Jews

A S WE have seen, the needs of the German Jewish immigrants were not entirely satisfied by the synagogue, as had been the case among the Sephardim; they founded their own charities and lodges. In the same way, the Russian Jews were not satisfied with the charities and lodges; their typical institutions became those for education and Jewish culture. They were the source of Zionism and Jewish nationalism, on the one hand, and of a wealth of economic and cultural organizations, on the other. Their life was thus even more secularized than that of the German Jew, but it was a Jewish secularism, not a German or American secularism. It was more of a group life than that of the German Jew, who restricted his special activities to a few interests such as the temple, the religious school, the charitable organization, the lodge. It included special newspapers and theatres, labor unions and community center buildings, with clubs and literary societies. All these peculiar institutions of the Russian Jew were in addition to their synagogues and charities, which largely resembled those of the earlier immigrants.

History of the Jews in the United States

I. THE SYNAGOGUES AND CHARITIES

SYNAGOGUES they had in abundance. Beside the one or two stately temples of the German Jews, arose in every city a multitude of little orthodox synagogues. The people of every province or city in eastern Europe established their own synagogue, where they came together to worship, exchange news of the home town, collect their contributions for charity, and conduct their whole social life as foreigners in a strange land. These synagogues were strictly orthodox in the Russian fashion, based entirely on Hebrew learning and Jewish law, and with no regard for outside culture or ideas. But in time, as the Russian Jews learned from their predecessors in America, many of them changed their viewpoint, joining the reform or conservative congregations. At the same time the strictly orthodox synagogues adopted a more modern point of view and formed a national association, the Union of Orthodox Jewish Congregations of America, on the pattern of the Union of American Hebrew Congregations, (which they would not join). They brought over Rabbi Jacob Joseph from Russia to be a chief rabbi for the Jews of New York, though that plan failed, owing to lack of united effort. But with their tremendous numbers, their growing wealth and Americanism, they both built up their own orthodox congregations, and overflowed in considerable numbers, bringing new blood and new devoutness into the older reform and conservative temples.

284

The Cultural Institutions of the Russian Jews

The same was true of the charities. The Russian Jew soon came to resent being the object of charity for the German Jew. He wanted to help himself, to have something to say about the mode of giving charity, to be influential in its control, if not quite independent. For example, the Russians wanted Jewish hospitals to serve kosher meals to patients; they wanted the children of orthodox Jews in orphan homes taught according to what their parents would have liked rather than according to the idea of the donors and governors of the orphan home, who might be reform Jews. They objected bitterly to the tendency of the Educational Alliance, which was placed in East Broadway, New York, to "Americanize" them, for they felt that their young people would pick up American ways quickly enough, and needed most of all to be taught Judaism. They felt, besides, that they did not want to become mere imitations of the German Jews; they had always lived an intense group life in Russia, with their own language, law, and many of the characteristics of a nation. The German Jews had wanted to become Americans of the Jewish faith, but the Russian Jews had been used to living as a Jewish nationality among the many nationalities of Russia, differing from them in culture; they wanted to continue, at least partly, in that type of life in America. Living closely together in communities of many thousands, even hundreds of thousands, they could easily do this. They became American citizens, entered politics, sent their children to universities; became active Americans; yet at the same time they kept up their Jewish life, not only in synagogue and charity, but in the cultural institutions typical of the Russian Jew.

II. YIDDISH AND HEBREW

THIS culture was of two types, according to its two languages, Yiddish and Hebrew. The popular form was, of course, in Yiddish, the language which was generally spoken by the immigrants. Yiddish theatres were founded, Yiddish newspapers established, Yiddish books printed. The language had begun to be a literary one in Europe, and now in America it developed a literature of its own. The Yiddish newspapers, which had been forbidden in Russia, are a typical example. There were attempts to start them in America as early as 1872, but the first successful one was the *Jewish Daily News,* established in New York in 1885 by Kasriel R. Sarasohn; this paper united with the *Jewish Morning Journal* in 1928. Just two years later another successful paper, the *Courier,* was established in Chicago. In 1930 there were four daily Yiddish papers in New York alone, two of them representing the orthodox and Zionist Jews, two the socialist and radical element; beside these, there were weekly and monthly journals. At the same time, the development of Yiddish fiction, poetry and drama in the United States has been remarkable.

The Yiddish theatre has been especially interesting, for it is strictly an American development, going far beyond anything ever done in that language in Europe.

286

The Cultural Institutions of the Russian Jews

Jacob Gordin

Its founder was Abraham Goldfaden, whose opera, *Shulamith*, is still often played. Its outstanding writer for many years was Jacob Gordin, who wrote seventy plays, some original and some translated from other languages. For some years the Yiddish theatre became more vaudeville than drama, but finally there came a revival. In 1918 Maurice Schwartz founded the Yiddish Art Theatre, which has since produced remarkable original plays by excellent writers. This company once attracted admiration from many general theatre-goers, who were unable to understand Yiddish, in which Schwartz acted, but went anyway for his interesting plays and brilliant acting.

But the religious interest of the orthodox immigrants was chiefly expressed in the Hebrew language, the language of prayer. So the Russian type of Hebrew schools, the little Cheder or room, the larger Talmud Torah or organized daily school, sprang up. At first, they were poor, disorganized, and gave the children a very bad education; later they were well systematized,

287

with fine, big buildings and well trained teachers; teaching every afternoon after public school; adding Jewish history, religion and similar topics to the study of the Hebrew language, and giving a far more solid Jewish training than a Sunday School possibly could. The first modern Talmud Torah in New York was founded in 1882. Above these elementary schools, there were attempts to found yeshiboth, or advanced schools for Talmudic study; the most modernized as well as most important of these today is the Rabbi Isaac Elchanan Theological Seminary in New York, which was founded in 1896, after the Russian immigrants had become numerous and many of them were already thoroughly established in America. The Maskilim, the modern Hebrew scholars of Russia, had an offshoot in America, too, so that the writing of Hebrew books, Hebrew periodicals, the development of Hebrew as a modern language, was another cultural activity of a certain group of Russian immigrants.

The whole process appears most clearly in the institutions for Jewish social life. At first there were settlements, educational and Americanizing agencies, started by the rich German Jews to help the poor Russian Jews grow to be like them. But the poor Russian Jews did not always respond. They began to develop their own neighborhood groups, having the synagogue or Hebrew school as a center. The characteristic Jewish institutions of the Russian immigrant came to be the community center or neighborhood center; this provided for social life and athletics, but its real purpose was the Hebrew school, which made it a cultural center for Jewish life. Their object was to adapt the young to American life as Jews, and to preserve their Judaism.

III. ZIONISM

THE German Jews had considered themselves a religious group only; but the Russian Jews felt that they represented a Jewish nationality. The great effort made in Germany to become German citizens; the deep impress received from the poetry and story of the Fatherland; the reform movement with its dropping of the prayers for the Messiah, the restoration of the sacrifices and the miraculous return to Palestine,—all these worked together in making the reform Jews turn against the national theory of Jewish life. Their motto, many times repeated, was laid down at the dedication of the first reform temple in the United States, at Charleston, in 1841: "This country is our Palestine, this city our Jerusalem, this house of God our Temple." They wanted to be exactly like all other Americans except for their religion. They felt that religion was the one element in the long history and life of the Jew which they needed and which must continue for them. In everything else, language, law, history, they identified themselves with American life; as Kaufmann Kohler, their outstanding thinker, phrased it, they considered the Jew a people, but primarily a religious people, whose chief distinction in the modern world is his religion.

289

History of the Jews in the United States

But the Jews of Russia came from a land where they felt themselves, and were called by others, the "Jewish nation." Eastern Europe did not have the western view of citizenship, shared on equal terms by all the inhabitants of a certain land; it had the older view, of many nationalities living under the same monarch. Among these many nationalities the Jews were counted as one. In addition, they felt that the government of Russia was their enemy; they felt themselves in exile in Russia, and longed eagerly for a return to the home of their ancestors in Palestine.

A different conception of Jewish life thus grew up in Russia, bred by the conditions of the Jews there and by their intense Jewish education and Jewish life. This was the idea of Jewish culture, of Jewish nationalism as a life of a people without a land but with its own learning, customs, loyalty and ideas. Religion without national life, they said, was not the old Jewish teaching, nor would it preserve the Jews as a people in the modern world, when they had no Ghetto forced on them to keep them separate.

But nationalism without religion, a nationalism of armies and governments, was not Jewish either, and has not been since the destruction of the Jewish state. Jewish nationalism, to these thinkers, was a life of a scattered people, who lived in their synagogues, schools and books; in their memories and in their hopes. They wrote in Hebrew or in Yiddish, two distinctly Jewish languages. Although not all the Russian Jews were nation-

alists, many of their writings led directly to Zionism; others of them expressed the idea of a Jewish nationality in dispersion.

It must be remembered that the Russian Jew coming
to America underwent the same process of change as the
German Jew had before him, but that he did not turn
into a German Jew. He began with a much different
background, and with a different outlook on Jewish life,
so that both the German and the Russian grew in the
same direction, but neither one came to imitate the other.
Hence, the Russian Jew in America, as in his former
home in eastern Europe, was ready and eager to take up
the new theory of Zionism when it was propounded.

The early nationalist writers included German Jews
such as Rabbi Hirsch Kalischer and Moses Hess; and
east European thinkers, such as Pinsker and Smolenskin.

Modern political Zionism was begun in 1896 by Theodor Herzl, a brilliant journalist of Vienna, who reported
the Dreyfus trial in France, saw how a Jew was hounded
even in that liberal republic, and was convinced that
the Jews needed a home land of their own. His first
step was to publish a book, *Der Judenstaat,* (The Jewish
State), in 1896; his second, was to call the first Zionist
Congress at Basle, Switzerland, in 1897. The aim of the
movement according to the Basle Program was: "The establishment for the Jewish people of a publicly and
legally assured home in Palestine." At the same time a
great Hebrew writer in Russia, known as Ahad Ha'am
(One of the People), founded cultural Zionism, the ideal

of a center of Hebraic culture in the ancient Land of Israel. The two hopes, the political center and the cultural center, also enlisted much interest of philanthropically minded Jews, who felt that Palestine might become a place of refuge for the oppressed of eastern Europe.

The Russian Jew in America was fertile soil for the development of this movement; he had the nationalistic sympathy, and in addition was building up wealth and power to support it. However, some of the American Zionist leaders had been reform Jews, even though the greater number of the reform Jews at first either opposed the movement or were indifferent to it. The first convention in the United States to form a Zionist movement was held shortly after the one at Basle; the first president was Professor Richard Gottheil of Columbia University, and the first secretary, Rabbi Stephen S. Wise. As the movement grew, it published organs in Yiddish and English, established branches for women, children and college students; further parties sprang up, of orthodox Zionists, Socialist Zionists, and so on. Two of these at least, are familiar to you,—the Young Judea clubs for children, and Hadassah, the women's branch, which takes charge of medical work in Palestine. Other leaders of great ability joined the movement: Judge Julian Mack, Justice Louis D. Brandeis of the United States Supreme Court, who was president of the organization in America before his elevation to that dignity, and Louis Lipsky, for several years president of the Zionist Organization of America and a member of the world executive committee,

292

who has given a life-time of devoted service as secretary, writer, speaker and worker for Zionism.

A great part of the program of Zionism was realized by the World War. The British government in 1917 gave out the famous Balfour Declaration: "His Majesty's government views with favor the establishment in Palestine of a national home for the Jewish people and will use its best endeavor to facilitate the achievement of this object." Naturally, this gave a great impetus to the movement in America, as in every land the world over. The various allied and associated powers in turn accepted this statement, so that patriotic American Jews, who might be personally opposed to Zionism, could no longer claim that the movement was in any way contrary to American loyalty. The Congress of the United States passed a resolution endorsing this program in 1922, the same year that the League of Nations adopted the British mandatory over Palestine, which included the Balfour Declaration. The Zionist movement is now one of the sincere expressions of a large group of American Jews.

IV. THE JEWISH LABOR MOVEMENT

WHEN the Russian Jews came to America, many of them happened to drift into the needle trades, the making of men's and women's clothing. At that time, these were largely carried on in sweatshops, small tenement workshops where the whole family might work on garments which the father took home from the jobber. The hours were terribly long, the conditions unhealthy, the pay too small to live on with any comfort at all. Most of the workmen were plain people, religious Jews who wanted to make a living and were not concerned with socialism or any other economic theory. But conditions drove them to organize in self-defense, and their leaders were largely of the young Russian intellectuals who have already been described, who believed in the rights of the working class; they showed them how to organize for their own benefit, and led them in the great strikes by which they won their rights and made a place for themselves in the American labor movement.

True, not all the leaders were radicals. One of the greatest leaders that American labor has ever had was a Jew (though of English, not of Russian origin), Samuel Gompers. For forty years he was president of the American Federation of Labor, the great federation of hundreds of separate unions, in which the Jews were only a small element. He believed in a conservative labor union policy, keeping out of politics, sticking to matters that concerned the laborers closely like wages and hours, bargaining for these when he could and striking for them when he had to. Gompers is important as a man and a labor leader, but not from the Jewish viewpoint; he had no Jewish interests himself.

The great labor union movement arose among the masses of Jewish workmen, of which those in the garment trades are the most important. The first Jewish union was formed as early as 1877, but the real growth came

The Cultural Institutions of the Russian Jews

MEYER LONDON

when there were more Jewish workmen and when they had worked together long enough to know each other and to realize their oppression. In the early nineties there was a great series of strikes in different branches of the needle trades, in which the workmen suffered severely but by which they learned to work together and won better conditions of working and of living. Many individuals rose out of the ranks of the workmen and opened factories of their own, but the masses found that they could only rise together.

One of the daring strike leaders of those days was Joseph Barondess, himself a Russian immigrant, who remained a leader of the Jewish masses until his death in 1928. Two others were Socialists, the writer Abraham Cahan and the lawyer Morris Hillquit. These men also were born in Russia, came to America at an early age, and therefore combined a thorough mastery of English and Yiddish, so that they were able to appeal directly to the Yiddish speaking workers and also to represent them to the American public.

History of the Jews in the United States

Cahan was famous as the editor of the *Forward,* the most popular Yiddish daily in the world, which sold 150,000 copies a day. It is a Socialist and labor paper in editorial policy, and prints both the Jewish and the general news of the day. Cahan also produced a number of books in both English and Yiddish, including fiction and works on history and economics.

Morris Hillquit wrote a *History of Socialism in the United States.* He has acted as the lawyer for many labor unions, occupied high position in the Socialist party, and he often ran for public office on its ticket.

So the Jewish labor unions found their leaders and their strength. The labor movement in America owes much to these immigrants who learned so quickly from their American neighbors, organized themselves, brought whole trades into the labor movement, and raised the level of living through the needle trades in many of the great cities of the country.

Part of the great Jewish labor movement is radical in politics and stands against religion, following the radical leadership which they accepted. A very large part of these Russian Jewish workmen, however, are still religious and Zionistic in their ideas and ideals, even though they have learned to work together in labor unions for their own benefit.

Review Questions

1. What were the Russian Jewish synagogues like?
2. Describe the Hebrew schools, elementary and advanced.
3. What is the Jewish Center movement? Why did the Russian Jews start their own institutions?

296

The Cultural Institutions of the Russian Jews

4. Give the purpose of Zionism; its development in America.
5. Why was a Jewish labor movement started? What was it like? How did it develop?

TOPICS FOR REPORTS

1. Zionism, its beginnings and development the world over.
2. The old arguments for and against Zionism among American Jews.
3. The Jewish labor movement, compared with the American Federation of Labor.
4. The Jewish Press, in Yiddish and Hebrew.
5. The Hebrew Schools; the Yiddish nationalist schools.
6. The reasons for the extremes of orthodoxy and radicalism among Russian Jews, with illustrations from their institutions.

REFERENCES FOR PUPILS

Most of the material for the previous chapter is useful here as well There are some additional books, of course.

Sampter, Jessie E., *Guide to Zionism*. Bloch.

Jewish Encyclopedia, art. on United States and various special articles.

The Outlook, January 5, 1916, art. on Zionism by Louis D. Brandeis (for Zionism), and Samuel Schulman (against Zionism).

Wiernik, Peter, pp. 297–305.

REFERENCES FOR TEACHERS

Gottheil, R., *Zionism*. Jewish Publication Society.

Stein, Leonard, *Zionism*. Adelphi Co.

Jastrow, Morris, *Zionism and the Future of Palestine* (the best statement of opposition to Zionism). Macmillan.

Schulman, Samuel, "The Searching of the Jewish Heart." *Menorah Journal*, April, 1918.

History of the Jews in the United States

Soltes, M., *The Yiddish Press as an Americanizing Agency*. Teachers College, Columbia University.

Dushkin, A. M., *Jewish Education in New York City*, pp. 63–99.

Park, R. M., *The Immigrant Press and Its Control*. Harper.

Hourwich, Isaac, *Immigration and Labor*. Putnam.

Levine, Louis, *The Women's Garment Workers*. Huebsch.

Friedlander, I., *Past and Present*, chaps. xv, xviii, xx, xxiv. Ark Publishing Co.

Hapgood, H., *The Spirit of the Ghetto*.

Publications of the American Jewish Historical Society.

> Eisenstein, J. D., "History of the First Russian-American Jewish Congregation," vol. IX, p. 63.

CHAPTER 19.

Outstanding Jews of the Second Half of the Century

THE second half of the nineteenth century offers a bewildering variety of interesting and important people, the lives of several of these extending over into the twentieth century. From all of them six very different people have been selected for special study: an encyclopedist, a woman poet, a Jewish leader in public life, a financier and philanthropist, a world organizer of farmers, and an American statesman. Of these one was of Sephardic descent, three were born in Germany, and two in eastern Europe.

I. MICHAEL HEILPRIN, 1823–1888

THE earliest of these, peculiarly enough, was of Polish birth, and one of the early Polish Jews in America. Michael Heilprin came to America in 1856, at the age of thirty-three, when he was a mature scholar and writer. His chief work was as writer for the *Nation,* for the last twenty years of his life, and as one of the editors of Appleton's *New American Cyclopedia*. He also wrote a monumental work on the *Historical Poetry of the Ancient Hebrews*. These things would not have been very remarkable except for the man behind them. He was a great scholar, a great lover of the Jewish people, a great fighter for freedom for all peoples.

Michael Heilprin was the sort of man who seemed to study everything and to remember everything; he had a really encyclopedic type of mind. He knew Hebrew,

© *Dodd, Mead & Co. From "Michael Heilprin and His Son" by Gustav Pollak*

MICHAEL HEILPRIN

Polish, Hungarian, French, and Spanish; he studied English from a copy of Gibbon's *Decline and Fall of the Roman Empire* before he came to this country, so that he might feel at home in the language as soon as he arrived. Two years after his coming here, a foreigner and unknown, he was already on the staff of a great encyclopedia, writing long articles on all sorts of difficult historical subjects and checking up and revising dozens of articles submitted by other writers. The writer on an encyclopedia is usually an unknown man; he works in the dark, but he is a great teacher of his age. Michael Heilprin did most of his writing in this anonymous way, both for Appleton's and for the *Nation*.

But he has been noted in this history for two things,

300

both connected with his historic sense and his love of freedom. The first was the struggle against human slavery. Heilprin had lived in Hungary as a young man and knew the fight for liberation in that land; he was a profound student of Jewish history, and shared the horror of oppression which the Jews suffered for so many centuries, and which they were still suffering in the lands whence he had fled to come to America. So he issued the most notable refutation of Rabbi Raphall's statement that the Bible and the Jewish religion approved of slavery.

This statement was most important at that time in two ways; it helped make sentiment for abolition, and it set the Jews right before the people of the country as not being altogether Southern sympathizers, as the prominence of Judah P. Benjamin might have made the Unionists believe. Throughout the Civil War, Heilprin lived in Washington, where he was able to keep in close touch with the great events of the time and to help the cause of abolition with his pen.

As we have seen, Michael Heilprin was a great Hebraist; he loved the ancient tongue which he had learned as a boy, and the people from whom he had sprung. His only active connection with the Jews, beside his writing, however, was with the colonization of the new Russian immigrants on the soil of America. He believed ardently that the Russian Jew, who had been forced to live in cities and become a trader, might again become a farmer in a free land

Hardly anybody believed this, so Heilprin was both original and courageous in making the effort. He was one of the organizers of the Montefiore Agricultural Aid Society, which raised money and assisted immigrants to settle on the land; he founded ten colonies of Jewish farmers in Oregon, North and South Dakota, New Jersey, and Kansas. He gave up his entire time to this work, laboring untiringly among the new arrivals who needed aid and the older settlers who might give money; in the end, he worked himself to death in this devoted service.

Of these colonies, all but one, Carmel, in New Jersey, have disappeared; the colonists were not experienced farmers. They met difficult conditions, or could not work together. But as a result of this effort, there are now thousands of Jewish farmers scattered through the United States, and Baron de Hirsch became so much interested in the problem that he gave millions of dollars to assist in this type of work.

While Michael Heilprin's labor for his people did not accomplish all he hoped, it had a fine influence on the future of the Jew in America.

The sons of Michael Heilprin were almost as well known in their day as their father: Angelo Heilprin, naturalist, traveller, writer, and lecturer at Yale; and Louis Heilprin, a quiet encyclopedic scholar after the pattern of his father but without his father's urge for public service. They were a great family and only a foreshadowing of what the East European Jew might some day accomplish in the United States.

Outstanding Jews, Second Half of the Century

REFERENCES

Jewish Encyclopedia, art., Agricultural Colonies.
Pollak, Gustav, *Michael Heilprin and His Sons*.
Wiernik, Peter, pp. 208–211.
Raisin, Max, pp. 296–300.
Mielziner, Ella M., Moses Mielziner, chap. on "Slavery and Judaism in America."

II. EMMA LAZARUS, 1849–1887

THE second of these interesting Jews is a young woman who was born in New York of Sephardic ancestry, and lived there during her thirty-eight years; before her early death she wrote poems which have made dear her name to the American Jew. Probably you have read and recited many of her poems in your religious schools, for she is a favorite writer on Jewish themes.

EMMA LAZARUS

Emma Lazarus, however, did not begin as a writer for the Jewish people. She began by writing poems in the best style of the day, on conventional themes of young poets, about nature and in imitation of the ancient Greeks. She was a friend of Ralph Waldo Emerson and of other noted men, who saw her genius and

303

encouraged it; but her work was not remarkable until she received her great inspiration from the persecution of the Russian Jews and from seeing some of them arrive in this new Land of Promise. The rich young writer came down from her aristocratic home to work among them. From that time she became a real Jew, full of enthusiasm and power. She began to study Hebrew, Jewish history, and the Bible; she went back to the sources of Jewish life. She wrote such inspiring poetry as "The Banner of the Jew" and "Gifts," which have expressed the Jewish spirit so well for the American Jews. She wrote the fine sonnet which was cast in bronze and placed at the base of the Statue of Liberty in New York harbor, a poem which every Jewish youth ought to know:

THE NEW COLOSSUS

Not like the brazen giant of Greek fame,
With conquering limbs astride from land to land,
Here at our sea-washed, sunset gates shall stand
A mighty woman with a torch, whose flame
Is the imprisoned lightning, and her name
Mother of Exiles. From her beacon-hand
Glows world-wide welcome; her mild eyes command
The air-bridged harbor that twin-cities frame.

"Keep, ancient lands, your storied pomp!" Cries she,
With silent lips. "Give me your tired, your poor,
Your huddled masses yearning to breathe free,
The wretched refuse of your teeming shore,
Send these, the homeless, tempest-tost to me.
I lift my lamp beside the golden door!"

Outstanding Jews, Second Half of the Century

Then there is her poem about the Russian massacres
of 1881, "The Crowing of the Red Cock":

Across the Eastern sky has glowed
    The flicker of a blood-red dawn,
Once more the clarion cock has crowed,
    Once more the sword of Christ is drawn.
A million burning rooftrees light
The world-wide path of Israel's flight.

Where is the Hebrew's fatherland?
    The folk of Christ is sore bestead;
The Son of Man is bruised and banned,
    Nor finds whereon to rest his head.
His cup is gall, his meat is tears,
His passion lasts a thousand years.

Each crime that wakes in man the beast
    Is visited upon his kind,
The lust of mobs, the greed of priest,
    The tyranny of kings, combined
To root his seed from earth again;
His record is one cry of pain.

When the long roll of Christian guilt
    Against his sires and kin is known,
The flood of tears, the life-blood spilt,
    The agony of ages shown,
What oceans can the stain remove,
From Christian law and Christian love?

Nay, close the book; not now, not here,
    The hideous tale of sin narrate,
Reechoing in the martyr's ear,
    Even he might nurse revengeful hate,
Even he might turn in wrath sublime,
With blood for blood and crime for crime.

305

History of the Jews in the United States

Coward? Not he, who faces death,
   Who singly against worlds has fought,
For what? A name he may not breathe,
   For liberty of prayer and thought.
The angry sword he will not whet,
His noblest task is—to forget.

Jewish Encyclopedia, art. on Emma Lazarus.
Wiernik, Peter, pp. 263–266.
Raisin, Max, pp. 289–291.
Abrahams, Israel, *Bypaths in Hebraic Bookland,* pp. 319–324.
Poems of Emma Lazarus, 2 vols. with memoir.

III. SIMON WOLF, 1836–1923

WE HAVE already heard of Simon Wolf as a young man in Washington during the Civil War. But he lived for eighty-seven years altogether, during the whole German and Russian periods of our history, and right up almost to the present day. His was an eventful life in an eventful time, and one deserving of mention by itself. He will be mentioned again in the next chapter, for in many cases of the violation of Jewish rights abroad, Simon Wolf was instrumental in bringing the matter to the attention of the American government.

He was brought to America when twelve years old, and all his life was the typical German liberal and humanitarian. He preferred serving others, whether as a public official, a lodge officer, or an unpaid advocate of Jewish immigrants or of German non-Jewish immigrants, to his own private law practice. He loved to speak and to write

Outstanding Jews, Second Half of the Century

SIMON WOLF

on these, his favorite topics. As he spoke and wrote extremely well, he was a favorite orator and literary representative of the Jews in America. For sixty years he was a sort of ambassador of world Jewry at Washington, sympathizing with every person and leading in every cause except Zionism, for which he had the dislike of his origin and his generation.

The record of his long life consists chiefly of the many offices he held. The real spirit of the man is revealed by reading any part of his big book, *The Presidents I Have Known, 1860 to 1918,* or by looking over his wonderful study of American Jewish history, *The American Jew as Patriot, Soldier, and Citizen.* The reader of these books is sure to feel the deep interest in the Jewish cause which led Simon Wolf to spend unending hours of unpaid labor making that list of over 7,000 Jewish soldiers in the Civil War. In these books appears the spirit of service, the desire to do something for other people, which brought him to Lincoln to plead the cause of the Jewish deserter; which led him before

History of the Jews in the United States

President Taft in 1911 to plead for the abrogation of the treaty with Russia; which made him for a period of over forty years the advocate of thousands of Russian immigrants who came before the Bureau of Labor for deportation.

He founded an orphan asylum at Atlanta, and the income from his books went to its support. He was president of the reform congregation in Washington, international president of the Independent Order B'nai B'rith, the Washington representative of that Order for a generation or more, officer of the Board of Delegates of American Israelites during its existence up to 1878, and after that the chairman of its successor, the Board of Delegates on Civil Rights of the Union of American Hebrew Congregations, for another thirty-three years.

In addition, Simon Wolf held two government appointments, Recorder for the District of Columbia, from 1869 to 1878 on appointment of President Grant; and Consul-General to Egypt in 1881 under President Garfield.

In the former case, he tells that he might not have accepted the position; but when his appointment was opposed because he was a Jew, he felt it his duty to fight for the place, to win it, and then to carry on its duties to the best of his ability, in order that he might justify his people as well as himself.

A liberal, a German, a Jew, a patriotic American— Simon Wolf was the typical man of his generation, and rendered a lasting service to his country.

308

Outstanding Jews, Second Half of the Century

REFERENCES

American Jewish Year Book 5685, art. "Simon Wolf," by
  Max J. Kohler, reprinted in Wolf's *Selected Addresses
  and Papers.*
Jewish Encyclopedia, art. on Simon Wolf.
Wolf, Simon, *The Presidents I Have Known.*

IV. JACOB HENRY SCHIFF, 1847–1920

JACOB H. SCHIFF was another German who found his
career in America, and who was probably the best known
Jew of his generation in this country as financier, philanthropist and leader of the Jews. Simon Wolf was thin,
nervous, excitable; but Jacob Schiff was more the German as we imagine him, short, solid in build, conservative
and systematic in mind, loyal and at the same time
sympathetic in his sentiments.

He came from an aristocratic background, an old
family of rabbis and business men in Frankfort on the
Main, Germany, the most aristocratic Jewish community
of Europe. At the age of eighteen he left for America,
and ten years later was admitted as a member of the
firm of Kuhn, Loeb and Co., private bankers. His entire
business career was as a member of this firm, for most
of the time as its head. In this capacity, he loaned
money for the building of great railroads, and financed
the undertakings of men such as Harriman and Hill, who
opened the empire of the west to settlement. He financed
many other business enterprises, and through their success he and his firm became immensely wealthy, until
they were the second private banking firm in America.

309

History of the Jews in the United States

In this business career, it is interesting to note that his far-sighted knowledge of conditions and his personal sympathies went hand in hand. He travelled across America several times, and understood the expansion of railroads through the west. His firm loaned huge sums to Japan during the Russo-Japanese War,

JACOB H. SCHIFF

for which he was later awarded a high Japanese decoration; but he refused to deal with Russia on account of her general medievalism, and especially her unjust treatment of the Russian Jews. Even during the World War, his firm loaned money to individual Allies, but would not allow a cent of it to go to Czarist Russia, and participated fully in the Allied loans only after the Russian Revolution, when it was certain the money would not be spent to help the persecutors of the Jews.

Such an immensely wealthy and successful business man could help Jewish causes on an unprecedented scale if he wished; Jacob Schiff was the sort of man who actively sought out worthy causes to help. He was himself well educated in Hebrew and in Jewish lore, so that he

310

was equally interested in the promotion of Jewish learning, in helping of Jews in distress, and in the advancement of the Jews in general culture and in Americanism.

He was the most remarkable builder of institutions there has ever been among American Jews. Here are a few illustrations of this rather extravagant claim. In New York alone he erected buildings for the Young Men's Hebrew Association, the Jewish Theological Seminary, and one of the buildings at Barnard College. He made possible the building for the Semitic Museum at Harvard University, established Jewish departments in the New York Public Library and the Library of Congress, furnished the money for the translation of the Bible into English and for the translation of the Jewish Classics— and so on.

There is no use expanding such a list, but it is important to notice that all these gifts and many more did not go out carelessly or without his personal knowledge; he sat on the boards of many of these institutions, met their patients, talked with their workers. In the Montefiore Home, of which he was president for many years, and which was his pet charity, he used to spend many hours talking to the patients, eating their regular fare with them, not only helping them from outside, but trying to see the world from the angle of their poverty and misery.

The third important work of Jacob Schiff was Jewish leadership; he did not seek this like Simon Wolf, for

History of the Jews in the United States

he was not by temperament a public man, but it was forced on him because of his great wealth and influence, and also because of the confidence which people had in him.

He was one of the founders in 1906 of the American Jewish Committee to protect Jewish rights the world over, and was one of the leaders in gaining abrogation of the Russian treaty with the United States in 1911, because the Russian government would not honor the American passport if it was carried by a Jew. He was interested in the cultural and economic development of Palestine, but never joined the Zionist movement, because he felt that his interest in and loyalty to Jewry was essentially a religious one.

The clue to all Jacob Schiff's good works is found in the fact that he was a good Jew, pious in his home life, observing the Jewish customs carefully, loving Jewish learning, feeling a little more sympathy for the Jewish cause than he did for the many non-Jewish causes to which he also gave money. There was a warmth of feeling about him, for he gave of his heart as well as of his wealth.

REFERENCES

Jewish Encyclopedia, art. on Jacob H. Schiff.
American Jewish Year Book 5682, art. by Cyrus Adler, "Jacob H. Schiff, A Biographical Sketch," pp. 21 ff.
Adler, Cyrus, *Jacob H. Schiff, His Life and Letters,* 2 vols. (an important work on the man and the period in which he lived).

312

Outstanding Jews, Second Half of the Century

THE next man whom we shall study, David Lubin, was another man of wealth (though not as wealthy as Jacob Schiff), who also used his leisure for public work. But instead of giving as a philanthropist to many causes and establishing hundreds of worthy works on a solid basis, he devoted himself to one life enthusiasm, a world-wide movement for the farmers of every land. Jacob Schiff was a quiet, steady thinker, a business man, who considered every matter that came before him with the same sane judgment; David Lubin was a

DAVID LUBIN

dreamer, an enthusiast, who forgot himself in one great cause.

Some of this may be traced to his background in Russian Poland where he was born in 1849. When he was an infant four days old, the wick of the Sabbath candle flew off and burned his face, leaving a scar that lasted

313

all his life. His mother cried at the injury done the baby, but the mystical rabbi of the little community scolded her; the child was marked for God's service; he should be named after David the king and in days to come was destined to do a great work!

When David was just six years old, his parents brought him to New York, for as we know, a few Russian Jews were coming to America as early as 1855. The adventurous youngster attempted to join the army during the Civil War, tried to run away to sea, and finally left school at the age of twelve and went to work. From that time on he shifted for himself, making a trip across the continent to San Francisco, joining a prospecting expedition in Arizona, when he was lost two days in the desert without food or water, then returning east to his family. In 1874 when he was twenty-five years old, David Lubin went to California again and opened a store in Sacramento. In that rough mining camp, he had the first "one-price" store, refused to bargain with anybody about the price of goods, and won everybody's respect for his honesty and fair dealing. As the business grew he became interested in broader problems of transportation, tariff, and especially of farming. He was one of the early advocates of the parcels post, which is now such a convenience; he studied soils and methods by which the California farmers might raise the best products for the market, and then how they might best transport and sell them so as to get a fair return for their hard work. His knowledge of the Jewish prophets and the lessons

314

they had taught, influenced him in his love of right and fair dealing and he felt that the place to begin was in fair dealing for the farmer. So he worked, wrote, talked, argued for the cause in his state and throughout the nation.

At last he grew to feel that the problems and needs of the farmer were world-wide, that no permanent good could come until they were studied from the standpoint of how much food was produced the world over, where it was, how much it cost to bring it to market, where it was needed and who was to eat it. In other words, he believed that the welfare of the people who raise the food products of the world and those who eat them can be advanced together or not at all, and that this must be done over the entire earth if it is to attain any results. So he decided to induce some monarch of a great nation to found an International Institute of Agriculture. This Jewish merchant of California, without special influence or standing, without any schooling, without the easy manners of the courts, a big rough man who had learned how to handle people in an Arizona mining camp, set out to conquer and convince the diplomats and rulers of the earth. The amazing thing is that he succeeded so completely.

The United States Department of Agriculture would not have anything to do with him because of his politics, so he went to Europe. Within three weeks of his arrival in Rome, he had an interview with the King of Italy; he convinced in turn ministers, professors, and newspaper

315

men, until in 1905 King Victor Emanuel III issued a letter, calling a conference of nations to found an Institute of Agriculture, and acknowledging his indebtedness for the idea to "Mr. David Lubin, a citizen of the United States." Three years later, nation after nation having been convinced, forty-five countries joined in what was the first permanent international cooperation in the world, the precursor of the League of Nations with its permanent bureaus. Nothing like this idea of the California merchant had ever been known before. Lubin shocked people who were used to court etiquette, offended those who were accustomed to diplomacy; but he convinced the practical men in industry and government both of his personal honesty and the greatness of his idea, and they worked for him and with him.

David Lubin was appointed the first representative of the United States in this Institute which he had founded. The King of Italy gave a splendid building for its use; the nations sent their official representatives and their technical experts, and the work began. Reports of crops of every kind, in every part of the world, gathered honestly, given out fairly for the benefit of the common people of every nation, and particularly of the farmers, this was the commodity in which the Institute dealt. This first international organization was the only international effort to continue throughout the World War, an indication of its importance as it grew. For ten years David Lubin sat in it as the representative of the United States, working equally for the American farmer and for the common man the world over. He wrote home about cooperative marketing and cooperative banking as he saw and studied them in Europe. He began various agitations and movements for the benefit of the farmers of the world. Most of all, he longed for peace, for that peace and justice of which the prophets dreamed so long ago, and he felt that the International Institute of Agriculture, which he had founded, would be a great step toward that mighty goal. He died in Rome, the city of his great effort and his great triumph, at the age of seventy, overflowing to the last with fiery enthusiasm, never ceasing his untiring labors for his cause.

REFERENCES

Olivia Rossetti Agresti: *David Lubin, a Study in Practical Idealism.*

VI. OSCAR S. STRAUS, 1850–1926

THE last of these outstanding Jews was from Germany, a lawyer and statesman, the first Jew to occupy a cabinet post in the United States, the first to be ambassador of the United States to a foreign land,—after Judah P. Benjamin, probably the most prominent Jew in American public life. He was more like Jacob Schiff in personality than any of the others, for he also was sober, systematic, and successful; his genius also was eminently of a practical sort, but with a constant search for the ideal which motivated the practical effort and made it appeal to him.

Twice before in this story we have come across his

317

name, once when his father, one of the "forty-eighters," went to Georgia and opened a store in Talbotton; once when the young man, then twenty-four years old, was one of the charter members of the Young Men's Hebrew Association in New York City. In between came the migration from Germany to Georgia, from Georgia

OSCAR S. STRAUS

to New York, the study in Columbia College and Law School, and entrance into active practice at the age of twenty-three. From that time on, the career of Oscar Straus was rapid and brilliant, in law practice and business, in scholarship, authorship, and finally in public service. His first book was *The Origin of the Republican Form of Government,* delivered as a lecture at the Y. M. H. A. of New York, in which he first worked out the connection between the constitutions of the Puritans and those of the Jews in the Bible. He later wrote several other books, particularly his autobiography, which is entitled *Under Four Administrations,* referring to the four presidents under whom he held office: Cleveland, McKinley, Roosevelt and Taft. Three times he was the

318

Outstanding Jews, Second Half of the Century

American representative to Turkey. His success the first time as a defender of the Christian missionaries and as intermediary for the Christians and Mohammedans was so marked that he was sent back twice more when danger threatened in the Near East, and he set the precedent that a Jew may prove the most appropriate ambassador to a Mohammedan country.

After his return from his second mission to Turkey, Oscar Straus was appointed one of the four American representatives to the permanent Court of Arbitration at the Hague, and was reappointed three times to this position by Presidents Roosevelt and Wilson, holding it 24 years. He was Public Service Commissioner of the State of New York and arbitrated many labor disputes, having the confidence of both labor and capital. The respect which he gained for himself was at the same time a tribute to the Jewish people, for Straus was known as an active and interested Jew. In fact, when President Roosevelt asked him to accept the post of Secretary of Commerce and Labor in his Cabinet, he did so with the words: "There is still a further reason: I want to show Russia and some other countries what we think of the Jews in this country."

Oscar Straus was a close personal friend and devoted follower of Theodore Roosevelt. He served in his cabinet, followed him into the progressive party, and ran on this ticket for Governor of New York State. This intimate friendship lasted until the death of the former president.

The public work of Oscar Straus led him from service

319

of the nation to the cause of world peace and service
of all nations. He held two positions in this cause, the
one at the Hague, and the chairmanship of the committee of the League to Enforce Peace at the Peace negotia-
tions at Paris, where he was an ardent supporter of the
idea of a League of Nations. A loyal Jew, he served his
people more without than within the Jewish fold. He carried their ideas to the world; working by books and
speeches, private organizations and public office to bring
about a reign of peace on earth. Peace between Christian
and Mohammedan, between capital and labor, between
warring nations, this was his practical work. His study
and writings were along the same line; studies in American government, in religious liberty, and a fine *Life of
Roger Williams,* the founder of religious liberty in
America.

REFERENCES

Oscar S. Straus, *Under Four Administrations.*
Yearbook 5688, art. by Cyrus Adler, "Oscar S. Straus," pp.
145–155.

REVIEW QUESTIONS

1. Sketch the life of each of the six Jewish notables in this
   chapter. Give his personality, what he accomplished, and
   his attitude toward Judaism.

TOPICS FOR REPORTS

1. Report on the life and work of some other interesting Jew
   of this period, such as Judge Mayer Sulzberger, Adolf
   Kraus, Leo N. Levi, Nathan Straus, or some other.

Outstanding Jews, Second Half of the Century

2. What is the value of a writer of book reviews and encyclopedias? Compare his work with that of the scholar as writer of books, or as teacher.
3. Look up the poems of Emma Lazarus; find several which you like to read to the class. Explain why you like them.
4. Look up one of the books of Oscar Straus, and report on it.
5. What work can a Jewish representative at Washington do? Explain several different kinds of service in this capacity; tell what they are worth.
6. Study the expansion of Jewish philanthropy in the United States, showing the part played by Jacob Schiff.
7. Study *one* of the problems which one of these men thought so important, such as farm cooperation, prices of farm products, arbitration in labor disputes, religious freedom, international peace, care for the sick, for orphans, cultivation of Jewish knowledge—give the meaning of the problem, how important you consider it, and whether you think the man in question estimated its importance rightly and approached it properly.

CHAPTER 20.

The United States As a Champion
of Jewish Rights

FROM Washington to Roosevelt we have noticed
official spokesmen of the American people giving
voice to a friendly and just attitude toward the Jews.
Now we shall see the official attitude of the government
of the United States, not only to Jewish citizens at
home, but also to oppressed Jews abroad. In both cases
the attitude of our government was broadly humanitarian; it befriended the Jews in many instances because it
was the friend and champion of the oppressed, because
it stood for liberty of thought and of speech in religious
and civil affairs.

Let us glance briefly at seven different occasions in
history when the question of Jewish rights came to the
fore, either the rights of Jewish citizens of the United
States in foreign lands, or those of Jews who lived in
those lands and were being oppressed there. In order to
understand these thoroughly, it would be necessary to
look up the background of the history in the different
lands; all that can be done in this book is to show the
part America played as champion of Jewish rights and
defender of the Jews.

322

United States Champion of Jewish Rights

I. TURKEY, 1840

THE first of these happened to be in Turkish territory in 1840; in that year in Damascus a monk named Father Thomas disappeared with his servant, and thirteen Jews were thrown into prison, charged with ritual murder. The accusation included all Jews the world over, for it was charged that the monk and his servant were killed so that their blood might be used for religious purposes, and that this was a Jewish custom. This horrible legend of the Middle Ages, through which so many Jews suffered martyrdom, was here employed to torture these poor victims, until four of them died in prison. Naturally, the Jews of the world were aroused in defense of their poor brothers, as well as in defense of their own good name and that of Judaism. The two leading Jews in the world at that time, Moses Montefiore, the great English philanthropist, and Adolph Cremieux, the minister of France, were sent to Syria to plead the cause of the Jews and of humanity; their plea was successful, the remaining prisoners were set free, and the terrible accusation was refuted.

Meanwhile, the Jews of America also were aroused, held great meetings, especially one in Philadelphia with Isaac Leeser as the main speaker, and wrote requests to President Van Buren that he use the influence of the United States. But the government had already acted before receiving the request; Secretary of State John Forsythe had written both to our consul in Alexandria

History of the Jews in the United States

and to our minister in Constantinople, David Porter, instructing them to use the good offices of the United States on humanitarian grounds. There was no claim of American citizenship or American interests, but simply that the United States did not want to see such cruel and unjust persecution. And the letter to our minister contains two sentences of great importance to American Jews: "The President is of the opinion that from no one can such generous endeavors proceed with so much propriety and effect, as from the representative of a friendly power, whose institutions, political and civil, place upon the same footing the worshippers of God, of every faith and form, acknowledging no distinction between the Mohammedan, the Jew, and the Christian. Should you find it necessary or proper to address yourself to any of the Turkish authorities, you will refer to this distinctive characteristic of our government, as investing with a peculiar propriety and right, the interposition of your good offices in behalf of an oppressed and persecuted race, among whose kindred are found some of the most worthy and patriotic of our citizens." The two important points here are that the United States is as much the country of the Jew as of the Christian; and that the Jews of the United States were officially and publicly acknowledged as good citizens.

In later times, when the Russian Jews fled to various parts of the world, some of them fled to Turkey, and General Lew Wallace (the author of Ben Hur), who was the American minister there at the time, assisted many of them to settle in the Turkish empire; the same problem was presented a few years later to Oscar S. Straus when he was minister in Constantinople. At that time the Turkish government welcomed Jewish immigration everywhere except to Palestine, and Mr. Straus had a very difficult task in defending the rights of the Jews of Palestine, protecting them from expulsion, and establishing the rights of those who happened to be American citizens.

II. SWITZERLAND, 1850–1860

THE second country in which the United States intervened in behalf of the Jews was Switzerland, but the circumstances were very different; this was in defense of the rights of Jews who held the American passport to enter Switzerland and to live there. At that time Jews could not become citizens of Switzerland, and so the government did not want to give rights to foreign Jews which were refused to native Jews; but our own government defended the rights of American citizens of any religion or race to equal treatment. This principle is most important because it recurred fifty years later in the far more important case of Russia.

As Jews were not permitted to reside in some of the cantons of Switzerland, the treaty which was negotiated with that country in 1850 allowed the cantons to discriminate against American Jews likewise, if they wished; no American Jews wanted to go to Switzerland at the time, but the leaders of our government refused to accept any treaty which discriminated among American citizens for any reason whatever. A later treaty got around the matter, leaving it to the cantons to decide; then an issue arose when one American Jew named Gootman was expelled from one canton. Year after year the American government took up the issue, argued, explained; President Lincoln even appointed a Jew as consul in Zurich as an object lesson. By 1862 the laws against the residence of American Jews were disused; ten years later the laws forbidding Jews to live in the various cantons were all repealed; and in 1874 the Jews of Switzerland were made full citizens. A great part of this result was due to the constant defense of the American Jews and of Jewish rights generally by the government of the United States.

III. ROUMANIA, 1878–1902

THE United States appeared in three other countries as the protector of the native Jews,—Morocco, Roumania, and Russia. In the second of these, it also insisted on an international treaty, and in the last it defended the American passport in a far more vigorous way than was ever necessary in the much smaller issue of Switzerland. In Morocco American consuls tried to protect the Jews of that country from mob violence in 1863, in 1872, and in 1880. And in 1906, when the Treaty of Algeciras was drafted, the American representative at that international conference, instructed by Secretary of State Elihu Root, took the lead by proposing a clause in the

United States Champion of Jewish Rights

treaty to ameliorate the conditions of the Moroccan Jews; this clause was supported by the agents of the other great powers and quickly passed.

So there was plenty of precedent for the United States to befriend the defenseless Jews of Roumania, laboring under discriminatory laws and in danger of mob outbreaks. Roumania, like all the Balkan states, is much younger than the United States, and was declared free of Turkey by the European powers after a revolt of its people. In 1870 this revolt had taken place, but the ratification by the powers had not, and Roumania and the United States had exchanged no official representatives. At this time President Grant was requested to appoint as consul-general to Roumania a prominent American Jew, Benjamin F. Peixotto, who had practised law in New York and San Francisco, and was former president of the B'nai B'rith, and founder of the Cleveland Orphan Home. To him the President mentioned particularly the Jewish problem in Roumania. He served in Roumania six years, doing his utmost, not only for our government, for there was very little commerce with Roumania for a consul to supervise, but especially in behalf of the Roumanian Jews. The B'nai B'rith supplemented his little salary to keep him in Roumania. But Roumania took her cue from Russia; the native Jews, who had lived there two thousand years, were considered aliens and therefore oppressed; they were accused of ignorance, of being non-producers, and many other insults were forced upon them.

The next step occurred in 1878, when the Congress of Berlin took up the question of recognizing Roumania as a sovereign kingdom. The American minister to Austria, John A. Kasson, suggested that the United States urge the inclusion of equal rights for the Roumanian Jews as a condition for this recognition; the Secretary of State approved, and the European powers incorporated the American suggestion in the charters founding the new nations of Roumania and Bulgaria. The latter country, which has very few Jews, lived up to this agreement from the beginning; the former, with its huge Jewish population, steadily evaded the agreement by one trick after another. But at least, one step had been taken; the equality of the Roumanian Jews was officially recognized by Roumania and approved by the great powers of Europe.

The next step occurred in 1902, when Theodore Roosevelt was President of the United States and John Hay, Secretary of State. At that time the persecutions in Roumania had begun to drive Roumanian Jews in considerable numbers toward America. Mr. Hay made this his reason for treating the problem as one in which the United States had a direct interest on account of immigration; he therefore addressed a letter to all the powers which had signed the Treaty of Berlin, pointing out that Roumania had violated the treaty, was still oppressing its Jewish subjects, and that these people were being driven to America as poor, ignorant, unhappy immigrants. His complaint was made on the double ground

328

of humanity and of American interests, and he appealed
to the Treaty for his authority. The note made a great
impression throughout the world, but Roumania continued to discriminate against the Jews.

The problems of the Roumanian Jews had not been
solved even in 1930. In 1913, at the close of the Balkan
Wars, the United States again brought up the matter
in international meeting, again was sustained, and again
results were nullified by the administration of the law
in Roumania. And though minorities were protected in
the Peace Treaties of 1919, today there are protests,
complaints, defensive propaganda, and the Roumanian
Jews still suffer as a hated minority in the land of their
birth.

IV. RUSSIA, 1879–1911

THE great issue with regard to Russia was the same as
with Switzerland, but multiplied many times because of
the great number of Russian Jews in America, the desire
of many of them to return to Russia for business or
personal reasons, and the fact that the conflict was not
between the small United States of the mid-century and
a little Switzerland, but between two of the great nations
of the earth.

But beside this legal and political issue, sympathy
with the condition of the Russian Jews themselves
was frequently aroused in the generous and sympathetic American people. The hard plight of the
Russian Jews was one influence in making the American government insist so constantly on the rights of

History of the Jews in the United States

American Jews in Russia. This sympathy burst forth in the early eighties, when the pogroms and the legal discriminations began; in the nineties, when there were renewed attacks on the Jews; but it reached its height after the terrible massacre of Jews at Kishinev on April 19th to 21st, 1903. This was a systematic pogrom, inspired by agents of the government, whose will was carried out by the mob and the police; it lasted three days, while the Jewish section of the town was laid waste, forty-seven Jews killed, over six hundred injured, and over two thousand families rendered homeless. The worst feature of this crime was the fact that it was carefully planned by responsible people, the mob was led by army officers and students for the priesthood, the police stood by watching, and finally when the word went out from headquarters, the riots stopped as if rehearsed.

All over the world sprang up a spontaneous burst of protest against Russia and of sympathy with the Russian Jew. In the United States, meetings were held in fifty cities, where Jew and Christian, public officials and ministers of many denominations, joined in a cry of protest. A hundred thousand dollars was raised in the United States for relief of the victims. And a great petition was prepared, requesting the Czar to bring about an end of religious persecution in his territory. This petition was signed by 12,500 Americans, including a large number of Senators, Governors and Mayors, three Archbishops and seven Bishops; President Roosevelt, after considerable thought, sent an inquiry about receiving the petition to the Russian government, but the Czar declined to receive it. However, the petition did not need to be officially received; it did its work as an expression of the true sentiment of the American people in the face of such terrible religious persecution.

After Kishinev, there were further pogroms, further relief funds, further immigration to America, often aided by relatives who were already fortunate enough to live in a free land. Nothing could be done to influence the attitude of the Jew-haters of Russia; the list of attacks on Jews from Kishinev to the World War makes monotonous reading. But the most important relation of the United States to Russia was not in the way of unofficial protest against local abuses, but of official action in order to change the attitude of Russia to American citizens, whether they were Christians or Jews.

The two countries had made a treaty in 1832, when the people of each had little occasion to visit the other, and when the United States had no particular connection with the Russian Jews. Besides, the worst period of oppression for the Russian Jews was still to come. So that the first test case of the American passport did not rise until 1879, when a naturalized citizen of the United States, a Jew, moved back to Russia and tried to buy real estate; this was against the Russian law, and the protest of the United States minister on his behalf did not help him. From that time on the argument continued for thirty-two years. On the Russian side was the point that Jews were prohibited from living in

331

certain cities, and engaging in certain trades in Russia, and that foreign Jews could not expect more rights than the Jews of Russia. On the American side was the argument that an American citizen is such without regard to his race or religion, that no foreign power has a right to ask questions or make distinctions between American citizens, and that the passport of the United States should take an American citizen anywhere in the world. Russia argued the meaning of the treaty, and the Russian government hated Jews and would not yield in their favor.

Time and again cases of American Jews arose, when they were refused passports, or when they were granted passports but were forced to sell their business and move out of Russia, or when the Russian police made arbitrary decisions and our minister intervened. As Russian Jews were moving steadily to the United States, the issue grew steadily more important; more of them wanted to return to Russia for business or to visit their relatives, and the sentiment against Russia was growing steadily stronger in the United States. The classic statement of American protest was written by Secretary of State James G. Blaine in 1881 to our minister in St. Petersburg. In this letter he outlined several cases that had already arisen, traced the Russian law with regard to foreigners in the past, and showed that discrimination against foreign Jews was a new policy at that time, though one on which America had already spoken clearly with regard to Switzerland. He particularly urged our

PETITION TO THE CZAR

representative to make plain what was due the citizens of the United States in return for the equal treatment given by this country to the people of Russia.

This condition continued, with diplomatic notes, arguments, and no change in the actual conditions. Finally, in 1910, when William Howard Taft was President, the American Jewish Committee decided to press the matter to an issue, and addressed a letter to the President on the basis of everything that had gone before. The B'nai

333

B'rith and other organizations took part in the movement. Judge Mayer Sulzberger of Philadelphia, Louis
Marshall and Jacob Schiff of New York, met the President and committees of Congress, which were taking up
various resolutions on the subject. When they were refused action at one of these meetings, one of the men
present remarked: "Well, we are still in exile," but Jacob
H. Schiff answered: "This means a fight." He realized
that in America the will of the citizens is supreme, and
that Congress had to be convinced that the Russian
action was a real violation of American rights. In
December, 1911, another resolution was introduced by
Representative William Sulzer of New York, a non-Jew,
was passed in the House by a vote of 300 to 1, in the
Senate by 72 to none, and the treaty of 1832 was ab-
rogated by President Taft. The government of the
United States had taken a decisive action, not only to
befriend the Jews, but to defend its own citizenship,
whether held by Jew or Christian, against any discrimination or attack from without.

V. PERSIA, 1897–1921

PERSIA is a smaller country, and one that has not attacked the Jews to any great extent. But even here the
United States intervened at two different times to protect the Persian Jews. The first was in 1897, when our
minister protested to the Shah at a time of mob violence
against the Jews, and urged him to protect them; our
secretary of state approved his action when reported.

334

United States Champion of Jewish Rights

The second occasion came when a Jew, Rabbi Joseph S. Kornfeld, was American minister to Persia, from 1921 to 1924. During that period a threatened attack on the Jews was averted by the prompt and wise action of the Jewish minister, who was compared by the Persian Jews to a second Mordecai and given every honor in their power to bestow.

VI. VERSAILLES PEACE CONFERENCE, 1919

AT THE Peace Conference which closed the World War, Jewish problems were among the many which had to be faced and solved if possible. Hence Jewish delegates came from many lands to lay before the Peace Commissioners the two great Jewish problems, the homeland in Palestine and the Jewish minorities in eastern Europe. The one needed a charter, the other needed protection, as we have seen. This history cannot take up these great problems of world Jewry in full, but must consider the American side of them—what the Jews of America attempted, and what President Woodrow Wilson approved and incorporated in the treaties of peace.

A number of Jewish organizations sent representatives to Paris in 1919, either to express their ideas or to observe the course of events; the two most important of these were the American Jewish Congress, represented by Louis Marshall, Judge Julian W. Mack, Rabbi Stephen S. Wise and several others, and the American Jewish committee, represented by Dr. Cyrus Adler, and Louis Marshall. These joined with the Jews of various other

335

nations in a Conference which met to discuss the two great problems for which they were all assembled; they also waited directly on the President of the United States to present him their requests as American citizens. President Wilson took several actions as a result of all this; first of all, he included the Jewish problems among the hundreds of questions that had to be considered. The Peace Conference took up, not only the question of Palestine, in which Great Britain had so great an interest, but also the question of the Jews of the various nations of eastern Europe, which was important to them alone. As to this latter problem, several different solutions were proposed; one was an arrangement for the Jews to be treated as a minority group with its own rights in the newly formed nations, such as Poland and Czecho-Slovakia, and the older ones, such as Roumania Another was to follow the American system, of equal rights for every person as a citizen, whatever his religion or race might be. And these solutions were complicated by serious charges and denials of the persecution of the Jews in different lands, the administration of the law, violence by mobs, and economic boycott to starve them out.

President Wilson took action on every one of these points, and was one of the men who tried to lay the foundation of a new era in eastern Europe, as in other parts of the world. The Polish leader, Paderewski, challenged the Jews on the facts, and asked for an investigation commission of Americans; President Wilson appointed as chairman of this commission a Jew, Henry

336

United States Champion of Jewish Rights

Morgenthau, who had previously served with distinction as ambassador to Turkey. At the same time a British commission was appointed, headed by another Jew, Sir Stuart Samuel. Both these commissions reported that the facts of Jewish persecution were clear enough; they differed in regard to causes, as the Morgenthau commission held that the Polish government was not responsible directly, and hence these were not pogroms after the Russian model. The commission spent nine weeks in Poland in the summer of 1919 and presented its official report to Congress in December, 1919.

Meanwhile, the cause of the Jews in eastern Europe had been incorporated in the various treaties, and President Wilson had a full share of responsibility for this, as for every action of the peace conference. He had received the Jewish delegates to hear their opinions as early as March, 1919, and the treaties with Germany and Poland, which were signed in June, included clauses covering the question, as did all the treaties later signed with other nations, including Austria and Roumania. Everywhere the rights of the Jews and other racial, religious and linguistic minorities were officially protected by law, whether the local government enforced that law or not, and everywhere American influence had been decisive in the result.

In the Polish treaty, the most important on account of the number of Jews concerned, the civil and religious rights of every person in Poland were guaranteed, whatever his religion, his race, or his previous nationality, and all were made citizens by law; these were the rights of individual citizenship according to the American, liberal idea. In addition, certain rights of a minority people, which American Jews do not need or desire, but which the Jews of Poland felt were important for them, were also protected: rights to have their own schools, their own Sabbath day, and so on. And all these rights, of both kinds, were protected by the League of Nations. No wonder that President Wilson seemed the savior of Europe, the liberator of the Jews.

Palestine also came under consideration. Here the President's interest was known in advance through a letter to Rabbi Stephen S. Wise, in which he declared his approval of the Balfour Declaration and his interest in the Zionist movement. Hence his approval was easily won for a British mandatory, which should advance the Jewish national center in Palestine, and which was finally sanctioned by the Conference of Allies at the San Remo Conference, in April, 1920. Again, as so many times before, America proved a champion of Jewish rights and of humanity before the nations of the world.

REVIEW QUESTIONS

1. Give several situations where the American government interested itself in the Jewish people.
2. Give different reasons for this interest.
3. What was the important issue with Switzerland? With Russia? Was there any difference between the two?
4. What was the important issue with Roumania? With Morocco? With Persia?

338

United States Champion of Jewish Rights

5. State the part played by Jewish representatives of the United States in protecting foreign and American Jews.
6. What was the official and the popular attitude of America toward pogroms?
7. What were the Jewish problems at Versailles? What had America to do with them?

TOPICS FOR STUDY

1. The conditions in each of the nations named in the chapter, to see why American help was needed. What sort of help was needed in each particular case? Did American aid solve the question? Why?
2. Was the American attitude toward Jews animated in any particular case, by: (a) humanitarian sentiments, (b) sympathy for the Jews as a people, (c) protection of American citizens, (d) regard for American immigration policy or other national policy?
3. Study the influence of Jews on American action regarding Jewish problems; see whether this influence was proper or excessive, and how it was exerted.

REFERENCES FOR PUPILS

Wiernik, Peter, pp. 306–18, 343–365.
Raisin, Max, pp. 193–196, 274–275, 336–339.
Wolf, Simon, *Presidents I Have Known*. Byron S. Adams.
Adler, Cyrus, *The Voice of America on Kishineff*. J. P. S.
Straus, Oscar S., *Under Four Administrations*, "The Paris Peace Conference," chap. xvi.
Morgenthau, Henry, *All in a Lifetime*, chaps. xvii, xviii.
Luzzatti, *God in Freedom*, art. by Max J. Kohler on "The Abrogation of the Treaty of 1832 between the U. S. and Russia, and the International Protection of Religious Minorities."

History of the Jews in the United States

Goodhart, Arthur L., *Poland and the Minority Races* (account of the Morgenthau Commission to Poland). Brentano.

REFERENCES FOR TEACHERS

Adler, Cyrus, *Jews in the Diplomatic Correspondence of the United States*. (This is also published as vol. xv of the Publications of the American Jewish Historical Society.)

Singer, I., *Russia at the Bar of the American People*.

Margolis, M. L. and Marx, A., *History of the Jewish People,* chap. xcviii.

American Jewish Year Book.
"The American Passport in Russia," vol. 5665, p. 283.
"The Passport Question in Congress," vol. 5670, p. 21.
"The Passport Question," vol. 5672, p. 21.
Kohler, Max J., "Jewish Rights at International Congresses," vol. 5678, p. 106.
"The Peace Conference and the Rights of Minorities," vol. 5680, p. 156.
"The Peace Conference and Rights of Minorities," vol. 5681, pp. 108, 406–408.

Publications of the American Jewish Historical Society.
Ezekiel, Jacob, "Persecution of Jews in 1840," vol. VIII, p. 141.
Jacobs, Joseph, "The Damascus Affair and the Jews of America," vol. X, p. 119.
Strook, Sol M., "Switzerland and American Jews," vol. XIV, p. 7.
Kohler, Max J. and Wolf, Simon, "Jewish Disabilities in the Balkan States, American Contributions Toward Their Removal," vol. XXIV, entire.

Sears, L. M., *History of American Foreign Relations* (on abrogation of the Russian Treaty), pp. 496–498. Crowell Co.

Kraus, *Reminiscences and Comments*.

Adler, *Jacob H. Schiff. The Memoirs of Count Witte.*

CHAPTER 21.

The American Jew in World War I

THE earlier wars of the United States were fought when there were few Jews in the country, and those few did their full duty and more for America in its need. What are the facts about the more recent wars, when the Jewish community of the United States had grown to huge size, and consisted of many different groups and factions, from many different lands? We shall now glance very briefly at the part played by American Jews in the Spanish-American War of 1898, and more carefully at their contribution during the First World War, from 1917 to 1918; we shall see that the fine record of earlier days was far surpassed by the splendid contribution of American Jews during these later wars.

I. THE SPANISH-AMERICAN WAR

THE first call for volunteers to fight for America after the great increase of the Russian Jews came with the Spanish-American War. For this war fairly accurate, but by no means complete, statistics exist; it is known, for example, that the War Department gave 4,000 furloughs for the holydays, so there must have been at least that many Jews in the service. There were records of about

341

thirty Jews who were army officers and twenty who were officers in the navy. Of these army officers, four reached the rank of Major, while in the navy the highest rank attained during the war was that of Commander. Fifteen Jews were among the crew of the Maine, the destruction of which occasioned the war; a half dozen served in Roosevelt's famous regiment, the "Rough Riders"; the first man to fall in the Battle of Manila was a Jew, Sergt. Maurice Juster of the First California Volunteers.

There were three Jewish naval officers who later reached the rank of Rear Admiral, though all of them were much younger and lower in rank at the time of the war. One of these was Lieutenant Joseph Strauss, who later held an important position in the World War. One was Lieutenant Commander Edward D. Taussig, who occupied Wake Island (Oceania) for the United States, and was the first American officer in charge of the island of Guam; he was retired as Rear Admiral in 1909. The third was Lieutenant Commander Adolf Marix, like the other two a graduate of the United States Naval Academy at Annapolis, who was in command of the battleship Maine before her catastrophe, was secretary to the court of inquiry on the explosion, and prepared the report which was laid before President McKinley; he was then promoted to Commander and cited for gallantry in two engagements in Cuba; he was retired as Rear Admiral in 1910.

The record is short because the war itself was short, and the forces engaged in it small. But it is a fitting prel-

The American Jew in World War I

ude to the tremendous outpouring of men and enthu.
siasm by the American Jews during the World War.

II. THE WORLD WAR

IN THE World War there were fully 200,000 Jews in the
American army, navy and marine corps, more Jewish
soldiers than the entire Jewish population of America at
the time of the Civil War; enough Jewish soldiers to fill
six complete divisions. The names of 150,000 men with
their units, were gathered by the War Records Office of
the American Jewish Committee, and check-ups show
that this is at least 25 per cent short of the total. This is
over 4 per cent of the total army, while the Jews number
just 3 per cent of the population of the nation; the 40,000
Jewish volunteers may account for this rather remarkable
excess for an unmilitary people. And beside these, 2,700
Jews who were not American citizens, left to fight with
the Judeans in Palestine.

Of course, all the Jews, German and Russian, found
their sympathies enlisted against Russia from the beginning. But when the United States entered the war and
Russia dropped out of it, Jewish sentiment, always
friendly to England and France, became entirely pro-
Ally. The vast majority of American Jews supported
the war as ardently as any people in the United States.

Of course, there were some pacifists among Jews, as
well as among Christians. Some, from Russia, had experienced military oppression and seen military service
in their childhood, and felt that the whole system was

wrong from the beginning. Some were convinced of the injustice of war and its uselessness in advancing the cause of justice among peoples. As only Quakers and similar religious sects were exempt from military service, all other pacifists were imprisoned or offered alternative service, and often were very badly mistreated. Many of them showed as great heroism on behalf of their beliefs as the soldiers did in fighting for their country.

Of the Jewish soldiers, 48 per cent were enrolled in the infantry, the hardest and most dangerous branch of all, while only 27 per cent of the entire army were in the infantry; evidently, the Jews did not flock to the easy or the safe jobs, as some of their enemies have since said. The Jews had a larger proportion than the non-Jews in infantry, medical corps, and signal corps; a smaller proportion in cavalry and engineers; about the same proportion as the non-Jews in the quartermaster corps and the ordnance corps.

Ten thousand Jews were commissioned officers, more than the entire number who served in the Civil War, and 1,000 of these were in the navy,—a high proportion, considering how few West Point graduates or professional soldiers there were among the Jews. Almost all of them entered the service for the war only, directly from the various walks of civil life. The highest of all in rank was Rear Admiral Joseph Strauss, who had risen from Lieutenant in the Spanish-American War until now he was Rear Admiral, in command of the mine laying squadron in the North Sea; he was the second highest

The American Jew in World War I

Jew serving in any of the Allied forces, ranking next to Lieutenant General Sir John Monash of the Australian Corps. Brigadier General Charles Henry Lauchheimer was the highest officer in the entire Marine Corps. While in the army there were 100 colonels and lieutenant colonels, 500 majors, and other ranks in proportion.

Whatever type of facts we examine, the results are the same: the Jews in the service were almost identical with their non-Jewish comrades. About 2,800 Jews died in service, and 10,000 others were wounded. The Jewish graves were designated by the Magen David, the six-pointed star, instead of the cross. Over 1,100 citations for valor were conferred on American Jews, 750 of these by the American command and 350 by other allies. 150 American Jews can wear the Distinguished Service Cross, 174 the Croix de Guerre, 4 the Medaille Militaire, and 3 the Congressional Medal of Honor, the rarest of all decorations, which was conferred on but 90 men during the entire war. Of these three, Sergeant William Sawelson, of the 312th Infantry, was killed in the act of heroism for which the medal was awarded; the other two, Lieutenant Sydney G. Gumperts of New York and First Sergeant Benjamin Kaufman of Newark, N. J., came through alive. Their official citations and those of many others with lesser decorations amaze us by their picture of a type of heroism that belongs to the age of chivalry. Here are parts of them: "Sergeant William Sawelson, for conspicuous gallantry and intrepidity above and beyond the call of duty. Hearing a wounded man in a shell hole some distance away calling for water, Sergeant Sawelson left shelter and crawled through heavy machine-gun fire to where the man lay, giving him what water he had in his own canteen. He then went back to his own shell hole, obtained more water, and was returning to the wounded man, when he was killed by a machine-gun bullet." "Sergeant Gumperts started with two other soldiers toward a machine-gun nest. His companions became casualties from a bursting shell, but he continued on alone in the face of direct fire, jumped into the nest and silenced the gun, capturing nine of the crew." "First Sergeant Benjamin Kaufman in the Argonne forest led a patrol to silence a machine-gun. He became separated from his patrol, and a bullet shattered his right hand. Without hesitation he advanced on the gun alone, throwing grenades with his left hand and charging with an empty pistol, taking one prisoner and scattering the crew, bringing the gun and prisoner back to the first aid station."

A specially touching fate was that of Michael Aaronsohn, a student in the Hebrew Union College, who volunteered in the combatant service and was totally blinded by a bursting shell on the field of battle. Aaronsohn recovered his strength but not his sight, and resumed his education, actually graduating as a rabbi. He has proved an excellent worker for Judaism, and also for the cause of his fellow-wounded in the World War.

The present author served in the army in France as a First Lieutenant Chaplain, so that these dry military records glow for him with the light of many incidents remembered. The Jewish soldier was a typical American soldier, neither more nor less; it is not necessary to claim more and less would be untrue. The Jewish soldiers were loyal, courageous, and reliable in the great emergency, exactly as their comrades of other groups; and this can be proved, not only by statistics, but also by personal memory and by the evidence of their fellows who fought side by side with them.

Certain units had a great many Jews; the highest percentage were in the Seventy-Seventh Division, the National Army unit from New York City, which was 40 per cent Jewish. One of the dramatic incidents of the war happened in this division, that of the famous Lost Battalion, which was surrounded by German troops and cut off completely from communication with the American lines for almost a week. When a courier was needed to break through the Germans and carry word back as to the location of the unit, the volunteer who managed to carry the message through was Abraham Krotoshinsky, a Jewish immigrant boy, and in peace times a barber by trade; here, in the Argonne forest, he saved his battalion and won for himself the Distinguished Service Cross.

Naturally, there was official recognition of the Jewish religion during the World War, as there had been in the Civil War, and it was correspondingly greater than at that time. In the Civil War there had been four Jewish chaplains to serve the soldiers; in the World War there were twenty-five, of whom twelve served in France and thirteen in the camps in the United States. Chaplain Elkan C. Voorsanger was promoted to the rank of captain for distinguished service, and was Senior Chaplain of the 77th Division, over all the religious work of that unit. In addition, there was one Jewish chaplain in the navy.

The work of the chaplains was important for several reasons. In the first place, it meant official recognition that the Jew was serving in the army beside his Christian fellows, that he deserved his own religious service as much as they. Then, it brought the Jewish boy a friend who understood him, was able to lead him in prayer, and also to help him in the hundreds of needs that arise when young men, many of them immigrants, are far away from home. The business of the chaplain was to act as a friend and helper of the soldier, to speak for him at headquarters, to visit him in the hospital, to follow him on the field of battle, and finally when the battle was over, to stay behind and see to the burial of the dead. Of the great number of Jewish soldiers in all the various units of the army, some at least had their own chaplains to stand beside them in battle, hospital, and burial ground.

III. CIVILIAN WORK

THE most important Jewish organization for war work was the Jewish Welfare Board, organized in April, 1917 by a number of national Jewish organizations, to represent the Jews of America, as the Young Men's Christian

GRAVES OF JEWISH SOLDIERS WERE
MARKED WITH MAGEN DAVID

Association repre-
sented the Protes-
tants and the Knights
of Columbus, the
Catholics. Its chair-
man was Colonel
Harry Cutler, of Prov-
idence, R. I., who
practically worked
himself to death
through his tremen-
dous service in this
organization during
the entire war; its vice
chairman was Dr. Cy-
rus Adler, of Philadel-
phia, of whose activ-
ities we have heard in several other connections in this
book.

This Board was one of the seven war-work organizations sharing in the joint drive for funds, together with
those of Christian and non-sectarian character; it worked
throughout under the direct recognition and supervision
of the military authorities. It was never one of the greatest organizations for civilian service to the troops, but in
its smaller field was one of the very useful ones. In the
camps and cantonments at home it established 200 different centers, with 500 workers, and erected 48 buildings for its work. In France it established centers in

the chief places where Jewish soldiers congregated, with 57 different centers administered by 102 men and 76 women. The first to establish this work overseas was Congressman Isaac Siegel, chairman of the Jewish Welfare Board Overseas Commission. Besides, the Board worked closely with the Jewish Chaplains, offering facilities and bringing supplies for them as well as for its own workers.

The climax of the welfare work in France came at Passover, 1919. I had been in France since August, 1918, and it was my second big opportunity for a Jewish service. The first was at the fall holy days, during the

JEWISH SOLDIERS IN FRANCE AT SEDER
Conducted by Chaplain Louis I. Egelson

350

doubtful days of the war; I held services in a Y. M.
C. A. hut for five hundred Jewish soldiers, some newly
arrived from the United States, some wounded in hospitals, and some in the engineers and quartermaster
corps. Everyone was full of uncertainty about his own
future and was likewise full of longing and fervor. Seven
months later, on Passover, the war was over, troops
were moving toward home; there was a gaiety, a thank-
fulness in the spirit with which we observed our ancient
feast of freedom. At this Passover the Welfare Board
arranged for the Passover meal and the entertainment of
the Jewish soldiers.

Since the close of the war the Jewish Welfare Board
has devoted itself to the development of Jewish community centers in most of the large cities of the country,
though it still keeps a military department for the benefit
of the Jews in the regular army and navy.

Beside this official representation of Jews in the war
from the American side, there was personal participation
of a great many persons of importance. A long list of
names might be given here, but it is only necessary to
study a few. For example, Professor Felix Frankfurter of
Harvard was a special assistant to the Secretary of War;
Eugene Meyer, Jr., was an officer of the War Finance
Corporation, and so on. In particular, there were three
Jews of the seven members on the Advisory Commission
of the National Council of Defense, which was placed in
charge of the entire industry of the United States, to
direct all the factories of the country into the channels

which were most valuable in the emergency. These three Jews were Samuel Gompers, President of the American Federation of Labor, an outstanding leader of American workmen for a generation or more; Julius Rosenwald of Chicago, a philanthropist of the Jacob H. Schiff type, and head of Sears, Roebuck & Co., the great mail-order house; and Bernard M. Baruch, a New York financier, who was later appointed chairman of the War Industries Board, with final authority over all the industries of the United States in their relation to production for the war. Mr. Baruch accompanied President Wilson to Paris as his chief economic advisor on all the business matters that came up in the treaties; since that time he established the annual Institute of Politics at Williams College, a real contribution to the understanding of national and international problems. These men happen to be outstanding in their ability but not in their loyalty; in that they were simply representative of the bulk of their fellow-citizens, Jews as well as Christians.

REVIEW QUESTIONS

1. Give figures on the participation of Jews in the Spanish-American War. Was this a large proportion of the army? Of the Jews of the United States?
2. Do the same for the World War.
3. Name one man who took part in both wars; state his special interest for us.
4. Trace the resemblance or difference between the Jewish soldier and other American soldiers, as in this chapter.
5. What was the importance of the chaplains? Of the Jewish Welfare Board? What did each do?

The American Jew in World War I

6. Name three soldiers mentioned in the chapter; tell their distinction.
7. List three civilians, with their distinction.

TOPICS FOR REPORTS

1. The work of the Jews of some other country in the World War. Compare with those of the United States.
2. A fuller biography of one of the men mentioned in this chapter.
3. Further names of interesting people, active during the World War.
4. An essay on the American Expeditionary Forces.
5. A study of the Judeans, the Jewish forces that served in the British army in Palestine.

REFERENCES FOR PUPILS

Wiernik, Peter, pp. 331–334, 417–20.
Cohen, George, *The Jews in the Making of America,* pp. 103–119. Stratford.
Levinger, L. J., *A Jewish Chaplain in France.* Macmillan.

REFERENCES FOR TEACHERS

American Jewish Year Book.
Adler, Cyrus, "List of Jewish Soldiers in the Spanish-American War," vol. 5661, p. 525.
Leavitt, Julian, "The Collection of Jewish War Statistics," vol. 5679, p. 103.
Leavitt, Julian, "American Jews in the World War," vol. 5680, p. 141. (This volume also has articles on the participation of French and British Jews in the war.)

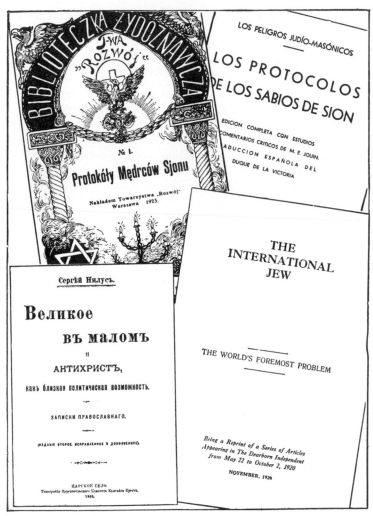

THE PROTOCOLS OF THE ELDERS OF ZION

Polish edition, *upper left;* Spanish, *upper right;* Russian, *lower left;* and the American edition, *lower right.*

CHAPTER 22.

Between Two Wars

I. ANTI-SEMITISM IN AMERICA

AFTER the First World War, the United States experienced its first organized movement against the Jews. As we have seen, individuals sometimes opposed them, from Peter Stuyvesant to General Grant, but most Americans were ready to welcome Jewish immigrants, and the government of the United States often defended Jews living in lands of persecution.

Not that Americans have always been hospitable or even just to foreigners. Every time immigration increased greatly some Americans would band together to oppose the newcomers. The first time such sentiments were given legal expression was in the Alien and Sedition Laws in the administration of John Adams. The second attack against newcomers was the Native American movement of the 1840's and the Know-Nothing Order of the 1850's. This was levelled against the Irish Catholics; riots occurred, a convent was burned in Boston, and candidates were nominated for office on the platform, "America for Americans." But the Irish soon became accepted as citizens and the excitement died down.

In the 1890's a new organization grew up, the APA or

American Protective Association, to "protect" America from the Catholic church, and especially from the Irish and German Catholics, who were in a majority amongst the immigrants in those days. Each of these anti-foreign movements was simply an expression of the fear of strangers, although the strangers, on each occasion, came here for the same reasons that had inspired the Pilgrim Fathers—the desire to worship in their own way, to make a good living for their families and to live in a free land.

After the First World War similar attacks were directed against the Jews. There were two reasons for this; first, because of the great increase in the number of Jews in America, many of whom looked different and spoke a language strange to the older American settlers; second, prejudices in certain American groups were stimulated by the rise of a virulent anti-Semitism in Europe. The medieval religious persecution of the Jews had died down in civilized lands during the nineteenth century, but many people still hated the Jews. A new type of anti-Semitism came with the invention of the race theory.

This theory arose in Germany about 1870; it held that all races differ from their inception, and that some are superior to others. The racists held that the Jews are Semites, and that they can never mix with the ruling Nordic race. Therefore they must be repressed by law or driven out of the country. Finally, the Nazis in unspeakable brutality slaughtered millions of Jews, using the race theory to bolster their war propaganda.

Of course, the whole racist theory is false from begin-

356

ning to end. No one race is better than any other so far as anybody has ever been able to prove. Most people of every race given equal opportunity reach an average level of intelligence and of morality. No race in the world is pure or unmixed; every nation is made up of tall and short people, dark and light ones, with different shapes of heads on the outside and different ideas on the inside. The accusations against the Jews are either not true at all, or are true of some Jews and of some Christians as well. They are likewise unjust, because no people should ever be persecuted for either their race or religion.

In Europe, anti-Semitism came to be important in politics. It was a weapon of the reactionary parties against any modern or liberal ideas, for they could blame these on the Jews. The Jew was always the scapegoat for political reaction from the Dreyfus case in France to the pogroms in Russia, to the losing of the First World War by Germany and the rise of the Communist party to power in Russia. It is equally true that the liberal parties in every country naturally defended the Jews, not so much because they were Jews but because they were citizens and entitled to the protection of the law.

The anti-Semites expressed their ideas in books and magazines, the number and violence of which are really amazing. The most famous of these was the *Protocols of the Learned Elders of Zion*. This pretended to be the minute-book of a secret meeting of the seventy Elders of Zion, plotting to overthrow the Christian nations and rule the world themselves. Plainly, the book is a clumsy and

357

History of the Jews in the United States

foolish forgery; but many people actually believed it to be true. Of course, there never were any Elders of Zion, and no Jews ever devised such a ridiculous plot. The book was actually published in Russia in the revolutionary year 1904 as one weapon of the Czarist government; it was based on a French book written in 1865 as an attack on Emperor Napoleon III.

After the First World War this movement suddenly appeared in America, and surprisingly enough some people were ready to accept it. The *Protocols* were reprinted in America by Czarist Russians, who tried to show that the Communist revolution was the work of the Jews. Henry Ford, then the great automobile manufacturer of Detroit, accepted the *Protocols* as true, and published a long series of articles attacking the Jews in his own weekly paper, the *Dearborn Independent*. Many Jewish leaders were attacked by name. Finally, one of these struck back. Aaron Sapiro, a lawyer who was organizing farmers' cooperatives, sued Mr. Ford and his paper for a million dollars, on the ground that his valuable work would be ruined by their lies. The trial was begun in Detroit in 1926 but it was never finished because Mr. Ford apologized to Aaron Sapiro and to the Jewish people as a whole. He wrote a letter to Louis Marshall, president of the American Jewish Committee, in which he said: "I deem it to be my duty as an honorable man to make amends for the wrong done to the Jews, as fellow-men and brothers, by asking their forgiveness for the harm that I have unintentionally committed, by retracting so far as lies

358

within my power the offensive charges laid at their door by these publications, and by giving them the unqualified assurance that henceforth they may look to me for friendship and good will." Naturally, this ended the matter in America, but the articles were still printed in many other lands in German, Spanish and many other languages. Thus the influential name of Henry Ford insured the continued spread of the evil.

A second move against the Jews was the effort made by some universities to cut down the number of Jewish students by establishing a Jewish quota. These schools claimed that the poor son of an immigrant, who was working his way through college to become a doctor or lawyer, was not as desirable as a rich young man, who wore better clothes and might have better manners. President Lawrence Lowell of Harvard University actually made such a proposal openly in 1922, but it was completely rejected by the Board of Overseers of the University, which held that the only qualifications for a student should be ability and character. Some colleges and many medical schools began secretly to limit the number of Jews in their faculties and student bodies.

The most conspicuous movement of the period was the rise of the Ku Klux Klan, a secret organization whose members paraded with hoods over their faces. The Klan took its name from a body of southerners organized some fifty years earlier, but they now opposed not only Negroes, but also Catholics, Jews and the foreign-born. They carried on this program by voting against members of

HATE MONGERS AT WORK

A leader of the Protestant War Veterans of America addresses a joint rally of the German-American Bund and the Ku Klux Klan.

these groups, by boycotting merchants, even by violence and murder. Between 1920 and 1925 the Klan claimed as many as a million members all over the country. But it was exposed in the newspapers, opposed at the polls, and finally many states passed laws forbidding masked organizations, which deprived the Klan of its mystery and started its rapid decline.

The great mass of Americans revolted against prejudice as much as against violence. In 1920, nine national Jewish organizations sent out a paper entitled, "An Address to Their Fellow-Citizens by American Jewish Organizations." It concluded: "Let not hatred and misunderstanding arise where peace and harmony, unity and brotherliness are required in order to perpetuate all that America represents, and to enable all men to know that within her wide boundaries there is no room for injustice and intolerance."

Leading Americans quickly responded. In January 1921, a protest against anti-Semitism was signed by 119 prominent American Christians, headed by former President William Howard Taft, President Woodrow Wilson and William Cardinal O'Connell. The Federal Council of Churches of Christ in America, the Protestant union of church bodies, defended the Jews and opposed intolerance of any kind. The National Conference of Christians and Jews was formed to work for good will and understanding through the churches and synagogues. Every president and most public leaders since that day have spoken out strongly against discrimination and for fair dealing among all Americans.

The hate vendors were promptly answered with literature and in other ways, such as the cartoons, above.

Between Two Wars

MORE disastrous for the Jews than all the anti-Semitic organizations were the new laws enacted to limit immigration, passed in 1921, 1924 and finally in 1929. The vast increase of the Jewish population up to 1914 came through immigration, sometimes as many as 100,000 Jewish immigrants arrived in a single year. The war and the difficulties of travel put an end to free entry into this country. There had long been limitations on immigration excluding certain persons, such as criminals, persons with infectious diseases, paupers, contract laborers, and finally also illiterates, those who could not read even their own language. But generally speaking, America needed new people to help build up the country, and was ready to welcome any refugees from religious persecution.

After the war the picture changed. American workers feared competition of low-paid foreign labor; some people feared the Catholic Church; racists pointed out that many recent immigrants had come from southern and eastern Europe, whereas formerly they had come largely from England, Ireland and Germany. Certainly, dislike of Italian Catholics and Russian Jews was one of the motives behind the laws restricting immigration. The new law limited total immigration to 150,000 a year, where formerly it had often exceeded a million. In addition, the law assigned a quota to each nation based on the number of those of similar birth or descent then resident in America. This provision resulted in a limitation of Jewish immi-

363

grants to about twenty thousand each year, for the Jews came chiefly from countries which had low quotas.

As this number is less than half of one per cent of the Jews in America, it is too small to be of any consequence in the total Jewish picture. The new immigration laws have actually introduced a new period in our history, a period in which American Jewry can no longer lean upon the numbers, the piety or the learning of Jews from other lands, but must become self-sufficient. New Jewish institutions of learning were founded, so that this period became the second great organizing period in American Jewish history, after the period of small immigration from 1865 to 1880. During World War I, America could no longer even import Hebrew Bibles and prayerbooks, and Hebrew presses were founded to produce them at home.

Jews of other lands were sadly harmed by these laws, for few of them could now look forward to founding new homes in America. The American Jews also suffered severely because they could not bring over their friends from abroad. Yet they gained strength through self-reliance in the pursuit of Jewish activities, which was thus forced upon them.

III. THE GREAT DEPRESSION

In 1929 began a depression which was the longest and most severe in the history of the United States. Millions of people were out of work and could find no way to earn a livelihood. Thousands of businesses went bankrupt, as customers could no longer pay for what they needed.

Between Two Wars

This situation affected the Jews even more than many other Americans. Some Jews were new in this country and were not yet solidly established. Others were engaged in the real estate business, where values went down far and fast, so that many saw their entire fortunes wiped out. The growing need appeared in the national demand for relief, which increased as much as 50 per cent the country over. At the same time the donors of charity were less able to help than they had been in days of prosperity.

Like other minority groups, the Jews found the competition for jobs especially hard when times were bad. Depressions always have this result; only when the mass of people are comfortable and happy can they share their prosperity with those who may differ from them in one way or another. In fact, the misery of great masses of people led them to look for a scapegoat for their troubles, and anti-Semitism was sometimes the answer.

The depression interrupted the normal activity and growth of Jewish institutions. Fewer people could afford to give money to synagogues, Jewish schools or charities; some could give less than they had formerly given. Some synagogues and Hebrew schools had to close; others retrenched at the expense of rabbis and teachers, who could hardly live on their lower salaries.

The first break in the years of hardship came with the election of Franklin D. Roosevelt as President in 1932; his "New Deal" administration undertook the work of rescue. First of all, the government had to take over much of the relief work which had formerly been carried on by

365

private agencies, both Jewish and Christian. Work projects for the government provided incomes for great numbers of people. The Jewish organizations turned to other types of work, such as family and vocational guidance, and service of the Jewish community as a whole.

The depression aroused many Jews to consider what types of work young Jews should enter, though pioneer thinkers had been working on this problem for a generation. Some turned toward farming, others toward professions like law and medicine where they felt they could be independent, and not have to ask anybody for a job. Jewish organizations, such as B'nai B'rith and various local federations, took up vocational guidance work, to aid Jewish boys and girls in selecting their future careers with care and intelligence.

In 1941, President Roosevelt ordered the establishment of a Fair Employment Practices Commission (known as FEPC), which lasted until 1946, all through the war period. This was designed to protect the rights of all minority groups to jobs; its chief work was to aid the Negroes, but Jews and many others were protected as well. By the time this federal organization came to an end, New York and New Jersey had passed similar laws for their own states. By 1960, sixteen states had agencies empowered to enforce state anti-bias laws. Such a movement does not abolish prejudice, but it does protect the rights of American citizens in a very important practical manner.

The Second World War finally ended the depression

and brought a wave of prosperity to the country. Millions of young men and women went to war instead of taking jobs. The rest were busy for long hours every week making the instruments of war and providing food for ourselves and our Allies. All groups of the population shared in this prosperity.

IV. EFFECT OF THE NAZIS ON AMERICA

EVEN before the Second World War another factor was changing the life of American Jews and of Jews the world over. This was the rise to power of the National Socialist party (the Nazis) in Germany. In January 1933, Adolf Hitler, their Fuehrer (or Leader), became chancellor, and in March dictator of Germany. His slogan was "Blood and Soil"; he taught that the Germans were the "master race" and the Jews the very lowest of mankind. The oppression of the Jews which followed was accompanied by an attack on every free or democratic movement. Members of the Socialist and Communist parties were locked up or killed; labor unions were taken over by the government; teachers in schools and colleges were replaced by Nazis.

But always the Jews suffered the first of all, and often the worst of all. In 1933 their businesses were boycotted. In 1935, through the Nuremberg Laws, they were deprived of their citizenship, which had been given them by the constitution of the German Empire in 1871. Little by little they were driven out of every type of business and profession. They had to live a real ghetto life, with their own

367

History of the Jews in the United States

schools, theatres and newspapers; finally they even had to wear a yellow badge as in the Middle Ages. In November 1938 came the climax; synagogues were burned, Jews were arrested in great numbers, many of them were killed, and the whole community was fined a total of a billion marks. This wiped out practically everything that the Jews of Germany still had left at the end of those terrible five years.

Naturally, as many Jews as possible left Germany for other lands, although everywhere immigration laws were an obstacle. Only ten to twenty thousand a year managed to enter the United States. But this small group included very valuable people: physicians, scientists, writers and rabbis. The most prominent Christian among the refugees was Thomas Mann, a Nobel prize winner for literature; the best known Jew was Albert Einstein, winner of the same prize for physics and one of the greatest scientists of all time. A University in Exile was organized in New York, whose professors were all eminent men and women (both Jews and Christians) who had fled from Germany, Italy and other lands of fascist oppression. This new wave of Jewish immigration, though much smaller than the ones before it, had a character all its own, for it included a large number of people of national and international reputation.

Hitler's war against the Jews began in 1933, while his war against other peoples began six years later. He formally declared war on the Jews of the whole world with the open intention of destroying them all. Every country

368

under Nazi domination accepted the Nuremberg laws, even Italy which had long shown tolerance to its ancient Jewish communities. Meanwhile, the Nazi propaganda extended to every nation in the world, including America. As always anti-Semitism was the entering wedge for an attack on free institutions and for a defense of fascism. The ultimate purpose of this propaganda was to bring about a Nazi state, with labor, education, in fact, every human action and thought, under the control of a single dictator. Labor unions and the liberal government in Washington were attacked, with the aim of undermining free elections and all American institutions.

The period from 1933, when the Nazis took over in Germany, to 1941, when the United States entered the war, was noisy with anti-Semitism. Probably the actual number of Nazi sympathizers, even among German-Americans, was always very small, but the German government backed them with money and influence, so that they were able to attract a great deal of attention. The German-American Bund tried to spread Nazi ideas; a flood of literature came from Germany, including the often-exposed *Protocols*. Certain groups of American "super-patriots" followed the lead, such as the Silver Shirts and the Christian Front. The issue entered national life with a body called America First, which advocated keeping out of the war; it defended Germany, and made the usual attack on the Jews. Father Charles E. Coughlin of Detroit preached over the radio every week and published a weekly magazine called *Social Justice,* spreading these and other dangerous slanders to an immense public.

This imported anti-Semitism differed from the economic discrimination of depression days, which was plainly a result of poverty. Now it was political propaganda, preparatory to Germany's making war on the United States. When the isolationist movements failed and the United States entered the Second World War, patriotic Americans turned strongly against the anti-Semites and most of their public activities stopped. Even Father Coughlin closed his paper and went off the air early in 1944. Only a few politicians, some of them members of Congress, dared to continue the attack on the New Deal as the "Jew Deal" and to defy the feelings of the vast majority of Americans.

For both Jews and Christians had protested strongly against Nazi persecution, and the government of the United States took an official position on the same side. The Federal Council of Churches of Christ in America adopted strong resolutions attacking Hitlerism, and appointed a "day of compassion" for the Jews to be observed in American churches. The Catholic Church in America, the American Federation of Labor, the CIO and many other national organizations condemned the Nazi persecution of the Jews. The National Conference of Christians and Jews, which had been organized in 1928 to work for good will in churches and synagogues, in 1934 founded an annual Brotherhood Week; the President and members of Congress and religious leaders in every denomination expressed their interest in and support of this venture.

A movement to rescue the victims of persecution was

Between Two Wars

also set on foot, but it was tragically ineffective, for every nation refused to change its immigration laws and admit the refugees until it was too late. As early as 1934 the League of Nations appointed a commission for the protection of refugees (Jewish and other); the first High Commissioner was James G. McDonald, an American. He resigned his post at the end of 1935, exposing in a powerful letter the folly of trying to save a few refugees while the Nazis daily increased the number of those who must seek new homes. In 1938, President Roosevelt called a meeting of thirty nations in Evian, France; they formed an Intergovernmental Committee, but did not find places where the persecuted Jews might settle. During the war, in 1943, representatives of the British and American governments met in Bermuda, but decided they would have to wait until after the victory to take any action.

The Nazi persecutions and the hopeless status of the refugees had two results; they convinced many Americans that Palestine was the last chance for European Jewry, and they inspired the collection of funds for relief. The Joint Distribution Committee, organized for the needs of the First World War, had to increase its appeal for funds because of the continually growing number of sufferers and the Jews of America have raised ever larger and larger sums, year by year. We shall read about this in detail in a later chapter. The difficulty of finding a permanent home for refugees led many who had never been Zionists to look to Palestine as the Jewish national home, where the unhappy wanderers might find rest at last.

History of the Jews in the United States

1. Describe the *Protocols*.
2. What is the race theory? Why is it wrong?
3. Give three forms of anti-Semitism in America after the First World War.
4. How is immigration limited? What were the effects of this limitation on the Jews?
5. Give two effects of the depression on American Jews.
6. Describe the Nazi type of anti-Semitism; give its connection with politics, in America and abroad.
7. How did Americans react to defend the Jews against the Nazis?

TOPICS FOR REPORTS

1. The Know-Nothing Party; the American Protective Association; the first and second Ku Klux Klan.
2. Make a collection of accusations against the Jews. Classify them: (a) Those which are untrue. (b) Those which apply to many peoples. (c) Those which apply to the Jews alone.
3. Give examples of leading Americans, past and present, who have shown friendship to the Jews.
4. Read the pamphlet, "The Races of Mankind," by Ruth Benedict; summarize the facts about races to the class.
5. Define propaganda; show the workings of propaganda attacking and defending the Jews.

REFERENCES FOR PUPILS

Clinchy, Everett R., *All in the Name of God*. John Day.
Parkes, James W., *The Jew and His Neighbor*. Smith.
Stegner, Wallace, *One Nation*, a series of pictures from *Look*, illustrating the status of minorities in America.
Gittelsohn, Roland B., *Modern Jewish Problems*, chapter VIII.

372

Between Two Wars

REFERENCES FOR TEACHERS

The American Jewish Yearbooks have a splendid summary, year
by year, of events and trends in the United States. Many
of these passages may also be read in part by the pupils.
Lasker, Bruno, *Jewish Experiences in America*. The Inquiry.
Myers, Gustavus, *History of Bigotry in the United States*.
Random House; this includes a section on anti-Semitism.

CHAPTER 23.

The Second World War
and Its Aftermath

WHEN the great war broke out, the American Jews were ready. They defended their country because they were Americans; in every field of military and civil service they did their share. And because they were Jews and felt for their persecuted brothers overseas, they redoubled their efforts to help them by the collection of money, by organization and by whatever influence they could achieve. The story from 1941, when the United States entered the war, until 1949, when this is being written, is a double story of the service of Jews to America and of their aid to Jews the world over.

It must be remembered that this was the first war since the destruction of the Jewish nation when all Jews were ranged on one side, for none fought in the ranks of the Nazis. American Jews and the Jews of every allied country knew that they were fighting not only for their own lands, but also for the oppressed Jews of the nations under the heel of the Nazis.

No wonder there was a special outpouring of enthusiasm among American Jews, both in the military service and in civilian war work.

374

The Second World War and Its Aftermath

THE National Jewish Welfare Board set up a Bureau of War Records to gather all possible facts about the Jews in the armed services. This bureau established committees in over a thousand cities and towns. The committees reported to the Bureau the activities of their fellow-townsmen in the armed services. Then studies were made in twenty different cities to check these reports and find out how nearly they were complete.

The total number of Jewish soldiers and sailors, WACS and WAVES, recruited from the Jewish population, greatly increased, now came to fully 550,000 during the time of actual fighting, and to 600,000 if we include all those who were inducted during the emergency, up to the end of 1948. This was the equivalent of thirty-seven full divisions of Jewish soldiers. We should expect to find that Jews were enrolled under the draft in exactly the same percentage as everybody else. Actually, this was so; in every city where a complete study was made the Jewish percentage in the services was found to be as high or higher than that of the general population. Between 11 and 12 per cent of all the Jews in America were enrolled in the Army and Navy. As very few Jews were eligible for exemption as farmers and not very many as workers in war factories, we are not surprised to see their percentage in the armed services so high.

These Jews were enrolled in every type of service and in every rank: 81 per cent were in the Army, 16 per cent

375

in the Navy, 2 per cent in the Marines and 1 per cent in the Coast Guard. Of the men in the Army, one out of six served in the infantry; the Jews were highest in percentage in the air force, medical corps and signal corps. Actually, 29 per cent of the Jewish soldiers were enrolled in the air corps, and one out of every five of these was a flyer, so that the proportion of Jewish flyers was far higher than we should expect.

About 20 per cent of all the Jewish service men were commissioned officers, almost double the percentage for the armed forces as a whole. Probably this was due to the fact that many Jewish boys had a good education and could qualify for commissions; as, for example, the very large number of Jewish physicians and dentists who enrolled.

Twenty-three Jews became Generals or Admirals during the war. There were six Major Generals, thirteen Brigadier Generals, one Admiral, two Rear Admirals and one Commodore. Of all these, the highest rank was attained by Admiral Ben Morreel, who attained the second highest rank in the United States Navy.

As so many Jews served in the dangerous branches, such as air corps, infantry, and marines, a very large number were killed or wounded. We know that 8,000 Jews were killed in action, another 2,500 died in service, and 18,000 were wounded in combat. Altogether, 35,000 Jews were casualties—killed, wounded, missing and prisoners.

The decorations awarded to Jewish service men amounted to at least 61,500, given to 35,000 different soldiers and sailors. It has been checked that these men were actually Jews; it is likely that there were many more Jews who received decorations but whose religion was not known to the Bureau of War Records. One Jew was awarded the Congressional Medal of Honor, Lt. Raymond Zussman of Detroit. In the fighting in the Rhone Valley, Lt. Zussman of the Tank Corps liberated a French town, killed seventeen Nazi soldiers and captured ninety-two single-handed; he was later killed in action. Seventy-four received the Distinguished Service Cross, thirty-seven the Navy Cross, and 2,400 the Distinguished Flying Cross. The Purple Heart was conferred on all the dead and wounded, 26,000 in all. Some men received many decorations, especially in the Air Forces. Probably the most decorated were Tech. Sgt. Abraham A. Todros of Brooklyn, who received thirty-one awards for his work with the French underground forces, and Capt. Edwin F. Radin of Brooklyn, the navigator of a B 26, who received twenty-nine, including the Croix de Guerre.

So great was the participation of the Jews in the service that the Jewish Welfare Board issued a two-volume work entitled *American Jews in World War II*. The first volume is made up of incidents of heroism in the various branches of the service and in various theatres of war; the second comprises lists of names of the dead and those awarded military decorations—enough to fill a whole volume!

The incidents of heroism are almost innumerable, and many of them attracted the attention of the entire American people. Major General Maurice G. Rose, son of a rabbi in Denver, Colorado, was commanding officer of the Third Armored Division on the advance in Germany. In March 1945, General Rose led a group of men on a patrol ahead of his troops; his car was stopped by a group of Germans, and when they suspected that he was about to resist, they shot him dead. He was one of the highest ranking officers killed in action in the war.

Another hero was Sergeant Meyer Levin of Brooklyn, a bombardier in the far Pacific. On the very first day of the war, Captain Colin Kelly was pilot and Levin bombardier in a Flying Fortress which damaged the Japanese battleship Haruna. Kelly was killed in the crash of the plane, but the crew bailed out and Levin took part in sixty bombing missions until finally he too was killed when his plane crashed at sea.

Barney Ross, one of the most popular prize fighters in the country and at one time champion, was a private in the Marines when he fought his greatest battle in November 1942 on Guadalcanal. For a whole night he warded off a Japanese attack almost single-handed, as most of his comrades had been wounded early in the fight.

One of the most touching radio messages was the one sent by Sergeant Irving Strobing from Corregidor just before its surrender to the Japanese. Its concluding words were: "The jig is up. Everyone is bawling like a baby. They are piling dead and wounded in our tunnel. Arms weak from pounding keys long hours, no rest, short rations, tired. Love to all my family and friends. God bless

378

The Second World War and Its Aftermath

By Dudley Summers for the NCCJ

THE FOUR HEROIC CHAPLAINS

'em all. Hope they'll be there when I come home. Tell Joe (a brother in the Coast Guard) to give 'em hell for us. God bless you and keep you. Stand by . . ." Strobing spent the subsequent years as a prisoner of war, until released by the advancing Americans.

We find such acts of heroism, not only in the fighting arms of the service, but also among the medical corps and the chaplains, men whose mission it is to heal and not to fight. The nation was deeply moved by the account of the last hours of Chaplain Alexander Goode, who died at sea with three other chaplains, one Catholic and two Protestant. The four were on the transport "Dorchester" in the North Atlantic in June, 1943, when the ship was struck by a torpedo. All four of them gave their life-belts to soldiers who could not find any in the confusion, and all four prayed together as the ship went down.

II. THE JEWISH CHAPLAINS AND THE JWB

FOR the first time in Jewish history, a very large part of the rabbis of a nation were called to take part in military service as chaplains, that is, as rabbis for the troops. When the reform, conservative and orthodox rabbinical conferences joined together to form CANRA (the Committee on Army and Navy Religious Activities of the Jewish Welfare Board), they sent out an urgent call for volunteers. All three bodies of rabbis cooperated, with the result that over a thousand rabbis offered themselves and 311 served as chaplains—267 in the Army, 43 in the Navy, and one in the U. S. Mercantile Service. This number was over ten times that of the First World War; the Navy alone had almost twice as many chaplains as all branches of the service twenty-five years before.

These men came from every seminary in the United States and represented all branches of Judaism. Seven of them were themselves refugees from Europe who had come to America and become American citizens; they were eager to serve in the war against the Nazis. They served in every theatre of war from Greenland to New Guinea and Korea, from India to North Africa and Germany. At first they worked in training camps and hospitals at home. Then the great majority of them accom-

380

The Second World War and Its Aftermath

CHAPLAIN CONDUCTS SERVICE (PACIFIC AREA)

panied their men overseas. They landed on dangerous beach heads; they took their part in battles in European and Pacific areas; some of them covered a thousand miles of the Burma Road as their area, while others flew from one Pacific island to another to serve the men of the Air Forces. Sixty-four of the Jewish chaplains were decorated for exceptional service. Nine died while in service, among them Alexander Goode in a ship at sea, Irving Tepper on the battle-field of Normandy, and Louis Werfel in a plane crash in North Africa.

Every chaplain of every religion had the same duties and faced the same dangers. But the Jewish chaplains had to cover far more ground than any other because the Jews were a small minority, scattered in every unit of the Army, Navy and Marines. In Europe they travelled about by jeep to meet their men, in the Pacific by plane or boat. One Jewish chaplain covered all of free China for an

381

entire year. Another had a congregation which extended from Newfoundland to Greenland, and on to Bermuda and the Azores. Others served on transports and hospital ships, or covered the ships and shore installations of an entire fleet in the Pacific. Every Marine Division had its Jewish chaplain, so that their territory covered all the island battles, from Iwo Jima to Okinawa, and also the occupation forces in Japan, Korea, and China.

A few chaplains occupied administrative positions at various headquarters, where they had charge of distributing Jewish supplies and advised commanding officers on the assignment of Jewish chaplains in the field. A few others were instructors in the chaplains' schools of the Army and Navy. Many served in hospitals both at home and abroad, bringing the consolation and the encouragement of religion to the sick and wounded.

When the Americans liberated the concentration camps in Germany, the first to aid the miserable prisoners were the Jewish chaplains. Many of these victims were Jews. Imagine the joy of these people, who had been imprisoned and starved for no other offense than that of being Jews, when they saw Army officers wearing the insignia of the Tables of the Law and the Star of David! When the chaplains arrived at the camps they went to work, giving every possible assistance to the sufferers. They obtained food and medical aid through the Army, prayerbooks from the JWB, they made lists of the survivors in order to facilitate the reunion of families, they distributed packages from friends in America. The chaplains were able to explain the needs of the Displaced Persons to the military authorities and to interpret the military orders to the newly liberated Jews.

Throughout the world the chaplains made contacts with Jews, from Australia and England to such out-of-the-way groups as the Jewries of India, Iran and China. Through their efforts many positive results were accomplished, such as an orphanage in France, a rebuilt synagogue in Manila, and a Hebrew school in Karachi, India.

The National Jewish Welfare Board expanded greatly in its activities during the war. It was one of the six agencies in the USO (United Service Organizations) which provided recreation, religion and education for the service men and women. The National Jewish Welfare Board took part in 250 USO operations in every part of the country. Some of these were clubs conducted entirely by JWB; others were jointly conducted with the YMCA, the National Catholic Community Service, or several of the religious organizations. In some cases a JWB worker was put into an area, where he found and served scattered Jewish men in the mountains, the deserts or along the seashore. At the peak of the Board's activities about 300 workers were in the field, while 626 Jewish communities cooperated through their local committees.

Overseas, the JWB was represented in the USO organizations of Hawaii, Panama, South America, Bermuda and the Philippines. Their representative in the Philippine Islands was imprisoned by the Japanese for three years because he was an American, but as soon as he was released by the American troops he reopened the club in Manila. In the war zones only a few representatives of the JWB were allowed, because the Red Cross was in charge of recreation in those areas. A half dozen workers went to Europe, where they opened religious hospitality centers in Paris, Heidelberg and Frankfurt. One man served in Australia and another in India, backing up the chaplains in every way possible.

An outstanding phase of JWB work during the war was CANRA, Committee on Army and Navy Religious Activities. This body worked on behalf of the three religious groups in American Jewry to secure Jewish chaplains to care for the religious needs of the Jews in the Army and Navy. CANRA recruited chaplains and recommended them to the military authorities; it aided the chaplains with advice, supplies and funds; it sent representatives to every theatre of war for formal visits of inspection under military authority. Since 1917, the Army and Navy recognized the JWB as the official agency for the Jewish religion in the armed services, parallel to the equivalent Catholic and Protestant religious bodies.

The most important events of the year for chaplains and JWB alike were the High Holy Days and Passover. Great congregations came together for these occasions in training camps at home as in foreign lands. By jeep, by plane, by boat the Jewish soldiers gathered to worship, whether in a great auditorium in Honolulu, a hut in the New Guinea jungles, or a captured Nazi stronghold in Germany. Meanwhile months ahead of time the JWB was

384

sending out supplies in readiness for the occasion. Special prayerbooks for the Holy Days, wine and *matzahs* for Passover—these were needed from the Himalayas to the Rhine. On the Passover of 1946, several chaplains held services for the first night in the Rhineland, but for the second night they found themselves across the Rhine, deep in Germany hurrying to keep up with the advancing armies. Four thousand soldiers attended a single Seder in Florence, Italy. Some chaplains prayed with the ancient Jewish communities of North Africa or Iran. Others brought the message of Israel to lands which had never known it before, to Iceland, Alaska and Guadalcanal.

One of the really amazing contributions of the JWB was the constant flow of supplies from New York and San Francisco to every part of the world. JWB became the largest publisher of Jewish books ever known, for the organization sent out 2,000,000 prayerbooks, half of them for Sabbaths, half for Passover and the High Holy Days. In addition, there were 700,000 abridged Bibles, 1,400,-000 Jewish calendars, 1,500,000 pamphlets—altogether, a tremendous amount of literature for the soldiers. Over a million *mezuzahs* were given out, together with quantities of other religious materials. Kosher food was sent all over the world for orthodox Jews in the armed services. Nine hundred thousand packages of *matzahs* were supplied for the six Passovers of wartime, also wine and other necessary materials. Much of this great purchasing and shipping business was accomplished with the aid of the Army and Navy, especially when the shipments went overseas.

History of the Jews in the United States

III. CIVILIAN WAR SERVICE

THE combined emotions of American patriotism and of loathing for the Nazis influenced the great mass of Americans, and particularly the American Jews into action. Civilian communities were extremely active during the war. Every Jewish Community Center and many synagogues opened their doors for the recreation of the soldiers and sailors; some of them even housed USO clubs. The many differing types of civilian war work attracted devoted Jewish men and women, boys and girls.

The B'nai B'rith may serve as an outstanding example, though every national and local organization had its own record of accomplishment. Over 21,000 members of the order and its auxiliaries served in the armed forces; 500 were killed and almost 500 were decorated. The National War Service Committee directed civilian activities; members of the B'nai B'rith sold over $700,000,000 worth of war bonds, donated 72,000 pints of blood, and provided 46,000 volunteer workers in civilian defense. They served ships, camps and USO clubs, made surgical dressings, provided Torahs for camps and ships, collected scrap metal by the ton, and raised funds for the Red Cross and the United Jewish Appeal as well as for their own direct contribution to the war effort.

The religious organizations published pamphlets on religious subjects for circulation among the troops, such as the Voice of Religion series of the Union of American Hebrew Congregations. The Jewish Publication Society

386

printed the many thousands of prayerbooks and other Hebrew works needed by the Jewish Welfare Board. Every Jewish body, large and small, contributed to the limit in the drive to win the war.

A small and very special group of Jewish scientists took part in the work of inventing and producing the first atomic bombs. The original idea of the conversion of mass into energy was based on studies made by Albert Einstein thirty years before. A letter from him brought the project before President Roosevelt for the first time. One of the two scientists who had first worked out a chain reaction in Germany was Lise Meitner, a Jewish woman; she afterward escaped to Sweden and passed on this experiment to Allied physicists. When the work on the bomb was organized, many Jews were among the scientists enrolled; refugees from Hitler like Prof. Leo Szilard of the University of Chicago and American Jews like Prof. Robert Oppenheimer of the University of California, the head of the laboratories at Los Alamos, New Mexico.

IV. THE DESTRUCTION OF EUROPEAN JEWRY

THE First World War had ruined the Jews of eastern Europe; the Second destroyed them utterly. The Nazis killed or imprisoned many millions of Poles and Russians, of French and Greeks, but they deliberately tried to exterminate the Jews of every land. In fact, they killed six million Jews, leaving only a million and a half alive west of the Russian border. Of the former, probably two million were massacred by the invading army. But fully four million were systematically slaughtered in the camps especially built for the purpose. Men, women and children were driven into gas chambers until the rooms were crowded; then gas was let in to choke them. The bodies were burned in great crematoria. Before their deaths, many of these helpless people were compelled to work for the Nazis, or they were used for medical experiments, or tortured in horrible ways. Whatever little they owned was saved for the use of the Germans; warehouses were filled with clothing formerly worn by the victims; there were whole rooms filled with baby clothing and shoes. Rumors of all this reached America but nobody could believe that any people in the world could be guilty of such brutality. After the liberation of the concentration camps General Eisenhower invited a delegation of editors and congressmen to see for themselves, and to tell the story to the American people. The complete proof was made public at the trial of the Nazi leaders in Nuremberg.

One of the German tricks to catch the Jews was to establish ghettos and then empty them gradually into the death camps. The largest of these was in Warsaw, where a half million Jews were herded together in a small section of the city, surrounded by a huge stone wall. The Jews within the ghetto organized their own schools and Zionist societies; the younger ones formed a military organization and gathered such weapons as they could from the Polish underground. Lists were issued weekly for those who were to be deported; one head of the Jewish community killed himself rather than prepare these lists for the death of his

The Second World War and Its Aftermath

fellow-Jews. Finally, in April, 1943, when only 40,000 were left in the ghetto, the remnant made ready to resist. When driven back by their fire, the Nazis brought up tanks and planes; they set fire to the four corners of the ghetto; they searched daily, not only for fighters, but for any living Jew whom they might kill. For six weeks the Jews resisted until the last little band of defenders gave up their lives in the tradition of Bar Kochba.

Every Jewish institution in the great East European reservoir of Jewish life and learning was destroyed. Synagogues were burned, schools were closed, Jewish leaders and scholars were either dead or had fled to foreign lands. No longer would world Jewry look to Poland and its neighbors for Jewish ideals and Jewish leadership. Tragically, without our doing anything about the matter, the leadership of world Jewry was transferred to America, which by the end of the war held almost half the Jews of the world.

We wonder that any Jews escaped the horror in Europe. Some escaped overseas at an early date; others, suffering terrible hardships, found their way to Russia or through Russia to China; some fled to Spain or Switzerland; the Jews of Denmark were ferried across the narrow but dangerous seas by their fellow Danes to a haven in Sweden. Probably the largest number survived in lands like Hungary and Roumania which were always anti-Semitic, but had not strictly followed orders to deport all their Jews to the death camps in Poland. Others emerged after years of fighting in the underground; some were

389

hidden, at the risk of their own lives, by brave and generous Christians. Many Catholic priests and the Pope himself gave shelter to hunted Jews, and especially to Jewish children. A starving and fearful remnant of the prisoners in the concentration camps were still found alive when the Allied armies dashed up in the last days of the war.

V. AMERICA AND THE JEWS

THE survivors in Europe were at first cared for by the Allied armies, then by UNRRA (the United Nations Relief and Rehabilitation Administration) and by JDC. The Jews of America began to raise larger and larger sums for their aid. The 1946 collection of the UJA (United Jewish Appeal) amounted to the vast sum of $100,000,000, followed in 1947 by $125,000,000 and in 1948 by $150,000,-000, totals unprecedented in the story of private giving. Only governments ordinarily raise and disburse such huge amounts of money. American Jewry achieved a stronger organization during the war through the American Jewish Conference, which included almost all the national organizations and local communities. Finally, Zionist sympathy increased tremendously among both Jews and Christians, who saw the great need of the survivors from Hitlerism for a home in Palestine and realized that there was no other safe place where they might go. The Jews wanted to escape from Europe, the graveyard of their families and friends. Most of them longed, above all, to live as Jews in the Jewish homeland. Their well-wishers in Amer-

390

ica tried to back them up in the fulfillment of their well justified desire.

As early as January, 1944, President Roosevelt had appointed a War Refugee Board to save the victims of Hitlerism. The first executive director of this board was John W. Pehle, the second, Brig. Gen. William O'Dwyer (afterward mayor of New York City). This body worked largely in connection with underground anti-Nazi forces in various countries. They succeeded in rescuing some Jews from the Balkan states and took them to Palestine, bringing others from France to Spain. They provided temporary relief for some in neutral Sweden and Switzerland, and helped in the establishment of refugee camps in North Africa.

In the same year, President Roosevelt established a "free port" for a thousand refugees at Oswego, N. Y. The majority of these were Jews, and Jewish organizations helped to establish decent conditions for human living in the camp. At the end of the war, those who wished were permitted to remain in the United States.

The number of immigrants entering through the usual channels was very small, chiefly because of the problems of wartime, but also due to the strict immigration laws. The President directed that these laws be applied in a humane fashion at the close of the war, but only 13,000 Jews entered our borders during the first post-war year. Probably the most important move to aid the survivors was the proposal of President Truman to the British government that they admit 100,000 to Palestine imme-

History of the Jews in the United States

diately. We shall see in the chapter on Zionism how this project was held up by successive investigations, but there is no doubt that it was the boldest move made by any world leader to aid the Jewish refugees.

President Truman also requested the Congress to pass laws permitting war refugees, both Jews and Christians, to come to America above the quota. In 1948, Congress passed such a law, admitting within two years 205,000 of the displaced persons, as they were officially called. But this law was hedged in by so many restrictions that it would actually admit very few, and the smallest number of these would be Jews. From 1949 to the present, efforts have been made to liberalize our immigration laws, but without success.

Of indirect aid to the Jews was the threat of punishment for their persecutors which President Roosevelt delivered in 1944. This could no longer help the Jews of Germany or Poland, but it probably was an important factor in saving many of the Jews of Hungary, who were being threatened with extinction. When the Nuremberg trial of the Nazi leaders was held in 1946, one of the four charges was that of "crimes against humanity," and under this heading the atrocities toward the Jews were proved conclusively by hundreds of documents written by the Nazis themselves as well as by the testimony of survivors. Perhaps this great trial, and especially the opening address of the American Supreme Court Justice, Robert Jackson, set a new standard for international morality, as it was intended to do. Genocide, the slaughter of a whole people,

392

was declared a crime, even if conducted as a part of military operations. It is most important also that the Nazis were charged with crimes against the German Jews even before war was declared; previously such matters had always been exempt on the ground that one nation might not interfere with the internal affairs of another.

VI. THE UNITED NATIONS

WHEN the United Nations came together for their organizational meeting in San Francisco in April, 1945, the Jews were not officially represented as a nation. But Secretary of State Stettinius, who led the United States delegation, invited forty-two national organizations to be his consultants. Among these two were Jewish, the American Jewish Conference, represented by Henry Monsky, and the American Jewish Committee, represented by Judge Joseph Proskauer. A number of other organizations sent unofficial representatives, who were able to discuss Jewish matters with the official delegates of various nations. The Jewish people were not recognized as a national entity, but American Jews now had the most direct recognition they had ever been given by an international body.

Two chief projects were advanced by the Jewish representatives. The first was Zionism, and on this they had to be content with a negative victory. They could not secure an endorsement of Jewish nationalism, but they did prevent a resolution by the Arab representatives which would have left out groups without governments of their own. The other was the proposal for an international Bill of

Rights, similar to the Bill of Rights in our Federal Constitution, to protect fundamental rights of men and women everywhere in the world. So far as it was effective, such a Bill of Rights would, of course, protect the rights of all minorities, including the Jews. The United Nations Organization decided that such a declaration should be worked out. A year later the Economic and Social Council appointed a Commission on Human Rights to take up the matter; Mrs. Eleanor Roosevelt, American delegate, was elected chairman of the Commission, and its report was adopted by the General Assembly of the U. N. in 1948.

The first official international recognition of the Jewish Agency as the spokesman for Jewish interests in Palestine was given in May, 1947. Rabbi Abba Hillel Silver of Cleveland, Ohio, then president of the Zionist Organization of America, made a dignified and powerful statement before the Political Committee of the United Nations, the committee which had been selected by the Security Council to investigate the problem of Palestine. The Jews did not have the same standing as the Arabs, for these had several member nations of the United Nations to speak for them. But the Jewish Agency was invited to attend the meeting of the special committee and to present its side of the matter.

The United Nations appointed a committee to study the situation in Palestine and also the problem of the Jewish refugees in Europe. This committee recommended the partition of Palestine into Jewish and Arab states. The report was accepted by the General Assembly on No-

The Second World War and Its Aftermath

vember 29, 1947, which has thus become one of the great dates in Jewish history. It marks the reestablishment of the Jewish nation in Palestine, which was destroyed by the Romans almost two thousand years ago.

From this time on, events moved rapidly. Great Britain gave up the mandate for Palestine in May, 1948. On the very same day, May 14, 1948, the State of Israel was proclaimed in Palestine, with Chaim Weizmann as president and David Ben Gurion, leader of the labor party, as premier. Through the summer and fall Palestine was invaded by various Arab armies, but the Jewish forces beat them in hard-fought battles. Meanwhile the United States, Russia, and many other countries recognized the new nation, and the United Nations tried to arrange for peace between Israel and the Arab states. On January 25, 1949, the first national election was held in Israel, by then recognized as a modern democratic nation.

VII. JEW AND CHRISTIAN IN AMERICA

IN THE last chapter we have seen how the Nazi program included bitter attacks on the American Jews, as well as on all Jewry. When the United States declared war on Germany all such direct propaganda had to stop. The great majority of Americans then came to realize the real nature of this German anti-Semitism, that it had always been a part of the fascist attack on our democratic institutions. Religious, labor and political organizations condemned anti-Semitism bitterly as a part of the Nazi view of life.

History of the Jews in the United States

Father Coughlin went off the air in 1944. Thirty pro fascists and anti-Semites were indicted for sedition and brought to trial in 1944, but the judge died and the government never started the trial over again. In the presidential campaign of 1944 some people tried to attack the Roosevelt administration through the person of Sidney Hillman, the labor leader, who was secretary of the Political Action Committee, and was known to be a Jew, born in Lithuania.

After the war, the greater freedom of utterance encouraged several propagandists to hold forth again. Gerald L. K. Smith toured the country, preaching extravagant race hatred. The Ku Klux Klan had a revival in the South and the Christian Front in Long Island, N. Y. A few members of Congress continued their attacks on minority groups, including the Jews.

On the whole, however, this whole movement was noisy and annoying rather than deep-rooted in American life. Many of the worst anti-Semites were defeated when they ran for office. Some of the trouble makers were jailed for inciting to riot, Mr. Smith among them. Yet when the national Fair Employment Practices Commission expired in 1946, only five states passed laws to prevent discrimination against any minority group in employment—New York, New Jersey, Indiana, Massachusetts and Wisconsin. Sixteen states now have such laws.

Discrimination against Jews and other minorities was exposed in some eastern universities, as when the American Jewish Congress brought suit against Columbia

396

University in New York, claiming that it was a "class institution" and because of discrimination it should not be exempt from taxes as a public institution. There was even talk of extending the discrimination common in medical schools to dental schools as well, but this was speedily stopped by the action of the dentists and their national organizations.

Anti-Semitism does not really belong in America; its recent outbreaks have been influenced by Nazi examples. A Gallup poll of the American people condemned the Nazi persecution of the Jews by 94 per cent. The labor organizations opposed anti-Semitism; the churches fought against it, both through the National Conference of Christians and Jews and by their own organizations. Brotherhood Week, organized by this body, became an important event, endorsed by presidents and governors and observed by 1946 in three thousand different communities. Some people organized into "exclusive" clubs and fraternities, which usually means that they exclude Jews from their social group, but this has little to do with business, politics or the broader phases of American life.

In the happiness over the victory, many people felt a grave disappointment that any anti-Semitism remained when we and our Allies had just beaten the great anti-Semites of the world. In response to this remaining prejudice, the Jewish organizations began two courses of action. First, some of them organized institutes to study the causes of prejudice and its method of development. They felt that we can thus approach a cure scientifically, just as the doctor, in treating a disease, first must know all he can about its origin and the different ways it affects patients. Second, Jewish organizations began to feel that it was their business not only to defend Jews from attack, but also to champion the cause of all minorities. Many Jews had always done this as became good citizens; now they did so as Jews. Only under a real democracy will the Jew have an equal chance for jobs, a right to education and an opportunity to share in every national activity. So Jewish organizations have become more aggressive in fighting for democracy, for rights for the Negro, for the rights of labor and for expansion of immigration. To be a good Jew it is necessary also to be a good citizen.

We have entered a new period in the history of American Jews, a period in which we are not only self-contained and self-reliant, but also a people to whom the Jewry of the world may turn for leadership. It is hard to imagine what the future will be like, though in the last chapter of this book we shall try to make a few guesses. But first we shall glance about the country, see how many Jews we now have in America, how they observe their religion, how they educate their children and how they are carrying on their life as Jews. Then we shall be entitled to a better guess as to how far their leadership will carry them and world Jewry in the years that lie ahead.

The Second World War and Its Aftermath

REVIEW QUESTIONS

1. Tell about the Jewish soldiers and sailors in World War II.
2. Why were the Jewish chaplains important? What did they do?
3. How did the Nazis destroy the Jews of Europe? In what ways did they attack the Jews of America?
4. What did America do for the persecuted Jews? What did the United Nations accomplish for them?

TOPICS FOR REPORTS

1. Study the report of some national Jewish organization, or one in your own city; report on its civilian war work.
2. Tell the experience of one Jewish chaplain or soldier, preferably one whom you know, though you will find fine material in the references below.
3. The Nuremberg trials.
4. There are many books describing the experiences of persons who survived the concentration camps, a few also about the Warsaw ghetto. Read one of these and tell the story to the class.
5. In what ways is the new period for American Jewry different from others in the past? Give examples of various kinds.

REFERENCES FOR PUPILS

Blumenthal, L. Roy, *Fighting for America*, 1945.
Kaufman, I., *The American Jew in World War II*, 1947, both published by the National Jewish Welfare Board.
Rontch, Isaac E., *Jewish Youth at War*, letters home from men and women in the service.
Golub and Green, *A Short History of the Jews*, Book IV, chapters VII, VIII, IX. Union.

History of the Jews in the United States

The Black Book, the Nazi Crime against the Jewish people, a source book compiled by the World Jewish Congress, the Jewish Anti-Fascist Committee (Russian), the Vaad Leumi (Palestinian) and the American Committee of Jewish Writers, Artists and Scientists.

Gottschalk, Max, and Abraham Duker, *The Jews in the Post-War World,* Dryden.

Elbogen, Ismar, *A Century of Jewish Life,* Jewish Publication Society, 1944, a volume which brings Graetz up to date, including the Nazis in the last chapter.

Hobson, Laura, *Gentleman's Agreement.* Simon & Schuster.

400

PART III
Trends in American Jewry

CHAPTER 24.

A Bird's-Eye View of American Jewry

THE story of the Jews of the United States up to 1961 is now told. But many of the questions of greatest interests are still unanswered. It is therefore necessary to turn from narrative to description, to make a rapid survey of the American Jews of the present day. This part of the study is not history in the narrower meaning, for it no longer tells the story of men and women who have completed their work. It is applied history, history still going on about us.

We have studied the Jews of the United States piecemeal according to their migrations to America, and now we shall glance at them together, as they live today. We shall want to know something about their numbers and their wealth, where they live and what they do; about the various institutions by means of which they practice their religion, teach their children, care for their brothers in need, and protect the name of Jew. In addition, we are interested to learn about prominent Jews of our own day who are active in politics and business, in literature and scientific discovery, in the labor movement and in philanthropy.

History of the Jews in the United States

THERE is no exact census of the Jews of the United States because the Bureau of the Census is forbidden to ask any question about religion. But we have a fairly accurate idea of how many Jews live in this country. For some years there were exact figures on Jewish immigration; in many cities the Jews have made a census of their own communities; and every ten years there has been a special census of religious bodies conducted with the cooperation of the various church organizations. We therefore have a fair idea of how many Jews live in the United States, but not exactly how many. The latest complete study was made in 1937, and since that time the numbers have been only estimated.

In 1959 fully 5,367,000 Jews live in the United States, or 3 per cent of the total population. This means that we are a very great body of people, but only a small part of the American people as a whole. We are by far the largest body of Jews left in the world after the Second World War; the second is that of the Soviet Union, which is probably about two million. We comprise almost half the Jews alive in the world today. Because of our free institutions and because America suffered less than Europe from the two great wars, the Jews of America stand out in world Jewry for their more modern education and their greater wealth.

As we have seen in our history, the great mass of the Jewish immigrants, fully 2,000,000 souls, came here in

404

the thirty-three years between the pogroms in Russia and the First World War. Since that time, only 20,000 Jews have entered this country per year for a period of over thirty years. This means first, that the numbers or the types of Jews in America will no longer be influenced by the flood of immigration. The annual increase of the Jewish population by immigration is less than half of one per cent, or too little to make any real difference. It means also that most of the Jews now living in America were born here, the children or grandchildren of immigrants. The immigrants themselves, who came here thirty or forty or fifty years ago, have grown old and many of them have died, leaving a Jewish population who were almost all born and educated in the United States.

Over two million of the five million American Jews live in New York City, which holds the greatest Jewish community ever gathered together in any city in the world. Originally the new immigrants lived on the lower East Side, crowded together in high tenements, where they had not enough room for either health or comfort. But in the course of years they moved to many other sections of the great city. By 1959, fully 854,000 Jews were living in Brooklyn and 493,000 in the Bronx, leaving Manhattan far behind with about 339,000. Some live in huge apartment houses, some in new sections with small houses set among trees. But great masses of Jewish people still live in poor and crowded sections because they cannot afford to pay for decent homes.

Some Jews live in every state and territory of this

History of the Jews in the United States

country but their number is not always proportional to the population of the state. The Jews are primarily city people, and always have a larger percentage living in the great industrial states, with their large cities. Still, we find Jews living in 10,500 different places in the United States. There are Jews in every city of 25,000 or more and in most of the smaller cities as well; in fact, 90 per cent of all cities and towns in America include Jews according to the record of the religious census. About 150,000 Jews live in tiny groups consisting of 100 Jews or less, most of them without a congregation or any other Jewish communal activity.

But 70 per cent of all these Jews live in the twelve largest cities in the country. After New York comes Los Angeles, which has grown very fast, and now has 400,000 Jews. Next come Philadelphia with 330,000 and Chicago with 282,000. Eighty-seven per cent of the Jews live in ten states which have over 100,000 Jews each, and all of which include great cities.

Contrast this to the 150,000 Jews scattered in tiny groups in 7,700 villages and country districts. In the big cities of 100,000 or over, the Jews make up 11 per cent of all the inhabitants, while in the rural places they are less than half of 1 per cent of the population.

The important thing about this distribution of the Jews is that it differs from that of the American population as a whole. Practically every minority group lives in one or another section of the country and engages in

406

A Bird's-Eye View of American Jewry

some special type of work. For example, the Swedes have settled in Minnesota and surrounding areas and are largely farmers. The Poles have centered in the Pittsburgh area and many of them work in the coal mines and steel mills. The Jews live chiefly in the big cities and engage in trade and manufacturing. The scattered Jews in the smaller towns are chiefly merchants, while the comparatively small number living in the rural districts are farmers.

Since immigration has come to a virtual end the Jews are not increasing faster than the American population as a whole. In fact, because many of them have small families, their percentage of the American population as a whole may actually decrease within a few years. The American Jews are steadily becoming an older group; they have an insufficient number of children to keep down the average age level and to make the group grow in numbers.

II. SOCIAL CLASSES AMONG JEWS

As WE have learned, the Jews came to America from many lands at different periods but most of them started out extremely poor. In the time that has elapsed since the first immigrants arrived, some few of them have made great fortunes, while very many have established themselves on a more modest scale. Now they belong to every class of society from the richest to the poorest. The few very wealthy Jews are not, by any means, among the richest men in America; their fortunes do not compare

History of the Jews in the United States

with those of the DuPonts, the Rockefellers or the Mellons.

At the other end of the social scale are many very poor Jews, who are barely able to make a living, and must appeal for assistance whenever they face illness or unemployment. The great Jewish charities grew up during the days of immigration, when the newcomers needed help to get a start in the new world. But it has always been necessary to aid the very poor with money and advice.

The great majority of Jews are similar to the great majority of other Americans. They are neither very rich nor very poor; they make a reasonable living and are able to save a little money. They are self-supporting but not wealthy; these are the greatest supporters of the synagogues and the Jewish schools.

The Jews like every other group in America include farmers, workers and business men. The chief difference is that they have a smaller percentage of farmers, about the same proportion of workers, and a larger proportion of business men than the general population. That is what we mean by saying that the Jews are a middle class group, not that most of them are engaged in business, but that their percentage in small business enterprises is unusually high.

There are now about 100,000 Jews living on farms in the United States and the number has been growing slowly but steadily. This is remarkable, as the general trend in American life is to move from the farms to the cities; yet a number of city bred Jews have been settling on farms.

408

A Bird's-Eye View of American Jewry

The Jewish Agricultural Society was founded in 1900 to give information, advice, loans and every kind of aid to Jews who wish to settle on the soil. It reports that Jews are now farming a total of a million and a half acres, in almost every state. Many are specialists; others are engaged in general farming.

The Jews in small towns are largely engaged in business, either as owners or employees. Many of them came at the time of the German-Jewish migration; first they were peddlers; then they sought fixed locations to settle into business. Other immigrants who arrived later have opened stores or factories in small towns.

In the largest cities, and especially in New York, the majority of Jews are workers. In New York, where over a fourth of the population is Jewish, many trades have more than 25 per cent of Jewish workers. Almost half of all the painters and plumbers, half of the plasterers and over half the sheet metal workers in the New York unions are Jewish. At one time almost all the workers as well as employers in the garment industries were Jewish, but now many young Jews have gone into other lines of work, and non-Jews have entered the men's and women's clothing industry. Even now, however, about half of the garment workers and many more than half of the employers are Jewish. In the fur trades it seems as though almost the whole business were run and worked by Jews. Very few Jews are employed in heavy industry, such as railroading, steel or oil. Jews are largely concentrated in the manufacture of consumers' goods.

History of the Jews in the United States

Many people have thought the Jews were important or even dominant in American business, but careful studies have shown that this is an error. Few Jews are engaged in banking, in the basic manufactures, or in public utilities, either as bosses or workers.

The Jews are largely massed in certain lines of occupation—in the garment industries, in retail trade, and in the field of entertainment. Many department stores belong to Jews, as do a large number of clothing stores, drug stores and groceries.

A very conspicuous group of Jews, though not very great in number, is engaged in the entertainment field—stage, radio, motion picture, and also in music. Some of our best known comedians, producers and concert violinists are included in this group. It would, however, be incorrect to say that the Jews "dominate" this field. If we want to be accurate, we can say only that the percentage of Jews in entertainment work is larger than that in the general population. They are by no means doing Jewish work or entertaining Jews; they are successful precisely because they are popular with the American people as a whole.

Finally, a considerable number of Jews have been entering the learned professions, especially in recent years. Comparatively few of them have gone into fields such as engineering or school teaching where they must rely upon some large organization for employment. Most of them have entered professions where they can set up their own offices, such as medicine, dentistry and law. The trend to

410

the professions is in part a result of the great respect for learning in the Jewish communities of Europe and the special privileges that were accorded to a lawyer or doctor. But certainly it is also a result of the ambition of many young Jews who are eager for learning or who want to improve their station in life, and also of their parents who are willing to make great sacrifices for their children's good.

In these few professions there are certainly many more Jews than would be expected in relation to our proportion of the general population, in spite of the great difficulty Jews experience in entering certain professional schools. But even here the Jews are a small minority of all lawyers, dentists and physicians, even though they have produced some of the outstanding men in these fields.

In former days social classes among Jews were established according to the country of their origin in Europe and to the number of years they had been established in this country. But nowadays few people care whether a family originated in Germany or England, in Russia or Roumania. Jews of all these groups are mingling in congregations, social organizations and philanthropic bodies. They are breaking down the old barriers by marriage, and very soon all these differences based on the old world will probably disappear. The new distinctions will be based on the standing of the family here and now—on occupation and wealth. We already have two large social classes, the workers and the small business men, and two smaller groups, the professional men and the very rich.

411

History of the Jews in the United States

IT IS very important to know not only how many Jews enter the United States or how many are born here, but also how many take part in Jewish activities and remain real Jews.

In their former homes in Europe the Jews had been under heavy pressure to join Christian churches, to inter-marry with Christians, and to leave the Jewish community. Some actually tried this way out, and were able to gain positions as judges, professors or government officials. Some of the younger intellectuals, not seeking their own personal advancement, looked to international socialism to solve the Jewish problem as part of the progress of mankind or to Zionism as a distinctive answer for the Jewish people itself.

Here in America the same forces do not make for "assimilation," as it is usually called. Very few Jews join Christian churches to advance their careers, though some have joined movements such as Christian Science or Ethical Culture because these answered some personal need.

Intermarriage also is a minor problem in America. Some Jewish young people marry Christians and bring up their children as Christians. This is especially common in small towns, where the Jewish young men and women are brought up among non-Jews and have very few Jewish friends. But even here it is not the rule, for most Jewish families in small towns have relatives and friends

412

in big cities not far away, and choose their wives or husbands among other Jews. Perhaps in several generations the tiny groups of Jews in small towns will disappear, but there is little evidence of such a process today.

Some years ago Professor Julius Drachsler made a careful study of thousands of marriage records in New York City. He found that every group except the Jews intermarried frequently with other groups, but that less than two per cent of the Jews intermarried with Christians. While the proportion grew somewhat larger in the second and third generation in America, it remained extremely small when compared with the total number of Jewish marriages. Most Jewish young people marry other Jews either because of loyalty to Judaism, or because most of their friends are Jewish, or because their parents wish it. Neither conversion nor intermarriage is a serious menace to Judaism in America.

But a great many American Jews are losing contact with their people and their faith. This is due to indifference, ignorance and laziness. We shall see in the chapters which follow that only half the adult Jews of America belong to synagogues, that only three-fourths of the Jewish children receive any Jewish education during their school years. This trend away from Judaism, as we shall also see, is combated by the activity of the religious and educational institutions, as well as many others, the clubs, lodges, and Zionist societies, which express Jewish ideas and tend to keep Judaism alive.

As citizens, Jews are rightly interested in many phases

413

of American life. It is only when they permit these other interests to take the place of Jewish loyalty, that they become useless to the Jewish people, and in the long run they might as well not be counted as Jews at all. Actually, the danger to the survival and the progress of American Jews is neither conversion nor intermarriage but indifference. Many Jews were torn out of this indifference by Hitler's persecutions in Europe and by the smaller threats of anti-Semitism in the United States. We do not know whether this kind of influence will actually make loyal Jews of many of them, or whether it is only temporary. As you read the chapters which follow this, one of the most important conclusions which you may look for is how far organized Jewish activity is overcoming the indifference of many individual Jews. Then you can make up your own mind exactly how important this indifference is, and how serious a threat it may become to Jewish strength and Jewish unity.

Review Questions

1. What is the number of Jews in the United States; their percentage of the Jews of the world; of the population of the United States?
2. Tell how the American Jews are distributed in city and country.
3. How are the Jews grouped according to occupation, social classes?
4. Are the Jews of the United States losing large numbers by assimilation? Give three ways in which Jews can be lost to the Jewish group.

A Bird's-Eye View of American Jewry

1. Study the Jewish population in your own state and city, compared with the total population.
2. Study the Jews in a particular line of business or profession.
3. A debate on intermarriage. Is it better that all peoples and religions should fuse into one? Is it better that each should keep its identity?
4. A study of your own family, from its arrival in the United States to the present day; where they lived, their occupations, their synagogue affiliations, etc.
5. Some literary studies of intermarriage, such as *The Melting Pot,* by Zangwill, *The Island Within* by Lewisohn, etc.

REFERENCES FOR PUPILS

The American Jewish Yearbook always contains statistics on the number of Jews, immigration, etc.
Look up the *Encyclopedia of Jewish Knowledge* (one volume) and *Universal Jewish Encyclopedia* (10 volumes) for articles on recent topics.
Edidin, Ben M., *Jewish Community Life in America,* chapter 1.
Gittelsohn, Roland B., *Modern Jewish Problems,* chapter IV.
Goldberg, Nathan, *Economic Trends among American Jews,* a pamphlet of the Jewish Affairs series.
Wise, James W. and Lee J. Levinger, *Mr. Smith, Meet Mr. Cohen,* chapter 1.

REFERENCES FOR TEACHERS

Drachsler, Julius, *Democracy and Assimilation.* Macmillan.
Robison, Sylvia M., *Jewish Population Studies,* 1943.
The Yearbook, vol. 43, pages 654–661, contains a fine summary of H. S. Linfield's Survey.
Davidson, Gabriel, *Our Jewish Farmers,* 1943.

CHAPTER 25.

How the Jew
Keeps His Judaism in America

THE oldest and strongest Jewish institution is the synagogue. In the ghetto the whole of Jewish life revolved about the synagogue; all Jews grew up as devout followers of the faith of Israel. We have seen how every group of Jews who came to America first of all founded religious institutions. So in surveying the great Jewish community of America today our first interest is in the religion of American Jews.

I. THE SYNAGOGUE IN AMERICA

WE HAVE no complete figures about synagogue membership in America. We know that there are about four thousand Jewish congregations in all, of all sizes, and of many different types of Judaism. Apparently, about half the Jews of America are regular members in good standing of these congregations, and this is about the same proportion as that of the general population who belong to the Christian churches.

Of course, some Jews may practice Judaism without belonging to a synagogue. Some may be too poor to pay the dues necessary for the upkeep of the institution;

416

others live in small towns, where no congregations exist.
Still others are not regular members but attend services
on the High Holy Days in temporary congregations. For
all the regular synagogues together have not sufficient
seats for the worshippers on these holy days. Many congregations provide overflow services; in the large cities,
especially in New York, innumerable halls and motion
picture theatres house temporary congregations. Thus the
great majority of Jews in America seem to have some connection with Jewish congregations, though only about
half the families hold regular membership.

When Jews first came to America, every group organized a small synagogue in its own neighborhood. Later
on these small synagogues grew and sometimes merged
to form great city congregations. But in late years as the
cities have spread out in area, new congregations were
formed in the new neighborhoods and the number of
synagogues has again increased.

For these four thousand congregations we have about
two thousand rabbis in America. Of course, many of the
smaller congregations cannot afford the services of a
rabbi, and must be satisfied with such other officials as
a cantor, a *schochet* (who slaughters cattle according to
orthodox Jewish practice), and a Hebrew teacher—sometimes all three function in one person. But it is true that
there is a shortage in America of men of proper training
and knowledge to represent Judaism adequately and to
serve Jewish congregations.

The great building period of the synagogues was during

the "boom" times of the 1920's. Two new seminaries were established during those days, and many national institutions erected new buildings. This activity ceased during the depression years of the 1930's, when many congregations had difficulty in paying their way, and during the war years when it was impossible to obtain materials and labor for anything except war work. But after the war building began again and an effort was made to meet the great need of a growing Jewish population. Many synagogues had now become inadequate for the work to be done, while others had been located in the wrong sections of growing cities.

The total value of synagogue buildings in the United States is at least $200,000,000, not including the new buildings in process of erection or planned at the present time by a large number of congregations. The so-called historical styles of the synagogues of the last two generations, many of them handsome structures, are passing. The earlier ones were built on the Greek, Colonial and other styles, and the later ones in the Byzantine style with great domes suggesting the mosques of the Orient. The newer synagogues are for the most part of functional design and of much greater simplicity in appearance, in consonance with contemporary American architecture. The largest structures have beautiful auditoriums and fine school and center buildings with extensive facilities for classes for children and adults, clubs and other activities. It may be added that the annual budgets of these synagogues come to a total of about $30,000,000, but cities

JEWISH TEMPLES RECENTLY BUILT

TEMPLE EMANU-EL, HOUSTON, TEXAS

TEMPLE SINAI, CHICAGO, ILLINOIS

TEMPLE BETH ISRAEL, LIMA, OHIO

TEMPLE B'NAI ISRAEL, MUSKEGON, MICHIGAN

and congregations differ so widely that total or average figures mean very little.

Some Jews prefer to use the name "temple," because they feel that their own house of worship takes the place of the ancient Temple in Jerusalem. Of course, they are not places for the offering of sacrifices like the old Temple; they are houses of worship, of study and of assembly, like the traditional synagogues of the past two thousand years.

What goes on in the synagogue building? Religious services and a religious school are common to all. In addition, many modern Jews feel that the synagogue should again be the center of the community life. Their Brotherhoods or men's clubs, their Sisterhoods, their young people's groups meet in the synagogue annex. Many of these buildings include gymnasiums and well-equipped stages for plays, and are therefore able to house the full program of a Jewish community center. At one time this type of activity was found in only the most liberal organizations, but now many conservative and orthodox congregations also conduct synagogue centers, either for their own members or for the entire community. Even those which do not adopt the entire program have many meetings, forums, and classes for young and old. Great numbers of Jews today feel that the synagogue should again be the center of Jewish life and activity, as it was in the past, not only for religion, but also for education, culture and social life. For most Jews, Israel is and has always been a religious people, and the synagogue comes first among Jewish institutions.

How the Jew Keeps His Judaism in America

II. REFORM JUDAISM

WE HAVE followed the slow growth of reform ideas among the German Jews, and the rapid rise of their institutions once these ideas had made headway. Now we shall see how great the institutions founded by Isaac M. Wise have grown.

The Union of American Hebrew Congregations, founded in 1873 with thirty-four congregations, reported in 1961 that it now included 630 congregations with more than 200,000 members. As most of these congregations count only grown men or women and usually heads of families as members, there must be at least three times that many persons directly connected with reform congregations.

Affiliated with the Union are three bodies whose local groups work with the congregations: the National Federation of Temple Sisterhoods, the National Federation of Temple Brotherhoods, and the National Federation of Temple Youth. The Union has two additional affiliates, the National Association of Temple Administrators and the National Association of Temple Educators. Their members are professionals who serve Reform Judaism.

The Union is thus a center of reform influence and of much of the Jewish leadership of the country. It includes almost all the reform congregations, from the twelve great temples consisting of over a thousand members each to very small synagogues which are able to engage a rabbi only for the fall Holy Days. As the oldest and best organ-

CINCINNATI CAMPUS, HEBREW UNION COLLEGE
—JEWISH INSTITUTE OF RELIGION

ized group in American Jewry, the Union set the pattern of organization and was long in the lead. In recent years, however, both the conservative and orthodox groups are becoming equally well organized, as we shall see later in this chapter.

The first task the Union undertook was to establish the Hebrew Union College in Cincinnati for the training of rabbis. This is now the oldest rabbinical seminary in America and one of the largest in the world. It has seven buildings on a beautiful campus near the University of Cincinnati. The combined Hebrew Union College-Jewish Institute of Religion has ordained 989 rabbis through 1960. The faculty, including the Los Angeles branch, numbers over sixty scholars, of whom thirty are HUC-JIR graduates. The total enrollment in all schools in 1960 was 832 students. A fourth school is being built in Jerusalem.

Over five hundred graduates of the Hebrew Union College are now occupying pulpits throughout the United States. It is their task to teach Judaism to their own congregations and to represent the Jewish people to the general community. Others are engaged in related types of Jewish work, such as that of the Hillel Foundations. One graduate of the College, Dr. Julian Morgenstern, was its president for twenty-five years, and was succeeded in 1947 by another alumnus, Dr. Nelson Glueck; other prominent alumni are Dr. Maurice N. Eisendrath, presi-

THE HOUSE OF LIVING JU-
DAISM, THE NEW HEAD-
QUARTERS OF THE UNION OF
AMERICAN HEBREW CON-
GREGATIONS, IN NEW YORK

423

NEW YORK CAMPUS, HEBREW UNION COLLEGE
—JEWISH INSTITUTE OF RELIGION

dent of the Union of American Hebrew Congregations, and the late Dr. Judah Leon Magnes, for many years chancellor of the Hebrew University at Jerusalem. Several alumni are serving as rabbis in England, Canada and South Africa.

The last link with the founders of the Hebrew Union College was broken when Dr. David Philipson died in

424

How the Jew Keeps His Judaism in America

1949 at the age of eighty-seven. He was a member of the first class, was enrolled when he was only thirteen years old. He was rabbi in Cincinnati for fifty years, taught at the College and sat on its Board of Governors. He wrote several books, including an important history, *The Reform Movement in Judaism*.

DAVID PHILIPSON

The Hebrew Union College has a famous library and museum on its Cincinnati campus. Recently the College opened its doors to a group of lay students who wish to study the Hebrew language and Jewish literature without planning to become rabbis. It has a number of fellowships for Christian ministers who desire a thorough knowledge of the Bible in its original language.

In 1922, a great period for building new institutions, a second rabbinical seminary was organized under reform auspices. This was the Jewish Institute of Religion, founded by Dr. Stephen S. Wise, rabbi of the Free Synagogue in New York City. In thirty years the JIR graduated over two hundred rabbis, most of whom are now serving reform or conservative congregations. Now New York City has

425

three rabbinical seminaries, representing the three branches of American Judaism.

In 1948 the two reform seminaries were merged; they are now known as the Hebrew Union College-Jewish Institute of Religion. Dr. Nelson Glueck was made president of the united seminaries, which continue the work of training rabbis in both Cincinnati and New York.

At the same time the College-Institute sponsored the Hebrew Union Schools of Education and Sacred Music in New York. This is both a training school for teachers and principals in Jewish schools and for cantors in any type of synagogue. The School of Sacred Music is the only one of its kind in the world.

Because New York is the great Jewish center in the United States, the Union of American Hebrew Congregations moved to that city in 1951. A beautiful and efficient building was erected on Fifth Avenue, called the House of Living Judaism, to serve as headquarters for the entire reform movement. The decorations of the structure are based on traditional Jewish themes.

The Union conducts many activities to aid its own congregations and to further Judaism as a whole. The Department of New Congregations sends out rabbis to help organize new congregations, both in small towns and in growing sections of metropolitan areas. The Department of Synagogue Activities cooperates with the synagogue federations in New York and Chicago, provides information for the secretaries and boards of congregations how best to

426

carry on their duties, and furnishes professional advice on the building of new synagogues.

Certainly the best known products of the Union are the textbooks for Jewish schools, which are prepared under the Commission on Jewish Education. The Central Conference of American Rabbis joins with the Union in this work. The Commission has prepared a complete curriculum for the Jewish school from kindergarten through high school, with some material for teacher training and adult classes as well. It has published books for study, workbooks, teachers' guides, entertainments for the holidays, and books for outside reading. It is constantly producing new and interesting books in all these different fields, for both pupils and teachers. This book is one of its products. The newest phase of this work is the Department of Audio-Visual Aids, which prepares recordings, filmstrips, and motion pictures for the use of both religious schools and congregations. The latest development has been in the area of adult education. This Department has sponsored national and regional workshops as well as special summer seminars. Special leaders' guides to help study groups and textbooks for individuals or adult classes have been planned and are beginning to appear. An effort has also been made to create adult education committees in every congregation.

The Union and Conference together have likewise a Commission on Information about Judaism, which publishes short and interesting leaflets on many subjects of

History of the Jews in the United States

Jewish interest. A great number of these were circulated among the armed forces during the war. In peace times they go to thousands of educators, ministers and other Christian leaders.

A very interesting project of the Union consists of the "Institutes on Judaism" conducted by rabbis for Christian ministers in many cities throughout the country. These short courses make for the better understanding of Judaism by the ministers who teach thousands of Christian congregations about religion. In time they should lead to a larger amount of knowledge and good will between Jews and Christians, who worship the same God in different ways.

We have already mentioned that the Union has three auxiliary bodies for men, women, and young people. The oldest of these is the National Federation of Temple Sisterhoods, organized in 1913. In many cities Jewish women had for years gathered together for religious and charitable purposes, and they eventually felt the need of establishing a national body. There are now 584 local Sisterhoods, with 105,000 members. Ten years later the National Federation of Temple Brotherhoods was instituted to unite the men's clubs of reform synagogues the country over and to stimulate the formation of new ones; this now has 420 groups, with a membership of 65,000. The third body to be incorporated in the Union is the National Federation of Temple Youth, which in 1961 included 400 groups, with 20,000 members.

The objective of all these projects is to make the syna-

gogue the center for the entire family. The school provides for the child in the kindergarten up through the
religious school and high school; there are educational
and social projects for young people and for both parents
in their own social groups, and all worship together at the
synagogue service. In addition, each group has selected its
special tasks. The Sisterhoods not only provide entertainment and study for their own members; they raise
money to help the Union in its Jewish educational work
and for scholarships at the College-Institute and they
aid the local religious schools. The Brotherhoods build
up temple attendance in their own congregations; in addition, they have also taken over the Jewish Chautauqua
Society, which brings speakers on Jewish topics to hundreds of colleges the country over.

The Central Conference of American Rabbis, which
was founded by Isaac M. Wise in 1889, has become one
of the largest and most important rabbinical organizations in the world. It had 785 members in 1960, most of
them reform rabbis, but it also included some of more
conservative opinions. At its annual meetings many scholarly papers are given; in addition, practical problems of
reform Judaism are considered. The decisions of the Conference set the standard for reform Jewish congregations
in this country and abroad. The Union Prayer Book,
published by the Conference, is generally used by reform
congregations in this country just as the traditional
Hebrew prayerbook is used by the orthodox. In the
interest of unity many congregations gave up the prayer-

books written by their own rabbis, and Isaac M. Wise set the example by giving up his own Minhag America in its favor. The Conference has likewise published the Union Hymnal, a Haggadah for Passover, and many other religious works.

III. CONSERVATIVE JUDAISM

THE second group of Jews who set out to develop their institutions in America were those who adopted conservative or traditional Judaism. Their school for rabbis, the Jewish Theological Seminary of America, was founded a decade after the Hebrew Union College, in 1886, and was located in New York. At first it met with many difficulties, but in 1902 the Seminary called to its presidency one of the great Jewish scholars of the world, Dr. Solomon Schechter, who before his death in 1915 put the JTS on a firm basis.

Solomon Schechter was a man of remarkable personality and had a most unusual career. He was born in a little Roumanian town in 1850, and grew up in strictest orthodoxy. In this environment he studied until he became a master of the whole field of Jewish literature. Then he moved to Vienna and became acquainted with modern learning. Still later he was called to Cambridge University in England, where he was Reader in Rabbinics. At this time occurred the great, romantic event of his career, the unearthing of the *Genizah* at Cairo, Egypt, a development that changed the course of his studies.

In olden times the Jews would never destroy a Hebrew

book, but when one became worn out, it was put away in a secret hiding place, a *Genizah*. Two English ladies who had travelled in the Orient brought Dr. Schechter some scraps of parchment and papyrus for an explanation. Much to his surprise, he found that one of these scraps contained a passage in Hebrew

SOLOMON SCHECHTER

from the book of Ben Sirah in the Apocrypha, a book which had previously been known only in the Greek language. Naturally, this discovery excited scholars the world over, and Dr. Schechter determined to find the source of this wonderful literary treasure. It proved the key to unlock other thrilling mysteries.

He discovered the source finally in Egypt, in the old synagogue at Cairo. He found thousands of ancient manuscripts, some of them complete books, but most pages and torn bits of pages. His later study was based on these manuscripts which he brought back to Cambridge. He actually unearthed the Hebrew original of Ben Sirah and published it. He and other scholars have been steadily finding in these manuscripts unknown books of Jewish

431

literature and unknown facts of Jewish history. This study is still going on after fifty years.

This man, of strong personality and wide reputation, reorganized the Jewish Theological Seminary. He organized the United Synagogue of America in 1913, a union of congregations for the "promotion of traditional Judaism in America." His teaching was a middle-of-the-road doctrine, holding to the old but trying to reinterpret it for the present day. His chief emphasis in all his writing and teaching was on what he called "catholic Israel," the Jewish people as a whole all over the world.

At Dr. Schechter's death, he was succeeded by Dr. Cyrus Adler, a very different person. Cyrus Adler was born in the little town of Van Buren, Arkansas; his entire training was acquired in America, for he studied Semitics at Johns Hopkins University. He was by profession, then, a Hebrew scholar, and for some years worked at the Smithsonian Institute in Washington. His name first became prominent when he was sent to Turkey and Egypt in 1890 to arrange for exhibits at the Chicago World's Fair. From that time on, people found that he was an excellent administrator. When Moses Dropsie died in 1905, he bequeathed funds for the foundation of the Dropsie College for Hebrew and Cognate Learning and asked in his will that Dr. Adler be the first president of that institution.

At Schechter's death ten years later, Adler was appointed president of the Seminary as well, and for twenty-five years he was president of both institutions, commuting between Philadelphia and New York to administer the

432

How the Jew Keeps His Judaism in America

two colleges. He was prominent in the Jewish Publication Society, the American Jewish Historical Society, the Jewish Welfare Board, and many other organizations. In 1929, he succeeded Louis Marshall as president of the American Jewish Committee. It was an unusual position for a Jewish scholar to function as

CYRUS ADLER

the head of a body of wealthy and prominent business men who had united for a public service. Dr. Adler died in 1940 and was succeeded as president of the Jewish Theological Seminary by Dr. Louis Finkelstein, who had long been a professor there.

The conservative Jews have parallel organizations to those of the reform Jews. The Rabbinical Assembly of America has 750 members; 708 congregations belong to the United Synagogue of America; the Women's League has 760 bodies; the Men's Clubs include 328; and the United Synagogue Youth 521 groups. This is a large and rapidly growing body. In many cities, in fact, the conservative synagogues are growing more rapidly than those of any other group.

433

THE JEWISH THEOLOGICAL SEMINARY OF AMERICA

The Seminary had 706 graduates in 1960; it conducts both a rabbinical school with 104 students and a school for Jewish teachers, with 265 students. It conducts classes on Jewish studies both in New York and in its branch in Los Angeles. The Seminary now possesses the greatest Jewish library in the world, with 200,-000 books and 10,000 old manuscripts. It has a Jewish

How the Jew Keeps His Judaism in America

THE JEWISH MUSEUM, NEW YORK CITY

Museum, in the former home of Felix M. Warburg, who willed his Fifth Avenue mansion for the purpose. Since 1938 the Seminary has conducted an annual Institute for Religious and Social Studies, where prominent men, both Jews and Christians, read papers on the great world problems.

435

Probably the best known activity of the Seminary is the "Eternal Light" radio program, which has been broadcast weekly since 1943. Its programs, which deal largely with Jewish history, Jewish stories and Palestine, are listened to all over the United States and in some foreign countries. It has received many awards as an outstanding educational program on the radio.

IV. RECONSTRUCTIONISM

AN OFFSHOOT of conservative Judaism is a new movement known as Reconstructionism. The Jewish Reconstructionist Foundation was established in the 1940's by Dr. Mordecai M. Kaplan, a professor at the Jewish Theological Seminary, on the basis of his own study and writings. His theory is that Judaism is not simply a religion, but a complete civilization, including language, customs and community life as well as religion and literature. He and his followers feel that Jewish life in America must be reconstructed to have strong democratic communities, including all these different phases of Jewish activity, and not religion alone. They are also ardent Zionists, for they feel that American Jewry needs a center of completely Jewish life as its inspiration and guide.

Many of the adherents of this philosophy are Dr. Kaplan's own students at the Seminary. But he has also influenced some reform Jews as well. The organization has a national magazine, *The Reconstructionist,* a Jewish Reconstructionist Fellowship to promote study groups, a prayerbook, and various other works.

436

How the Jew Keeps His Judaism in America

In practice the Reconstructionists are strictly observant, as are the leaders of conservative Judaism generally.
But their theory of a religious civilization, with its emphasis on Jewish art, literature and social life with the well-
spring in Palestine, is opposed by many religious leaders,
who see the synagogue as the chief center for Jewish life
and religion as its primary purpose.

V. AMERICAN ORTHODOXY

THE last group to reach unity and national organization
in America is orthodoxy. It always had the largest numbers, but for many years its followers were poor and disorganized, and their synagogues too numerous and too
small to exert any real influence. As they were the latest
comers to the United States, they were last to become well
established financially, and also the last to learn American
methods of organization. The result is that about three-
quarters of the American synagogues are orthodox, but
they are not all joined in a single body, like the reform or
conservative groups.

The Union of Orthodox Jewish Congregations of
America was formed in 1898, and now serves 3,100 congregations. It also has a Women's Branch; a national
association of men's clubs, called Koheles; and an association of junior congregations, called Ner Mitzvah. But this
is not the only orthodox body, for there is also a Union
of Sephardic Congregations, founded in 1929, and the
National Council of Young Israel, founded in 1912. This
last body includes 87 congregations, with 50,000 mem-

YESHIVA UNIVERSITY, NEW YORK CITY

bers; it represents a very devout and active group of orthodox Jews, who wish to give dignity to their services, and at the same time to maintain strict orthodoxy. The majority of orthodox congregations, especially the small and scattered ones, do not belong to any national organization, and thereby forfeit a great deal of help and encouragement. But as time goes on, they will probably come to realize the importance of joining such bodies.

The same is true for the rabbis. The Rabbinical Council of America and the Union of Orthodox Rabbis are both large bodies; the former consists largely of American trained rabbis, while many in the latter group were born in Europe and received their rabbinical education there.

438

How the Jew Keeps His Judaism in America

A number of *yeshivoth* now exist in America, some of which ordain rabbis. The oldest and most generally recognized is the Rabbi Isaac Elchanan Theological Seminary in New York, which was founded in 1896. In 1928 this seminary was recognized by the state of New York as Yeshiva College to teach regular college subjects and give degrees. It is now known as Yeshiva University; the president is Dr. Samuel Belkin. Instead of studying rabbinic subjects in one school and the general field of learning in another, as is done by students of the other seminaries, students of the Yeshiva can receive their entire religious and secular training in a Jewish institution. This is the logical extension of the all-day Hebrew school which does the same thing for young children. Some students at Yeshiva University are in the rabbinical department, others in the school for Hebrew teachers, and many others are merely taking a general course, as in any college.

In 1922, another orthodox seminary was founded in Chicago, the Hebrew Theological College, with Rabbi Saul Silber as president. Other smaller institutions exist throughout the country, of which some are becoming generally recognized and their rabbinical ordination accepted. Some of these have been transferred from Europe since the growth of the Nazi movement in 1933; they are very aggressive in spreading the doctrines of orthodoxy, or in their favorite phrase, "Torah-true Judaism." They sponsor Hebrew day schools, publish literature, and win many adherents, especially among people who have themselves immigrated from eastern Europe.

439

History of the Jews in the United States

Orthodoxy is strongest in the east, particularly in New York City, where people can live a strictly observant life if they desire. It is weakest in the small towns of the west and south, where Jews have more contacts with Christians and are most deeply influenced by American conditions. Many strictly orthodox congregations have accepted new customs unknown in Europe, such as sermons in the vernacular, Sunday schools for the children, and confirmation for girls. The growing trend is toward combining orthodox Judaism with American methods of organization.

VI. RELIGIOUS UNITY OF ALL JEWS

EVERYBODY knows that all these differences among synagogues are comparatively trivial; what is most important is that the synagogue is a place where Jews worship God. All rabbis are preachers and teachers of Judaism. All rabbinical seminaries teach their students the Bible, the Talmud, Jewish history, and those other subjects which it is necessary for Jewish religious leaders to understand. All Jews agree in their main ideas about God and man. Practically all Jews disagree with Christians on the interpretation of these same points.

So it is only natural and right that Jewish religious leaders should join together for the sake of the great ideals they share. The primary bond of union among rabbis and congregations of different types is the Jewish faith and the conviction that the synagogue should remain the central Jewish institution. Many Jews do not accept this last point, for they prefer non-religious or "secular" institutions and they organize such groups as Jewish charities, lodges, or Zionist societies. Still others try to combine the two approaches to Jewish life.

Probably before the First World War nobody would have urged orthodox, conservative and reform Jews to work together on a religious basis. There was too much bitterness between the reformers, who attacked orthodoxy in order to establish their right to make changes, and the orthodox, who felt that reform Jews were not really Jews at all. But for most Jews those feelings have passed. Reform and conservative institutions no longer need to attack others in order to establish their own rights; they are recognized by Jews everywhere. During the First World War all Jews joined in a common effort to rescue their brothers overseas, and that effort has continued for over thirty years. In the committee on religious activities of the Jewish Welfare Board, representatives of orthodox, conservative and reform rabbinical bodies worked together to find proper chaplains for the United States Army and Navy, to recommend these rabbis of all three groups to the military authorities, and to help them in their religious work in the armed forces.

In 1926, the Synagogue Council of America was organized to carry out this idea of the religious unity of Jewry. It is made up of representatives from six organizations, three of them conferences of rabbis and three unions of congregations. Its main purpose is to strengthen the Jewish religion in America. It has no control over the bodies which compose it, for they would accept no au-

441

thority of this kind. But it has proved a valuable forum for the discussion of many matters concerning the Jewish religion and it has taken action on some of them. In its work the Synagogue Council cooperates with the Catholic and Protestant church bodies and with the National Conference of Christians and Jews.

REVIEW QUESTIONS

1. How many Jews take part in religious activities in the three types of synagogues?
2. In what chronological order did the three religious groups organize? Why?
3. What are the necessary institutions of a local synagogue? Of a national organization of synagogues?
4. Show how the American Jews are coming closer together in their religion, and in their religious institutions.

TOPICS FOR REPORTS

1. Describe your own synagogue, with the meaning of the ceremonial objects you see. Visit a synagogue of another type, and describe its resemblances and differences. Pay especial attention to the two services, and the details in which they differ.
2. List the meetings and other activities that go on in your own synagogue for a month. Show their relation to the religious purpose of the congregation.
3. Describe a visit to one of the rabbinical seminaries or to one of the great synagogues of the country.
4. Report on one of the interesting essays by Solomon Schechter, such as "A Hoard of Hebrew Manuscripts," "Memoirs of a Jewess of the Seventeenth Century," etc.
5. What is the attitude of the three groups in Judaism toward such ideas as: the Sabbath, kosher food, music in the

442

How the Jew Keeps His Judaism in America

synagogue, *bar mitzvah* and confirmation, Palestine, the Messiah?
6. Invite your rabbi to tell the class about his own seminary, and what he studied there.

REFERENCES FOR PUPILS

Edidin, Ben M., *Jewish Community Life in America,* chapter 5.
Pilch, Judah, *Jewish Life in Our Times,* pages 7–22.

REFERENCES FOR TEACHERS

The American Jewish Yearbook has a summary of events of each year, including an article on Religious Activities in the United States. In addition, the Yearbook lists all national Jewish institutions, including seminaries, unions of congregations, and the like. The use of the Yearbook for this and subsequent chapters will not only provide information, but will also keep the material up to date.
Karpf, Maurice J., *Jewish Community Organization in the U. S.,* pages 51–57.
Freehof, Solomon B., *Reform Jewish Practice.* Hebrew Union College Press.
Gordis, Robert, *Conservative Judaism.* Behrman.
Steinberg, Milton, *Basic Judaism.* Harcourt-Brace.
Jung, Leo, *The Jewish Library,* a series of volumes written from the orthodox point of view.

CHAPTER 26.

Jewish Education in America

IN ALL our study of the past we saw that wherever there was a synagogue there was also Jewish education. For everybody knew then, as now, that Jews must teach their children what Judaism is if they are to continue living as Jews. The present day synagogue is very closely connected with the school; in fact, most synagogues conduct schools for the children of the congregation. But there are also many schools for those who belong to no synagogue or who want a different type of Jewish education. Everybody who believes anything himself, or who belongs to any group at all, would naturally like his children to share his knowledge and his beliefs. This chapter will follow up the question: how does a child receive a Jewish education in America? But we shall go beyond this to cover the whole field of Jewish education for young people and adults as well, so that we shall have a general picture of Jewish education in this country.

I. ELEMENTARY JEWISH EDUCATION

JEWISH schools in eastern Europe were all-day schools which taught all the subjects it was considered important for the pupils to know, but especially the Hebrew lan-

Jewish Education in America

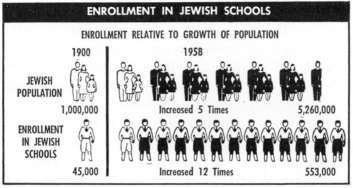

ENROLLMENT IN JEWISH SCHOOLS

ENROLLMENT RELATIVE TO GROWTH OF POPULATION

	1900	1958	
JEWISH POPULATION	1,000,000	Increased 5 Times	5,260,000
ENROLLMENT IN JEWISH SCHOOLS	45,000	Increased 12 Times	553,000

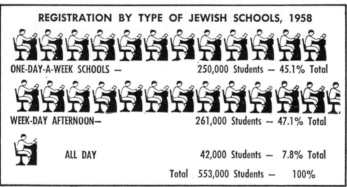

REGISTRATION BY TYPE OF JEWISH SCHOOLS, 1958

ONE-DAY-A-WEEK SCHOOLS — 250,000 Students — 45.1% Total

WEEK-DAY AFTERNOON— 261,000 Students — 47.1% Total

ALL DAY 42,000 Students — 7.8% Total

Total 553,000 Students — 100%

guage and the Jewish religion. This was necessary, as there were no public schools in those countries before the Russian Revolution, and Jewish children were often not admitted to the few schools which existed. The first Jewish schools in America, as we have seen, were likewise schools for general education.

But as the public schools grew up in America, about a century ago, Jewish parents sent their children to them so

445

that they might have an American education. Since that time most Jewish schools have been supplementary to the public school, and are held either on Sunday mornings or on week-day afternoons, to teach Jewish subjects only. Only in the last few years has there been a new though small growth of all-day Jewish schools.

In 1958, the attendance at all three types of Jewish schools was 553,000. This is a very large number, but it is not much more than one-half of all the Jewish children in America. Does this mean that the remaining number learn nothing at all? Not at all; some of them belong to clubs or community centers where they celebrate the Jewish holidays and learn something of Palestine. Some may have private teachers to teach them Hebrew. Others have attended Jewish schools for a year or two or will attend them before the age of bar mitzvah. Probably three-fourths of all the Jewish boys and girls receive a little Jewish education at some time in their lives.

The cost of this whole system of Jewish education is over $60,000,000 a year, for American Jews believe in Jewish education and want their children to understand their religion and their history. About one fourth of this money is paid by the Jewish Federations in various cities; the rest is provided by the congregations and by the parents themselves.

The first Jewish Sunday school was founded by Rebecca Gratz in 1838. Today practically every reform and conservative congregation has a Sunday school, and many orthodox congregations as well. Here the children meet

Jewish Education in America

once a week for two or three hours to study the Bible, Jewish history, Jewish religion, and sometimes Hebrew. Many of these schools meet once or twice on week-days also, so that the pupils may really learn sufficient Hebrew to read the Bible and prayerbook intelligently, and even to speak a little in Hebrew as in any modern language.

These schools used to be shoved out of the way in basements or corners of synagogues. But every new synagogue now provides good schoolrooms, with an assembly hall and often a gymnasium and library. The number of well trained teachers is growing every year, though there are still not enough of them. Altogether, 250,000 children were attending Sunday schools in 1958.

But a great many Jewish parents felt that one or even two periods a week were not enough to teach the tremendous background of Jewish life, and especially the Hebrew language. So the next group, about 261,000 children, attend Jewish week-day schools after the public school is over. Some of these schools meet three or four or even five times a week. They aim to give a complete Jewish training, based on the Hebrew language, and including the subjects taught in the Sunday school. Some of them even have clubs, choirs and scout troops, conduct their own services on the Sabbath and give their own entertainments on the Jewish festivals. While most of these schools are conducted by congregations, many and especially the largest of them are communal schools, known as Talmud Torahs.

About seven thousand of these week-day pupils are

447

attending schools where Yiddish rather than Hebrew is the basis of study. These did not begin as religious schools, fostered by congregations. They were founded by national organizations of workers, who were primarily interested in the Jewish people rather than in the Jewish religion. The first of these was founded in 1910; now there are 182 such schools in the country, including several high schools and one Teachers Institute and People's University.

The Yiddish schools, which had always been close to the life of the Jewish people, slowly grew more Jewish in the religious sense. The bitter experiences of Hitlerism and the war years speeded up this change, until many of them are very similar to the congregational schools in their teaching. They observe the Jewish festivals, teach Jewish history and customs, and some of them teach the Jewish religion as well.

The most intensive Jewish school is the all-day school, something like the Catholic parochial schools. The first of these was founded in New York in 1886, but there were very few until the past few years. In 1958 there were 214 Jewish all-day schools, called yeshivoth, with about 42,000 elementary and high school pupils. Greater New York alone has 136 of the all-day Jewish schools, with about 31,000 students altogether. The other 78 schools and 11,000 pupils are scattered through the rest of the country. The students in these schools study all the necessary school subjects and also a great deal of Hebrew and of Jewish history; many of the all-day schools are strictly orthodox.

Most American Jews prefer to have their children at-

Jewish Education in America

tend the public schools and receive their Jewish education through the synagogue or other Jewish organizations. But we all know how difficult it is to learn the great background of our people's life and faith in a few hours a week. The present trend is to improve our Jewish schools by providing better buildings, better training for the teachers, newer and better textbooks, and by adding an extra afternoon or two to the instruction of the Sunday school. Another trend is for the Hebrew school to work in connection with a Jewish community center, so that the children may enjoy their club activities at the same school where they receive their formal instruction.

Hebrew high schools exist in New York, Chicago and several other large cities, where graduates of the week-day Hebrew schools may become well educated adult Jews, or even prepare for careers in Jewish work. Hebrew is taught in fifty-three high schools in New York, where over five thousand students take it as a regular subject. Of course, Hebrew has always been a recognized college subject, and many American universities offer courses in Hebrew.

II. EXTENSION EDUCATION

BUT Jewish education reaches a great many people who are not enrolled in school. This is not intensive but extensive education, not to teach a few people a great many things, but to teach a great many people a few things. Naturally, such education can be of many kinds, for children or adults, for orthodox or reform.

449

History of the Jews in the United States

The leading agency here is probably the National Jewish Welfare Board, which is the guiding spirit for three hundred Jewish Centers throughout the country. Each Center has its clubs, classes, festival celebrations, lectures and concerts, and exerts a broad educational influence on every family and on the community as a whole.

The Union of American Hebrew Congregations and the United Synagogue conduct youth groups in their various congregations. These groups provide Jewish interests for the young people beyond religious school age. The Zionist Organization has a whole series of youth groups, Young Judea for boys and girls, Masada for young men, Junior Hadassah for young women, and also the Student Zionist Organization for college students. The B'nai B'rith Youth Organization conducts groups for boys and girls, for young men and women; in addition, the Order sponsors the Hillel Foundations in colleges. The National Council of Jewish Women, which conducts educational work for its own members and social work in the community, also sponsors the Council of Jewish Juniors for young women.

The various Brotherhoods and Sisterhoods of congregations all have their programs for their own members. In addition, the reform group sponsors the Jewish Chautauqua Society which sends Jewish speakers to college campuses. Both the conservative and reform groups have recently organized national bodies for adult Jewish studies to bring Jewish knowledge to men and women throughout the country.

The Jewish Welfare Board has sponsored a Jewish

Jewish Education in America

Book Council and a Jewish Music Council, to make the Jewish public better acquainted with Jewish books and Jewish music.

One of the very interesting methods of extension education is through the summer camp, where Hebrew studies and Jewish games and songs can become a part of the general camp program. Some of these have become real centers of Jewish learning, either for boys and girls who have a Hebrew school background, or for young people who are active in Jewish youth organizations. Other camps give the children an opportunity to enjoy the cultural side of Jewish life through song, dance and handwork, subjects which are often not a part of the school curriculum.

III. ORGANIZING JEWISH EDUCATION

WE HAVE seen how many ways there are for young Jews to get a Jewish education, how these ways differ very widely, and how little system exists in the whole project. A few years ago there was no system at all. Any person who knew Hebrew himself and wanted to teach it opened a school called a Cheder. If the poor parents of the neighborhood sent their children, they could pay only very small fees, and so the school was small and poorly kept and the teacher was half starved. Meanwhile, Sunday schools met in dark basements with teachers who had little knowledge but much enthusiasm.

This picture began to change in 1910, when Dr. Samson Benderly founded the Bureau of Jewish Education in New York City. This organization studied the daily Hebrew schools and began to work out many methods for improving them. One of Dr. Benderly's outstanding contributions was in the raising of disciples, many of whom today hold important educational positions in the United States.

In New York, the Jewish Education Committee is carrying on this work. Probably you know its magazine for children, called *World Over;* this is only a small part of its efforts toward the improvement of school buildings, the training of teachers, and the attempt to place Jewish education on a higher plane in the community. In thirty-nine other cities Bureaus of Jewish Education have been established, fully half of them between 1940 and 1946. This indicates that interest in Jewish education is steadily rising and that many cities are trying to organize their separate Hebrew schools and congregational schools into a school system, something like that of the public schools.

A number of national organizations help in this work. The American Association for Jewish Education is making studies, experimenting with methods, and pointing out the way to organize city-wide bureaus and to improve the schools. The Department of Education of the Union of American Hebrew Congregations, which we mentioned in the last chapter, is the leading publisher of textbooks for Jewish schools. This book is one of the many published under the auspices of its Commission on Jewish Education. In addition, the Union conducts teachers' institutes, advises congregations and local communities, and con-

452

ducts experiments in Jewish education. In such ways as these the week-day schools and Sunday schools are coming closer to each other and learning to teach American boys and girls more and more about Judaism.

Even city-wide celebrations of the Jewish holidays have been tried, with many schools taking part. In New York the Hebrew schools have held an art exhibit and organized a Jewish Children's Theatre.

IV. SCHOOLS FOR SPECIAL PURPOSES

AN IMPORTANT part of this whole movement is the work of twelve training schools for Jewish teachers in different parts of the country. As young men and women plan to become full-time teachers in Jewish schools, they need a special course of study just like public school teachers. At present all these teachers' seminaries are insufficient to supply the teachers needed in the Jewish schools, but they seem to be growing steadily.

Adjoining the historic Mikveh Israel Synagogue and the Gratz College for Teachers in Philadelphia stands the beautiful building of Dropsie College for Hebrew and Cognate Learning. This institution was founded in 1905 by Moses Dropsie; it does not prepare a man for a career as rabbi or Hebrew teacher; it is intended only for advanced students who wish to specialize in Jewish or Oriental studies. Dr. Cyrus Adler was president of Dropsie College from the time of its foundation until his death; he was succeeded by Dr. Abraham Neuman.

Another important Jewish college is the Yeshiva Uni-

453

versity in New York City. This began in 1896 as a theological seminary; now it is a university, with the Albert Einstein Medical College and Stern College for Women. It gives all the usual university degrees. As you can guess from its history, this university is strictly orthodox in its background, and every student is required to study a great deal of Hebrew as part of his college course. There are also special courses for rabbis and for Hebrew teachers.

In the fall of 1948, Brandeis University was opened at Waltham, Mass., near Boston. This is the first non-sectarian university under Jewish auspices in America. There

THE CASTLE, ON BRANDEIS UNIVERSITY CAMPUS

454

is no discrimination with regard to faith or race, either amongst faculty or students. But it is a Jewish enterprise, for the board of directors and most of the contributors are Jews, and the president is Dr. Abram L. Sachar, who had been for twenty years national director of the Hillel Foundations. This is not a school to teach Judaism; it is simply a university. It is intended to be a Jewish contribution to higher education in America.

Among the many other schools which we might mention, we shall discuss only one more, the National Farm School in Doylestown, Pennsylvania, near Philadelphia. This school was founded in 1896 by Rabbi Joseph Krauskopf of Philadelphia, one of the earliest graduates of the Hebrew Union College. He felt that American Jews should have a chance to return to the soil after many centuries of city life, and that Jewish boys should have an opportunity to study agriculture. This school, which is open to both Jews and Christians alike, provides both high school education and practical farm work without any cost. The boys pay much of their tuition by keeping up the large farm and at the same time they also get their practical experience in farming.

V. JEWISH UNIVERSITY STUDENTS

THE first complete survey of Jewish students in colleges and universities was made in 1935 and another one covered the same ground in 1946. In both surveys the Jewish students had more than double the proportion of the Jews in the general population: they were 8.8 of all students in the earlier and 8.2 per cent in the later study. Because of the steady increase of college students as a whole, however, this meant an increase of Jewish students from 105,000 in the earlier study to 161,000 in the later one. This great body of young people consists two-thirds of men and one-third women; it includes students in many professional branches as well as those in colleges of liberal arts.

Naturally, these young people need organizations of their own, especially in those colleges which include a thousand Jews or more. Many of them are living away from home, and lack both family and synagogue environment, as well as the many groups to which they may have belonged.

The first Jewish organization to be founded on the campus was the fraternity, which provides congenial homes and social life. The first such fraternity was the Zeta Beta Tau, founded in 1898 as a Zionist club. But as Jewish students were not admitted to most of the non-Jewish fraternities, other groups of both men and women students followed, until in 1954 the Yearbook listed 27 fraternities and sororities, with a total membership of 93,000. Of course, not all these are students at any one time, as many of the organizations count both student and alumni members.

Next came the Intercollegiate Menorah Society, founded at Harvard University in 1906 for the purpose of studying Jewish life and ideas. For a long time the Menorah Society had many student branches; at present

Jewish Education in America

HILLEL BUILDING, OHIO STATE UNIVERSITY

its chief work is the publication of an excellent magazine, the *Menorah Journal.*

The nationwide Student Zionist Organization is another active body today, with many chapters. The members conduct discussions, make a study of Israel, and do practical work for the Zionist cause.

Today, however, the college field is dominated by the B'nai B'rith Hillel Foundations, which have 235 chapters in various universities in the United States and abroad. The first Hillel Foundation was organized at the University of Illinois in 1923 to provide a religious and social center for the Jewish students. By 1961, this single experimental house had grown to 91 full-time Hillel Foundations and 140 part-time counsellorships. This was effected through the backing of the B'nai B'rith, which adopted Hillel in 1924 and made it a national movement.

A Hillel Foundation has a house with a full-time direc-

457

tor, almost always a rabbi. Its program includes religious services, social events, classes, discussions, and everything which the students themselves desire. In other words it functions as a Jewish community center for the student body. In 1954 the Foundations owned 62 buildings, many constructed for this special purpose, and were planning campaigns for seven more. The most remarkable student center is the Sara Delano Roosevelt Memorial House at Hunter College, New York, which is used by Protestant, Catholic and Jewish organizations for their work. The Hillel students themselves have been raising money for student welfare funds and have brought a number of European refugee students to American universities.

Another body which is active on the college campus is the Jewish Chautauqua Society, which was founded in 1893 by Rabbi Henry Berkowitz of Philadelphia to spread Jewish knowledge, on the pattern of the many Chautauqua groups which were so popular at that time. When its original activity declined, the National Federation of Temple Brotherhoods took over the organization and directed it toward the campus field. In 1953, the Society furnished lecturers on Jewish subjects to 450 colleges and 100 youth camps, gave Jewish books to 625 college libraries, and brought a fair and honest knowledge of the Jew to a great body of intelligent Christians.

VI. JEWISH BOOKS

EVERYBODY knows that you do not have to receive your education in school from teachers; much fine learning is done in libraries from books. About a hundred books are published in the United States every year on Jewish subjects, ranging all the way from scholarly works to fiction for old and young. This is a great many more than were published annually a dozen years ago. Among the striking changes are the increase in the number of books for children and young people, and the improvement in the quality of the content and the general make-up and printing.

Some of these Jewish books are produced by Jewish publishers, some by general publishers, and some by Jewish organizations whose aim it is to spread Jewish knowledge. In 1927, at the suggestion of Rabbi S. Felix Mendelsohn, a small group of Jewish educators began a movement for a Jewish Book Week. The Jewish Book Council of America was formed in 1940 to sponsor Jewish Book Month each November and emphasize the importance of Jewish books. Many cities take part in this activity through meetings and exhibits, and some public libraries as well as many Jewish Centers welcome the emphasis on the Jewish book. Since 1944, the Jewish Book Council has been a part of the Jewish Welfare Board, which has also sponsored a Jewish Music Council to carry on the same work in the field of Jewish music.

One of the leaders in publishing Jewish books is the Jewish Publication Society of America, with headquarters in Philadelphia. This Society each year publishes the *American Jewish Yearbook,* as well as scholarly books, fiction and books for young people. These are distributed to its members, who live all over the country. The Publica-

AMERICAN BIBLE TRANSLATORS

tion Society has produced great works like Graetz's *History of the Jews* and Louis Ginzberg's *Legends of the Jews;* it gave Israel Zangwill, the English novelist, encouragement in his early days and published his great Jewish novel, *Children of the Ghetto.* One of the important projects of the Society is the Jewish Classics series, which includes a number of great Hebrew works of the past, printed with the English translation on the page opposite the Hebrew text.

Probably the most significant work of the Jewish Publication Society was the English translation of the Hebrew

Jewish Education in America

Bible. The old King James version was thoroughly Christian in its viewpoint, and was sometimes wrong in its interpretation of the Hebrew. No previous Jewish translation, however, could equal it for beauty. The Society's version was the result of seven years of work by seven editors, both reform and conservative, representing the Hebrew Union College, the Jewish Theological Seminary and Dropsie College. Professor Max Margolis of Dropsie College was editor in chief; the reform members of the board were Rabbis Kaufmann Kohler, David Philipson and Samuel Schulman, while the conservative members were Dr. Cyrus Adler, Dr. Joseph Jacobs and Dr. Solomon Schechter. This board of Jewish scholars produced the splendid English translation of the Bible which we all use in the synagogues today, and which is accepted by English-speaking Jews the world over.

Two great Jewish encyclopedias have been produced in the United States; if you have ever looked up any of the subjects in this book or your other religious school work, you certainly know one or the other. The *Jewish Encyclopedia,* consisting of twelve volumes which appeared in the early years of the twentieth century, is one of the great storehouses of Jewish learning, with hundreds of articles on the Bible, Jewish history, religion, biography, literature—every possible phase of Jewish life. The *Jewish Encyclopedia* was originally an idea, conceived in the mind of one man, Dr. Isidore Singer, an immigrant from Europe who felt that the time had come to put down the knowledge of the Old World in a form understandable

461

to the New. He interested two men, a Christian publisher and a Jewish philanthropist. The latter was Jacob Schiff, an enthusiastic patron of Jewish learning, who made it possible for him to gather together a board of editors, to engage scholars from all over the world to write special articles, and finally to have the work printed.

The *Universal Jewish Encyclopedia* came out thirty years later, when the march of history had outdated the *Jewish Encyclopedia* in modern topics, though it is still authoritative in every other field. The *Universal Jewish Encyclopedia* was devised by Rabbi Isaac Landman of Brooklyn, who acted as editor as well as promoter and brought the work into being. It consists of ten volumes, and when you look at it you are impressed at once by its attractive appearance and its wealth of illustrations.

Many Jewish organizations further Jewish learning by instituting research groups and by their publications. The American Jewish Congress produces not only books but also the series of pamphlets entitled *Jewish Affairs,* which you will find most helpful for reference. The American Jewish Committee has a big research bureau which has produced important works. The American Jewish Historical Society meets each year to hear papers on various phases of American Jewish history; much of the information in this book comes from the published yearbooks of the Society. The Historical Society was founded by Cyrus Adler in 1892; in 1961 the Society moved to new headquarters in New York City.

A dramatic story underlies the serious historical and

linguistic studies of the YIVO, or Yiddish Scientific Institute. This organization was founded in Vilna in 1925, built up a great library and established connections with universities and scholarly bodies throughout the world. Then came the war; YIVO managed to move to New York in 1940 and continued its work in the New World. It has amassed a great collection of materials relating to the Jewish persecutions during the war, and its exhibits in New York and other cities have attracted wide attention. YIVO publishes a magazine and books on Jewish topics in both Yiddish and English.

Finally, we must mention the *Histadruth Ivrith,* or League for the Hebrew Language. This was a small organization of Hebrew scholars from its foundation in 1916 until the outbreak of the Second World War. But by that time many Jewish scholars had fled to America, and Hebrew, as well as Yiddish, had a rebirth here. The Histadruth now has Hebrew-speaking groups of adults and young people, a camp and a Hebrew theatre. This group also publishes a Hebrew magazine and Hebrew books on modern topics, just like the Hebrew-speaking Jews of Palestine.

VII. THE JEWISH PRESS

STILL another means of learning about Judaism, and especially about the important events of our own day, is through the Jewish press. We have seen its small beginnings in German, English and Yiddish. Today it is a large and important factor in American Jewry, for the

463

History of the Jews in the United States

Yearbook of 1960 lists 201 periodicals published in the United States. It is interesting to see what languages Jews are reading nowadays, for 154 of these papers are written in English, 20 in Yiddish, 3 in both English and Yiddish, and 9 in Hebrew. Yiddish is slowly giving way to English in this country, but Hebrew is surviving on a small scale as a universal Jewish language. Two of the papers are written in German, while some thirteen of the periodicals use English in combination with some other language.

Three daily newspapers are in Yiddish. At one time there were more Yiddish dailies than now and they had a much larger circulation. But even today many thousands of immigrant Jews read these as their only source of news. They feature both Jewish and world news, and in addition have many serious articles which are more like magazine articles than the news stories in our English papers.

Of the fifty-six weekly newspapers, fifty-three are in English. They are the chief source of Jewish news for people the country over, who get their world news from the daily papers and the radio. Following the lead of such historic papers as the *American Israelite* in Cincinnati and the *American Hebrew* in New York, these weekly newspapers are now being published all over the country.

Many organizations publish valuable magazines, such as the *Jewish Frontier, Commentary, The National Jewish Monthly* and *The Jewish Veteran*. Other papers are written for special groups of readers, for children, social workers, Jewish educators, or physicians.

On the whole, the Jewish press provides the general

464

Jewish Education in America

public with information on the latest Jewish events, on news of importance to the Jewish people, while some of its publications give material of lasting value in various fields of Jewish scholarship.

REVIEW QUESTIONS

1. Describe three kinds of elementary Jewish schools.
2. Why do we have city-wide and national organizations for Jewish education?
3. Describe two different types of schools for adults.
4. Why do Jewish college students need Jewish organizations of their own? Describe two of these.
5. List three great works of Jewish scholarship produced in America.
6. List three societies for Jewish learning, conducted in different languages.

TOPICS FOR REPORTS

1. Place your own school in this survey; visit a school of a different type and compare the two.
2. What is the purpose of Jewish education: to teach Judaism, or Jewish national life, or to adjust the Jew to American life?
3. A visit to some Jewish educational institution in your vicinity.
4. List some books published by the Jewish Publication Society: check those you have read. Which did you like best, and why?
5. Compare the JPS Bible with some Christian version: notice the different order of the books; read selected passages in both, and note the differences.
6. Bring various Jewish periodicals to class: see what they contain; read the most interesting items to the class.

465

History of the Jews in the United States

REFERENCES FOR PUPILS

Wiernick, Peter, pp. 282–285, 339–342, 375–379.
Universal Jewish Encyclopedia has many articles on Jewish education and on special topics treated in this chapter.
Edidin, Ben M., *Jewish Community Life in America*, chapter 4.
Engelman, Uriah Z., *Educating the Jewish Child*, Jewish Affairs pamphlets, vol. 1, no. 11.
Gittelsohn, Roland B., *Modern Jewish Problems*, chapter IX.

REFERENCES FOR TEACHERS

The Yearbook each year contains a list of Jewish periodicals, of Jewish books published in America, and an article on Jewish education during the previous year.
Jewish Education, published by the American Association for Jewish Education.
The Jewish Teacher, published by the Union of American Hebrew Congregations.
Engelman, Uriah Z., *Hebrew Education in America*. J.T.S.P. University Press.
Pilch, Judah, *Jewish Life in Our Times*, Behrman House, chapter 8.
Karpf, Maurice J., *Jewish Community Organization in the United States*, chapter V. Bloch.
Gamoran, Emanuel, *Changing Conceptions in Jewish Education*. Union.
Soltes, M., *The Yiddish Press, an Americanizing Agency*.

466

CHAPTER 27

How the Jew
Cares for His Own in America

YOU remember that when the first Jews were admitted to New Amsterdam in 1654 an agreement was made between them and Peter Stuyvesant. The Jews agreed that they would care for their own poor and would not be a burden on the tiny community. Since that time philanthropy has become a major effort of the American Jewish community which now consists of five million people. In fact, to some Jews charity has become more important than religion.

Of course, in Jewish tradition, charity has always been an important part of the religious life. For three thousand years it has been a living factor in every Jewish community, providing aid for the needy, hospitals for the sick, and temporary homes for travelers. Sometimes special funds were collected to redeem captives who had been enslaved by pirates and held for ransom. But the highest type of charity, according to the sages, was to help the poor to help themselves. Education, employment and loans are better than outright gifts of money, for they preserve the self-respect of the recipient. In Jewish tradition, charity was always connected with justice (in fact, the same word, *zedakah,* is used for both), for it was felt

467

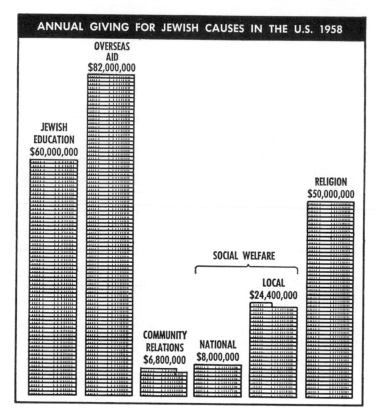

ANNUAL GIVING FOR JEWISH CAUSES IN THE U.S. 1958

OVERSEAS
AID
$82,000,000

JEWISH
EDUCATION
$60,000,000

RELIGION
$50,000,000

SOCIAL WELFARE

LOCAL
$24,400,000

COMMUNITY
RELATIONS
$6,800,000

NATIONAL
$8,000,000

that all wealth comes from God, and that everyone should be willing to share his good fortune.

I. HOW JEWISH CHARITY DEVELOPED

IN THIS country the early synagogues were the centers for all the needs of the community, religious, educational and philanthropic. But little by little as the communities grew

How the Jew Cares for His Own in America

new groups were formed to care for special needs, such as those of the poor or orphans or the sick. Many such organizations grew up, backed by people of much kindness and good will but without any special knowledge of the best ways to accomplish their purposes. In the 1860's, relief moved on from the first stages of almsgiving to a wider conception of charity. Twenty years later the German Jews began to help the new Russian Jewish immigrants, at first with relief, and later with the establishment of settlements and Americanizing agencies which were to assist the immigrants to feel at home in the new land. Thus there sprang up a great variety of small specialized organizations, with little cooperation and often in direct competition with each other.

The Russian Jews, in turn, went through the same process. They did not like to receive charity from the earlier settlers but wanted to help each other, and very soon they began to do so, often organizing a complete set of philanthropic societies which duplicated those of the German Jews.

The next step was for these different societies to join together in a Federation of Jewish Philanthropies. Federation made for a better system in meeting the needs of the community; it made it possible to employ trained social workers and other experts. But at first the societies organized by German Jews were the only ones to be federated and these were under their own leadership. The Russian Jews, especially when they grew to be the majority in American Jewry, were not willing to be controlled

469

by German Jews. Sometimes they even formed a federation of their own, so that a city like Chicago for a time had two different federations of Jewish philanthropy. The final stage came with the union of the two federations, or in some cities, with the union of the many small organizations. This enabled the Jewish community to form a united approach to the problems of all its members, both in raising funds and in spending them in the best way.

The depression of the 1930's marked a radical change, not only in Jewish philanthropies, but in all private charity. The millions of persons who were out of work presented too great a problem for all the private agencies together. City and state relief organizations helped and finally the federal government stepped in so that people might not starve in rich America. Millions of families were tided over the emergency by direct relief and by work projects of the government.

During this time of depression when help was most needed, it became the duty of the federal government to administer relief and the difficult task was taken away from the private agencies, both Christian and Jewish. The Jewish agencies found two important outlets for their activities. In the first place, they catered to special needs which were not served by the government. They gave advice and leadership to people who felt that they could not work out their difficulties by themselves. The agencies often gave additional money for special needs, for they were not limited by law in the same way as the government organization. Secondly, they turned to the needs of

470

the Jewish community itself, to Jewish Centers, Jewish education, and the needs of Jews overseas.

As a result of the slow process of the earlier years, and the speeding up of the depression days, the Jewish philanthropies are now well organized in almost every city and in the country as a whole. They are also more Jewish than ever, serving primarily the needs of the Jewish community. At first, the many small organizations served different groups with special needs—the poor, the sick, the immigrant. Today they conceive their united task entirely differently; they aim to serve the Jewish community as a whole, both its unhappy members, those who have serious problems, and its normal members who need to live together and work together as Jews.

II. TYPES OF PHILANTHROPIES

LET us glance hastily at some of these different organizations and the work they are doing. We naturally think of the relief society which provides food, clothing or money for people who cannot earn enough to support themselves, or who are ill or out of work. Many Jews in America, as we have seen, are bitterly poor; if their work stops for even a few weeks, they must ask for aid. Even towns with small Jewish communities have relief societies, for there is usually at least one problem family and occasionally there are transients who require a little help.

The first special Jewish organization for philanthropy in the United States was the Hebrew Benevolent Society of New York. It was founded in 1822 when the need arose

471

to visit a Revolutionary war veteran, who was old and ill, and asked that somebody visit him in the hospital. The little group formed then grew to be the largest Jewish organization of its kind in the world, the Jewish Social Service Association of New York.

The old charity society has now changed its name and purpose. It is usually known as a family welfare society or personal service bureau. Its chief aim is not to give money, but to provide the advice and encouragement which will help a family to become self-supporting. Often mental problems or family disagreements can be remedied. Vocational training, employment bureaus, and free loan societies are all working toward the same ends. The fact is that American Jews have no paupers, no people who have been used to receiving charity. We are people who have always cared for ourselves, even though we may have been very poor in Europe, and have had to learn to face new conditions in America. The Jewish immigrant may cease in ten years from being a recipient and become a giver of charity. The chief task of a Jewish welfare society is to help people to help themselves.

There are certain groups of people who cannot care for themselves, such as orphans, very old people, and the sick. The Jewish community of America has taken care of these special needs very well. We have already studied the organization of the first orphan homes; now there are about fifty-five organizations for child care throughout the country, which assist around seven thousand children. Most of these are not orphans, but come from

472

broken homes, where because of illness or for other reasons they cannot be cared for properly.

The old idea of a good home for orphans was the biggest possible building, to house the largest number of children. But newer and far better homes, like the one at Pleasantville, N. Y., or the Bellefaire Home at Cleveland, consist of many small cottages, where small groups of children can live like so many families, each under the guidance of a cottage mother. About one-third of the children cared for by the Jewish organizations are housed in these institutions of both the older and newer types. But fully two-thirds are boarded out in foster homes, where they are able to live with a real family, and are visited by the social worker once in a while to see that they are getting on well.

Another 76 agencies care for the aged who are too

BELLEFAIRE HOME, CLEVELAND, OHIO

473

old to work and too poor to live in hotels. Of course, many old people live with their own children, and many are supported by social security or old age pensions, but some require special care, especially if they also happen to be sick. Some 12,000 people live in these institutions for the aged.

The largest project in the whole field of Jewish social service is the health work, especially the 70 Jewish hospitals located in large cities all through the country. Fully half the money spent goes for health work. Many people may not realize the need for such effort by the Jewish community. Everybody understands the need for Jewish family welfare societies, because Jews have special problems connected with the Jewish religion, or the use of the Yiddish language, or their old-world background. In the same way, Jewish children should be brought up as Jews, and the Jewish aged feel most at home in a Jewish environment. Although medical treatment can be given by any good physician, whether he or the patient is a Jew or a Christian, many patients prefer kosher food and a Jewish institution.

The chief purpose of the Jewish hospital is to serve the needs of the Jewish community as a whole and not only the need of the individual patient. Jewish physicians who are not always admitted to Christian institutions find in the Jewish hospital facilities for training and practice. The Jewish hospital provides an important part of the medical care of the whole city in which it is located because both Jewish and non-Jewish patients are treated there. The

How the Jew Cares for His Own in America

PART OF MT. SINAI HOSPITAL BUILDINGS

largest of these Jewish hospitals is Mt. Sinai in New York, but many others rank with the best health centers of the country. In addition, Jews have founded several hospitals of national scope, two for tuberculosis in Denver, one for tuberculosis in Los Angeles, and one for blood diseases in Hot Springs, Ark. The last, as well as the National Jewish Hospital in Denver, were founded and are largely supported by B'nai B'rith.

In several large cities there are organizations for Jewish delinquents, notably the Jewish Board of Guardians in New York. Some Jewish children, living in the slums, fall into bad company. Every effort is made to save them from a life of crime, and often these efforts meet with success. The number of Jewish criminals is actually very low everywhere in the United States. This is largely due to organizations like the Jewish Big Brothers and Big Sisters who befriend needy and delinquent children, and the chaplains and social workers who aid Jewish prisoners.

History of the Jews in the United States

A new phase of Jewish social work is vocational guidance. Sometimes this service is associated with an employment agency, which tries to find jobs for Jewish boys and girls. Because there is discrimination in many fields, such Jewish organizations are useful and necessary. Many Jewish Centers provide guidance classes and conferences with experts, in order that young people may choose their life work as intelligently as possible. The B'nai B'rith sponsors a Vocational Service Bureau, which publishes valuable information on various trades and professions.

Another special service is aid to immigrants. In 1885, when the Russian migration was mounting, the Hebrew Immigrant Aid Society (known as HIAS) had its beginning. During that time, when the newcomers were poor and ignorant of American ways, it was most important to have a friend to welcome them. HIAS has a representative at Ellis Island to meet the immigrant, to aid him in finding his family, and to get a start in this strange new world which he is entering. HIAS works with foreign agencies and also has its representatives placed in many points of prospective immigration abroad to instruct the people there in just what preparations they must take if they wish to come to America. In doubtful cases HIAS represents the immigrant, explains his story to the American authorities and even carries certain pleas to the higher courts in Washington.

The National Council of Jewish Women has devoted much attention to the immigrant, especially to women and girls who come to this country. The organization

476

follows them to their destination, and sees that they are properly received there. In addition, the Council conducts classes in English and such other topics as are required for people who wish to become citizens.

After the adoption of immigration restrictions, all this work was cut down until the Nazi persecutions made it necessary for vast numbers of Jews to move from their native lands. In 1939, when this movement was at its height, a joint body was formed, known as the National Refugee Service, which shared in the United Jewish Appeal, and spent the money acquired from this fund to help new Americans to become settled throughout the country. In 1946, this body was still further expanded, and adopted the name, United Service for New Americans.

We have rapidly surveyed many kinds of social service, extended for the most part to individuals and usually to persons who are in trouble. Now we want to talk about an entirely different type of work, service to the whole Jewish community, young and old, rich and poor together. This is the Jewish center movement, and we shall have to go back a good many years to find its small beginnings.

III. THE JEWISH CENTER MOVEMENT

IN MANY cities nowadays the largest and most important Jewish institution, next to the synagogue, is the Jewish Center. We want to see how this movement came into being, and where it stands today.

The present Jewish Center movement had a double beginning, in the Young Men's Hebrew Association and the

History of the Jews in the United States

YMHA BUILDING, 92ND STREET AND LEXINGTON AVE., NEW YORK CITY

settlement house. It now includes and unites many different types of agencies, all of which are committed to work for the Jewish community. Back in the 1870's groups of young men founded YMHA's in order to further their Jewish life, both cultural and social. The first of these, established in New York and Philadelphia, were copied in many other cities, and YWHA's were organized for young women. The Jews followed the Young Men's and Young Women's Christian Associations, which were already well established.

Then came the East-European immigration, and Jews began to establish settlement houses to serve as centers of education and social life, and to help the immigrants become Americans. The idea of the settlement, which also was originated by Christians, was for better educated people to settle among the poor and underprivileged in order to help them. The Maxwell Street Settlement in Chicago, founded in 1893, and the Educational Alliance in the East Side of New York, founded in 1889, were followed by many smaller institutions.

478

How the Jew Cares for His Own in America

These settlement houses provided immigrant aid, classes in English, clubs for young people and children, athletics, religious services, and all kinds of meetings for young and old. They undoubtedly made a great contribution to the welfare of the newcomers. But they were founded and controlled by German Jews outside the immigrant neighborhood, and the Russian Jews soon objected to having their own neighborhood centers organized and controlled by people from uptown.

To overcome the objection a new type of Jewish Center grew up among them. It was usually organized around a synagogue or a Hebrew school, and it added all the social, athletic and educational features which the people needed and could afford. In 1921, the National Jewish Welfare Board absorbed the small and struggling Federation of YMHA's and a truly national movement began.

By 1961, the JWB included 350 Jewish Centers, with 675,000 members. Some of these organizations used other names, such as YMHA, Jewish Community Center, and the like. But all of them accepted certain general principles. They were to serve, not one group, such as young men or young women, but all elements in the community. They were not philanthropic organizations, where the rich might give money and the poor enjoy the benefits, but community centers for all Jews, rich and poor alike. The careful study of the Jewish Centers, made in 1947 by Prof. Oscar Janowsky of the College of the City of New York, laid special stress on the Jewish value of such institutions. They can be of abiding value to the

History of the Jews in the United States

YM AND YWHA BUILDING
PHILADELPHIA, PA.

Jews of America if they not only bring Jews together in a congenial social environment, but actually offer them Jewish education and ideals. We have proceeded very far from the social club or the settlement house in establishing real institutions.

In addition, many communal organizations throughout the country have established social centers which come fairly close to the Jewish Center idea. There are synagogue centers, orthodox, conservative, and reform, which provide social and educational activities for their own members and often for everybody in the neighborhood. The more secular groups and the Yiddishists have their own centers and cultural agencies in the larger cities.

In many medium-sized Jewish communities the Jewish Center is a real factor for unity. Members of all synagogues belong to it, and the Jewish Federation pays the excess expenditure over and above the membership dues. Since the close of the war great sums of money have been raised to erect new and up-to-date centers in a number of cities. There is even a World Federation of YMHA's and Community Centers whose purpose it is to spread the

How the Jew Cares for His Own in America

Jewish Center movement throughout the world. Six countries belong to this World Federation, and several others benefit by its work, but the lead belongs to the Jewish Welfare Board which represents the great Jewish Center movement of America.

IV. FEDERATIONS AND WELFARE FUNDS

WE HAVE seen how the many Jewish organizations for various philanthropic purposes joined together in federations. This avoided constant appeals for money from the Jewish public and the different agencies learned to work together. In the past there had often been competition, not so much as to which organization could do the best work, but which could raise the most money. Now with a joint campaign once a year much more money is raised, competition is replaced by cooperation, and the public is kept informed about the different agencies and what they are trying to accomplish.

There are about four thousand Jewish philanthropic agencies of all kinds and sizes in the United States; they spend about $35,000,000 a year. This includes all those in the Federations and some outside. The first modern federation was formed in 1896 in Cincinnati, and is still functioning successfully. In Chicago and Baltimore the Federation represents a union of an orthodox and a reform federation forming a joint organization. The New York Federation of Jewish Philanthropies includes 116 different agencies; it is by far the largest in the nation. The usual federation includes organizations for family welfare,

481

for children, the aged, and also hospitals, Jewish Centers, and employment agencies. Many of them include bureaus of Jewish education. None of them include synagogues, for each of these are intended to serve a different section of the Jewish population and each has its own point of view and its own means of support.

The first purpose of the Federations was to raise money jointly, and in this they were most successful. We must notice that beside the monies donated by the Jewish communities much is received from other sources such as membership dues in Jewish Centers, fees in Hebrew schools, the money paid by patients for hospital care, and mothers' pensions paid by the states. The Community Chest movement in the general community has followed the same lines of development as the Jewish Federation; in some cities the Jewish agencies are part of the Community Chest, while in others they remain separate organizations.

By 1930 there were sixty-six Jewish Federations in the United States. By 1958 the Yearbook listed 54 Federations, Welfare Funds and Community Councils in 234 cities throughout the country. Most cities with large Jewish communities have central bodies to raise money for philanthropy; in many of them these bodies do other work as well, such as coordinating Jewish activities and taking the lead in filling the needs of the Jewish community.

When the local needs were provided for, the communities found that they were still receiving many appeals

Courtesy Chicago Jewish Chronicle

FOODLESS DINNER

In Campaign of Joint Distribution Committee, where wealthy American donors heard of the privations of European Jewry. No food was served. Note the mourning decorations.

from Jewish sources outside of the community; there were national organizations for religion, education and philanthropy, and a growing appeal for overseas work. The next step was the organization of a Welfare Fund to collect the money and divide it up among these outside causes. Sometimes this work is also done by the local Federation but usually it is undertaken by a separate body. You may be confused by the names of the organizations in your own city, because many different titles are used throughout the country. But wherever you live, you will probably have both a Federation and a Welfare Fund, whatever they are called.

A number of Jewish communities have gone a step further in organization by forming Jewish Community Councils. The Council brings together all Jewish organizations, religious, philanthropic and social, on a democratic basis. Its purpose is to achieve unity among all the Jews in the city that they may solve their common problems together. The Community Council has committees on relations between Jews and Christians, on Jewish education, on the growing needs of the community for new buildings and new services. In fact, the Community Council takes an interest in any problem that the Jews of that particular city feel is important to them. One of the achievements of the Community Council is that it has taken control out of the hands of the small body of wealthy people who give large sums for Jewish causes, and turned over the administration of affairs to the Jewish masses, the people who belong to the synagogues and the lodges. In this way

How the Jew Cares for His Own in America

the Community Council works, not only for unity, but also for a growing democracy in Jewish life in America.

V. THE NATIONAL ORGANIZATION OF
JEWISH PHILANTHROPY

In 1899, just at the beginning of modern scientific social service, the National Federation of Jewish Charities was organized. Its immediate purpose was to stem the stream of transients who wandered from one city to another, asking for charity on their way. This conference later adopted a better name. They called themselves the National Conference of Jewish Social Service and included a variety of different organizations and activities. The Conference meets every year to consider problems connected with different types of social work.

In 1932, as a result of the growing federation movement, the Council of Jewish Federations and Welfare Funds arose. By 1961, the Council included 216 agencies covering some 800 communities in America. Its chief interest is the organization of Jewish communities to serve the many needs of the Jewish people in this country and abroad. At one time the Council made an effort to budget national and international Jewish philanthropies, much as is done by the Federations and Welfare Funds in their own cities. This did not work out at the time because many people feared that the group in control might favor some projects at the expense of others, for example, that Zionism or Hebrew education might be neglected. We shall need to achieve a greater measure of unity in American Jewry first, then national budgeting will be a logical development.

The Jewish social workers also have their professional organizations. For fifteen years, from 1925 to 1939, the Graduate School for Jewish Social Work functioned in New York; it trained social workers in the special tasks of conducting Jewish social agencies and organizing Jewish communities. This training was most important, as the Jews have special problems of their own, which other schools of social work do not consider. The school finally closed for lack of funds, but ever since then leaders in social work have been trying to find a substitute. In 1947 a Training Bureau for Jewish Communal Service was organized, but this also did not last.

REVIEW QUESTIONS

1. What is the Jewish idea of charity? Why do we have special Jewish philanthropies in America?
2. Discuss the effects of the depression on Jewish charities.
3. Name three types of Jewish philanthropy; tell why they are needed, and how they work.
4. What is the reason for Jewish Centers? How do they work?
5. How do Federations operate? What are their advantages?

TOPICS FOR REPORTS

1. The need for trained Jewish social workers; how they receive their training.
2. Various methods of collecting charity; the special place of Federations and Welfare Funds among them.
3. Methods for organizing the local Jewish community, with special reference to the Jewish Community Council.

486

How the Jew Cares for His Own in America

4. Describe a "drive" for some cause, as it works in your community.
5. Study some philanthropic institution or Jewish Center; visit it, read its literature, describe how well it fulfills its purpose.
6. A study of biblical and talmudic charity; show how the same ideas are being applied today.

REFERENCES FOR PUPILS

Articles on Charity in *Jewish Encyclopedia* and *Universal Jewish Encyclopedia*.

Pilch, Judah, *Jewish Life in Our Times*, pages 155–165.

Edidin, Ben M., *Jewish Community Life in America*, chapters 6, 8, 11.

REFERENCES FOR TEACHERS

Bogen, Boris D., *Jewish Philanthropy*. Macmillan.

Karpf, Maurice J., *Jewish Community Organization in the United States*, chapters VI through VIII, XI.

Jewish Social Service Quarterly, official publication of the Jewish social workers.

The Jewish Center, a quarterly magazine on Jewish Centers, and its recent successor, *The Circle*, a popular monthly publication of the Jewish Welfare Board.

CHAPTER 28.

How American Jews
Are Organized for Many Purposes

WE HAVE discussed those Jewish organizations which were created for the three main purposes of advancing religion, education and philanthropy. But Jews, like other people, have many motives for forming organizations. If you make a list of Jewish organizations in your own city, you will find very many beside those we have already discussed. You will find social clubs, labor organizations, lodges, and societies for cooperating with Christians. Probably you yourself belong to one or another youth group. Your parents are probably members of several Jewish societies of different types.

In the Yearbook for 1960 there is a list of 303 national Jewish organizations of many varieties. Of these, 119 are religious and educational; 17 deal with community relations and 30 with Jewish culture. Some 112 deal with the area of social welfare: 65 with aid to Israel, another 15 with other aid overseas, and 32 with social welfare in America. Then there are 25 social organizations: six of them fraternities and sororities, 11 lodges for men and women, and 8 *landsmannschaften,* groups of people who came from the same country or community of the Old World and formed social and aid societies in America.

There is no one organization which can include all American Jews, but there have been many attempts to work out unity on one basis or another, and we shall consider these also as part of the picture. The fact is that all Jewish organizations are voluntary and depend on the particular interest of their adherents in order to carry out their purposes. Any Jew who is not interested can simply stay out of a particular synagogue or lodge, or even out of organized Jewish life as a whole. In small communities, where people know their neighbors, practically all Jews are a part of the Jewish community life, but in the larger cities a great many people who consider themselves good Jews take no part in any Jewish movement at all.

I. SOCIAL ORGANIZATIONS

LIKE all other people, Jews like to come together for pleasure among a congenial group. So most cities with fairly large numbers of Jews have their smaller social clubs in addition to the inclusive Jewish Centers. Some are city clubs for social purposes, some are country clubs for golf and tennis, and most of them are exclusive, serving their own members alone. But the more progressive clubs do have some educational meetings, and insist that their members belong also to a synagogue or to the Federation.

Some of these social groups also belong to national bodies. For example, we have mentioned the national fraternities and sororities, most of which have their local

489

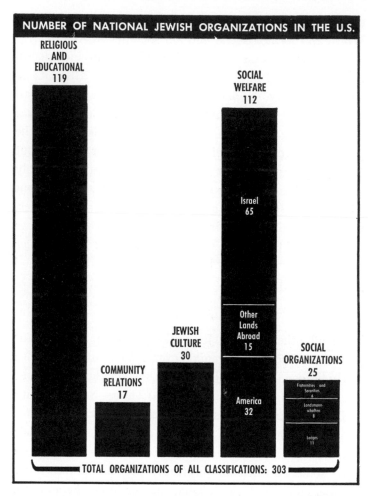

chapters in the various colleges. These provide housing
and social life for their members; they stand for brotherhood and forge a link between their members as these go

on from one college class to the next. Some of them include Jewish features in their programs.

At least a half million Jews belong to fraternal orders and *landsmannschaften,* proving that these groups play a very important role in Jewish life. The latter began as little groups of people who came from the same city or province in Europe and enjoyed meeting with each other and talking over old times. They eventually organized for mutual benefit in case of sickness or death. There are now as many as four thousand of these local bodies, and in the course of time they banded together in national organizations—a federation of Polish Jews, of Roumanian Jews, and so on. They have also done much practical work for the people who remained in the old home, raising large sums of money, and even sending their own representatives across the seas to supervise its distribution.

The oldest and largest of the fraternal orders is the B'nai B'rith, which we have mentioned often in the course of this history. In 1961, there were fully 470,000 members including the various groups of men, women, and young people. B'nai B'rith began as a secret order, and provided cultural programs for its members. These were poor German Jewish immigrants of the 1840's, who also needed mutual aid. It then developed to a philanthropic organization, and finally entered the fields of Jewish education and self-defense. At present the best known activities in its program are the Hillel Foundations in American universities (which we have already mentioned) and the Anti-Defamation League (which we shall treat later in this chapter). The B'nai B'rith has long dropped the element of secrecy from its meetings and even from its initiations, though it still lays stress on the meetings and work of the local lodges. It has produced a number of Jewish leaders during the past century. The president of the Order now is Label A. Katz of New Orleans, Louisiana, who has placed strong emphasis on every phase of Jewish education. Two of its former national secretaries have been famous as social workers, Dr. Boris D. Bogen, who had been in charge of the work of the Joint Distribution Committee in Soviet Russia after the First World War, and Dr. I. M. Rubinow, who had headed the first Zionist Medical Unit to Palestine at the same period. Both of these men made important contributions through the B'nai B'rith to the Jews of America.

Another important Jewish fraternal order is the Independent Order B'rith Abraham, organized in 1887 and numbering 11,000 members in 1961. This body also is important in the field of philanthropy. In recent years Jewish workers have developed their own lodges, of which the largest is the Workmen's Circle, with 65,000 members.

II. ORGANIZATIONS FOR WOMEN AND YOUNG PEOPLE

WE HAVE several times mentioned the existence of special organizations for women and young people, in connection with religion, the Jewish Centers, and the fraternal orders. As a matter of fact, practically every national organization with a cause to promote has its women's auxiliary, while many of them sponsor youth groups as well.

How American Jews Are Organized

This was not always so. In the early days men were the only active workers in Jewish affairs, as in American life in general. Many men were horrified when women began to form organizations, hold meetings, and make speeches. But women won a higher place in America from year to year until finally they won the right to vote on complete equality with men.

The first national organization of Jewish women was the National Council of Jewish Women, founded at the World's Columbian Exposition of 1893 by Mrs. Hannah Solomon of Chicago. At this fair the Jews were invited to send representatives to the Congress of Religions; the synagogues and rabbis were represented, but no organization of Jewish women existed. So a few prominent women attended, and while there they organized the Council. In 1961, the Council had 329 sections with 122,000 members. True to its origin, it does not stand for any one group in Judaism, but is simply a woman's club, with Jewish members and Jewish interests. We have already seen how active the Council has been for many years in giving aid to immigrants; it has accomplished other social work, as for the blind and deaf, and for Jewish farm women. It has also done religious work, such as the establishment of religious schools.

Today women's organizations function in every field exactly as do the men's. The Federations of Sisterhoods are religious; other bodies are social, or charitable, or educational. About half the pupils in Sunday schools and 40 per cent of those in week-day schools are girls. Many of the teachers are young women, born and trained in America. The largest body of Jewish women in America is Hadassah, the women's branch of the Zionist movement, with 300,000 members.

Beside Mrs. Solomon, two other Jewish women of her generation became important leaders. One was Rebekah Kohut; both her father and her husband were prominent rabbis. She was born in Hungary but brought up in California. For many years she was a leader in the Council of Jewish Women, the Emanu-El Sisterhood in New York, and many other public movements. Her highest honor was the post of president of the World Council of Jewish Women between the two World Wars. Her own life story, *My Portion,* is a fascinating book; it illustrates the period of German Jewish immigration and describes many later developments.

The other outstanding woman of her time was Henrietta Szold, best known as the founder of Hadassah. She was born in Baltimore in 1860, the daughter of Rabbi Benjamin Szold. For many years she was secretary of the Jewish Publication Society, translating books from the German, editing its Yearbook, and doing a great amount of scholarly work. In 1912, after a visit to Palestine, she gathered together a group of women and formed the first chapter of Hadassah. From that time on, Miss Szold became the leading woman Zionist in America and finally the most prominent Jewish woman in the world. She organized the Zionist Medical Unit which went to Palestine after the First World War. She was national president of

How American Jews Are Organized

Hadassah for many years, and later honorary president for the rest of her life.

In 1920, when she was almost sixty years old, Henrietta Szold went to Palestine, where she lived for the last twenty-five years of her life. She was at the head of the medical, the educational and the social service work of Palestine at

HENRIETTA SZOLD

various periods as well as a member of the Zionist executive. In her old age she organized the Youth Aliyah, by means of which 100,000 children have already been saved from Germany and other lands of persecution to be brought up as free citizens of the Jewish homeland. When she died, at the age of eighty-four, she was recognized the world over by Jews and Christians alike, as a great person and an outstanding Jewish leader.

We cannot even list all the types of Jewish youth organizations which have grown up within the past few years. Every Jewish Center has its clubs; the Zionist bodies, the synagogues, the B'nai B'rith, and even the Workmen's Circle have their youth groups. Many thousands of Jewish young men and women belong to these

495

various bodies both for their own pleasure and education, and for the benefit of the Jewish people as a whole. But still larger numbers of Jewish youth have no such affiliation, so we cannot be sure just how much all the organizations together will help the young people or the cause of Judaism.

III. THE JEWISH LABOR MOVEMENT

IN CHAPTERS 17 and 18 we read about the mass immigration of Russian Jews and how they became workers in industry; how they were at first exploited in sweatshops but how they later organized labor unions to defend their cause. The final fight to establish union standards in the needle trades was won in a series of strikes in New York in 1910. The International Ladies Garment Workers became the greatest of these unions, and still remains one of the pillars of the American Federation of Labor, with David Dubinsky as its president.

At about the same time makers of men's clothing were striking in Chicago, and the Amalgamated Clothing Workers of America became powerful under the leadership of Sidney Hillman. This union was a member of the old Congress of Industrial Organizations. Many other unions were organized among furriers, hatmakers, and so on. At the beginning some of these unions were almost exclusively composed of Jews, but now half of their membership is composed of the various races and groups in America, though many of their leaders are still the Jews who led the original fight for unionization.

496

How American Jews Are Organized

The Jewish unions have shown originality in many respects, and their program has often been followed by the American labor movement as a whole. They have been concerned for the general welfare of their members besides the immediate object, which was the improvement of wages and hours. They have established health centers, banks, and a housing program; they have become active in providing recreation and education for their members and their members' families. They have developed unemployment insurance, which has proved a lifesaver for thousands of people. The manufacture of women's garments especially is a seasonal trade, and many of the workers had to work overtime for half the year and then be idle the other half. In 1921, the ILGWU devised an insurance plan, by which the workers and employers paid into a fund, and any workers long unemployed would draw from it.

Probably the most significant innovation was the permanent arbitration board set up to solve grievances, make rules for the trade, and as far as possible prevent strikes. The purpose of this board is to abolish the old system of constant bickering for advantage between workers and employers, and among the employers as well. A system of orderly government is introduced into an industry, with a board of arbitration composed of appointees of the unions, of the employers, and an impartial arbiter as chairman. The manufacturers are assured of regular operation and the workers of security, while America is thereby made a more peaceful and orderly land.

History of the Jews in the United States

The Jewish labor unions have had many important off-shoots. In 1915, they organized the People's Relief Committee, which became one of the three agencies that formed the Joint Distribution Committee. In 1934, at the time of the Nazi persecutions, they organized the Jewish Labor Committee to represent labor in the fight against anti-Semitism and fascism. This body is composed of over a hundred unions and several hundred other labor and progressive organizations; all these total several hundred thousand members.

Beside the labor unions, which work chiefly for economic betterment, the Jewish workers have developed three large fraternal orders, with different points of view on Judaism as well as on politics. These are the Workmen's Circle (or Arbeiter Ring) with 65,000 members, the Jewish People's Fraternal Order, with 47,000, and the Labor Zionist Order, with 25,000. All these have local lodges, educational programs, sick benefits and insurance.

The oldest is the Workmen's Circle, which began with one lodge on the East Side of New York in 1892, exactly as the B'nai B'rith had started fifty years before. In 1900, it was reorganized as a national fraternal order. In general, this order stands for socialism and for Jewish rights, but not for Zionism. Most of its activities are conducted in the Yiddish language, including its many schools for children and its lecture courses for adults. It maintains for its members a medical department, a social service department and ten summer camps.

How American Jews Are Organized

The *Farband* or Labor Zionist Order was at first called the Jewish National Workers Alliance. This is a Zionist order, cooperating with the labor movement in Israel. Since its founding in 1912 it has grown in membership and broadened its work, for it now sponsors various benefits for its own members, study and musical groups, and schools for the teaching of both Yiddish and Hebrew.

The newest of the three is the Jewish People's Fraternal Order, which is the Jewish branch of the International Workers Order. This is a leftist group; the Jewish section was organized in 1930 by a group who had withdrawn from the Workmen's Circle. At first its only interests were along political and economic lines, but during the Second World War it also became active in the field of Jewish education. Most of its lodges conduct their business in Yiddish, though some are now using English. Beside many schools for children it conducts a Jewish Educational Institute in New York for adults.

IV. JEWISH DEFENSE AGENCIES

MOST Jewish organizations, whatever their main purposes, are also concerned with defending the good name of the Jew and with protecting Jewish rights, both at home and abroad. But there are a few agencies which deal specially with this type of problem, and which are usually known as defense agencies.

Their beginnings may be traced to the protest meetings and joint action among American Jews at various times when Jews were in danger overseas, as in the Damascus

499

case of 1840. After a number of similar occasions, the
Board of Delegates of American Israelites was set up in
1859. The Board worked as a separate organization for
almost twenty years, when it was finally amalgamated
with the newly formed Union of American Hebrew Congregations. From 1878 to 1925 the Board worked in this
new form and was finally disbanded because new organizations had grown up specifically for this work. For many
years the Washington representative of the Board, as well
as of the B'nai B'rith, was Simon Wolf, of whom we have
heard before.

In 1906, after the Kishinev massacre, the American
Jewish Committee was formed to defend Jewish rights.
This was a committee consisting of some of the ablest and
most influential American Jews. At first most of them
came from the reform congregations. Its strength lay in
the personality of its leaders, who were not elected by any
body of American Jews. The first president was Judge
Mayer Sulzberger of Philadelphia; then Louis Marshall
of New York, a famous international lawyer; third, Dr.
Cyrus Adler, president of the Jewish Theological Seminary. The latest president is Louis Caplan of Pittsburgh.

The American Jewish Committee was one of the leaders
in the abrogation of the Russian treaty in 1911. It was
active in defense of Jewish rights all through the Nazi
period. The organization is not committed to the Zionist
program, but it has defended the right of Jews to immi-
grate to Palestine and to buy land there, and has strongly

supported the United Nations program on Palestine. It is active in working for a declaration on human rights under the UN charter. The Committee works also through radio and the press toward the education of Americans in general on the rights of minority groups. It favors laws to protect these rights in such matters as immigration, employment and education. It fosters the study of problems of discrimination, and publishes pamphlets and books. Of late years the Committee has extended its influence by working directly in local communities and by organizing chapters in the larger cities.

This Committee failed to satisfy the Jewish masses in America; they felt that it was a limited body consisting of reform Jews, and did not represent their views on Zionism or on Jewish rights in eastern Europe. In fact, this dissatisfaction represented the same split between the German Jewish leaders and the Russian Jewish masses which we have often seen in philanthropy and community organization. So in 1916 there was organized an American Jewish Congress, to serve only during the war period and the peace conference. In 1917, over 300,000 Jews voted for delegates to this Congress, which finally met in Philadelphia in December 1918. The Zionists held a majority, and the chairman of the meeting was Judge Julian Mack, at that time president of the Zionist Organization of America. Both the Congress and the Committee were represented at the Paris Peace Conference, and worked to establish the rights of Jews the world over. In 1920, the Congress met again, to receive reports and to adjourn.

But there were many people who wanted to see the organization continued, so that in 1922 it was reorganized. During the whole of the following period Dr. Stephen S. Wise was the leading spirit of the Congress and it has been consistently Zionist in its ideals. The supporters of the Congress point to two differences between itself and the Committee; the Congress represents the masses of Jews, who are chiefly of Russian origin, and it appeals to the general public rather than to select leaders. For example, the American Jewish Congress fostered mass meetings and parades against Hitlerism; it backed the boycott against German goods during the Nazi period; now it is carrying to the courts cases of discrimination against American minorities. It is working on the problem of job discrimination against minorities. In these movements the Congress is defending not only Jews, but also Negroes or any other minority groups, for it believes that American democracy demands fair treatment for all, and that the Jew cannot defend himself alone without defending all the oppressed. The Congress also has an active publication program including the Jewish Affairs series which we have often cited.

A third defense agency which has grown in proportion to the need is the Anti-Defamation League of the B'nai B'rith, founded in 1913 by Sigmund Livingston of Chicago. For many years the League carried on a limited but important campaign against anti-Semitism in newspapers, magazines, movies and the stage. Then came the Ku Klux Klan and the work of the League broadened into politics and public relations. With the rise of the Nazis the League became one of the chief American agencies for the education of the non-Jewish public in the understanding of the Jew and in the proper relationship of all groups living together in a democracy. The chief weapon of the League for years has been publicity of every type, including radio, films, pamphlets, public meetings, and cooperation with schools, labor unions and business groups. Since 1945, it has joined with other organizations in advocating laws in defense of minorities. The chief strength of the League is its backing by the hundreds of B'nai B'rith lodges throughout the country. Every lodge has an Anti-Defamation Committee which keeps in touch with the local situation and appeals to the national organization for help when it may be needed.

We have already mentioned the Jewish Labor Committee, which was formed in 1934, when Hitler was already in power. This Committee has been able to defend Jewish rights through the cooperation of the great labor unions of the nation. Its special interest is the protection of Jews and other minorities in industry.

One of the very interesting Jewish organizations, which has made defense work one of its activities, is the Jewish War Veterans of the United States. This is a veterans' organization to whose membership only men or women who have served in the armed forces are eligible. It was formed by a small group of Civil War Veterans in New York in 1896 and remained small for a long time. But the membership was increased by veterans of the Spanish-

History of the Jews in the United States

American War and became really important with the large growth of membership after the First World War. It is now the second oldest veterans' organization in America, and generally recognized as a representative body. It takes care of the claims of veterans under the G.I. Bill of Rights. It has posts in many parts of the country, and because it is a patriotic body it is able to do much for Jewish rights in American life.

One of the ways in which Jewish rights are best protected is through cooperation with Christians in civic and educational groups which tend toward good citizenship. There are many of these, of all different kinds of membership and with diverse purposes. We shall mention only one of them here, the National Conference of Christians and Jews. This began as a committee of the Federal Council of Churches of Christ in America (the Protestant federation), but soon became a separate organization, with Protestant, Catholic and Jewish co-chairmen. It works largely through the churches and synagogues, teaching people to respect each other's religious faith. Its most interesting method of expression is the use of teams of three ministers of the three faiths to conduct panel discussions before schools, in army camps and over the radio. In addition, it sponsors a national Brotherhood Week every February, which is widely supported, not only by ministers, but also by newspaper editors, mayors and even presidents of the United States, for everybody realizes the need of brotherhood among all Americans. This is one of the best methods of defending Judaism,

504

for it is conducted by both Christians and Jews together, and it speaks in the name of religion to the members of the churches. Dr. Everett R. Clinchy, past head of the Council, is likewise organizer of an International Council of Christians and Jews, which held a meeting in Switzerland in August 1947 to form a program for the post-war period.

We must note the two latest trends in defense of Jewish rights. One is the scientific study of the problems involved, such as: what makes people hate those of a differ-. ent race or religion? What kind of people join these hate movements? How can we best counteract them in a free country like America? Several of the organizations we have mentioned have set up special groups to study such questions, and are publishing their studies. Another is the cooperative method of meeting problems as they arise. In 1944, the big defense agencies together with a number of city organizations formed the National Community Relations Advisory Council. By combining the knowledge and the power of the various groups, the Advisory Council is able to offer to any city the proper methods for coping with any local problem that may arise.

In these various organizations there have been a number of outstanding personalities. Here we shall discuss briefly the lives of two, whose names have appeared often in this history and who have accomplished important work for their people.

The first of these is Louis Marshall, who was president of the American Jewish Committee from 1917 to 1929.

505

He was born in Syracuse, N. Y., in 1856, the son of Jewish immigrants. He practiced law for many years in New York City, where he became recognized as one of the great constitutional lawyers of his time. He was a man of broad interests; he worked so hard to preserve the forests of America that Syracuse

Louis Marshall

University named its forestry building after him. He defended the rights of the Negroes in several important legal cases. He was the only man to serve as a member of three constitutional conventions of New York State.

, In Jewish life he was such an outstanding leader during the first quarter of the twentieth century, that when Israel Zangwill, the English novelist, visited America, he remarked that "American Jewry was ruled by Marshall Law." He was interested in the welfare of all Jews everywhere, rather than in a single party; he was at the same time president of the reform Temple Emanu-El and the conservative Jewish Theological Seminary. He was a devout Jew, with a good Hebrew background, and he was eager that every Jewish child have a religious education.

How American Jews Are Organized

Mr. Marshall is best known for his work in defense of Jewish rights. He was president of the American Jewish Committee for twelve years. He was one of the organizers of the Joint Distribution Committee. He led in the movement to abrogate the Russian treaty in 1911. Because he was the leader of the American Jewish delegation to the Peace Conference of 1919, following the First World War, he was elected chairman of the joint meeting of Jews from many countries.

His last great work was the formation of the Jewish Agency for Palestine, in which he represented the non-Zionists and Dr. Chaim Weizmann the Zionists. This was a difficult task, for many Zionists objected to sharing their work with those outside the movement, while many non-Zionists wanted to have nothing to do with it. Only two such strong personalities could bring the two groups into line and work out an agency by which all Jews might help in the development of Palestine. This was achieved in Zurich, Switzerland, in August, 1929; Mr. Marshall, who was seventy-three years old, fell ill and died a month later.

The second man we wish to consider is Rabbi Stephen S. Wise, leader of the American Jewish Congress and of the Zionist Organization of America. Dr. Wise was born in Hungary in 1874 and was brought to America as an infant when his father, a leading rabbi of that day, took a congregation in New York. He himself occupied pulpits in New York and Portland, Oregon, until 1906, when he founded the Free Synagogue of New York City.

History of the Jews in the United States

Dr. Wise had many claims to fame. He was known as one of the great orators of the United States and for many years he was constantly traveling about to speak to large audiences of both Jews and Christians. He was a leader in liberal movements for many years, defending the rights of labor and of the poor.

STEPHEN S. WISE

He was one of the men responsible for the resignation of a corrupt mayor of New York City. He was one of the founders of the Zionist movement in America and the first secretary of the organization. He served twice as president of the Zionist Organization of America, and through his friendship with President Woodrow Wilson he had much to do with the favorable action on Zionism at the Versailles Peace Conference. He founded the Jewish Institute of Religion in 1922 to provide a liberal seminary for rabbis in New York City.

As a Zionist and a leader of the Jewish masses Dr. Wise found the American Jewish Congress a congenial organization. Since its foundation he had been its chief leader and for much of the time its president. Its policy has al-

508

ways been militant and its program has included human rights for all people. This was in line with his own aggressive and liberal temperament. In 1936, he founded the World Jewish Congress, which included Jews from twenty-six nations. As president of the American Jewish Congress, Dr. Wise was elected president of the World Jewish Congress as well. Dr. Wise died in 1949, at the age of 75.

It is no wonder that two such men as Stephen S. Wise and Louis Marshall were often opposed in matters of policy, for they differed greatly in both personality and ideas and their organizations reflected their differences. Louis Marshall was a lawyer, conservative by temperament, wedded to no one party in Judaism but devoted to Jewish interests in general. Stephen S. Wise was a rabbi, an eloquent preacher, with very definite ideas on both general and Jewish affairs. In American public life he was a liberal, in Jewish life a Zionist and a defender of Jewish rights at home and abroad.

V. JEWISH UNITY IN AMERICA

IN SPITE of these many organizations which represent every kind of Jew and every interest of Jewish life, no one organization exists which can speak for American Jewry as a whole. The Synagogue Council of America combines all the chief religious bodies and has brought them closer together in their discussions on Jewish religious questions. The Council of Jewish Federations and Welfare Funds can discuss problems of philanthropy and pass resolutions leading to improved methods of fund-raising. The United Jewish Appeal raises tremendous sums of money and divides them among the various causes. But no one body can today represent American Jews, can state what they think of Palestine, or of Jewish education, or even of Jewish rights.

As we have seen, the trend is constantly in the direction of unity, but unity is not yet achieved. The first important attempt at unity in a big city was the Kehillah, or Jewish Community of New York City, organized in 1909. All kinds of societies were represented in it, synagogues, lodges and philanthropies. It succeeded in putting into effect a number of important Jewish activities, of which the most lasting was the Bureau of Jewish Education. The president of the Kehillah was Dr. Judah Leon Magnes, an able leader, who later became the chancellor of the Hebrew University in Jerusalem. But the Kehillah failed because there was no real community among New York Jews; they were too many in number and had too diverse interests. Probably New York will be the last, rather than the first city in the United States to have an effective Jewish community organization.

Up until now every attempt to organize all American Jews for self-defense, for Jewish rights abroad, or for cooperation with the non-Jews has failed. Every national Jewish organization had its leaders, its policies, and its own methods; each one considered its own the best. Yet everybody knew that when two Jewish groups made different demands on our government, or when they followed opposite policies in a crisis, the Jews as a whole

How American Jews Are Organized

Judah L. Magnes

suffered. So many efforts have been made for greater unity.

First came a Joint Consultative Council of the four big defense agencies, but this council had no authority. Then came the General Jewish Council, with the same bodies. But they soon fell out over their different methods, and so the group broke up.

In 1943, Henry Monsky, then president of B'nai B'rith, issued a call for a war-time organization to speak for American Jewry. This was the American Jewish Conference, which held its first meeting in August 1943 in New York City. Here five hundred delegates met, one hundred and twenty-five representing the national Jewish organizations and 375 elected by Jewish communities throughout the country. This was the nearest to complete unity that American Jewry has yet seen.

The Conference did a most useful piece of work. It adopted unanimously two programs, one for the rescue of the persecuted Jews of Europe and one for equal rights in the years after the war. It also passed against a small minority a plan for Palestine which included a

511

History of the Jews in the United States

demand for a Jewish commonwealth. Everyone was agreed on the need for Jewish immigration into Palestine, but some objected to this further point. The result was that the American Jewish Committee and some groups of less importance resigned from the American Jewish Conference, which then

HENRY MONSKY

represented a large majority of American Jews but no longer the complete Jewish community.

Now, we all know that when two bodies compete for control there can be no unity; in fact, such factionalism is often worse than no leadership at all. At the San Francisco meeting called to form the United Nations, the American Jews had to be represented by two bodies, the American Jewish Conference and the American Jewish Committee. In most matters they agreed, but complete unity had not been achieved. There was also a difference of opinion as to whether the Conference should take up questions concerning Jews in America, or should leave these to the separate bodies.

The Conference met annually until the fall of 1947, when it was proposed that it become a permanent organ-

512

ization. But many of the leading groups objected, so the Conference was disbanded in 1948. The latest attempt at meeting the problem of unity is the Presidents' Conference, an informal group of seventeen presidents of national Jewish bodies. They were called together to work with the Jewish Agency for Israel, in 1954, so the presidents may consult on important Jewish problems; but the national organizations are still not united.

Certainly, the Jews of America require many organizations for their different needs and to express their differing ideas. But they also are growing closer to each other through the years, so that they should now be ready for some over-all basis of union. Most Jews in this country are now born and educated in America. Practically all their organizations include the newer and the older elements in the community. In many cities it has proved possible to bring together all the Jews on the basis of representing their many organizations. Perhaps one day these *local* examples may point the way to the formation of a unified, representative, *national* organization.

REVIEW QUESTIONS

1. Make a list of objectives for which Jews have joined together.
2. What is the purpose of a Jewish social club? Describe one.
3. Describe the three stages of development of Jewish fraternal orders.
4. Describe two Jewish women's organizations in your city, with their purpose, officers, and national affiliations.
5. Tell of three organizations which are defending Jewish

rights; describe their methods, and tell which you think most effective.

1. List the Jewish organizations in your city, fitting each into its place in the description given here.
2. How can the Jews of your city be represented by a joint organization? What changes would be necessary for this purpose?
3. Present a biography of one of the leaders of a Jewish organization, such as Henrietta Szold, Louis Marshall or Henry Monsky.
4. Study the set-up of a Jewish labor organization; describe its work of a Jewish nature, of an economic and political nature.
5. Study the problem of defending Jewish rights in America and in Europe; the dangers to these rights, the best methods of fighting for them, by laws, education, and cooperation with non-Jews.

REFERENCES FOR PUPILS AND TEACHERS

Much of the material for this chapter will have to be dug out of current periodicals. Some appears in the *Universal Jewish Encyclopedia*. The Yearbooks give a list of national Jewish organizations, a full report of the American Jewish Committee, and a summary of the year's chief events.

Richards, Bernard G., *Organizing American Jewry*, Jewish Affairs pamphlets.

Edidin, Ben M., *Jewish Community Life in America*, chapter 10, The Jew and His Neighbors; chapter 13, Community Organizations.

Pilch, Judah, *Jewish Life in Our Times*, Part Two, chapter 2, Organizations for the Solution of the Jewish Problem.

Karpf, Maurice J., *Jewish Community Organization in the U. S.*, pages 62–66; 130–135.

How American Jews Are Organized

Levinger, Elma Ehrlich, *Fighting Angel, the Story of Henrietta Szold*. Behrman.

Monsky, Daisy, and Maurice Bisgyer, *Henry Monsky, The Man and His Work*. Crown Publishing Co.

Solomon, Hannah G., *Fabric of My Life*.

American Jewish Yearbook, vol. 5681, pages 21–55, art. on Louis Marshall by Cyrus Adler.

See also the various periodicals published by the national Jewish organizations, such as:

American Jewish Monthly, by the B'nai B'rith.

Congress Weekly, the American Jewish Congress.

The Jewish Veteran, by the Jewish War Veterans of the U. S.

The Committee Reporter, by the American Jewish Committee.

The Bulletin of the Anti-Defamation League of B'nai B'rith.

CHAPTER 29.

The American Jews and World Jewry

THE Jews of America, like every other people on this
continent, have always felt a close tie with their
relatives and friends abroad. People wrote letters, sent
money to the "Old Country," and helped their families to
come to America. The *landsmannschaften* were active in
befriending the Jews of a particular country or province.
Generous givers often donated moneys, not only for the
needy in America, but also for the Jews of Palestine and
of other foreign countries.

Some Jewish organizations have been international in
their membership. Such different bodies as the World
Union for Progressive Judaism, the Agudath Israel (a
strictly orthodox body), the World Jewish Congress, the
World Zionist Organization, all have active branches in
America. During the Nazi persecutions American Jews
met with leaders of the Jews of Great Britain, France and
other countries to discuss the problems of the Jews of
Europe. Even a few German Jewish representatives succeeded in attending these conferences. Only the Jews of
the Soviet Union were absent. But in August 1943, the
Russian Jews were officially represented by a delegation
to America, who for the first time since the Russian Revolution brought Russian Jewry back into the orbit of world

516

Jewry. Communist policy has since isolated the Jews of Communist lands once more.

American Jews have worked with Jews in other lands in two main endeavors; the great relief organizations and the Zionist movement. Both of these received a considerable impetus at the outbreak of the First World War, when the need in Eastern Europe was terrific and the claims of the Jews to Palestine first received international hearing. Again, during and after the Second World War, the sums of money raised for these two purposes exceeded any ever raised by the Jews in America, and probably any given by a similar group of five million people anywhere in the world.

I. THE JOINT DISTRIBUTION COMMITTEE

WHEN the First World War broke out in 1914, it brought untold misery to the Jews of eastern Europe, caught between the contending armies. Thousands of people had to flee from their homes. The Russians often accused the Jews of treachery to the land of the Czars. Massacres that outdid a thousand Kishinevs were committed, both during the war itself and during the Russian civil war which followed.

The American Jews responded to this need at once. In October 1914, two committees were organized to raise funds for relief in Europe: the American Jewish Relief Committee, sponsored by the American Jewish Committee, which appealed largely to the reform Jews; and the Central Relief Committee, which appealed chiefly to the orthodox and Zionists. The next year the People's Relief Committee representing Jewish labor organizations joined the fund-raising groups. For the first time all elements in Jewish life were hard at work for the same purpose.

They soon found that though they might raise money separately they had to spend it together, so they joined together in the American Jewish Joint Distribution Committee, usually known as the JDC. In the first ten years of its existence this organization sent fully $59,000,000 to Europe and Palestine. At first the work was largely relief, but after the close of the war the JDC tried to help the victims to reconstruct their own lives. Hospitals, schools, loan societies and similar organizations had a share in the funds, as well as homes for orphans and soup kitchens for the hungry. One year Julius Rosenwald of Chicago offered to give a million dollars or ten per cent of the quota. In 1918–19 the Jews made their first appeal to the American people for aid, and met with a splendid response. Governors, editors, millionaires and bishops assisted in this drive for suffering humanity.

Among the many who ran grave risks in this life-bringing work, two gave up their lives. Professor Israel Friedlander of the Jewish Theological Seminary and Rabbi Hyman Cantor, a graduate of the Hebrew Union College, were killed by bandits in the Ukraine while on a mission of mercy for the JDC.

In 1926, a new project was undertaken in Soviet Russia to help Jews settle on the soil. The Russian government took the land from the great estates which had been con-

518

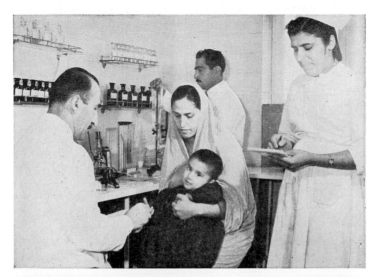

AID TO JEWS OVERSEAS

The great Jewish agencies help tens of thousands of needy Jews with food, clothing, medicine, rehabilitation, and resettlement. As only one part of its far-flung program, the Joint Distribution Committee maintains modern clinics in Teheran, Iran (*top*): Another agency, ORT, teaches valuable skills in special vocational schools abroad. Shown here is an ORT school for typewriter mechanics in Paris.

fiscated, and offered it to poor workers and traders whose livelihood had been ruined by the Russian Revolution. These groups included a considerable number of Jews, so the JDC launched a $25,000,000 appeal for three years, of which a great part was to be spent in this constructive work. Jewish farmers were established in the Ukraine and the Crimea, and a beginning was made of the Biro-Bidjan project in eastern Siberia.

By 1930, the work of the JDC was declining, and it was thought that the organization could soon be closed. But then came Hitler and the German Jews needed help to emigrate and some even needed relief in their old homes. As the Nazis overran one country after another, the need grew year by year. People in enemy countries were aided by the use of borrowed money, making it unnecessary to send American funds out of this country. Those who had escaped to Spain or Switzerland could be aided directly, and often helped to migrate to Palestine, America or Canada. In far-off Shanghai, China, some 12,000 refugees from Hitler had been caught in the midst of the Japanese war; large soup kitchens were established, barracks were organized for living quarters, and the JDC representative, who had been imprisoned because he was an American, continued to direct them from his prison cell.

At the close of the war it became possible to save the Jews who yet remained alive in Europe. This meant working in the liberated countries and the free countries of Europe, in Asia, South America, or wherever Jews had survived or had fled. It meant care for the orphans, the aged and the sick, as well as helping families to reunite and men to make a living. Food, clothing, medicine and tools were needed and had to be purchased and shipped. Jews in Displaced Persons camps needed homes. Many thousands pleaded to leave the lands where they had lost everything, and to start over again in some free country, preferably in Palestine. In fifty nations Jews were in misery and needed help of every possible kind.

This work began in camps and refuges under the auspices of the American Army and of UNRRA; the JDC sent supplementary food and clothing. Within a year the JDC was able to proceed by itself and to undertake the constructive tasks which might make the Jews of Europe again proud and self-sustaining. Workshops were opened for those preparing to emigrate, schools for children who had not seen the inside of a school for five years or more. In the peak year, 1947, the JDC spent the vast total of $69,200,000 for its work the world over. Altogether, in the forty-six years from 1914 through 1959, the organization had spent over $660,000,000 for relief and reconstruction in foreign lands, and even greater needs were expected in the years ahead.

II. OTHER RELIEF AGENCIES

WHILE the JDC was by far the greatest Jewish relief agency in the world, others which certainly deserve mention were working along with it. Some seventeen other organizations had a combined budget of about $26,000,-000 for the year 1958, so we must realize that they included a tremendous variety of projects for the benefit of Jews abroad.

The HIAS (Hebrew Immigrant Aid Society) is working with the JDC to get visas, provide funds, and help Jewish refugees to safe homes. It has offices in 31 countries besides America, where it aids the new Americans to establish themselves.

ORT is another organization designed to serve a special purpose. It was formed in St. Petersburg in 1880 to train some of the Jewish shopkeepers and peddlers to become artisans and farmers. The initials are of three Russian words, meaning Society for Industry and Agriculture, but they are now used for the English name, Organization for Rehabilitation through Training. The work of the ORT has grown steadily, as Jews found increasing need to learn trades and agriculture. Many graduates of its schools have been able to settle in Palestine and to go to work at once. Because of the great poverty of the Jews of Europe since the war, ORT is finding more than ever to do; thousands of young Jews who have never had a trade are now eager to learn one and to migrate as skilled workers. ORT receives most of its money from American Jews to continue its activity in Europe.

Another body which originated in Russia in Czarist days is OZE—the Jewish Health Society. Because of the weakness of so many survivors of the war, and their susceptibility to various diseases, this society has an immense job and its work is most important.

In 1939, the Union of Orthodox Rabbis in America

formed the *Vaad Hatzala,* or Rescue Council, to aid the Jews of Europe. This body has sent great quantities of kosher food, especially since the close of the war, is maintaining synagogues and schools, and assisting orphan homes for children who were saved by Christian families during the Nazi terror. It is especially active in aiding rabbis and yeshivah students and in sponsoring orthodox schools for Jewish children.

Among many other projects, we may note one by the Synagogue Council of America, by which American synagogues are asked to "adopt" and aid a ruined synagogue in Europe. An effort is also being made to find and to rescue the thousands of Jewish books and art objects which were seized and scattered by the Nazis.

Practically every lodge and synagogue in America has aided in the work of rescue in one way or another. Thousands of individuals have been sending packages as well as helping the established organizations. For everyone recognized the great emergency, and everyone was ready to help as far as he could.

III. THE ZIONIST MOVEMENT

WE HAVE noticed the beginnings of the Zionist movement in America (chapter 18) and its gradual development through the period of the First World War and the establishment of the British mandatory in Palestine. Since that time interest in Palestine and sympathy with Zionism have been increasing rapidly in the United States. In 1948, the Zionist Organization of America had 250,000

History of the Jews in the United States

CHAIM WEIZMANN

members; with Hadassah and other Zionist groups the total of registered Zionists was fully 700,000.

In the beginning, adherents of the Zionist movement were recruited largely from among Russian Jews, and many of the German Jews in America opposed the movement. The first great change came in 1914 when Louis D. Brandeis became the chairman of the organization; even after he was appointed to the Supreme Court in 1916 he continued his interest in Zionism, though he could no longer hold any office. After the war, Louis Lipsky became president of the ZOA and remained its leading figure until 1930. In that year the movement was reorganized to bring both groups into the administration, and it has been steadily growing in influence.

The Second World War, when millions of Jews were killed and thousands of others sought escape to a Jewish homeland, gave a new impetus to this growth of the Zionist organization. During the Nazi persecutions Palestine received more Jewish refugees than any other country in the world. The growth of the Yishuv (the Jewish

524

community of Palestine) was accompanied by the development of farming, industry, education, and the continued enrichment of Jewish culture. Jews the world over looked on Palestine as a place of refuge for the persecuted, while an ever growing number came to sympathize with the idea of a Jewish national home.

A great step forward was taken in 1929, when Zionists and non-Zionists joined in forming the Jewish Agency for Palestine, the official body to deal with the mandatory power, Great Britain. This was accomplished by the cooperation of Dr. Chaim Weizmann, then president of the World Zionist Organization, and Louis Marshall, a non-Zionist who was president of the American Jewish Committee. Through the Jewish Agency great numbers of Jews who did not believe in a Jewish state (or political Zionism) were able to cooperate in the practical work of immigration to Palestine and of building up the country. The non-Zionists are interested because they find an inspiration in the Hebrew University, in a Jewish center for art and culture; because they want Jews to flourish in any part of the world; and because they too love the ancient land of Israel. The Zionists, who have been working for Palestine through all these years, are willing to share in the control of the movement because the Agency is thereby strengthened and given added power to work for the people of the land and to speak with greater authority in international discussions.

A significant step was accomplished by the adoption in 1942 of the "Biltmore Program" (named for the New

York hotel where the meeting was held) by the American Zionists. Here for the first time the term, Jewish Commonwealth, came into prominence, instead of the phrase, Jewish National Home, which had been used in the Balfour Declaration. The Biltmore Program made the Zionist demands stronger and more definite.

After the war the Jews pressed for a fulfillment of this program, but the Arabs and the British opposed it. At first there was a British commission of inquiry, then an Anglo-American one, finally a commission of the United Nations. This last recommended the partition of Palestine into Arab and Jewish states, and the United Nations accepted the proposition. The dealings with the international body were largely carried on by Rabbi Abba Hillel Silver of Cleveland, Ohio, at that time president of the ZOA, and a leader of the Jewish Agency. The greatest forward step of all was the proclamation of the State of Israel in May, 1948.

The proclamation of the State alone would not, however, have brought any security to Israel were it not for the ability and the enthusiasm of the Haganah which became the army of the new State. Its series of victories against the Arab nations that attacked it and the political wisdom of the representatives of Israel in negotiating with other nations finally resulted in the admission of the new State to the United Nations in May, 1949.

A poll taken in 1945 showed that 80 per cent of American Jews favored a Jewish commonwealth in Palestine, 10 per cent opposed it, and the final 10 per cent were

526

undecided. A similar poll among non-Jews showed 75 per cent in favor. We can see this trend in the Central Conference of American Rabbis, the reform body. For many years the Conference had opposed Zionism, but in 1935 it passed a resolution of neutrality, saying that its members might properly favor or oppose. In 1943 it went even farther, declaring that Zionism and reform Judaism are not opposed in theory.

At the same time great numbers of Christians came to sympathize with Zionism. Before the State of Israel, both Democratic and Republican parties favored its establishment. In 1952 both national conventions adopted resolutions favoring Israel, and both candidates for president approved aid to the new state.

Not that all Americans, or even all Jews, are agreed on this any more than on many another proposition. In 1942, the anti-Zionists organized the American Council for Judaism. The group was small, but it included some members of influence, such as its national chairman, Lessing Rosenwald of Philadelphia. It does not oppose Jewish immigration to Palestine or relief for the Jews there, but it does object to political Zionism or to any form of a Jewish state. Several reform congregations, led by one in Houston, Texas, took a definite stand against Zionism but the Union of American Hebrew Congregations opposed an attitude which would exclude any Jew from membership in a congregation, because of his feelings with regard to Palestine.

In addition to the Zionist districts all over the country,

527

there are a number of other groups interested in Palestine, some of them affiliated with the ZOA and some altogether separate. The largest of all is Hadassah, the women's branch, which was founded by Henrietta Szold in 1912 and which by 1948 had over 250,000 members. Hadassah is doing effective work for the health of Palestine. Among its major projects are hospitals, dispensaries, school lunches, and trade schools. Its most ambitious project is the Hadassah-Hebrew University Medical Center, a great cluster of modern buildings just outside Jerusalem. But even better known is the Youth Aliyah begun by Miss Szold in her old age. Its purpose was to take Jewish children away from the dangers of Europe before and during the war and to train them in the colonies of Palestine.

The Student Zionist Organization mobilizes the Zionist sentiments of college students, the Junior Hadassah, the young women; the Masada, the young men; and the Young Judea, the Jewish children of America. These all have a double purpose, to educate their own members to a love of Palestine and to do practical work including the raising of money for the Land of Israel.

The Mizrachi is a body of orthodox Jews who are also Zionists; their program is to develop Palestine along orthodox religious lines. The Poale Zion, or Labor Zionists, are affiliated with the Histadrut, the Israeli Federation of Labor; they believe that the State should develop as a socialist country. Both these groups have auxiliary groups of women and youth.

528

The American Jews and World Jewry

During the war an American Zionist Emergency Council was organized to bring together the ZOA, Hadassah, Mizrachi and Poale Zion for a common purpose, the defense of Jewish rights in Palestine. It was supported by Jews and Christians in large numbers. The American Palestine Committee, consisting altogether of non-Jews, cooperated ably with the Emergency Council in its appeal to the President, the Congress, and American public opinion.

There is still another group of Zionists not affiliated with any of these. It is known as the Revisionist group, who were not satisfied with the British mandatory or the policy of the World Zionist Organization, but demanded a maximum program of Jewish rights and Jewish power in Palestine. They have had many members in eastern Europe but have always been very few in America. During the war the Revisionist group in America was known as the Hebrew Committee for National Liberation and was headed by Peter Bergson. It carried on much propaganda among the American people, but accomplished little directly in Palestine.

Most of these organizations collect money for use in Palestine. But the two special fund-raising agencies in the United States are the Jewish National Fund to buy land in Palestine and the Jewish Foundation Fund for immigration, farm settlement, and industry. It is worth noting that one-third of all the Jewish owned land in Palestine belongs to the Jewish National Fund and is thus the property of the Jewish people forever, being only leased to the settlers for use. In 1925, these two agencies combined in an annual drive, known as the United Palestine Appeal. This merger was very important, as by that time the greater part of the money for Palestine had to come from the United States. As the Jews of Europe became poorer and as the war finally destroyed their sources of income altogether, America became the chief source of funds for Palestine. This brings us to the subject of how the great sums of money were raised which we have been talking about throughout this chapter.

IV. THE UNITED JEWISH APPEAL

In 1933, the first year of Hitler's rule in Germany, American Jews began to insist that they unite their efforts to help the Jews of Europe and of Palestine. So the United Jewish Appeal was organized to combine the JDC and UPA in the various cities. Most local Jewish communities formed Welfare Funds, which in one annual campaign raised the money for these overseas needs and also for various national Jewish causes. Later on the National Refugee Service (now the United Service for New Americans) was added to the national appeal.

The success of this annual campaign has been amazing, even in depression years. People wanted to help all three causes, but they did not want them to compete for money. Each organization, of course, needed money badly and wanted as large a proportion of the funds collected as it could get. Several times the United Appeal was interrupted because of the difficulty in allocating the funds,

530

The American Jews and World Jewry

but the Jews of America insisted on a single campaign, and have supported it loyally.

Every year more money was raised than the year before. In the five years, 1939 through 1943, the average was $15,000,000 per year. In the next two years the total was $60,000,000, so that in seven years the American Jews gave over $137,000,000 for overseas needs, besides all they gave for their own national and city institutions. Of this great sum, $66,000,000 went to the JDC for its work in every country in the world, $43,000,000 to the UPA for its work in Palestine, and $14,500,000 to the United Service for New Americans, to be spent in America.

With the end of the war, fabulous sums were needed, and the Jews of America undertook to give them. Of course, it was impossible to meet all the needs of over a million Jews in Europe alone, many of whom were half starved, untrained for work, without homes and with small chance of finding any. In 1946, the Jews of America were asked to provide a hundred million dollars and actually raised the entire sum. Nobody had ever imagined before that such sums might be raised by the free gifts of private persons, without government loans or taxation. The national leader was Henry Morgenthau, Jr., former Secretary of the Treasury of the United States. In 1947, the goal was $170,000,000; it was not reached, but the total subscribed was $125,000,000, far more than even the year before.

For 1948, with the rapidly rising needs for migration to Israel and for the establishment of the Jewish

History of the Jews in the United States

institutions there, the amount raised was $150,000,000. So great a sum would have been considered utterly impossible only a few years ago. In 20 years, from 1939 to 1958, the United Jewish Appeal has raised fully $1,150,-000,000. From this and other organizations, over a billion dollars was sent from America to Israel in the State's first thirteen years. Approximately two million people have been helped from year to year, some in their homes, others to migrate to another land, still others with loans, new homes and a fresh start in life. These are much greater sums than we are spending on all our Jewish needs at home, for they spell life or death to many thousands of Jews, and also sustain the State of Israel.

In addition to the great sums given to aid the building up of Israel, further money is being loaned to that government by Americans who purchase Israel bonds. The first drive for the bond sale began in 1951 and raised $200,-000,000 in three years. Sale of bonds has raised $364,-000,000 in America up through 1959.

From the creation of the State of Israel on May 15, 1948, until August 1, 1961, exactly 1,000,000 immigrants arrived.

Review Questions

1. Name at least three contacts of American Jews with Jews in other lands.
2. Discuss the growth, the decline, the second growth of JDC.
3. What is Zionism? List at least five Zionist organizations, with their purposes.
4. What is the value of the United Jewish Appeal? How is the money raised? How is it spent?

The American Jews and World Jewry

1. The sums raised for the UJA in your city; if it is a Welfare Fund city, study the Welfare Fund budgets to obtain this information.
2. How a financial campaign is run; consult leaders in your city. Work out a campaign, with methods, for your own school to take part in the coming national drive.
3. The development of Palestinian Jewry since 1920; this may be a class project, with each person taking a different aspect.
4. Present the arguments on Zionism of any one of the following organizations: the Zionist Organization of America, American Council for Judaism, American Jewish Committee, Mizrachi, or Poale Zion. This may be developed into a debate or panel session.

REFERENCES FOR PUPILS

Edidin, Ben M., *Jewish Community Life in America*, chapter 11, Helping Jews in Other Lands; chapter 12, Building Palestine.

Pilch, Judah, *Jewish Life in Our Times*, Part Two, chapter 3, Organizations for the Rehabilitation of Jewish Life; chapter 8, Zionism and Palestine.

See the *New Palestine* and literature of the United Jewish Appeal.

REFERENCES FOR TEACHERS

As always, the *American Jewish Yearbook.*

There is much fine literature on Palestine, such as:

Revusky, Abraham, *Jews in Palestine*. Bloch.

Crum, Bartley, *Behind the Silken Curtain*, the story of a member of the Anglo-American Commission on Palestine. *The Palestine Yearbook.*

CHAPTER 30.

Jewish Contributions to
American Culture

W E SHALL now take note of what has been accomplished by a few outstanding Jews in various fields of American life: in literature and the theatre, science and art, industry and business, philanthropy and politics. Generally speaking there is little that may be called Jewish in the work of these individuals; most of the writers and painters, for example, show very little Jewish influence. But they are interesting to us as fellow-Jews; they show how a Jew may succeed in America; they indicate what Jews have contributed to American life as a whole.

Naturally, we must also notice the Yiddish and Hebrew writers, who are Jewish in language as well as by birth, and who have brought a distinctive Jewish element into American writing. We cannot list all the Jews who have written books from Mordecai Noah to the present day; there are entirely too many of them, and not all of them are worth remembering. We cannot even list the non-Jews who have written sympathetically about the Jews, such as Mark Twain, or those with a little Jewish background, such as Bret Harte, the first important writer of western stories, who was one-fourth Jewish.

534

Jewish Contributions to American Culture

JEWS have probably made a greater contribution in literature and music than in any other field of American life. The number of well-known writers is so great that again we cannot list them all, but shall simply mention some outstanding people for our general information. The student can follow up any field in which he is particularly interested.

Probably the most influential Jew in recent American literature has been Gertrude Stein, a queer genius who was read, criticized and imitated for almost fifty years. She was reared in San Francisco but lived most of her life in France. Her writing was "experimental," which means that she tried out many different ways to use words so as to convey her meaning. Some of her stories and autobiographical writings are very simple and clear, but others are extremely difficult to understand. As an old woman she experienced the hardships of the Second World War in France, winning the hearts of the French people and the American soldiers alike by her broad interests and kindly spirit.

Another important figure in American literature for many years has been Louis Untermeyer, poet, translator and editor of anthologies. Mr. Untermeyer was born in New York in 1885; he began his career as a successful business man but soon retired from business to give all his time to writing. He made the best translation of the poems of Heine in the English language. His many col-

535

lections of poetry, his essays on other poets and his lectures over a period of years have been important in directing public attention to American poetry. Mr. Untermeyer has written on some Jewish themes, especially the poems in *Roast Leviathan,* which are based on rabbinic legends, and his one novel, which deals with the life of Moses.

A younger man whose poems have won a Pulitzer Prize and much general popularity is Karl Shapiro. Most of his best poems were written in the South Pacific, where he served in the American Army for several years. Abraham Klein has written poems of essentially Jewish content. Muriel Rukeyser won attention as a very young woman by her poems, and is now one of the recognized poets of the country. Dorothy Parker is equally well known as a writer of humorous verse and of short stories, in both of which fields she has won distinction. Jessie Sampter, who died in Palestine, wrote chiefly on Jewish topics, especially on the Land of Israel.

Among the many Jews who have written fiction, we shall note first two women who were born in the Middle West and have been among the leading novelists and short story writers of the last generation, Edna Ferber and Fannie Hurst.

Miss Ferber began writing stories when she was a newspaper reporter in Milwaukee. One of her early books, *Fanny Herself,* tells of her own school days in Appleton, Wisconsin, a very different picture of Jewish life than that given in the usual ghetto novel of New York.

536

Jewish Contributions to American Culture

In later days she wrote the story of her life under the title, *A Peculiar Treasure*. One of her many novels, *So Big*, was awarded the Pulitzer Prize in 1924. Another, *Show Boat*, has become a popular musical play and motion picture. She has written a number of successful plays.

Fannie Hurst had a much harder start in establishing herself as a writer. She went to New York as a young woman, determined to write stories. Her parents urged her to return home. She held on for two years before a single story was accepted. After that, her success came rapidly. One of her best known short stories is *Humoresque*, the tale of a poor Jewish boy who became a famous violinist. Her many novels deal with different phases of American life, including a Jewish group modelled after the people among whom she grew up in Hamilton, Ohio.

Ludwig Lewisohn, critic, translator and novelist, is of special interest to us because he has written much on Jewish problems. He was born in Germany in 1882 and was brought to America when he was still a young child. Here he grew up in the South with no Jewish interests, but with a wide interest in literature. He became a university instructor in German, but felt that he could not succeed in that profession because he was a Jew. Some other Jews, who have given their life to university teaching, have disagreed with him in this. Mr. Lewisohn has told his own story in two volumes: *Upstream* which tells about his non-Jewish beginnings, *Midchannel* about how he found himself as a writer and a Jew. He lived for some years in Europe, then returned to the United States and became editor of the *New Palestine*. He died while a professor at Brandeis University.

Zionism is the motivating force in Lewisohn's life. His works are divided sharply into two groups. His critical works deal with American literature as a whole; he is generally recognized as one of the most understanding students of literature and one of the finest stylists in America. His novels deal almost altogether with Jewish problems, often with his own problem, that of the Jew who has returned to his people after years of wandering. Two of his best known novels are *The Island Within* and *The Last Days of Shylock*. As he wrote: "Jewishness tracks you through the universe; it lies in ambush from without and from within."

Many other Jews in America have written excellent and interesting stories; one need only mention such names as Ben Hecht and Robert Nathan, Irving Stone and Meyer Levin. The last of these has written much about Palestine, where he lived for several years. Laura Z. Hobson, author of *Gentleman's Agreement,* wrote a fine study of anti-Semitism in America which attracted wide attention, both in book form and as a motion picture. Several Jewish novelists such as Michael Gold, Albert Halper and Howard Fast write on social questions, emphasizing the economic problems of the poor. And several famous European writers have come to America, such as Franz Werfel who died in Hollywood, and Lion Feuchtwanger, who continues to write historical novels.

Some Jews appear in every field of literature, and of

these a few are really important writers. Waldo Frank is not only a novelist, but also a leading expert on South America. Emil Ludwig is famous for his many biographies, especially for those of Napoleon and Goethe.

Maurice Samuel is a prolific translator and has written excellent works on Palestine as well as several novels; probably his best known book is *The World of Sholom Aleichem*, which told about that excellent Yiddish humorist and the Russian Jewry from which he sprang. Of late years there has been a great increase in books dealing with Jewish topics, and especially books about Israel. Three of the most interesting have been *Exodus* by Leon Uris, *The Magic Barrel* by Bernard Malamud, winner of the 1959 National Book Award, and *Good Bye, Columbus* by Philip Roth, which won the same prize in 1960.

In the field of journalism there are several well-known names, though more of writers than of publishers. Jews who write for the papers range from Walter Winchell to Walter Lippmann. The founder of the *New York World* was Joseph Pulitzer, born in Hungary, not an active Jew but a great newspaper man and a great lover of humanity. He founded the School of Journalism at Columbia University and left money in his will for the Pulitzer Prizes, the highest awards for writers in America. Adolph Ochs, because of his positive Jewish attachments was a very different person. He was for many years owner and publisher of the *New York Times*. Mr. Ochs was born in Chattanooga, Tenn., and rose through the ranks from

History of the Jews in the United States

newsboy to printer, until finally he became the owner of the newspaper; then he moved to New York, where he made the *Times* one of the great newspapers of the country. He was a very active Jew, and raised a great endowment for the Hebrew Union College.

II. YIDDISH LITERATURE

WE HAVE seen in our study of the Russian Jews in America how they brought with them the Yiddish language, and published newspapers, books and plays in Yiddish. The language expressed the folk life of the East European Jews, and they continued to use it for several generations, even though they also knew English. These Yiddish writers have contributed a special element to America because they have written from a Jewish background. Many of them have become well known in English translations, and one of them, Sholom Asch, is probably the Jewish writer best known to the American reader.

There have been many Yiddish writers of importance in America. Yehoash (Solomon Bloomgarten) was known as the poet of the Jewish national hope. He translated into Yiddish such different works as Longfellow's *Hiawatha* and the Hebrew Bible. He wrote a dictionary of Yiddish. During the same years Morris Rosenfeld wrote poems about the workers in the sweatshops of New York.

A favorite Yiddish writer was the beloved humorist, Sholom Aleichem, whose short stories were printed in newspapers and magazines and then collected into volumes. His real name was Solomon Rabinowitz, but he took the pen name which means "Peace be to you" and is used in daily life as "hello." He was born in Europe but did most of his writing in New York. It was typical of him that he requested his family to observe the day of his death by reading his happy tales and by laughing as they did when they first heard them. There has been a revival of interest in Sholom Aleichem since the publication of several translations of his works.

Chaim Zhitlowsky was a leader of the Jewish Socialists, who lived the last forty years of his life in America. He believed firmly in the value of the folk speech, for he was devoted to the ideal of Jewish nationalism. So he wrote for the newspapers, edited one himself, and wrote many books on Jewish life and world philosophy.

In the theatre, two of the leading authors have been David Pinsky and Perez Hirschbein. Pinsky is especially well known because one of his plays, *The Treasure,* was performed on Broadway and several of his books have been published in English. Among critics, such men as Joel Antin and Samuel Niger are especially recognized.

But the best known and most powerful writer of Yiddish in America has been Sholom Asch. Like most of these other writers, he was born in Europe and came to America because this was the freest land in which to live, as well as the one where a Yiddish writer might best reach a large audience. He has written many plays and novels, some on Jewish history, some on the life he knew in Europe, some on Jews in America. These have been translated into many languages, so that he is really a world

541

figure; at the same time, he has been most popular with American readers and has had several books in the "best seller" class. Among these were *Three Cities,* dealing with the Russian Revolution, and *East Side,* about a poor Jewish neighborhood in New York. He has also written *The Nazarene,* a life of Jesus, and *The Apostle,* a life of Paul, which were very popular among Christians, but were much criticized by Jews. Asch is a wonderful story teller, and hundreds of thousands have been fascinated by his books.

III. HEBREW LITERATURE

THE most limited branch of Jewish literature in America is written in the Hebrew language. Yiddish is the declining, English the growing language of the Jewish masses. But modern Hebrew began primarily with the intellectuals, and only a limited audience exists for books in the ancient tongue. The *Histadruth Ivrith,* with some thousands of members, has been promoting Hebrew culture in America since 1916, and its influence has been growing rapidly during the war and post-war years. Many Hebrew scholars and writers have come to America during the Hitler persecutions and the Second World War. At the same time, the rapid development of events in Palestine and the constant stream of Hebrew books published there have encouraged the study of Hebrew and the reading of Hebrew books in America as well.

These works include textbooks, stories for children, poems and novels for adults, as well as eleven periodicals.

Jewish Contributions to American Culture

The majority of them, however, are serious works intended for students. Some of them are collective works, such as the *American Hebrew Yearbook,* or *Hatekufah.* This last is a collection of fiction, essays and poems, and also contains translations of classic works from other languages; it was the life work of the famous patron of Hebrew learning, Abraham Stybel, who began his work in Russia, went to Germany, then Palestine, and finally to America.

Probably the outstanding Hebrew writer in America for a generation was Reuben Brainin, who was known the world over for his many volumes of essays, biographies, novels and short stories. During his long life Brainin has written in the Russian, German, Yiddish and Hebrew languages, for he was born in Russia, educated in Vienna, and lived in many lands before settling in America. He was one of the earliest supporters of Theodor Herzl and helped him prepare for the first Zionist Congress. His long and very active life was largely devoted to the Zionist cause.

But many other Hebrew writers have lived in America, some of whom were born and educated here. The first yearbook of *Hadoar* had eighty contributors, all of them living in America, and a considerable number American-born. Simon Halkin was awarded a prize in 1948 for a book of Hebrew poems. In addition he has written on the Jew in America and has translated some of Shakespeare's plays into Hebrew. Ephraim Lisitzky has written Hebrew poetry for forty years, dealing with many phases of American life, not only with the Jews, but also the Negroes and the American Indians. Other well-known writers are Israel Efros the poet, Harry Sackler the short story writer, and Daniel Persky the essayist and critic. Of the many scholars who wrote on rabbinic subjects, probably the most famous was Professor Chaim Tchernowitz, who wrote under the name of Rav Tzair, and edited the only Hebrew monthly in America, *Bitzaron*.

IV. THE THEATRE

JEWS are even more conspicuous in the entertainment world than in literature. We find them in considerable numbers in the theatre, radio and motion pictures. They are actors, writers, producers, and theatre owners. As a rule, they are simply interested in putting on a good show, but sometimes a Jewish element enters into their work as well. There are even sufficient people with Jewish interests to organize a Jewish Theatrical Guild of America, with two thousand members, for the purpose of "perpetuating Judaism in the theatre." The Rabbis' Sons Theatrical Benevolent Association was founded by Al Jolson and Harry Houdini, and is restricted to the sons of rabbis, cantors, and other officials of the synagogue.

One of the pioneers of the American theatre was David Belasco, playwright and producer, who brought realism to the American stage. Belasco was born in San Francisco; he was a poor boy who began by selling peanuts in the theatre, became an actor, moved to New York, and became a leading figure in the theatre for a generation. He wrote many successful plays, including *The Girl of the Golden*

544

West, which was made into one of the first American operas.

But he is best known as a master in stagecraft, an experimenter with lights, scenery and everything that would make a play resemble real life. Audiences were once used to seeing a library represented by books painted on the scenery; Belasco used real books, and selected the very volumes that would appear in that kind of a home, or doctor's office. Probably his most popular production was *The Auctioneer,* a play of Jewish life where David Warfield acted the title role, full of smiles and tears; this play was revived again and again by popular demand.

Early in the twentieth century the Frohman brothers were equally well known as theatre owners and producers. Then came the Neighborhood Playhouse on the East Side of New York, where Alice and Irene Lewisohn worked with the young people of the neighborhood and succeeded in influencing the whole of the American theatre. One of their most notable productions was *The Dybbuk* by Ansky, a beautiful play of the Chassidim, the Jewish mystics of eastern Europe. Other Jews are associated with the Theatre Guild, an outstanding group which has produced many of the fine plays of our time.

A number of Jews are recognized as playwrights today, such as S. N. Behrman, Paddy Chayevsky, and Lillian Hellman. Billy Rose and Oscar Hammerstein II are well-known producers.

Jews are likewise prominent in Hollywood, though they certainly do not control the movies, as some people think.

History of the Jews in the United States

Some of them were among the early pioneers of the motion picture industry like Carl Laemmle and the Warner Brothers. Louis B. Mayer is widely known as the president of M.G.M. Among the famous actors are such people as Edward G. Robinson, Al Jolson, and Paul Muni.

Other Jews are active in radio and television. David Sarnoff of the Radio Corporation of America was one of the pioneers. We have Norman Corwin, a writer, Eddie Cantor and Jack Benny, actors, and the impressive weekly programs of "The Eternal Light," which bring Jewish traditions before a vast American audience.

V. MUSICIANS

Music is a very old Jewish art. It is often mentioned in the Bible, and was highly developed in the synagogue melodies of the Middle Ages. So it is not surprising that at the present day concert audiences in the big cities are largely made up of Jews, while Jewish artists are found in every type of musical activity, from swing to symphony, as composers, performers, and conductors.

A surprising number of the leading concert violinists have been Jews, including several who began as child prodigies. Mischa Elman was born in Russia during Czarist days, played in public at the age of five, and was a concert player by the time he was twelve. At that time his work was so remarkable that the government gave him special permission to study in St. Petersburg. When he was seventeen years old he came to America; since that time he has been a popular concert artist, and has toured

546

the world, giving concerts in Europe, Asia, and the Orient.

Another man with a very similar career is Jascha Heifetz. He was born a few years later than Elman in Vilna, played in public as a child of five, and studied with Auer in St. Petersburg. Since 1917, he has been an American, winning a great following by his exceptional technique. One of his concert tours took him to Soviet Russia, where he was much appreciated.

Yehudi Menuhin, a San Francisco boy, sprang into prominence just as suddenly and almost as young. He was born in 1917; at the age of six he gave his first great concert in San Francisco, at eight he played in New York, and at ten in Paris. Since that time he has developed into one of the great musicians of our time.

Younger violinists who have gained national recognition include Nathan Millstein and Isaac Stern. The most prominent Jewish musician today is Leonard A. Bernstein, conductor of the New York Philharmonic Orchestra. He is best known for his brilliant television programs, but has also composed music for the stage. Among the many other musicians, probably the best known is Benny Goodman, famous for his dance band, who has repeatedly played with symphony orchestras as well.

If we turn to composers, there is a wide range. Some of the favorite composers of popular music have been Jewish, such as Irving Berlin and Jerome Kern. George Gershwin was one of the first who used jazz themes for operas and symphony compositions and ushered in a new age of American music. Though he died some years ago,

547

Moses J. Ezekiel

his works are still constantly performed over the radio and on the stage.

A strong contrast to these men was Ernest Bloch, a Swiss Jew who was frequently influenced by Jewish themes in his serious compositions. His *Israel* and his *Sh'lomo* are based on the sad minor music of the synagogue and express the tragedy of Jewish life. Another well-known composition is *America,* which won a national prize in 1928 for the best symphonic work by an American. This symphony expresses the spirit of America, as understood by a Jewish immigrant.

VI. ARTISTS

JEWISH artists are neither so numerous nor so famous as Jewish writers or musicians, but a few of them have been outstanding. The most prominent of the nineteenth century was Moses J. Ezekiel, who was born in Richmond, Virginia in 1844 and died in Rome, Italy in 1917. He was a Confederate soldier in the Civil War when only seventeen years old. He then won a prize which enabled him to

548

"The Talmudists" by Max Weber

study sculpture in Rome. He lived there most of his life, in the ancient Tower of Belisarius. He was knighted by the King of Italy and the Emperor of Germany, and won many medals for his work. In 1876, he created the statue of Religious Liberty which the B'nai B'rith presented on that centennial year, and which stands in Fairmount Park, Philadelphia.

A very interesting personality who died recently is Jo Davidson, famous for his portrait busts of prominent men and women. He first became well known when he made a bust of President Woodrow Wilson and then was commissioned to portray the Allied generals and statesmen after the First World War.

Among painters who are generally recognized are William Zorach, Max Weber and Marc Chagall. All these have used Jewish themes from time to time. Chagall is intensely Jewish in his entire work. He is an immigrant, who was born in Poland and studied for many years in Paris. The little Jewish village in which he lived as a child, with its houses, its old bearded scholars, its active young people, is a theme which appears again and again in Chagall's paintings.

VII. SCIENTISTS

AMERICAN Jews are important in science, not so much by numbers as by outstanding contributions. In practically every branch of scientific work there are a few eminent Jews, working with their non-Jewish colleagues toward an understanding of truth. This number was increased when

550

Jewish Contributions to American Culture

the Nazis persecuted European Jews, and many great thinkers had to flee for their lives to other lands. Some of these joined the faculty of the Hebrew University in Jerusalem; others the "University in Exile," a part of the New School for Social Research in New York; others are scattered the world over.

ALBERT MICHELSON

Three American Jews have been awarded the Nobel Prize for scientific work: Albert A. Michelson, professor of physics at the University of Chicago, in 1907; Albert Einstein, in 1921, when he was still a member of the Prussian Academy of Sciences in Berlin; and Karl Landsteiner, a medical researcher at the Rockefeller Institute in New York, in 1930. This is the greatest international honor for any scientist.

Dr. Michelson had a remarkable record as one of the finest and most original men in the physics laboratory. He was a graduate of the Naval Academy at Annapolis, where he was always more interested in pure science than in gunnery. He spent his entire active life at the University of Chicago, where he taught and conducted his original

551

ALBERT EINSTEIN

research, and where he was the first recipient of the "Distinguished Professorship" of the University. He invented the most delicate instruments imaginable to measure the speed of light, the length of the light ray, and the light coming from distant stars.

His work gave the clue for the theory of relativity to another Jew, Albert Einstein, at that time a mere clerk in the patent office in Berne, Switzerland. Probably the work of these two men has affected our knowledge of the nature of the world more than any discoveries since those of Newton. They have worked on parallel lines. Albert Einstein was the theorist, working out his ideas by means of mathematics, while Albert Michelson was the laboratory worker, devising means by which these theories can be tested and proved.

Albert Einstein himself came to America to live in 1933, after twenty years of brilliant work and of high honors in Berlin. But the Nazis made him a prime target of their propaganda, because he was both a Jew and a pacifist. They seized all of his property and threatened his life.

552

Jewish Contributions to American Culture

They even spread the story that this kindly man, whose chief interest was in abstract science, was really the head of an international organization to fight Hitler. Einstein accepted a position at the Institute for Advanced Study in Princeton, N. J., founded by Louis Bamberger and Mrs. Felix Fuld, and headed by Dr. Abraham Flexner.

Several American Jews have been awarded the Nobel prize in recent years, among them the physicists, I. I. Rabi of Columbia University in 1944 and Felix Bloch of Stanford in 1952. Another physicist of national reputation is Robert Oppenheimer, who headed the atomic bomb project at Los Alamos during the war. He became involved in a controversy with Lewis Strauss, then chairman of the Atomic Energy Commission, and was deprived of his clearance for secret government work. He had by that time joined the Institute at Princeton. Still another national figure is Admiral Hyman Rickover, designer of the atomic submarine.

A number of Jews have achieved eminence in the medical sciences, which have been a traditional Jewish field of interest since the Middle Ages. There was Dr. Abraham Jacobi, one of the German immigrants of 1848, who lived a stirring life on two continents, and finally died at an advanced age, a leading American physician. He established the first child clinic in America. Later came Dr. Simon Flexner, who made many discoveries working in the Rockefeller Institute. He then became director of the Institute for fifteen years. Dr. Flexner was a member of a famous family from Louisville, Ky.; one of his brothers,

History of the Jews in the United States

Abraham, was the president of the Institute for Advanced Studies, and another, Bernard, was a prominent lawyer and civic worker.

Among other medical scientists have been Bela Schick, discoverer of the Schick test for diphtheria; Joseph Goldberger, who discovered the cause of pellagra, but lost his

EMILE BERLINER

life in the effort, and Jonas A. Salk, who devised the Salk vaccine for polio.

In psychology there was A. A. Brill, the first to bring the works of Sigmund Freud to America. Kurt Lewin was both a great man in this field and an active Jew; he worked very hard in the effort to understand and explain the problems of anti-Semitism—how it is that some people grow to hate those who are different from themselves. Among anthropologists, the leader for many years was Franz Boas at Columbia University. Among philosophers, we had Morris R. Cohen at the College of the City of New York; present leaders include Sidney Hook and Horace M. Kallen.

There have been Jewish inventors, too. Probably the

554

Jewish Contributions to American Culture

most important of them was Emile Berliner, who was born in Germany in the 1850's and spent his whole working career in America. Early in life he invented the telephone transmitter which is still used. This brought him a fortune, and he was enabled to devote the rest of his life to the studies which interested him. Some of them led to new inventions, such as improvements on talking machines and motion picture projectors, a method for duplicating phonograph records, and the first helicopter, which his own son flew in 1910.

REVIEW QUESTIONS

1. Name two Jewish writers in English; one in Yiddish; one in Hebrew.
2. Is there anything especially Jewish in the writings of American Jews?
3. Discuss the place of Jews in the American entertainment world.
4. Name two Jewish musicians, telling about their work.
5. Name two Jewish scientists in different fields; tell why they are important.

TOPICS FOR REPORTS

1. What is the future of Yiddish in America? Of Hebrew? Give reasons for your opinion.
2. Read a story of Jewish life by Sholom Aleichem; by Ludwig Lewisohn; by some other author in English or Yiddish. Report on the story while some other pupil reports on the author.
3. Find Jewish columnists or other feature writers in your local newspaper; which ones are nationally syndicated?
4. The Jews in music, a historical study.

555

5. A concert of Jewish music, by piano or victrola; play compositions of synagogue music, folk tunes from eastern Europe and from Palestine.
6. Jewish art in Palestine; exhibit and discussion.
7. Report on the life and work of any one man in this chapter.

REFERENCES FOR PUPILS

The Universal Jewish Encyclopedia, articles on many persons mentioned in the chapter.
Many Jewish periodicals have articles on Jews in art, science, etc., in their New Year numbers.
Roth, Cecil, *The Jewish Contribution to Civilization.* Union.
Lotz, Philip H., *Distinguished American Jews.* Association Press.
Levinger, Elma Ehrlich, *Albert Einstein.* Julian Messner.

REFERENCES FOR TEACHERS

Who's Who in America contains brief biographies of many outstanding Jews.
Who's Who in American Jewry, Jewish Biographical Bureau; this work contains brief biographies of 2,500 Jews, it is now out of date.
American Jewish Yearbook includes occasional articles on leading Jews, as well as lists of names. For example:
vol. 24, pp. 112ff., "Jews of Prominence in the United States."
vol. 25, pp. 195ff., "Jews Who Have Received the Nobel Prize."
Art. on the same subject in vols. 33 and 34.
Many persons mentioned in this chapter are memorialized in books and articles, such as the following:
Frank, Philipp, *Einstein, His Life and Times.* Knopf.
De Kruif, *Hunger Fighters,* a chapter on Dr. Joseph Goldberger.
Kagan, Solomon R., *Jewish Contributions to Medicine in America.*

CHAPTER 31.

Jews in American Industry
and Public Life

A S WE saw in chapter 24, the Jews are a cross-section of American society. In this cross-section every class is represented, but often in different proportions than in the general population of the United States. In this chapter we shall follow up this fact, and shall note some of the more prominent of the Jews who have made contributions in various economic and political fields.

I. AGRICULTURE

THE basis of the life of a nation is agriculture, for the farmer grows the food which everyone needs. America used to be almost entirely an agricultural people; now over half its people live in cities, but farming is still the biggest business of all. But the Jews who came to America were not farmers, as their ancestors had been in Palestine two thousand years ago.

During most of those two thousand years Jews were not permitted to own or till farms. They were forced into sections of certain cities; they were restricted to those occupations which were undesirable to others, such as peddling, money lending, and dealing in old clothes. By their own enterprise they found other occupations also, so that they usually were able to make a living. But one sign of the unnatural life in the ghetto was the lack of farmers among them.

In modern times, when the general trend is away from the farm and toward the cities, the Jews have turned the opposite way. In Palestine they have established successful farm colonies as the basis of the new national life. In Russia a considerable number of Jews settled on the land after the Revolution. The land was given to them by their government and funds came from America. And in America, too, there has been a small but steady increase in the number of Jewish farmers. The early attempts at founding Jewish colonies on American soil were largely failures, but many individuals discovered that they had an ability and a liking for farm life. At present about 100,000 American Jews are living on farms, a small percentage of the total farming population, but a remarkable growth considering that there were no Jewish farmers at all fifty years ago.

We have already heard of David Lubin, the farmers' friend. In more recent times a similar role has fallen to Aaron Sapiro, the lawyer who sued Henry Ford for a million dollars. Mr. Sapiro's work was principally to aid farmers to cooperate, that they might sell their products to greater advantage. The most successful group of this kind has been the orange growers of California, but similar groups have grown up in other parts of the country, largely under his stimulating leadership. Even in agriculture, Jews have produced national leaders.

558

Jews in American Industry and Public Life

II. LABOR

THE first leader of the American Federation of Labor and one of the greatest labor leaders in America was Samuel Gompers, an English Jew. He was born in 1850, came to America with his parents at the age of thirteen, and entered the trade of cigar-making. At that time wages were very low

© U. & U.

SAMUEL GOMPERS

and workers were completely at the mercy of the bosses. Young Gompers joined one of the first unions in the cigar business and was soon made its president.

In 1886, when the American Federation of Labor was founded, Samuel Gompers was elected its president at the salary of one thousand dollars a year. For the next thirty-eight years he was president of the Federation, until he died in 1924. He developed it and made it into a great national body; he set its policies, many of which are still in effect. He had little interest in Jewish affairs, for he devoted his entire life to one cause, the welfare of the workers. He fought for the right of labor to organize; he led great strikes for better wages and living conditions.

559

History of the Jews in the United States

At the same time he opposed the socialists and others who wished to organize a labor party. He felt that labor, as any other group in America, should work for its own interests through the two great political parties. During the First World War Gompers was an adviser of President Wilson; after the war he

SIDNEY HILLMAN

was bitterly opposed to Communism. In brief, he stood for trade unionism as a part of the existing American system, and for the advance of labor within the system.

In more recent times a number of great labor unions have grown up, which have a large Jewish membership and Jewish leaders as well. The outstanding personality among these was Sidney Hillman, president of the Amalgamated Clothing Workers of America. He was a contrast to Gompers in almost every respect. He was intensely Jewish. Hillman was born in 1887 in Lithuania; his grandfather was a rabbi, and he began to study for the same profession. But he became interested in the revolutionary movement when only eighteen years old, was imprisoned for almost a year, and left Russia for the United States.

Jews in American Industry and Public Life

At twenty-two years of age he was working in a clothing factory in Chicago for six dollars a week. Then came a strike against the intolerable conditions in the industry, and young Hillman was one of the men who arranged a new type of settlement with the company, a contract which included a constitutional set-up in the industry and provided for an impartial arbiter to settle any disputed questions. He was the first president of the Amalgamated Clothing Workers when they became a national union and remained head of the union for thirty-two years until his death in 1946. He was one of the organizers of the Congress of Industrial Organizations (the CIO).

During the Second World War, Mr. Hillman was President Roosevelt's leading labor adviser, and occupied several important national offices. The best known of these was head of the labor division of the War Production Board. He was largely instrumental in the tremendous production of American factories for our own armies as well as those of our Allies.

In 1943, Hillman took a step which marked him as one of the most progressive leaders of American labor; he was the founder and first chairman of the Political Action Committee of the CIO. This put him into active politics, and he became one of the important people of the 1944 presidential campaign. In fact, he became the marked man of that campaign, as a labor leader and a Jew. But labor backed him, and the success of President Roosevelt was also a success for Hillman and the labor vote.

When he died in 1946, Mr. Hillman was at the height

of his powers and was recognized as one of the leaders in American political and economic life. After his death the Amalgamated Clothing Workers established the Sidney Hillman fund of a million dollars for scholarships and awards for public service.

III. BUSINESS

JEWS are largely known to the outside world as business men, for few non-Jews know much about the work of any individual Jew, but everybody knows some Jewish-owned store or factory. As the German Jews scattered through the country, many of them established retail stores, and some of these have now grown into great enterprises. The largest retail store in the United States is Macy's in New York, which belongs to members of the Straus family. Various other great department stores in different cities are likewise owned by Jews.

These are by no means the greatest business enterprises in America. The greatest factories and banks are owned by Christians, rather than Jews. The wealthy Jews—and there are a number of them—come in the second group of great American fortunes and not at the very top.

The most important financial institution that is controlled by Jews, though by no means the largest bank in America, is Kuhn, Loeb and Co., of New York. We mentioned it in connection with the life of Jacob H. Schiff, who was its president for many years. Other partners have been Felix M. Warburg, a leader in Jewish philanthropy, especially in the Joint Distribution Committee, and Paul

562

Jews in American Industry and Public Life

M. Warburg, the first governor of the Federal Reserve Bank of the United States. Kuhn, Loeb and Co. has played a very important part in building railroads and in other such enterprises, which have made possible the developing of new sections of the United States. It has also granted loans to foreign governments in time of war.

Another great enterprise is that of the Guggenheim family, who pioneered in copper mining in Wyoming. They bought mines and built smelters, so that they were able to carry through mining operations and deliver metals ready for use. As the country grew, mining became more and more important, and the Guggenheims accumulated vast wealth. One member of the family, Simon Guggenheim, became United States Senator from Colorado; he also established the famous Guggenheim Fellowships, which enable outstanding American scholars and artists to do their specialized work. These fellowships are awarded without distinction of race, creed, sex or color.

IV. PHILANTHROPY

In every period of our history, we have noted some outstanding philanthropists, who aided Jews and Christians alike. Beginning with Judah Touro and continuing in the tradition of Jacob H. Schiff we find a larger and larger group as we approach our own day.

Nathan Straus (1848–1931) was a brother of Oscar S. Straus the diplomat, and was himself a successful business man. He became more and more interested in public welfare, until he finally retired from business and gave all his

NATHAN STRAUS

time to helping others. His greatest philanthropy was the Straus Milk Fund in New York City, which saved the lives of thousands of babies; it lowered the death rate in New York and became an influence on state and national governments the world over.

All this began in 1892 when Mr. Straus's cow died, and the veterinarian found that it had suffered from tuberculosis. Mr. Straus then began to think, not only of the danger to his own family, but also of the danger to people everywhere, for no dairies were then supervised, and any infant might be drinking infected milk. The great Pasteur had not long since shown that disease germs might be killed if the milk were sufficiently heated. Mr. Straus began a movement to pasteurize the milk, sell it very cheaply to poor people, and even give it away for poor babies. Today we can hardly understand the fierce opposition to this movement; some people felt that their business was being harmed, while others were suspicious that Mr. Straus himself might want to gain some advantage. But he triumphed in time. Milk inspection became a duty of every state government, milk was pasteurized, and the children of the nation were saved from illness and death.

Both Mr. and Mrs. Straus became Zionists when they visited Palestine. His second great benevolence was toward Palestine, where he opened two health centers, a Pasteur institute, soup kitchens and workshops. During drives for Palestinian work and for

JULIUS ROSENWALD

war relief, the kindly old man would go from one meeting to another, inspiring other people to give, and invariably making another donation himself, as he went along. He gave of himself as well as his money, generously, for he truly loved his fellow men.

Julius Rosenwald (1862–1932) was another who was well known both for his great success in business and for giving away much of his fortune. He was born in Springfield, Illinois, and became head of Sears, Roebuck & Co., the great mail order house. When he began to make large gifts for philanthropy and education he worked out original ideas as to how these might be most useful. He held, first, that every gift should stimulate activity, and not merely do things for people; second, that every gift should be used up within a generation, and no endowment should last forever.

His outstanding field of work was in raising the standard of Negro education in the United States. He became a trustee of Tuskegee Institute and other Negro schools because he saw the great need of the Negro race for better education. He offered to build a Y.M.C.A. or a public school for any community that would itself raise a certain amount toward the building and guarantee its future upkeep. In this way he helped to build over four thousand modern school buildings for Negroes in the South.

In his own city of Chicago, Mr. Rosenwald founded a museum of industry, one of the greatest in the world; he was a trustee of the University of Chicago and gave millions toward its building program.

Mr. Rosenwald gave to Jewish causes in the same way. He was president of Sinai Temple of Chicago. He was also honorary president of the Jewish Charities and gave generously for its work. He gave a half million dollars to the Hebrew Union College, and a million dollars to the Joint Distribution Committee in one year, 1918. He was especially interested in helping Jews to settle on the land in Russia after the First World War, and offered five million dollars for the purpose if others would make up a similar sum. With the cooperation of the Russian government, this project was successfully carried out, but the Second World War ruined the Jewish farm settlements in the Crimea and the Ukraine.

Always Mr. Rosenwald insisted that the money he gave

Jews in American Industry and Public Life

be spent within roughly twenty-five years, because he felt that he knew what was needed for his own time but not for the distant future. Later generations would know their own needs, and would have to provide for them.

We cannot possibly list all of the important philanthropists. Samuel Fels endowed a foundation for the study of human beings; Louis Bamberger and his sister founded the Institute for Advanced Study at Princeton; Bernard Baruch founded the Williamstown Institute of Politics at Williams College; Nathan Goldblatt gave a million dollars to the University of Chicago for the study of cancer. The first planetarium in America was given to Chicago by Max Adler; the second to Philadelphia by Samuel Fels.

V. JEWS IN SPORTS

EVERYONE is interested in the great athletes of the country. While Jews cannot claim as many of these as of actors or musicians, there are a few who have been outstanding performers.

In the nineteenth century, Joe Choynsky was one of the great boxers who fought such men as Corbett. In the twentieth, Bennie Leonard was for many years lightweight champion and retired undefeated to take up the practice of dentistry in Brooklyn. Leonard had the reputation of being one of the cleverest boxers of all time. He was likewise a loyal and active Jew.

For a brief time Max Baer, who is half Jewish, was heavyweight champion. Barney Ross of Chicago accomplished the very unusual feat of holding championships in two weight divisions at the same time. He was an extremely popular champion because of his personality as well as his athletic ability. Ross was badly injured during the war, when he was one of the marine heroes on Guadalcanal.

A number of Jews have won distinction in baseball, but the most successful of them all was Hank Greenberg of the Detroit Tigers, for several years one of the heaviest hitters in the country. Greenberg interrupted his baseball career by entering the service early in the war; though he played well since his return to civil life, he never reached the excellence of his earlier performance.

In football a number of Jews have been selected on all-American teams, and some of them are nationally known. Such men as Benny Friedman, Marshall Goldberg and Sid Luckman were outstanding players in their college days, and have stayed in the sport, either as coaches or professional players.

Nat Holman was a famous basketball player and coach, who was followed by many Jewish boys. In fact, the excellent teams of the New York City colleges include many Jewish players.

In practically every department of sports, some Jew has made his mark. There are enough of them to warrant a book which has been written on this very topic.

This book even includes chess, a game in which Jews have excelled for centuries. Samuel Reshevsky, once top player in the United States, began as a child prodigy, making tours through the country and playing simultaneous matches with groups of adult players. In 1958, Bobby Fischer, then 15 years old, won the U.S. chess championship, and still holds it today.

VI. JEWS IN PUBLIC LIFE

FROM early in the history of the nation, there have been a few Jews who have achieved success in public office. Their numbers have always been small; even now their percentage in Congress is half that of their percentage in the general population. In the early history of this country we have followed the great career of Judah P. Benjamin, United States Senator and Confederate Secretary of State, and later, that of Oscar S. Straus, Secretary of Commerce and Labor, three times Minister to Turkey, and member of The Hague Arbitration Tribunal. In modern times these have been followed by Henry Morgenthau, Jr., for twelve years Secretary of the Treasury, and Louis D. Brandeis, Associate Justice of the Supreme Court.

Mr. Morgenthau's father had been ambassador to Turkey during the First World War. The son was a follower and close friend of Franklin D. Roosevelt, who brought him into the Treasury Department on his election and appointed him Secretary of the Treasury in 1934. He held this position until 1945, after President Roosevelt's death. Since he has left public office, he has been chairman of the United Jewish Appeal, has visited Palestine and Europe, and has done great work for the Jewish people. During the past few years he has been chairman of the Israel Bond Issue in this country.

569

History of the Jews in the United States

Mr. Brandeis was the first Jew to occupy the highest judicial position in any nation, though since that time Lord Reading has been Chief Justice of Great Britain and two other Jews have been appointed on the Supreme Court of the United States. Louis D. Brandeis was famous as a lawyer, a judge and a Zionist leader. He was born in Louisville, Ky., in 1856, of a well-known family of German Jews. He was named after his uncle, Lewis N. Dembitz, a member of the national convention that nominated Lincoln for president in 1860, and a scholar and writer on Jewish topics. Brandeis studied law at Harvard and practiced in Boston for about forty years, making a great fortune.

During those years of legal practice he became known as the "people's lawyer" because of the many liberal movements he defended in the courts, as well as the new method he worked out for presenting them. The method was to give, not only legal arguments, but all the facts he could from the life of the people. He defended the Oregon Law limiting the number of hours a woman might work in factories, showing the Supreme Court of the United States just what the effects were of twelve hours of work every day, and how much the working women were suffering at that time. He attacked both the railroads and the insurance companies for unfair and monopolistic practices.

In 1916, President Woodrow Wilson appointed Mr. Brandeis as associate justice of the Supreme Court. The appointment met with bitter opposition in the Senate, not because he was a Jew, but rather because of his liberal

Jews in American Industry and Public Life

Assoc. Press   ˉ *Harris & Ewing*   *Wide World*
FELIX FRANKFURTER   LOUIS D. BRANDEIS   BENJAMIN N. CARDOZO

opinions, which had made him both friends and enemies. After a long investigation, he was finally confirmed by the Senate, and served on the court for thirty-three years until he retired because of old age. In court he was frequently counted in the liberal minority, for Brandeis and Oliver Wendell Holmes often dissented from the majority judgments when these set property above human rights.

It is interesting to note that Brandeis had at first little interest in Jewish problems but later in life he became the leader of American Zionists; in fact, he occupied that position at the time of his appointment to the Supreme Court. In 1910, he was chairman of the arbitration board which settled the garment workers' strike in New York and set up an orderly system in that industry. Thus he became familiar with both the Jewish workers and the Jewish employers, and was able to arbitrate between them. This led him to a study of Jewish problems, and he joined

571

the Zionist movement in the same year. Four years later, when the First World War shifted the center of the Zionist movement to America, he was made chairman of the Provisional Executive Committee for Zionist Affairs. From that time to the end of his life he was an active Zionist, though as a justice of the Supreme Court he had to leave the public leadership to others. He was especially interested in the liberal aspect of Zionism, for he hoped that the Jews might develop in Palestine a purer democracy than any other in the world. Louis Brandeis died in 1941 at the age of 85, just two years after his retirement from the bench.

During six of these years in which Louis Brandeis occupied the bench, two of the nine justices were Jewish, for in 1932 President Hoover had appointed to the Supreme Court Benjamin Nathan Cardozo, at that time chief justice of the New York State Court of Appeals. Cardozo was a descendant of an old Sephardic family; he had devoted his whole life to the study of the law, and was recognized as an outstanding legal authority. For that reason his appointment was urged by people from every walk of life; he met no opposition in the Senate and his years of service on the Court contributed greatly to American law. He died in 1938, at the age of sixty-eight.

A third Jew was raised to the Supreme Court in 1939, when Professor Felix Frankfurter of the Harvard University Law School was appointed by President Roosevelt. This was a notable appointment, not only because he was a Jew, but also because he was foreign born, having been brought to this country as a child from his native Vienna, and further because he was not a judge but a famous professor of law. Frankfurter who was a friend and follower of President Roosevelt was intensely interested in liberal legislation; he was also an active Zionist for many years. During his service on the Court, however, he has not been as liberal as his two Jewish predecessors; he has been rather a reconciling influence between the extremes of opinion.

One of the outstanding American personalities of the two World Wars was Bernard Mannes Baruch, a millionaire from Wall Street who never ran for office but has been confidential adviser to six presidents beginning with Woodrow Wilson. Mr. Baruch was born in South Carolina in 1870; his father was a physician who had served in the Confederate army. His mother came from a family of Sephardim who had been in America for nine generations. The young man stood six feet three, was an athlete, but failed to enter West Point because he was deaf in one ear. So he was graduated from the College of the City of New York and went to work for a brokerage house at three dollars per week. By the time he was thirty-three he was reputed to be worth three million dollars. He was a member of the New York Stock Exchange until 1917, when he left it for official duties.

At that time President Woodrow Wilson appointed him a member of the Council of National Defense. He afterwards became chairman of the War Industries Board and accompanied President Wilson to the Paris Peace Conference. After the war he bought an estate in his native state, invested in various industries, and prepared to grow old gracefully. But the Second World War came, and President Roosevelt called him back to Washington again.

Now he became a really famous figure—the tall old man whom reporters called "elder statesman" and "park bench statesman," the latter because he liked to sit informally in one of the Washington parks to talk over the problems of government. He headed commissions which wrote two important reports, one on synthetic rubber, the other on post-war plans. In 1946, he held his latest and most important post, as the United States representative to the United Nations Atomic Energy Commission. This was a highly controversial subject, and only the great respect in which Mr. Baruch was held made it possible to appoint the commission and to go ahead with its work.

Mr. Baruch is also a notable donor to various philanthropic causes. He founded the Williamstown Institute of Politics at Williams College, and has taken part in many other projects for human welfare. His greatest single gift was one of a million dollars in 1944 for a research foundation in physical medicine, especially for the benefit of veterans. As this had been his father's medical specialty, we may realize that personal interest as well as general humanitarian motives lay behind his act.

Still another outstanding Jew in American life is David Eli Lilienthal, formerly chairman of the Tennessee Valley Authority and of the Atomic Energy Commission. Mr. Lilienthal was born in Illinois in 1890, of immigrant parents. He studied law at Harvard, and then practiced in Chicago, specializing in public service and labor problems. He did notable work for the city of Chicago in its fight with the telephone company, and he was made a member of the Wisconsin Public Service Commission. Then, when Congress established the TVA to develop the waters of the Tennessee River and its tributaries, President Roosevelt appointed him as one of the directors in 1933. He was chairman of the whole project from 1941 to 1946, making a great reputation for his efficiency in public office and for TVA's independence of all political influences.

In 1946, with the enactment of a law to guard the newly discovered atomic power as a public trust, President Truman appointed David Lilienthal as chairman of the Atomic Energy Commission, which was to control the expansion of this vast almost unlimited new field. The bitter opposition he met in the Senate was probably not due to his being a Jew, but rather to his fine record of public service and his opposition to political control. His final confirmation by the Senate was hailed everywhere as a triumph of good government, as well as a deserved personal vindication.

Another member of the first Atomic Energy Commission was Lewis L. Strauss, a New York banker who rose to the rank of Rear Admiral in the Second World War. Later he served as Commission chairman. He was appointed Secretary of Commerce, but was not confirmed by the Senate.

At various periods ten Jews have served in the United States Senate and about 70 in the House of Representa-

575

tives. Eleven of these served in the Eighty-seventh Congress, elected in 1960. These men have not been elected because they were Jews, but simply because they were leaders in their own parties in the states where they happened to live. Many of those states have few Jewish voters, as we can see by the list of Senators. These were: David Levy Yulee, Florida, 1845–61; Judah P. Benjamin, Louisiana, 1853–61; Benjamin Franklin Jonas, Louisiana, 1879–85; Joseph Simon, Oregon, 1879–1903; Isador Rayner, Maryland, 1905–12; Simon Guggenheim, Colorado, 1906–13; Herbert H. Lehman, New York, 1950–56; Jacob K. Javits, New York, 1957–; Richard L. Neuberger, Oregon, 1955–60; Ernest Gruening, Alaska, 1956–.

Several of the Jews in the House of Representatives have won national respect for their achievements. Adolph J. Sabath of Chicago was first elected to Congress in 1907; when he died in 1952 he had served in Congress for 45 years, setting a record for length of service. He was a Democrat and an active "New Dealer," a staunch supporter of the programs of President Franklin D. Roosevelt.

A man of similar prominence in earlier days was Julius Kahn of San Francisco, who served in the House for thirty-three years. He was a picturesque personality, who was an actor in his youth and then turned to politics. He was a Republican, was chairman of the Committee on Military Affairs during the First World War, and was therefore closely concerned with the passing of the draft bill and of other laws governing the conduct of the war. At his death in 1924, his widow, Florence Prag Kahn, was

Jews in American Industry and Public Life

© U. & U.

JULIUS KAHN

elected in his place, and served in the House for twelve years. Mrs. Kahn was a striking personality in her own right, with a strong sense of humor and great understanding of national affairs. She was the only Jewess ever to hold a Federal elective office.

Another representative of long standing was Sol Bloom, a New York City Democrat, who served from 1923 to his death in 1949. Mr. Bloom also began his career in San Francisco in the theatre, but moved to New York and went into politics there. He has been active in the foreign affairs of this country, and was a member of the United States delegation at the formation of the United Nations in San Francisco in 1945. He was chairman of the national committee on the George Washington Centennial in 1932.

One of the tragedies of American public life was the death of Representative M. Michael Edelstein of New York on the floor of the House in 1941. Congressman Rankin of Mississippi had made a bitter anti-Semitic speech, which Edelstein answered ably. But his heart

577

failed, and he died at the end of his speech before help could reach him.

In the history of the United States nine Jews have served as governors, 7 by election in their own states and two by appointment as governors of territories. It is curious that four of these were in office at the same time in 1933. The first governor was Edward S. Solomon, a Brigadier General in the Civil War, who was appointed governor of Washington Territory by President Grant in 1870.

Then came a long gap until, in close succession, four western states with very few Jews in their population elected Jews as their chief executives. First came Moses Alexander of Idaho in 1915, then Simon Bamberger of Utah in 1917, Julius L. Meier of Oregon in 1930, and Arthur Seligman of New Mexico in 1930. None of these men were professional politicians, but all were merchants in their own states, civic leaders of prominence, who were called to high office because they had won the respect of their Christian fellow-citizens. Mr. Bamberger, in fact, was the first non-Mormon ever to be governor of Utah. We are also interested in the fact that the first two of these men were born in Germany and settled in the far west, while the other two were American born.

The two governors who followed were elected in great states, with large Jewish populations. Henry Horner was governor of Illinois from 1933 to 1940, when he died in office. He had formerly been a judge in Chicago, was a famous student of the life of Abraham Lincoln, and all his life was a leader in Jewish affairs.

578

Jews in American Industry and Public Life

HERBERT H. LEHMAN   HENRY HORNER

The most prominent of the governors was Herbert H. Lehman, governor of New York State for five terms, from 1932 to 1942. He was a member of a well-known Jewish family in New York, who owned the Lehman Brothers Bank. One brother, Irving Lehman, was a judge in the New York State Court of Appeals from 1908 to his death in 1941; he was for many years president of the National Jewish Welfare Board. Another, Arthur Lehman, was for several years president of the Federation of Jewish Philanthropies of New York City.

Herbert H. Lehman himself had a long and distinguished career in public service. He had been a colonel in the First World War. He was first elected lieutenant governor of New York for two terms, then governor for five terms, the longest period of any governor of that state. He resigned in 1942 to become director of foreign relief operations for the United States at the request of his close friend President Roosevelt. Then when UNRRA was organized to carry on relief and rehabilitation work for the United Nations, Mr. Lehman was chosen director general by the representatives of many nations; for three years (from 1943 to 1946) he conducted the most important task in the world, that of bringing help and hope to the war-shattered nations and their millions of refugees. He has always been a leader in Jewish work of this same type, such as the Joint Distribution Committee, and also in other Jewish organizations, such as the American Jewish Committee, his own congregation, Temple Emanu-El of New York, and the Jewish Theological Seminary. He is certainly one of the outstanding Jews in America.

In 1949 Mr. Lehman was elected to the United States Senate on the Democratic ticket; he made a remarkable record as a Senator, working for liberal immigration laws as well as fair treatment of all groups of American citizens.

The second Jew to be appointed governor of a territory was Ernest Gruening, governor of Alaska from 1939 to 1952, and later elected Senator when Alaska became a state. And the seventh elected governor was Abraham A. Ribicoff of Connecticut, 1955–1961, who resigned to join the cabinet of President John F. Kennedy.

President Kennedy, in fact, is the first who has appointed two Jews as members of his cabinet, Governor

580

Jews in American Industry and Public Life

Ribicoff as Secretary of Health, Education and Welfare, and Arthur J. Goldberg as Secretary of Labor. Mr. Goldberg is a lawyer, who has represented various national labor unions, and has been active in arbitration of controversies between the unions and the employers.

It is notable that the number of Jews in American public life has increased during the very time of Nazi anti-Semitism. The anti-Semites were deeply resented by American public opinion, from the President to the voters. While never very numerous, outstanding Jews became congressmen, ambassadors, judges, to serve America and, incidentally, to enhance the reputation of the Jew.

REVIEW QUESTIONS

1. How many Jewish farmers are there in America? Why do they prefer farm life?
2. List three Jewish labor leaders; tell about the life of one of them.
3. Who are the richest men in the United States? Are there any Jews among them?
4. Name three Jewish philanthropists; what is each known for?
5. What are the highest positions held by Jews since the beginning of the nation? Name the men who held them.
6. List five Jews in public life, with their positions.

TOPICS FOR REPORTS

1. List the leading Jewish business firms in your city, with interesting facts, such as: type of business, when founded, from what land the founder came, whether their families are still in the firm, their connection with Jewish life.
2. Find similar information about Jewish labor groups in your city, such as labor unions, Workmen's Circle.

581

3. In the classified telephone directory, check different types of business conducted by men with Jewish names; note in which businesses most Jews are concerned, which (if any) have none at all. A group project.

4. In the World Almanac or other reference work, check lists of recent philanthropies and of philanthropic foundations for Jewish names.

5. Debate: should Jews become conspicuous in public office? Many people were alarmed by the way in which Morgenthau, Baruch, Lehman and Frankfurter were attacked by anti-Semites, and felt that they should not have taken office.

6. The connection between political success and Jewish leadership.
   a) See how often the same man may be in both fields.
   b) The reasons for what you find.

References for Pupils and Teachers

De Haas, Jacob, *Encyclopedia of Jewish Knowledge.*
Universal Jewish Encyclopedia.
> Both of these works are recent enough to include in their brief biographies the men mentioned in this chapter.
Who's Who in America.
Who's Who in American Jewry.
Wise, James Waterman, and Lee J. Levinger, *Mr. Smith, Meet Mr. Cohen,* chapter 7.
Irving, Henry, *Bernard Baruch.*
Bloom, Sol, *Autobiography.*
Mason, Thomas Alpheus, *Brandeis, a Free Man's Life.*
De Haas, Jacob, *Louis D. Brandeis,* a Biographical Sketch; this covers Brandeis' Jewish activities.
Gompers, Samuel, *Seventy Years of Life and Labor,* an autobiography.
Whitman, Wilson, *David Lilienthal, Public Servant.*

Jews in American Industry and Public Life

Wise, James Waterman, *Jews Are Like That,* includes essays on Louis D. Brandeis and Nathan Straus.

Ribalow, Harold U., *The Jew in American Sports.* Bloch.

The American Jewish Yearbook contains excellent brief biographies of many of the men under discussion. See the following:

Louis D. Brandeis, by Louis E. Levinthal, vol. 44.

Benjamin Nathan Cardozo, by E. J. Nathan, vol. 41.

Henry Horner, by H. M. Lautman, vol. 43.

Sidney Hillman, by A. H. Raskin, vol. 49.

Julius Kahn, by Harry Schneiderman, vol. 27.

Julius Rosenwald, by Pauline K. Angell, vol. 34.

Nathan Straus, by D. de Sola Pool, vol. 33.

Each *Yearbook* includes a list of Jews in American Public Service, past and present. See vol. 49, pages 725–730.

CHAPTER 32.

The Future of the American Jew

T HIS chapter is not a venture in prophecy; it is merely an attempt to apply the lessons of our history to the period that is just ahead, the post-war period.

I. NATURE OF THE POST-WAR ERA

THE post-war era is one in which the American Jews must develop their own Jewish life, without any substantial immigration from abroad. Our numbers are likely to stay roughly at over five million in the foreseeable future.

Earlier we noted that most American Jews lived in the great cities, but since World War II this has been changing. New suburbs have arisen around the cities, attracting very many Americans, most of them middle-class with young families. Among these are many young Jews with growing children.

This has greatly influenced Jewish life. The chief effect has been the rise of many new synagogues, middle-sized neighborhood institutions. Newcomers are joining in great numbers; their children are flocking to congregational schools. Some observers consider this to mean a great increase in religion because it applies to all three branches of Judaism.

584

The Future of the American Jew

Other Jewish organizations and institutions—B'nai B'rith, Hadassah, Jewish Centers and others—are also spreading to the suburbs. But the greatest growth is among the synagogues, their schools, and affiliated groups.

Another factor for our consideration is the destruction of European Jewry, which leaves America by default as the chief headquarters for the Jews of the world. We are raising great sums of money for the support of the remnants of European Jewry, for their immigration to Israel, and for the new life they are entering there. We are using our influence as Americans to support these great policies to which our country has been most friendly. We in this country must also preserve Judaism and Jewish learning, for the great centers of the Old World are no more.

This new period is highlighted by the emergence of the State of Israel. This fact changes Jewish life the world over, including America. Of course, we are citizens of the United States, not of Israel. We have no political relationship at all to the new state. We do not even use the same name, for we are Jews, while the citizens of Israel are Israelis. This last term even applies to non-Jews who live in Israel and have become its citizens. But we are the supporters and sympathizers of Israel. Immigrants come to Israel from all the world, but especially from the lands of persecution and sorrow. Money likewise comes from all the world, but especially from the lands of prosperity and freedom. This means that American Jews contribute most of the funds to build the Jewish state, its homes, its farms, and its factories, but on the whole, few American

History of the Jews in the United States

Jews are settling in Israel. The Zionists of America represent practically all American Jews in this enthusiastic support for Israel. But even this great body can have no authority in Israel itself, which has its own government and conducts its own affairs.

II. OUTSIDE PRESSURE

THE center of the problem of anti-Semitism seems to have shifted from personal feelings and actions to the broader sphere of law and government. Some of the most vicious propagandists still speak and write against the Jews, but their followers are very few. It is notable that in the presidential campaign of 1944, considerable anti-Semitism was contained in the attacks on Sidney Hillman, while nothing of the kind existed in 1948. Apparently, most Americans have no direct hostility to Jews or to any other body of fellow-citizens, though many of them have personal prejudices against any individuals or groups who are different from themselves. Only if another depression should come is such prejudice likely to turn into direct and dangerous discrimination.

Of course, we know that the anti-immigration movement was in part anti-Jewish, and that the laws it produced are here to stay. Some states have Sunday laws which prevent a man from closing his place of business on Saturday and keeping it open on Sunday. This causes great hardship to orthodox Jews and also to the Seventh Day Adventists, a Christian denomination which observes Saturday as its day of rest. Many states permit or even

586

enforce the reading of the Bible in the public schools, which means that Jewish children have to learn the New Testament as a part of the supposedly non-sectarian public school education. Of late years a widespread movement has developed to give an hour or more of public school time to educate children in religion. Usually these classes are not conducted in the schools or by the regular teachers; the children leave school to study religion in their own churches. Some Jewish schools have even taken part in this work when it is adopted by the public schools of their own city. But this also is a dangerous invasion of the right to keep our own religion in our own way. It means that American institutions, the city government and the public schools, are being used for sectarian teaching.

The struggle against these and even more serious abuses has become, not a Jewish affair, but a struggle for a better and purer democracy throughout America. For example, many homes have what is called a "restrictive covenant" in the deed, which forbids their sale to Negroes, Jews, or various other groups. But in 1948, the Supreme Court of the United States outlawed any such clauses, and declared that the courts must not enforce them. This means that owners of property may sell only to selected persons if they wish, but they cannot bind others legally to do the same.

The problem of admission to colleges and medical schools has eased. In 1959, 19 per cent of all American medical school students were Jewish.

History of the Jews in the United States

The struggle of American Negroes to win equal rights has had some effects on Jews. In 1954, the U.S. Supreme Court ordered integration of white and Negro students in public schools. Some southern legislatures and groups opposed this decision, and sometimes violence erupted. In 1957 and 1958 bombings damaged some schools, homes, and religious institutions, among them eight synagogues.

Some of this violence may have been caused by a feeling that Jews favored public school integration. But in most cases, the major explanation lay in the character of those people who hate others so strongly they want to throw bombs. They do not always limit their hatred to Negroes; they are just as likely to hate Jews or anyone that seems to them to be "different."

The majority of Americans reacted strongly against this violence. The bombings halted, but tensions over the struggle for equality continue. Negro groups, often joined by sympathetic white groups, strived for equal rights by such techniques as the "sit-ins" and "Freedom Rides."

III. JEWISH ACTIVITIES

THE number of Jews by birth will probably remain about the same in this country for some years to come, with but little increase. The number of Jews who participate actively in Jewish life may decline. But if so it will certainly not be caused either by intermarriage or conversion to Christianity. Intermarriage exists and in small towns affects a large percentage of the Jews. But most Jews live

The Future of the American Jew

in large cities, and most of the Jewish young people are marrying other Jews, so that intermarriage remains a very small drain on the totality of Jewish families.

Practically no Jews are joining Christian churches, though some seem to find religious and moral satisfaction outside the synagogue rather than within. Some turn to Ethical Culture, following its distinguished founder, Felix Adler, who was himself the son of a rabbi. Others find hope in Christian Science, with its teaching of the cure of illness by faith. Still others seek the fulfillment of their social ideals in political movements like socialism.

It remains that the real loss to Judaism comes through indifference and ignorance of what Judaism is. The real hope for the Jews is in Jewish education, which teaches children and young people why they are Jews, and how they can prove their loyalty to their people.

In fact, Jewish institutions are increasing in number, size and activity. The synagogue itself is showing both an external and an internal growth. First, new congregations are constantly being organized, new synagogues built, while the national organizations and seminaries are steadily increasing their membership and their influence. Meanwhile, all three groups—reform, conservative, and orthodox—are perfecting their organizations, devising new and better methods for their worship, their schools and their social life.

In general, the attitude today seems to seek a common basis of understanding among American Jews. Most of the reform synagogues are bringing back old Jewish cus-

toms, discontinued a century ago either because of care-
lessness or because some early reformers objected to cere-
mony in general. The Sabbath candles, the Seder, the
teaching of Hebrew, and many other customs are now
practiced in reform congregations, often with changes
which will make them more consistent with the liberal
outlook. At the same time, orthodoxy is becoming, on the
whole, less European and more American—though there
is still a very aggressive body of orthodox Jews who insist
that their viewpoint is the only possible one. The old-
fashioned orthodox rabbi of eastern Europe usually opposed any modern education, but spent all his time studying Torah and Talmud. The modern orthodox rabbi is a
broadly educated man, with a university degree. Both he
and his congregation recognize the need of new adjust-
ments so long as these do not contradict the Torah. Many
orthodox synagogues use a modern Hebrew education, in
place of the old method of learning by rote; they have
introduced English sermons; they use instrumental music
at meetings, though not in the religious service. Here in
America we seem to be working out a new type of Judaism, which will tend away from extremes and will bring
all Jews nearer together.

This trend has shown up most clearly in the organization of the Synagogue Council of America. In this group,
all three bodies of Jews are actually cooperating, not for
Jewish relief or Jewish defense, but specifically for the
advancement of the Jewish religion. The members of each
group have grown to respect their colleagues in the other

groups, and their competition is no longer a matter of opposition or even of hostility, as it was in older days, but simply a healthy rivalry concerning which may best bring Judaism to a greater number of Jews and thus serve their people best.

The same is true of Jewish education. The European influence appears in the all-day Jewish school, which is a growing though as yet a small factor in the whole of Jewish education. The daily Hebrew school is coming nearer to the public school in its buildings, textbooks, and methods. It often meets in a Jewish community center and the children enjoy the club work and other center activities. Always it has added new courses, such as music, handwork and current events. The congregational schools, whether reform or conservative, are no longer satisfied with one period a week for the study of Jewish history. They are also teaching Bible, ceremonies and current events; they have added extra hours during the week so that they may have time to teach the Hebrew language to their pupils. The Federations and other community agencies are recognizing the needs of Jewish education, are contributing money for the purpose, and are steadily strengthening its effectiveness. We still have far to go, but Jewish education is increasing, both in the number it reaches and in the amount it is able to teach them.

Jewish philanthropy is taking a new position in modern American life. The last depression removed from the Jewish agencies much of their relief work; the state is now taking care of old age pensions and unemployment insur-

591

ance. But the Jewish communities are turning to youth activities, Jewish community centers, and the development of Jewish culture in America. The National Jewish Welfare Board has worked out a policy which emphasizes Jewish values, so that the Jewish center movement is not simply a group of settlement houses or neighborhood social centers, but a positive Jewish factor in the various communities.

Finally, the greatest philanthropic drives ever made for the aid of human beings have been conducted year after year by the United Jewish Appeal in order to rescue the Jews of Europe and to aid the new State of Israel. This effort has been a tremendous influence on all Jews, from the richest to the poorest, from the great cities to the tiniest village. It brought to them all a sense of kinship with their fellow-Jews, the personal contact with the world-wide needs of the Jewish people. The hopeful fact is that the time of greatest collections for overseas work is the very time when we can see the end of the need.

The displaced persons have now left Europe almost to a man. The persecuted Jews of Yemen and Iraq have all gone to Israel, with many from other backward lands. Israel has been established, and is being put on a sound basis by the sacrifices of its own citizens with help from the Jews of America. Investment in government bonds and private industry in Israel is already taking the place, in part, of the great campaigns for gifts to that country. The time will soon come when we need no longer support our brethren overseas, but can give our attention to strengthening Jewish religion and culture.

The Future of the American Jew

THE dominant trend today among American Jews, and the one great need which still remains unsolved, is Jewish unity. The prejudice against each other among Jews from various parts of the Old World is dying out. Jews whose parents came from different lands marry as a matter of course; old German or Sephardic congregations are electing as rabbis the sons of immigrants from eastern Europe. The latest immigrants have become quite as prosperous and quite as American as the descendants of the earlier groups.

It is not that Jews will ever lack different parties and different opinions, but that all of them are learning that they need each other, and each group is learning to respect the others. There was a time when orthodox Jews would want to excommunicate a reform leader, or when all religious Jews would join against the non-religious or secular Jew. Today Jews are becoming readier to admit to the Jewish fold anyone who considers himself a Jew, even though he may express his loyalty in unusual ways.

We have seen how the religious bodies have worked out a method of cooperation, how the various appeals for overseas needs are coordinating their activities, how the defense agencies are growing nearer to a common program. The Council of Jewish Federations and Welfare Funds has become more than a social work agency; it is taking an active part in solving some of the over-all problems of American Jewry. It can do this better than many

593

other bodies because it actually represents many Jewish communities, rather than being simply a national organization for a single purpose.

We have seen also how the most effective body for unifying American Jewry—the American Jewish Conference—came to an end because of the opposition of some of its own members. Meanwhile, the leading Jewish organizations pursue different and often opposing policies, tending to break American Jewry into two groups, each of which tries to lead and to represent the Jews of America as a whole. We may have to wait for the development of Jewish unity in the local communities before we can gain it in the national sphere. When enough Jewish communities have their community councils or other unified bodies, then the representatives of these can come together really to represent American Jewry as a whole. This may come sooner than we think, for the unifying process is going on steadily in many American cities, and all Jews feel the need of working together in the face of the great problems which confront us.

We must therefore face the future, trying to apply the lessons of the past. We are uncertain what may come, yet we are filled with hope because we know what America has done for the Jew and what the Jew has returned to America; how Judaism has helped in founding the ideals of America, and how Judaism is needed by the Jew himself. We are filled with loyalty for this nation which has been a better homeland than any the Jews have ever known since they were driven out of Palestine almost two

594

The Future of the American Jew

thousand years ago. At the same time we feel loyalty to the wandering folk of Israel and to the vision of God which kept them brave and true through all their trials. We feel love for the ancient land of Palestine and deep sympathy for the new State of Israel there. We hope to unite within ourselves the religion and culture of Judaism and the freedom and democracy of America.

REVIEW QUESTIONS

1. What is the special situation of the American Jews? Name three characteristics of the present era.
2. What is the effect on Jewish numbers of (a) anti-Semitism, (b) intermarriage, (c) indifference?
3. What trends are evident in (a) the synagogue, (b) Jewish education, (c) Jewish philanthropy?
4. What are the indications of growing Jewish unity? Why have we not yet achieved it?

TOPICS FOR REPORTS

1. Judaism and Americanism. An essay or a class project.
2. Jewish education. This may be a panel, with such topics as:
    a) What kind of Jewish education is best in America?
    b) How far does our own Jewish training help us?
    c) What should we know to be well informed Jews?
3. Minority groups in America.
    a) The nature of prejudice.
    b) Disabilities of various minority groups.
    c) Methods to improve American democracy.
    d) What can the Jew do?

REFERENCES FOR PUPILS

Gittelsohn, Roland B., *Modern Jewish Problems*. Union.
Edidin, Ben, *Rebuilding Palestine*. Hebrew Pub. Co.

History of the Jews in the United States

The Voice of Religion pamphlet series. Union.
Jewish Information Series, JWB.
Jewish Affairs Pamphlets, American Jewish Congress.

REFERENCES FOR TEACHERS

Janowsky, Oscar I. (editor), *The American Jew*, a composite portrait, Harper, 1942. Various phases of American Jewish life, such as religion, education, and culture, discussed by different writers.

Cohon, Samuel S., *Judaism—A Way of Life*. Union; the reform point of view.

Steinberg, Milton, *A Partisan Guide to the Jewish Problem*. Bobbs Merrill; Reconstructionist point of view.

Waxman, Meyer, *A Handbook of Judaism*. Bloch; an orthodox statement.

The Palestine Yearbook gives annually the latest facts on Zionism and especially on Palestine.

The American Jewish Yearbook has annual summaries of events and special articles.

Consult Jewish magazines for a constant flow of relevant articles; see especially *Commentary, Liberal Judaism,* the *Menorah Journal,* the *National Jewish Monthly,* the *New Palestine,* the *Jewish Frontier.*

596

New Books, 1930–1961

IN THESE many years, a large number of important new works have been published which deal with the topic of our study. Many of these have already been mentioned in connection with the various chapters in Part III. Here are some other important titles, though by no means all of them.

Two works are indispensable: *The Universal Jewish Encyclopedia*, 12 volumes; and Jacob De Haas's *Encyclopedia of Jewish Knowledge*, 1 volume. Both of these are recent and include many events and persons not in older works, such as the *Jewish Encyclopedia*.

GENERAL WORKS

Dubois, Rachel D. and Emma Schweppe, *The Jews in American Life*, Nelson, 1935.

Foner, Philip S., "Jews in American History," 1654–1865, a pamphlet, International Publishers, 1945.

Fredman, Joseph G. and Louis A. Falk, "Jews in American Wars," a pamphlet published by the Jewish War Veterans.

Friedman, Lee M., *Jewish Pioneers and Patriots*, Jewish Publication Society.

————, *Pilgrims in a New Land*, Jewish Publication Society.
Two books with interesting sketches of great variety, which will serve as source material for many parts of this history.

Grayzel, Solomon, *Story of the Jewish People*, contains a chapter on America.

Handlin, Oscar, *Adventure in Freedom*, three hundred years of Jewish life in America.

Ish Kishor, Shulamith, *American Promise*, Behrman.

History of the Jews in the United States

Learsi, Rufus, *History of the Jews in America.*
————, *Israel,* Behrman.
Marcus, Jacob R., *Early American Jewry,* 2 vols.
————, "The Jews in American Life," a pamphlet, American Jewish Committee.
————, *Memoirs of American Jews, 1775–1865,* 3 vols.
Masserman, Paul and Max Baker, *The Jews Come to America,* Bloch.
"Our People, the Jews in America," a pamphlet published by the International Workers Order.
Standard Jewish Encyclopedia, 1 vol., ed. by Cecil Roth.
"The Story of the Jews in the United States," a pamphlet in the JWB Information Series; probably the best brief summary for general use.

Books on Special Topics

Bentwich, Norman, *Solomon Schechter,* Jewish Publication Society.
Carvalho, Solomon Nunes, *Incidents of Travel and Adventures in the Far West.*
Edidin, Ben, *Rebuilding Palestine,* Behrman.
Goldberg, Isaac, *Major Noah, American Jewish Pioneer,* Jewish Publication Society.
Goldstein, Israel, *A Century of Judaism in New York,* the history of Congregation B'nai Jeshurun from 1825 to 1925, printed by the congregation.
Goodman, Abram V., *American Overture,* tells of Jews in the colonies, Jewish Publication Society.
Grinstein, Hyman B., *The Rise of the Jewish Community of New York,* Jewish Publication Society.
Huhner, Leon, *The Life of Judah Touro,* Jewish Publication Society.
Janowsky, Oscar I., *The American Jew,* a composite portrait, Harper.
————, *The JWB Survey,* National Jewish Welfare Board.
Jewish Frontier Anthology, contains many articles of interest.

598

New Books, 1930–1961

Kohn, Eugene, *The Future of Judaism in America,* The Liberal Press.

Korn, Bertram W., *American Jewry and the Civil War.*

Marcus, Jacob R., *Early American Jewry,* two volumes on the colonial period.

Schappes, Morris U., *Documentary History of the Jews in the United States, 1654–1875.*

Wischnitzer, Mark, *To Dwell in Safety,* the story of Jewish migrations.

Zuckerman, Nathan, *The Wine of Violence,* an anthology of anti-Semitism, Association Press, 1947.

STORIES FOR YOUNG PEOPLE

Leonard, Oscar, *Americans All,* Behrman.

Levinger, Elma Ehrlich, *The Golden Door,* Bloch.

————, *Jewish Adventures in America,* Bloch.

Audio-Visual Aids

FILMS

The American Jew: a Tribute to Freedom. Kinescope, 16 mm. sound, black and white. Anti-Defamation League of B'nai B'rith.

The Gift. Kinescope, 16 mm. sound, black and white. National Academy for Adult Jewish Studies.

Lawyer from Boston. Kinescope, 16 mm. sound, black and white. National Academy of Adult Jewish Studies of the United Synagogue of America.

The Life of Henrietta Szold. 16 mm. sound, black and white. Hadassah.

The Pugnacious Sailing Master. Kinescope, 16 mm. sound, black and white. National Academy of Adult Jewish Studies.

Sons of Liberty, 16 mm. sound, color. Jewish Education Film Library.

FILMSTRIPS

David Einhorn: The Father of the Union Prayerbook. Color, 41 frames. Union of American Hebrew Congregations.

Haym Salomon—Financier of the Revolution. Color, 30 frames. Filmstrip House.

Isaac Mayer Wise—Master Builder of American Judaism. Black and white, 36 frames. Union of American Hebrew Congregations.

The Jews in America (Two Parts). Full color, 49 frames. Jewish Education Committee of New York.

The Jews Settle in New Amsterdam—1654. Color, 37 frames. Union of American Hebrew Congregations.

Judah Touro—Friend of Man. Color, 36 frames. Union of American Hebrew Congregations.

Major Noah. Color, 40 frames. Jewish Education Committee of New York.

Rabbi Stephen S. Wise: a Twentieth Century Prophet. Color, 43 frames. Union of American Hebrew Congregations.

The Story of Haym Salomon. Color, 31 frames. American Jewish Archives.

Three Hundred Years: Memorable Events in American Jewish History. Color, 45 frames, with 12-inch long-playing recorded narration. Union of American Hebrew Congregations.

Through the Years: Jewish Women in American History. Color, 43 frames. National Federation of Temple Sisterhoods.

To Live by That Heritage. Black and white, 31 frames. Theodor Herzl Institute.

600

INDEX

Index

Index

Carabajal, Luis de, 42, 44
Cardozo, Benjamin N., 571f.
Catholic church, 370
Catholics, prejudice toward, 355f., 361, 363
Cayenne, 50
Central Conference of American Rabbis, 427, 429f., 527
Central Relief Committee, 517
Chagall, Marc, 550
Chaplains, Jewish, 202f., 347f., 380ff.
Charities, Jewish, 245ff.
Charleston, South Carolina, 93, 95, 142, 214f.
Chassidim, 268, 545
Chautauqua Society, 429
Chayevsky, Paddy, 545
Cheder, 287, 451
Chicago, 182f., 196, 406, 481
Chicago, Univ. of, 551f., 566
Chicago World's Fair, 432
Choynsky, Joe, 567
Christian Front, 369, 396
Cincinnati, 14, 150, 184, 422, 425, 481
Cincinnati, Univ. of, 422, 425
Civil War, Jews in, 199ff.
Civilian work, Jewish, 348ff.
Cleveland, 153, 250
Clinchy, Everett R., 505
Cohen, Alfred M., 492
Cohen, Jacob, 62, 149
Cohen, Morris R., 554
Columbia University, 539
Columbus, Bartholomew, 32
Columbus, Christopher, 23, 27ff.
Commentary, 464
Commission on Human Rights, 394
Commission on Information about Judaism, 427

Commission on Jewish Education, 427, 452
Committee on Army and Navy Religious Activities, 380, 384
Committee on Civil Rights, 588
Communist party, 357
Community Chest, 482
Congress of Industrial Organizations, 370, 496, 561
Congress of Religions, 493
Congressmen, Jewish, 575ff.
Connecticut, 82-83
Conservative Judaism, 430ff.
Contribution to America, Jewish, 8, 9
Corwin, Norman, 546
Coughlin, Charles E., 369f., 396
Council of Jewish Federations and Welfare Funds, 485, 509, 593
Council of Jewish Juniors, 450
Council of National Defense, 573
Cremieux, Adolph, 323
Cresques, Judah, 29
Cromwell, Oliver, 49, 103
Curacao, 50, 53f.
Cutler, Harry, 349
Czarist government, 358

D

Damascus case, 323f., 499
Dandrada, Salvador, 62
Davidson, Jo, 550
Davis, Jefferson, 205, 206
Dearborn Independent, 358
Deborah, The, 231
Decree of Expulsion, 26
Defense agencies, Jewish, 499ff.
De Gama, Vasco, 31
De Leon, David Camden, 155, 200

603

Index

Index

Index

Index

Index

608

Index

Index

610

Index

Native American movement, 355
Nazis, 356, 367ff., 374, 387ff., 392, 502f., 520, 524, 552f.
Negroes, prejudice toward, 359
Neighborhood Playhouse, 545
Ner Mitzvah, 437
Neuberger, Richard L., 576
Neuman, Abraham, 453
New Amsterdam, 50, 467
"New Colossus, The," 304
"New Deal," 365, 370
New Orleans, Jews in, 150
New Palestine, 537f.
New School for Social Research, 551
New York City, 15, 405f., 409, 417, 426, 430, 440, 452, 506f., 510
New York Congregations
—B'nai Jeshurun, 142
—Emanu-El, 506, 580
—Shearith Israel, 67
New York Federation of Jewish Philanthropies, 481
New York Times, 539f.
New York World, 539
Newport, R. I., 72-79, 124-125
Niger, Samuel, 541
Noah, Mordecai Manuel, 161ff., 534
Nobel Prize, 368, 551
Nones, Major Benjamin, 89, 118
North Carolina, 134-135
Nuremberg Laws, 367f.
Nuremberg trials, 388, 392

O

Ochs, Adolph, 539
O'Connell, William Cardinal, 361
Oglethorpe, General, 94

Oppenheimer, Robert, 387, 553
Ordroneaux, Captain John, 154
Origin of American Jews, 9
Orphans, Jewish, 473
ORT, 522
Oswego, N. Y., 391
Ottolenghi, Joseph, 95

P

Paine, Thomas, 107
Palestine, 7, 338, 371, 394f., 437, 495, 512, 523ff., 558, 565
Paris Peace Conference, 501, 573
Parker, Dorothy, 536
Peixotto, Benjamin F., 327
Penn, William, 85, 131
Pennsylvania, 85-90
People's Relief Committee, 498
Persecution in Russia, 11
Persecution in Spain, 24ff.
Persia, 334, 335
Peru, 44f.
Philadelphia, 86, 88-90, 247, 406
—Congregation Rodeph Shalom, 142
—Orphan Asylum, 171f.
Philanthropic organizations, Jewish, 481ff.
Philanthropies, Jewish, 14, 467ff., 563ff.
Philipson, David, 233, 425, 427, 461
Pilgrim Fathers, 356
Pinner, Moritz, 195
Pinsky, David, 541
Pinto family, 82
Pinto, Solomon, 118
Poale Zion, 528f.
Pogroms, 269f., 357

611

Index

Index

Index

614

Index

W

Wallace, General Lew, 324
War Industries Board, 573
War Production Board, 561
War Refugee Board, 391
Warburg, Felix M., 435, 562
Warburg, Paul M., 562f.
Warfield, David, 545
Warner Brothers, 546
Warsaw ghetto, 388f.
Washington, George, 93
Washington and the Jews, 124ff.
Weber, Max, 550
Webster, Daniel, 204, 207
Weizmann, Chaim, 395, 507, 524f.
Welfare Fund, 484
Werfel, Franz, 538
Werfel, Louis, 381
William the Silent, 46
Williams, Roger, 73, 80, 108
Williamstown Institute of Politics, 567, 574
Willoughby, Lord, 51
Wilson, Woodrow, 335ff., 361, 550, 560, 570, 573
Winchell, Walter, 539
Wisconsin Public Service Commission, 575
Wise, Isaac Mayer, 180f., 184, 199, 207, 218ff., 429f.
Wise, Stephen S., 292, 335, 426, 502, 507ff.
Wolf, Simon, 186, 199f., 255, 306ff., 500
Women, Jewish, 493ff.
Women's League, 433
Workers, Jewish, 409
Workmen's Circle, 492, 498f.

World Council of Jewish Women, 494
World Federation of YMHA's and Community Centers, 480f.
World Jewish Congress, 509, 516
World Over, 452
World Union for Progressive Judaism, 516
World War I, Jews in, 343ff.
World War II, Jewish chaplains in, 380ff.
World War II, Jews in, 374ff.
World Zionist Organization, 516, 525, 529
World's Columbian Exposition, 493
Writers, Jewish, 535ff.

Y

Yehoash, 540
Yeshiva University, 438f., 453f.
Yeshivoth, 448
Yiddish, 7, 16
Yiddish Art Theatre, 287
Yiddish and Hebrew culture, 286f.
Yiddish Scientific Institute, 463
Yiddish school, 448
Yiddish theatre, 286f.
Yishuv, 524f.
Young Judea, 292, 450, 528
Young Men's Christian Association, 383, 566
Young Men's Hebrew Association, 14, 258f., 477ff., 480
Young People's League, 433
Youth Aliyah, 495, 528

615

Index